CHILD CUSTODY AND DIVORCE

THE LAW IN SOCIAL CONTEXT

SUSAN MAIDMENT

CROOM HELM
London & Sydney

KJ170

© 1984 Susan Maidment
Croom Helm Ltd, Provident House, Burrell Row,
Beckenham, Kent BR3 1AT
Croom Helm Australia Pty Ltd, First Floor, 139 Kings Street,
Sydney, NSW 2001, Australia

British Library Cataloguing in Publication Data

Maidment, Susan
  Child custody and divorce.
  1. Custody of children − England 2. Children
  of divorced parents − England
  I. Title
  344.2061'7   KD772
  ISBN 0-7099-1737-6

Printed and bound in Great Britain by
Biddles Ltd, Guildford and King's Lynn

CONTENTS

Preface
Acknowledgments

As a family lawyer interested in the law of child custody, i.e.
the law which seeks to protect children on the breakup of their
parents' marriage, I was aware that there was a body of knowledge about the family, marriage and divorce, relationships
between husband and wife, and parents and children, which
addressed itself to the same concerns as the law. This body
of knowledge found in the social sciences, I believed, was a
crucial tool for understanding the social context in which the
necessity for legal decision-making arose. The legal process
was after all only one particular step in a social process, in
this case the breakup of a marriage.

The purpose of this book was therefore to put the law of
child custody in its social context. At one level this purpose
was quite general. It was to make available to lawyers this
large body of knowledge about the social process in which the
legal process played only a small part. It seemed right that
intelligent, caring lawyers had some understanding of the
social context on which their legal practices and procedures
impinged. At this level then I wanted to present the social
science evidence which was relevant to child custody law simply
to widen the horizons of the lawyer and make him aware that he
was not operating in a social vacuum. It was not possible
however to limit myself to this task. I wanted to believe also
that somehow a greater social understanding of the legal process surrounding child custody would actually positively contribute to the legal decision-making process, i.e. that a
greater awareness and understanding of the social process in
which the legal decision-making arises would allow an evaluation of the quality of the legal decisions, if necessary to
make possible "better" decisions, decisions that were more in
accord with informed social science understandings of the
problem.

The focus of this book is therefore on social science
evidence and findings as they relate to children, and the
contribution that they can make to a greater understanding of
the issues that form the subject matter of child custody legal

decision-making.

The emphasis is on recent research findings which are less widely known, and these are necessarily selective. A comprehensive account of current knowledge is impossible given the wide ranging scope of the subject; so also is a detailed explanation of methodological issues. The research selected for inclusion will therefore necessarily reflect personal idiosyncracies and preferences; personal assessments of policy implications may also intrude. This is both unavoidable and excusable for the subject matter of this book represents not only an academic commitment, but also a search for a "better" legal system.

ACKNOWLEDGMENTS

I wish to record my gratitude to the Nuffield Foundation for having granted me a Social Science Research Fellowship, which allowed me to work full-time for one year on this book without carrying out my normal duties at the University of Keele. Without their financial assistance this book would not have been possible.

I also want to thank Freda Mainwaring of the Law Department at the University of Keele without whose co-operation throughout, the numerous drafts of this book would not have been typed; and Rowena Gay for her professional help in producing the final copy.

I dedicate this book to my husband and children.

If matters arise in our laws which concern other sciences
and faculties, we commonly call for the aid of that science or faculty which it concerns, which is an honourable
and commendable thing. For thereby it appears that we do
not despise all other sciences but our own, but we approve
of them and encourage them (Buckley v Rice-Thomas (1554)).

No single discipline has the omni-science which we all
seek in the constructive settlement of family disputes
(Payne, 1982).

The law and practice in relation to infants ... have
developed, are developing and must and no doubt will, continue to develop by reflecting and adopting the changing
views, as the years go by, of reasonable men and women,
the parents of children on the proper treatment and
methods of bringing up children (Lord Upjohn, J v C
(1970)).

I have the appalling responsibility of deciding the custody of R ... The case is extremely difficult ... There
is little to choose between the parents. It is transparent that there is a strong bond between the child and each
of the parents (Judge Kenneth Taylor, M v M (1980)).

Chapter 1

INTRODUCTION

THE NATURE OF THE PROBLEM

In 1981, 145,713 married couples were divorced, 60% of whom had children under the age of 16, and 159,403 children were involved in their parents' divorce (OPCS, 1983). 1,600,000 children are being brought up in one-parent families (Social Trends, 1982), a rise between 1971 and 1981 of 71% (NCOPF, 1983), and caused mainly by the increase in the divorce rate. It is estimated that one in four marriages are now likely to end in divorce, and that nearly one in five children are involved in divorce each year (Rimmer, 1981).

The enormity of the problem for the legal system has hardly begun to be appreciated. Yet for every decree absolute of divorce that is granted a judge has also made a declaration of satisfaction about post-divorce arrangements for the children and usually also a custody order, deciding which parent should be responsible for the children. Judges have always made custody orders, in previous times more often in circumstances of marriage breakdown arising out of death, more recently arising out of separation or divorce. And judges have always been criticised for the decisions they have made; dissatisfaction with custody decision-making has a long history.

One thesis of this book is that the nature of the divorce and custody decision-making process can only be understood when the legal structure is located in its social context. Why and how judges decide custody cases can only be properly appreciated within an understanding of the social process involved in marriage and divorce, of the changes in the social institution of the family and of the social expectations of parenting. And this social context itself must be seen in an historical perspective, for what society does and values today is inextricably linked with what was done and believed in the past. A sense of history brings with it a sense of balance. Judicial decisions which elicit immediate and automatic response of outrage may take on a different

1

light when viewed in a social and historical setting.

Although divorce has been possible in England and Wales since the end of the seventeenth century, it was only after the Second World War that divorce became socially acceptable and financially possible for all social classes (McGregor, 1957). Women's employment during the war, the social upheaval of the war, and, perhaps most importantly, the setting up of the Legal Aid scheme in 1950, all contributed to a social acceptance of divorce on a scale never before experienced. In the 1970s the liberalisation of divorce law by the Divorce Reform Act 1969 coincided with the formal breakup of marriage on an unprecedented scale, so that between 1970 and 1981 the number of divorce petitions filed rose from 71,676 to 169,076, from a rate per 1000 married total population of 4.7 to 11.8 (OPCS, 1983, provisional figure). Despite this pervasive experience of divorce, society has not come to terms with its own behaviour. Despite its prevalence, divorce is still not normally supposed to happen (Group for the Advancement of Psychiatry, 1980), so that there is neither preparation for it, nor, unlike death, officially recognised mourning for it. The lack of rites of passage for divorce, the lack of ceremony, has perhaps been even exacerbated in this country by the removal in 1977 of the judicial hearing for undefended divorces. Even the parties' "day in court", however cursory it was in practice (Elston et al, 1978) has been replaced with an anonymous administrative procedure whereby divorce petitions are processed by a registrar behind closed doors. Society has yet to create a terminology to describe the step-relationship and the wider family created by it (Mead, 1970), and the reconstruction of family life by remarried divorcees lacks adequate models (Burgoyne and Clark, 1982a; Hart, 1976). Courts are thus called upon to create the rules, the social structure for divorce, which society has failed to provide (Bohannan, 1970). Thus for example, divorced fathers appeal to the courts for enforcement of their right of access to their children, because society has been unable to create a social structure within which parenting can continue beyond the marriage which created it.

Recognition, that in a time of enormous social change in the institutions of the family, marriage and divorce, the judges are being asked to provide rules for the reorganisation of parent-child relationships, allows a perspective in which the frailties and human errors of which they may be guilty is tempered by an appreciation of the enormity of the task. The fact is that in child custody cases, the judges are asked to make decisions, which they not only dislike making, but which also encapsulate the social consequences of the divorcing process, not only in the immediate situation but also for the future. Whether a judge (or anyone else) is capable of such decisions, or whether it is right and fair for society to require of him such decisions are difficult questions.

THE WELFARE OF THE CHILD

There is a widespread belief in our society that divorce has damaging consequences for the children of the marriage and that such consequences ought to be minimised. In modern divorce law concern for the welfare of the child has therefore been elevated to an overriding principle according to which parental needs or desires will be determined. Thus no decree absolute of divorce may be granted until and unless the judge has made a declaration of satisfaction about the arrangements for the children (Matrimonial Causes Act 1973, s 41), and all questions concerning the custody or upbringing of a child must be resolved by the courts according to the principle that "the welfare of the child is the first and paramount consideration" (Guardianship of Minors Act 1971, s 1). The "welfare of the child" is therefore the yardstick by which parental freedom of action as regards their own future and the future of their children must be measured. The concept of the child's welfare has a long history, as will be explored in some detail in chapter 4. The concept is also notoriously indeterminate (Mnookin, 1975); it has no essential meaning. As Lord Upjohn perceived in J v C (1970), beliefs about a child's best interests or welfare have changed and will change according to current views on matters such as child-rearing and parenting. The "welfare of the child" principle is therefore now a deliberately indeterminate standard incorporated into the law in order to allow current social and cultural views about the needs of children, and also, it must be said, of their parents to be embodied in the legal decision-making process surrounding divorce. The Victorians who developed the principle may have believed that the welfare principle produced determinate rules for deciding custody cases in the same way that they believed in absolute rules governing the social order. To the late twentieth century observer, reared on social sciences knowledge, the relativity of social and cultural values is more apparent. A sense of history also serves to illuminate the social determinants for the content of the welfare principle.
　　Seen in this light, many of the current controversies over custody can be located within the changes in the structure of the family in contemporary society. Burning issues, such as whether fathers ought to get custody, whether access for the non-custodial parent ought to be enforced more efficiently, whether joint custody for both parents is more appropriate both for children and parents, merely reflect changes in the sexual division of labour within the family, whereby modern fathers participate more in their children's upbringing, as well as increased psychological understanding of the

3

emotional needs of children. Issues such as whether lesbian or homosexual parents ought to be allowed custody derive from changes in acceptable sexual behaviour. These current controversies are therefore merely reflections of the recognised diversity of family forms in modern society.

Historically the welfare principle reflected the dominant ideology of the family. The Victorian judges, who developed the welfare principle, favoured one dominant family form. The Victorian family was idealised as a patriarchy, in which the father's authority was supreme, and in which both the wife and the children knew their place in the home as his dependents. The law reflected and upheld the patriarchal family by denying the wife any legal rights over her children or her property, and by respecting the "sacred rights of the father" over his dependents and their property. The welfare principle itself incorporated this family ideology, so that children's needs were largely interpreted in accordance with the father's rights. The judges accepted in most cases that the father knew best what was for the welfare of his children, and were usually reluctant therefore to deprive him of custody as against the mother. Mead has noted the ability of societies to allow "a contrast between life as people believe it to be, and life as it is lived by some, if not all, members of that society" (Mead, 1970). Victorian society is a pre-eminent example of that discrepancy between ideals and practices. The law, which was largely made by and for the middle and upper classes, upheld the ideal and masked the diversity of family forms which in fact existed. Most aspects of the patriarchal family have now been eroded (although not entirely in tax and social security provisions); of particular importance in this context was the change in the law in 1973 which finally gave mothers and fathers equal parental rights over their children (Guardianship Act 1973, s 1). Other changes had occurred at the end of the nineteenth century, for example the right of married women to own their own property (Married Women's Property Acts 1870-1882). The difference between Victorian times and now, however, is current recognition of the enormous diversity of family forms which clearly exist in our society (Rapoport et al, 1982). It is this recognition, and with it the implication of a greater social acceptance of the diversity, that has contributed to current controversies about the children of divorce. If there is now no such thing as "a normal family", as sociologists currently argue (Oakley, 1982) then beliefs about the most suitable upbringing for children of divorce are bound to differ. Thus the criticism that, along with other policy-makers (Eversley and Bonnerjea, 1982), the judges in their custody decisions may be failing to appreciate this recognised diversity of family forms.

Alongside the ideology of the family as the context for determining the child's welfare, there has also been a competing notion of the child's "best interests". This child-

4

centred concept originated in the Court of Chancery which had assumed a jurisdiction in Equity to protect wards (Lowe and White, 1979). Until the 1840s the Equitable jurisdiction was largely limited to cases where the ward had property which needed protection, but gradually the concept of the child's welfare was enlarged to include the child's material welfare, for example, the material circumstances in which the ward was brought up, and by the end of the nineteenth century the judges were speaking of "moral and religious welfare" as well as "physical well being" (Re McGrath (1893)). Where the ward's care was in dispute between a parent and a non-parent, for example, a relative, guardian or children's home, or between non-parent and non-parent in the case of an orphan, the courts of Equity were also recognising "the ties of affection" (Re McGrath (1893)) as a justification for leaving the child in the care of the person with whom he was already living. Though this policy of respecting the emotional ties the child had formed was not always followed, and especially where it was the father who was seeking the return of his child, for example, from foster-parents (Re Thain (1926)), the judges in their wisdom were in these cases reflecting a common-sense understanding of emotional needs and attachment behaviour long before Freudian theories were current or theories of maternal deprivation from the 1940s onwards had articulated psychological explanations for the nature of personal relationships.

Although therefore the dominance of parental rights had already begun to be eroded in the case of disputes between parents and non-parents by the end of the nineteenth century, within the context of marriage breakdown followed by separation or divorce the interpretation of the child's welfare, although the guiding principle since 1857 when judicial divorce was introduced in this country, was inextricably bound up first with the ideology of the patriarchal family, and then with the ideology of marriage. Concern for the child's welfare, as expressed in the child-saving legislation of the latter part of the nineteenth century (e.g. concerning child labour, compulsory education, control of delinquency, child protection, sexual exploitation etc. (Walvin, 1982; Pinchbeck and Hewitt, 1973)), did not impinge in any way on the judicial task of family restructuring following separation or divorce. Over the nineteenth century the "sacred rights of the father" in respect of his children were only gradually with great difficulty displaced by the mother, as regards both custody and access, and until the end of the 1940s matrimonial guilt in the sense of responsibility for breaking up the marriage was a most powerful disqualification in the eyes of the judges losing a mother any claims to custody of her children. As a general rule, the judges took the welfare of the child to lie with upholding the father's position in the patriarchal family, and later to lie with the innocent party to the divorce by upholding the institution of marriage. To these judges

5

there was no dichotomy between the child's welfare principle and those other principles. In their world-view the child's welfare was actually served by upholding the institutions of the family and marriage, and in this they were merely reflecting the dominant social ideology.

The end of the Second World War saw two great changes in social values. Firstly, the concept of matrimonial guilt began to be seen as a quite separate issue from the qualities of parenting which a guilty spouse, and particularly a mother, could offer. Secondly, the psychology of child development turned its attention to the question of maternal deprivation and of attachment or bonding between children and adults. In the past thirty years or so enormous strides have been made in knowledge of the psychological mechanisms in the child's emotional development. Psychology, as social science knowledge generally, has now become a significant influence on social and cultural values, an integral feature of everyday life (Newson and Newson, 1974). Expert advice on childrearing, in particular in relation to the need of children for healthy emotional and cognitive development, abounds in modern society. The fact that this professional concern for children in psychology coincided with the demise of the matrimonial guilt principle, has made it possible for the legal system to incorporate the findings of psychology, and of other social sciences, into the judicial process of divorce. While there have always been theories of children's needs and of proper childrearing as long as there have been parents, it is only now that experts have provided a body of knowledge, which in turn, despite its gaps, its omissions, its contradictions, its susceptibility to fads and fashions (Dally, 1982), has become part of the social and cultural values of late twentieth century society (Newson and Newson, 1974). Despite the back-lash against the experts which has already begun (King, 1981; Sutton, 1981), for claiming an expertise and objectivity which is not and may never be justified by the state of knowledge in the social sciences, the judges may with some justice be faulted for failing to make themselves sufficiently familiar with, and for failing to take more into account in their decision-making, the substantial, if flawed and time-bound knowledge that presently exists. If the Victorian judges can be excused for pressing the moral and religious needs of children, values which were part of the social ethos of the time, then modern judges may be faulted for failing to grasp the enormous advances in the knowledge of child development and socialisation which inform the current social ethos. The intuitive approach of today's judges is proving to be unacceptable to a large body of litigants and critics, because it binds them to one ideology of the family and marriage which is time- and class-bound. A failure to recognise the diversity of family forms and childrearing practices, and the pervasive influence of social science knowledge nowadays makes

6

judicial decision-making in custody cases often appear anachronistic.

It is in the spirit of the foregoing analysis that this book will attempt to provide an understanding of the legal decision-making process concerning the children of divorce. A description of the legal process, in terms of both procedure and substantive law, i.e. the mainly judge-made rules and interpretations of the child's welfare principle, will be considered in a social science context in order to illuminate the sociological underpinning of child custody law, and also its implications in terms of child psychology and development. A contribution to the understanding of child custody law in its social context will also be provided by an historical account of how the welfare principle came to be written into statute law in the Guardianship of Infants Act 1925 (later codified in the Guardianship of Minors Act 1971), for the very origins of the statutory principle betray social and political purposes far removed from its apparent child-centred orientation. A recognition of this fact may place current dilemmas into a more balanced perspective.

THE NATURE OF THE SOCIAL SCIENCES

The theme of this book is that a social science approach to the custody legal decision-making process is required. It is inadequate to criticise the legal and judicial process from an intuitive, non-social scientific stance, because that is to act in the very way of which the judges are accused. Social science knowledge is therefore a necessary underpinning for the understanding of custody decisions in the past and present. A social history and sociological context, explaining the social structures of the family, marriage and divorce, husband-wife and parent-child relationships, introduces new perspectives and understandings that the legal decision-making process does not operate in a social vacuum. But the social sciences can contribute to the custody process more positively. A greater awareness and understanding of the social process in which legal decision-making arises may make it possible to evaluate the quality of the decisions, and to apply informed social science understandings to the problems of child custody. The theories and findings of child psychology and psychiatry, and of Freudian psychoanalysis, are nowadays reflected in modern social and cultural values, and as such must play a part in legal decisions. The focus of this book is therefore on social science knowledge relevant to children, and the contribution that it can make to a greater understanding of the issues that form the subject-matter of child custody legal decision-making.

While the basic concerns of the social sciences are philosophical in origin, the development of the social sciences from the mid-nineteenth century and their enormous

7

growth in the twentieth century has introduced a new dimension in the amount of empirical information available for explanation and understanding of social organisation. Yet, certain caveats must be entered against a blind acceptance of social science as omniscient, representing truth, objectivity and absolute knowledge. Earlier beliefs that social science could emulate natural science if only the methods of observation could be perfected, have now given way to a wide acceptance that the social sciences, as indeed the natural sciences, can never be value-free in either their inspiration or research methods (Ryan, 1970; Willer and Willer, 1973). Social scientists are influenced in their research by the social values and demands of the society in which they operate, and the very subject-matter of the social sciences, human behaviour, means that both the data and its measurement, the involvement of the researcher and the distortion involved in the act of describing, limit the ability of social science to explain and predict. Social science knowledge, and its reception, depends also on the social context and circumstances or fate of those who propound it, and of those who receive it. Thus theories may rise and fall, and explanations of the same facts differ.

As an example of the reception of social science knowledge, Bowlby's maternal deprivation theory (1951) that children need the care of a permanent mother-figure for their emotional health, became ascendant in the years following the Second World War, but has now been discredited by psychologists (Rutter, 1981). The sociological explanation for Bowlby's reception is, however, that it served economic and political interests in the post-war world to remove women from the labour market, and the maternal deprivation theory thus coincided with a political desire to get women back into the home (Wilson, 1977). Bowlby's theory also illustrates another problem of social science, that research findings may be methodologically unsound. It has been shown that Bowlby's effects of mother-separation in children in institutions, who were deprived of normal social intercourse, were extrapolated to ordinary children living in a conventional two-parent family (Morgan, 1975). The most interesting question about Bowlby then is why, despite this obvious methodological flaw, did Bowlby's theory become the received wisdom until the late 1960s. The answer has already been suggested: he was persuasive because he appealed to the prior beliefs and social interests of politicians (Wilson, 1977). This also underlines how research may be popularised and used long after it is no longer accepted in the academic community. Psychiatrists rejected Bowlby in the late 1960s, psychologists have always rejected Freudian analysis of the child's sexual development: yet popular belief in both is still current.

The preceding discussion has attempted to explain why, both as between social science disciplines or even within a single discipline, there are no unified theories of, for example, child development, child welfare (Kadushin, 1971), parent-child relationships, the family or divorce as social institutions etc. Thus:

> Theories (of developmental psychology) have risen and fallen, but there has been little integration of the insights of one into the structure of its predecessors. There has certainly been an accumulation of knowledge, but there has been little cumulative understanding of how this knowledge fits together to form an intelligible whole (Sutton, 1981: 51).

The reader of the social sciences must therefore be aware of the theoretical framework of the literature, which is an essential part of understanding the significance of the evidence. For example, the background of writers such as Bowlby (1951) or Goldstein et al (1973) in Freudian theories of child development, colours their opinions. Indeed, it is said that Goldstein et al illustrate exactly "the wrong way to employ social science to solve problems of social policy" for they urge legal reforms "based not so much on 'social science facts' as on 'social science issues in controversy', consulting a limited range of literature and ignoring evidence of the weakness of basic studies, used to support their proposition" (Katkin et al, 1974).

Social science evidence must be assessed not only for theoretical reliability, but also for its methodological reliability. The fact that research fails to prove a theory may lie as much in the inadequacy of the study as in the apparent disproving of the thesis (Shaffer and Dunn, 1979; Rapoport et al, 1977). Unreliability may include generalisations from particular research, of obvious flaws in research methods, e.g. use of self-reporting, of the influence of the investigator as a participant in the observation, of research used in ways that the researcher never intended, or research used selectively, or used after it has been discredited (Shipman, 1972).

To what extent then can the social sciences provide guidelines for policy-makers, in our case legal decision-makers (Skolnick, 1975)? Particular problems in using social science evidence in this practical way arise, for social science cannot provide "clear policy mandates waiting to be put into effect". This is true on a theoretical level; but on the practical level also, "the kinds of problems studied by social scientists may bear little relevance to the issues involved in policy decisions". Much research quoted in this book may have implications for the central concern (e.g. the rejection of the maternal deprivation thesis), but dangers exist in extrapolating research conducted with one purpose in

9

mind to a different context. Even where research is relevant, its results may be inconsistent, or "by no means unequivocal.. they may be accurate in one situation or for one group of people, but not another ... predicted effects have turned out to be non-existent, limited to certain conditions, or in a direction opposite to what was expected" (Skolnick, 1975). Research may also become outdated through a change in social conditions. For example, research on the effects of maternal employment on children conducted when its incidence was much lower than it is nowadays cannot be valid (Lamb, 1982). The same is true of earlier research on children of divorce (Levitin, 1979).

The temptation to extrapolate exists because there are some areas of central concern to this book on which there is little social science data. There was until very recently almost no research on child custody decisions, on custody and access arrangements; or on the relationship of children to their father, although there was an almost obsessive interest in the mother-child relationship (Rutter, 1981). Where studies did consider children of divorce, they had conceptual and methodological problems that made the validity of their findings and the accumulation of a coherent knowledge base problematic (Levitin, 1979). Clinical research studies concentrated on small, self-selected samples presenting to the clinician who used his own impressions and insights in reaching conclusions; single parent family studies tended to treat these families as deviations from the "normal" two-parent family, and failed to take account of multiple variables or mediating factors influencing child behaviour, such as poverty (Levitin, 1979). This book will therefore concentrate only on the most recent research of direct relevance to the children of divorce.

Changing social policy by using research findings, it has been noted, is exceedingly difficult to achieve and evaluate. The empirical evidence to support change may be slight, the change in policy may have "ripple effects" (unintended consequences) which are impossible to predict, and research findings can be diluted and distorted when filtered through the policy-making processes and adopted by practitioners. This is as true of judges and the legal process as of social workers and the political process (Fuller and Stevenson, 1979).

One may wonder, therefore, whether the raison d'etre of this book, to investigate and evaluate current social science findings relevant to the legal decision-making process as regards children of divorce, has not been persuasively nullified. Might it not be that those judges who eschew experts and their so-called expertise and applaud the virtues of old-fashioned "common-sense" are after all right? This book argues that lawyers are ill-advised to insulate themselves from the body of social science knowledge about children. Despite the rise and fall in theories, it can be claimed that there have been real advances of knowledge and thinking (Fuller and Stevenson, 1979). As will be seen, there are now certain well-established understandings concerning children's needs for emotional attachment to adults which are adhered to by proponents of disparate theoretical perspectives, whether they are psychologists, psychiatrists, psychoanalysts or sociologists. In other areas there may be less concordance, for example, on the importance of access. The judges, or whoever the decision makers are, need to be aware of these agreements or disagreements, to be aware that the issues they face have been investigated by social scientists even if the social scientists have not and never will provide absolute answers to these problems. The judges need to be aware that their own views of the needs of children, which they are in the privileged position to be able to impose, are the product of particular social interests. Thus the purpose here is not to prove the judges' views to be right or wrong (because such judgments can only be made on moral grounds), but to show that there may be other views which are the product of different social interests or based on empirical social research conducted in a professional attempt to understand and explain human behaviour. Courts need to:

refine their own critical apparatus for dealing with the evidence presented to them by child care experts. They should adopt a critical view of theories of child development (and take a sharp look at their own implicit assumptions), and if they are going to put trust in 'experts' they must have some appreciation of what constitutes the scientific method (Sutton, 1981: 101).

The aim of this book is to make decision-makers, be they judges, social workers, or parents themselves through private ordering of custody and access, aware of the often unstated assumptions about children; that what society believes is "best" for children consists of "indeterminate" and largely "speculative" ideas (Mnookin, 1975), often deeply "ambiguous (Skolnick, 1975), often not entirely child-centred; that decisions do not represent absolute truths but value judgments firmly rooted in prevailing societal experience and produced by particular social interests. Knowledge of the social sciences provides the awareness necessary to understand the nature of the legal decision-making process. Despite its limitations, social science knowledge exists, as a sophisticated version of common-sense based on observation of human behaviour. With a proper understanding of its inadequacies, it can only broaden the horizons, widen the perspective, and inform the decision-maker of the "best" evidence presently available. The analysis which follows will illustrate how interpretations of the "welfare of the child" have changed, and how they might change in the light of current social science knowledge.

Chapter 2

THE LAW OF CHILD CUSTODY

THE WELFARE OF THE CHILD IS THE FIRST AND PARAMOUNT CONSIDERATION

This book concerns the law of child custody which applies on the divorce of the child's parents, numerically the largest circumstance in which questions of custody arise nowadays. Custody orders may nevertheless be made in other contexts: by magistrates on the parents' separation (Domestic Proceedings and Magistrates' Courts Act 1978); by magistrates, County Courts, or the High Court in respect of legitimate or illegitimate children without any other proceedings between the parents (Guardianship of Minors Act 1971); and the High Court can make wardship orders giving the care of the child to any adult. In some cases non-parents (persons who are not biological parents) may be seeking custody of the child although until the custodianship procedure in the Children Act 1975 comes into force, the only way third parties can initiate proceedings for custody or care of a child is through wardship. Third parties may, however, be allowed to intervene in custody proceedings already started: step-parents may intervene in divorce proceedings as of right (Matrimonial Causes Rules 1977, rule 92(3)), and grandparents may apply for access as of right in the magistrates' courts (Domestic Proceedings and Magistrates' Courts Act 1978, s 14 and Guardianship of Minors Act 1971, s 14A). In divorce proceedings, a non-parent may be granted custody (Matrimonial Causes Act 1973, s 42); similarly in Guardianship of Minors Act proceedings (Re R (1974)) until the Children Act custodianship provisions come into operation (Children Act 1975, Schedule 3, para 75(1)) when the court will have to make a custodianship order in favour of a third party.

In all these proceedings, as in divorce, the decision of the court must be guided by the welfare principle. This principle was made the statutory criterion in the Guardianship of Infants Act 1925, now the Guardianship of Minors Act 1971, s 1:

Where in any proceedings before any court ...
(a) the legal custody or upbringing of a minor; or
(b) the administration of any property belonging to
or held on trust for a minor, or the application of
the income thereof, is in question, the court, in
deciding that question, shall regard the welfare of
the minor as the first and paramount consideration,
and shall not take into consideration whether from
any other point of view the claim of the father, in
respect of such custody, upbringing, administration
or application is superior to that of the mother, or
the claim of the mother is superior to that of the
father.

The welfare of the child is the criterion by which all
decisions concerning custody, access, education or upbringing
of children must be decided, and whether the adults before the
court are parents or non-parents (J v C (1970)).

In 1925 the reference to the welfare of the child as "the
first and paramount" rather than the sole consideration had
been intended by Parliament to recognise that "after all, the
infant is a member of a social unit, the family", and therefore it was legitimate for the judges, as they were already
doing, to also take into consideration "the conduct of the
parents ..., the wishes of the parents ..., the responsibilities of the father for his children ..., the special suitability of a mother to have charge of young children, questions
of religion, and matters of that kind" (Viscount Cave, House
of Lords, Vol 58, 1924, c 349). By 1969, the social values
and beliefs which informed the interpretation of the child's
welfare in 1925, in particular the father's absolute rights at
common law and the punishment of matrimonial guilt, were no
longer deemed by the judges to require legal recognition. The
changes in the ideology of the family and marriage which had
taken place in the intervening years meant that these social
values were no longer to be juxtaposed against a concept of
the child's welfare, but that understandings of the child's
welfare, whether intuitive or informed by sociological and
psychological knowledge, were to be incorporated within the
concept itself. The following statement by the House of Lords
represents the current law:

the words '... shall regard the welfare of the infant
as the first and paramount consideration' ... in their
ordinary significance ... must mean more than that the
child's welfare is to be treated as the top item in a
list of items relevant to the matter in question. I
think they connote a process whereby, when all the
relevant facts, relationships, claims and wishes of
parents, risks, choices and other circumstances are
taken into account and weighed, the course to be

followed will be that which is most in the interests
of the child's welfare as that term has now to be
understood. That is the first consideration because
it is of first importance and the paramount consideration because it rules on or determines the course
to be followed (Lord McDermott, J v C (1970)).

On this view the child's welfare is tantamount to being the
"sole" consideration, since all other considerations must be
subordinated or conduce to it.

In J v C the purpose of explaining the statutory language
was to justify granting custody of a child to foster-parents
who had cared for him for 8½ out of his 11 years of age
against the wishes of "unimpeachable parents" who through no
fault of their own had been unable to care for their own child.
But in the late 1960s the issue which exercised the courts
more often and deeply was to what extent the conduct of the
parents in the breakdown of the marriage was a relevant consideration. The judges' difficulty was how to resolve the conflict between two principles which they wished recognised: one
was the punishment of the guilty party; the other was the
maternal presumption that "as a general rule it was better for
little (children) to be brought up by their mother". In Re L
(1962) the Court of Appeal allowed a father's appeal against a
care and control order to the adulterous mother "as a matter
of simple justice ... Whilst the welfare of the children is
the first and paramount consideration, the claims of justice
cannot be overlooked" (Lord Denning). By 1969 the wish to
give care and control in wardship proceedings to an adulterous
mother led to an honourable attempt to reconcile "the welfare
of the child" with "the claims of justice":

> the word 'first' in the section implies that there
> are other circumstances that are to be considered
> in this process of consideration and weighing. In
> doing this, a special weight must be given to the
> welfare of the infant. This may so clearly point
> in one direction that it concludes the matter, even
> if every other consideration points in the opposite
> direction. On the other hand, it may be that the
> welfare of the infant would be equally served which-
> ever parent has care and control; or the balance may
> fall on one side by only a small amount. In those
> circumstances, the other considerations may be suffi-
> ciently strong to determine the matter. I do not
> think that one can express this matter in any arith-
> metical or quantitative way, saying that the welfare
> of the infant must, in relation to the other matters,
> be given twice the weight, or five times the weight,
> or any other figure. A "points system" is, in my
> judgment, neither possible nor desirable. What the

court has to deal with is the lives of human beings, and these cannot be regulated by formulae (Megarry J, Re F (1969)).

Following the judgment in J v C, the Court of Appeal more than once reaffirmed that to "balance the welfare of the child against the wishes of an unimpeachable parent or the justice of the case as between the parties was no longer to be regarded as good law" (Re K (1977); S(BD) v S(DJ) (1977)). Indeed the climate of judicial opinion had so changed that in Re K not only was the mother, despite her adulterous conduct, "not as a matter of law but in the ordinary course of nature the right person to have charge of young children" (Sir John Pennycuick L J), but the very validity of "the claims of justice" was doubted:

> I do not think that justice between parents in these cases is ever simple. On the contrary, it is a highly complex question which can very rarely be answered satisfactorily, and then only after exhaustive investigation ... So I prefer to keep an open mind as to where the justice of the case, as between the father and mother, lies. It seems to me that all experience shows that, particularly serious-minded people such as the mother in this case, do not break up their marriages unless their relationship with their spouses has deteriorated very severely indeed. So I hesitate to make moral judgments in this class of case; I do not find it particularly helpful (Ormrod L J).

In the present state of the law, then, the welfare of the child is treated as the only or sole criterion for the court. There may be many relevant facts to consider but ultimately the judge must exercise his discretion according to what he believes is for the child's welfare:

> In my judgment I must take account of all relevant matters; but in considering their effect and weight I must regard the welfare of the infant as being first and paramount. If it is objected that this formulation does little to define or explain the process, I would reply that it is precisely a process such as this which calls for the quality of judgment which inheres in the Bench; and this is a quality which in its nature is not susceptible of detailed analysis. There is a limit to the extent to which the court can fairly be expected to expound the process which leads to a conclusion, not least in the weighing of imponderables. In matters of discretion it may at times be impossible to do much more than ensure that the judicial mind is brought

to bear, with a proper emphasis, on all that is
relevant, to the exclusion of all that is irrelevant (Megarry J, Re F (1969)).

The result of this approach is twofold. While in one
sense it has elevated the child's welfare to the only consideration in custody cases and thus represents a highpoint in
child-centredness, nevertheless at the same time, the courts,
taking their cue from society, have denuded the principle of
previous social understandings, in particular about matrimonial guilt. The issue which will be addressed in later chapters is whether any new understandings have or ought to take
their place within the interpretation of the welfare principle.
At a time of rapid social change in family organisation and
sex-roles (Rapoport et al, 1982; Change in Marriage, 1982), it
may be that the judges are unclear as to the basis on which
they ought to make custody decisions. It is also apparent
that the lack of clear principles according to which the
child's welfare may be determined has opened the way for intuitive judgements by the judiciary for which they are criticised. It is important therefore to recognise that it is the
social flux which has caused the judicial diffidence. While
it will not be argued here that new principles ought necessarily to take the place of the old, it may be that the discretion of the judges ought to be informed by wider understandings of parent-child relationships and of the divorcing
and family restructuring process which the social sciences can
offer. In this way their wide discretion may appear less like
'palm-tree justice'.

THE WELFARE OF THE CHILD AND DIVORCE

Under the Matrimonial Causes Act 1973, s 41, a decree of divorce cannot be made absolute,

> unless the court, by order, has declared that it
> is satisfied -
> (a) that for the purposes of this section there
>   are no children of the family to whom this
>   section applies; or
> (b) that the only children who are or may be
>   children of the family to whom this section
>   applies are the children named in the order
>   and that -
>   (i) arrangements for the welfare of every child
>   so named have been made and are satisfactory
>   or are the best that can be devised in the
>   circumstances; or
>   (ii) it is impracticable for the party or parties
>   appearing before the court to make any such
>   arrangements; or

(c) that there are circumstances making it desirable that the decree should be made absolute
or should be granted, as the case may be,
without delay not withstanding that there are
or may be children of the family to whom this
section applies and that the court is unable
to make a declaration in accordance with paragraph (b) above.

The section applies to children under 16, or until 18 if they
are still undergoing education or training.

The child's welfare as a precondition to the granting of
a divorce reflects a modern belief that while parents may
choose divorce for themselves and must face the consequences
of their own decisions, children need legal protection against
their parents' actions. The legal justification for this fundamental intrusion into parental autonomy in the interests of
the children is the premise that children may be damaged by
their parents' divorce and that it is the responsibility of
the courts to protect them against such damage. It is not
clear whether such a responsibility can be meaningfully exe-
cuted in practice, and indeed the very premise requires elabo-
ration (see chapter 6).

There are two stages in the divorce process which lead to
the declaration of satisfaction with the arrangements for the
welfare of the child (a "s 41 declaration"). The petitioner
is required to submit with the divorce petition a **Statement as
to the Arrangements for the Children** (Matrimonial Causes Rules
1977, rule 8(2)), which states the proposed arrangements as
regards:

(i) residence /state where the child is to live with
particulars of the accommodation, what other persons (naming them) live there and who will look
after the child; and, if it is proposed that the
child should be in the immediate care of a person other than the petitioner, state whether or
not that person has agreed to this arrangement/.

(ii) education, etc. / state the school or other educational establishment which the child will attend, or if he is working, his place of employment, the nature of his work and details of any
training he will receive/.

(iii) financial provision /state who is at present
supporting the child or contributing to his
support and the extent thereof and whether it
is proposed to make any application to the court
for the financial support of the child and if so
what support is to be applied for/.

(iv) access /state any arrangements which have been
agreed for access and the extent to which access

is to be given/. _ _ _ _
The said child/ren/ is /are/ /not/ suffering from
serious disability or chronic illness or from the
effects of such illness /, namely, /state, in respect
of each child so suffering, the nature of the disability or illness and attach a copy of any up-to-date
medical report which is available/ /. The said
child/ren/ is /are/ /not/ under the care or supervision of a welfare officer, or officer appointed
by a local authority or other person or organisation
/, namely, /give details, and state the date of any
order for care or supervision and the circumstances
which gave rise to its being made/ /.

The information contained in the petitioner's Statement is
available to the judge as the basis for his s 41 declaration.
The judge is not informed of present arrangements, nor is it
necessary that the petitioner who submits the Statement be the
parent who currently has care of the child (Davis and Murch,
1977). Only the petitioner is required to attend, though both
parties are sent a notice of the date and time of the Children's Appointment. Prior to the Special Procedure for divorce
in 1977, the Statement was dealt with by the judge in open
court after granting the decree nisi of divorce, and this will
still be so in defended divorce suits. But in undefended divorces, which now represent 99% of all divorces (Judicial Statistics, 1981; Maidment, 1980), and which are now processed
administratively by the registrar of the divorce court without
an open court hearing under the Special Procedure (Matrimonial
Causes Rules 1977, rule 48), the judge holds a Children's
Appointment at which the petitioner must attend in order that
the judge may consider the arrangements for the children. The
judge may make the s 41 declaration, and may also at this
stage make custody and access orders if these are uncontested.
The central concern for children in the divorce process is
again evidenced, because it is the judge, not the registrar,
who must hold the Children's Appointment.
    The rules are silent about how the Children's Appointment
should proceed. The judge must be satisfied about the "welfare" of the child, defined to include custody, education, and
financial provision (Matrimonial Causes Act 1973, s 41(6)),
and these are the matters on which information must be provided in the petitioner's Statement. The judge's discretion
is unlimited, both as to the content of his decision and as to
the procedure adopted, except that the judge cannot refuse to
make a declaration of satisfaction on the ground that the
child's financial support is to be derived from the parent's
reliance on social security benefits. As long as the child is
being maintained financially, its source is not a reason for
refusing to make a declaration (Cook v Cook (1978); England v
England (1980); McDermott v McDermott (1980)). Nor is a

parent's intention to contest custody a reason for refusing to grant a s 41 declaration, because such a refusal would unnecessarily delay the granting of the decree absolute (Ashley v Ashley (1979)). In practice judges interpret their function idiosyncratically (Dodds, 1983). In one study (Maidment, 1976) 67% of declarations were that the arrangements were satisfactory, 31% the best in the circumstances, 1% impracticable to make arrangements and 1% exceptional circumstances justifying a decree absolute without a declaration. In a more recent study "satisfactory" or "best in the circumstances" declarations were made in between 77% and 96% of cases (Davis et al, 1983; similarly, Dodds, 1983). Where a declaration was not made (in 10% of cases) the hearing was adjourned, but this was not because the judge was not satisfied after having heard the parent, but because the solicitor asked for it or because the parent with care had not attended (Davis et al, 1983; similarly, Dodds, 1983). On adjournment, a welfare report may be ordered.

No explanation is evident for the distinction that judges make between the "satisfactory" or "best in the circumstances" standards. Judges also differ according to the procedure they adopt. In one study both parents attended in 40% of Children's Appointments (Gerard, 1981); in other studies only 21% (Davis et al, 1983) and 28% (Dodds, 1983): "It appears that the attendance of parents without care is regarded, at least in most courts, as being of little significance" (Davis et al, 1983). Some Children's Appointments are held on the same day as the pronouncement in open court of the decree nisi, others some weeks later; some (40%) take place in the judge's room, others (60%) in a courtroom; in some parties are sworn and give evidence in the witness box (Davis et al, 1983; Dodds, 1983). The average length of Appointments was 4½ minutes, although some only lasted 2 minutes; only 3% took more than 10 minutes, and this was related to solicitors attending (in 24% of the cases) (in Gerard's study (1981) 20% of parents were represented), husbands attending, or the availability of a welfare report. Judges varied in the amount and type of questions they asked; and there is "a lack of consensus between judges as to what are the appropriate matters for their concern in the Appointments" (Davis et al, 1983; Dodds, 1983). Judges also differ in their conduct of the Appointment; some display little sympathy or humour; some appear to "see their role in terms of a demonstration of moral authority"; others adopt a conversational manner, or a "benign, welcoming, friendly" manner (Davis et al, 1983).

As presently operated the cursory practice of Children's Appointments represents "rubber stamp welfare" (Dodds, 1983): "whilst the overt message is of the need to uncover problems, the way that Appointments are arranged and the way that they are sometimes conducted belies this" (Davis et al, 1983). But the s 41 declaration also represents a child protection philosophy which justifies state intervention in family life on the grounds of the welfare of the child. The rationale for this interference with family or parental autonomy, and the justification for a screening procedure to identify children and families "at risk" from divorce, and how that might be better achieved, will be explored in chapter 6.

THE CONCEPT OF PARENTAL RIGHTS

During marriage, or in the absence of any court order, both parents of a legitimate child, born or conceived within marriage, have equal parental rights. The law is contained in the Guardianship Act 1973, s 1, and its origins are traced in chapter 5:

> (1) In relation to the custody or upbringing of a minor, and in relation to the administration of any property belonging to or held in trust for a minor or the application of income of any such property, a mother shall have the same rights and authority as the law allows to a father, and the rights and authority of mother and father shall be equal and be exercisable by either without the other.

Since the parental rights are "exercisable by either without the other" they may be exercised separately, without agreement or even consultation or notification. The resolution of any disagreements on any question affecting the child's welfare is provided for in s 1(3), whereby either parent may apply to a court to settle the matter in difference. No official statistics nor reported cases on applications under this sub-section are available. Presumably the sub-section is not used in practice, for if disagreements are serious enough to require court resolution, the marriage itself is in danger, and questions concerning the children will therefore arise in the context of marriage breakdown.

The principle of equal parental rights is important, as a legal recognition of equality of the sexes, and as social recognition of the greater "symmetry" (Young and Willmott, 1973) within marriage. It also has important practical effects, not so much within the subsisting marriage, but in the period following marriage breakdown. Unless and until a court order for custody is made, both parents may exercise their rights independently. So, a father may remove children from the mother with whom they are living, for example, on their way home from school, or may refuse to return them after a visit. Indeed, a father who 'kidnaps' his own child, even taking him out of the country, in these circumstances does not commit an offence of taking a child by force under the Offences Against the Persons Act 1861, s 56, although his employees who aid him do

21

(R v Austin (1981)). The mother's emergency remedy against the father's action is to ward the child and ask for care to be ordered to her. What are the "parental rights and authority" which parents share? The word "authority" appears superfluous, since it has no legal meaning. "Parental rights" is a legal concept, but admits no easy definition. The present position commences in the statutory definition of parental rights (and duties) in the Children Act 1975, s 85:

... unless the context otherwise requires, "the parental rights and duties" means as respects a particular child (whether legitimate or not), all the rights and duties which by law the mother and father have in relation to a legitimate child and his property; and references to a parental right or duty shall be construed accordingly and shall include a right of access and any other element included in a right or duty.

The Government's intention to provide lasting statutory definitions is evidenced in section 89: "In any Act passed after the Children Act 1975, unless the contrary intention appears - (a) the expression 'the parental rights and duties', ... shall be construed in accordance with Part IV of the Children Act 1975". Section 89 creates no more content to the definition than does section 85, and section 85 is unhelpful in merely referring back to the common law. The only notable phrase in section 85 is its specific inclusion of a parental right of access. This was no doubt added as a counterweight to Wrangham J's description of access as "a basic right in the child" in M v M (1973). Section 85 has in this respect then only confirmed the scepticism that many felt about Wrangham J's well-intended change of emphasis. At the very least, access is now a "mutual right" of parent and child (Bevan and Parry, 1978).

The definition of parental rights and duties must thus be sought in pre-1975 common law. The legal relationship of parent to child is composed of rights and duties but the concept of parental rights and duties itself is vague, and imprecise, "a loose way of describing the conglomeration of rights, powers, liberties and (perhaps) duties which a parent has with respect to his child" (Eekelaar, 1973). Further, the experienced family law judge, Ormrod J has said: "If one were asked to define what are the rights of a parent a propos his child, I for one would find it very difficult" (Re N (1974)). Nevertheless, one can extract from the common law the various rights and duties most commonly said to be composed in the parent-child relationship:

1. Right to physical possession
2. Right to access (visit)
3. Right to determine education
4. Right to determine religion
5. Right to domestic services (compensation for interference with parental rights)
6. Right to discipline child
7. Right to consent to marriage between sixteen and eighteen
8. Right to consent to medical treatment under sixteen
9. Right to veto issue of passport, and give consent to emigration
10. Right to administer child's property
11. Right to succeed to child's property on death
12. Right to appoint a guardian
13. Right to agree to adoption
14. Right to object to local authority assumption of parental rights under the Child Care Act 1980, s 3
15. Right to consent to change in child's surname
16. Right to represent child in legal proceedings
17. Duty to secure education up to sixteen
18. Duty to protect
19. Duty to maintain
20. Duty to represent child in legal proceedings.

There is considerable doubt about the extent of some of these parental rights and duties (Eekelaar, 1973; Bevan and Parry, 1978; Justice, 1975). Some are imperfect or limited rights or more ambiguous in scope and significance than others. A fundamental limitation, however, on all of them (except perhaps the parental right to agree to adoption (Freeman, 1977)) is that the statutory principle that "the welfare of the child is the first and paramount consideration" will take precedence over any parental right in case of conflict (Eekelaar, 1973; Justice, 1975).

THE CONCEPT OF CUSTODY

Parents have parental rights by virtue of being natural guardians of their children. The term "guardianship in its fullest sense ... embraces a 'bundle of rights', or to be more exact, 'a bundle of powers'" (Hewer v Bryant (1970)) which a parent has over his child, i.e. the full parental rights which constitute the parent-child relationship:

These include power to control education, the choice of religion, and the administration of the infant's property. They include entitlement to veto the issue of a passport and to withhold consent to marriage. They include, also, both the personal power physically to control the infant until the years of discretion

23

and the right (originally only if some property was concerned) to apply to the courts to exercise the powers of the Crown as parens patriae (Hewer v Bryant (1970)).

At times "custody" has been deemed the equivalent of "guardianship" (Hewer v Bryant (1970)). In Re Agar-Ellis (1878) the father's right to control his daughter was said to include the right to determine the child's upbringing "as regards religion, education and other matters". In Condom v Vallum (1887) "custody or control" was said to include all the rights that a father had over his child including religion. Victorian judges, however, also used the word "custody" in another sense, the right to physical possession of the child (which is also included in "custody" in its wider sense). It was said that at common law custody denoted "charge of the infant's person" (Re W (JC) (1963)). "Custody", "care" and "control" were terms used alternatively or in combination to represent the same idea. Indeed, in the first Custody of Infants Act of 1839, the granting of custody to the mother clearly meant "care" of the child since at common law the father alone had the legal rights of guardianship. The Custody of Infants Act 1873 also refers to "custody or control".

But from about the 1930s the device appeared of splitting "care and control" from "custody" (Re W (JC) (1963); Allen v Allen (1948); Re Willoughby (1951)). The rationale for split orders was that

> The father, the innocent party, is given the custody of the child or children, but the care and control is left to the mother. That order is entirely realistic. By giving the father the custody, it recognises that he, the innocent party, is at least entitled to a voice in the bringing up of the child, and also to the consideration of the court when any question arises as to what is to be done for the child (Wakeham v Wakeham (1954)).

Care and control orders to the wife were a method of preserving the husband's right to "a say in the child's upbringing and education" (Clissold v Clissold (1964)). Subsequently the judges saw that split orders were undesirable because of the mother's practical difficulties where the father was entitled to make the decisions, for example, for medical treatment; "Normally it was better for a child to have one authority in its daily life" (S v S (1968)).

The demise of split orders resulted from practical considerations as well as from the fall of the matrimonial offence theory. But the concept of custody to which it had given rise remained: "The man in the street was apt to think that the one who had custody had superior rights in the

everyday affairs of the child" (Sachs L J in S v S (1968)).
This view was confirmed by Hewer v Bryant (1970) where Sachs
L J explained that "in its wider meaning the word 'custody'
is used as if it were almost the equivalent of 'guardianship'
in its fullest sense".
The recent practice of the Divorce Courts was thus clear.
A custody order was deemed to give full rights of decision-
making, as described in Hewer v Bryant (1970), to the custodian; "care and control" granted only the right of physical
possession. This distinction was clearly adopted in the first
legislative attempt to elucidate the meaning of "custody".
The Children Act 1975, s 86, introduced a new terminology,
"legal custody", and a new distinction, between the parental
rights relating to the person of the child and those relating
to his property:

> unless the context otherwise requires, "legal
> custody" means, as respects a child, so much of
> the parental rights and duties as relate to the
> person of the child (including the place and
> manner in which his time is spent); but a person
> shall not by virtue of having legal custody of a
> child be entitled to effect or arrange for his
> emigration from the United Kingdom unless he is
> a parent or guardian of the child.

S 87 introduced "actual custody", defined as the right to
"actual possession of the child" (and also the parental
duties). This equates quite clearly with the traditional
"care and control". The definition of "legal custody" however
gives rise to difficulties. The Children Act attempt to define "legal custody" was for the purpose of creating the new
legal relationship of "custodianship" for non-parents and this
is the reason for the distinction between personal and property parental rights. The definition, limited as it is to personal rights, might have been satisfactory if limited to cases
of custodianship. However, s 89 purports to give the definition a more universal significance by including s 86 (and s 87)
in the Interpretation Act 1889, now 1978. The intention was
to provide a standard term with a standard meaning for the
future, i.e. to take "legal custody" out of its limited context of custodianship. This intention is also evident in the
use of the terms in the Domestic Proceedings and Magistrates'
Courts Act 1978, and in s 1 of the Guardianship of Minors Act
1971 as amended by s 36(1)(a) of the Domestic Proceedings and
Magistrates' Courts Act 1978. There are two problems with the
definition, however. Firstly, "legal custody" as defined does
not equate with the wider use of the term "custody" in matrimonial proceedings. Sachs L J's definition of custody in
Hewer v Bryant (1970) clearly includes the power to administer
the child's property: "legal custody" according to the

Children Act 1975 does not. So there are now two separate, perhaps concurrent concepts available for use. Secondly, s 86, while making the distinction between parental rights which relate to the person of the child and those which do not, does not, with a few minor exceptions, tell us which are which. S 86 does specify that "legal custody" includes "the place and manner in which the child's time is spent", and that the parent does have the right to effect or arrange for the child's emigration from the U.K. Further, schedule 3, paragraph 7 includes in "legal custody" the parental right to give consent to marriage; and schedule 3, paragraph 5 includes the parental right to object to a s 3 resolution under the Child Care Act 1980. Otherwise, parental rights are not specified. It has been suggested that the parental rights of succession to and administration of the child's property are clearly not included in "legal custody", and that the right to give agreement to adoption, the right to appoint a testamentary guardian, and the right to change the child's surname are probably also not included in "legal custody" as not relating to the person of the child (Bevan and Parry, 1978). On another view, the right to appoint a testamentary guardian clearly is an incident of "legal custody" (Bromley, 1976).

The definition of "legal custody" does nevertheless suggest a new distinction between custody and guardianship. If custody according to the Children Act 1975 only means "legal custody", i.e. parental rights relating to the person of the child, then the other parental rights, i.e. including those relating to the property of the child, belong to the parent whether or not he has "legal custody", i.e. qua guardian. This emphasis on the rights of the guardian (whether parent or not) over the child's property was certainly in the minds of the Act's framers (Houghton Committee, 1972), but the neatness of this scheme, i.e. custody entailing personal rights, guardianship entailing property rights, unfortunately failed to coincide with the well-established divorce court practice. Sachs L J in Hewer v Bryant (1970) clearly believed that custody included "administration of the infant's property". Whether the statutory definition supersedes Sachs L J's version for all purposes is unclear. The attempt in ss 86 and 89 to provide a standard statutory definition for "legal custody" is therefore more confusing than elucidating.

In addition to the confusion of terminology and definitions in the Children Act 1975, the Guardianship Act 1973 which replaced the father's common law rights of guardianship with equal parental rights (and which was not intended to affect the legal position arising when a custody issue came before a court, which continued to be governed by the welfare principle in the Guardianship of Minors Act 1971), has also belatedly caused more confusion, or possibly even a deliberate attempt to revert to the earlier limited meaning of "custody" as physical possession or care of the child. In Benson v

Benson (1980) the mother had a custody order, but the father had succeeded in getting an order allowing him to choose the daughter's school. Allowing the mother's appeal, Ormrod L J for the Court of Appeal thought it was quite wrong to allow one parent "particularly not the parent who had the formal custody" to choose or make a decision about the child's education. "The situation was perfectly simple: it was for the court to decide the future education of the child when the parents could not agree". This view, that the custodian had no right of decision-making since the non-custodian could seek a ruling from the court, was repeated in Dipper v Dipper (1980). At first instance, care and control had been granted to the mother, with (sole) custody to the father. The judge justified this "somewhat unusual order" on the grounds that: "I do not want these children to be removed from their schools without the father being notified and he will have the say about their future upbringing". The Court of Appeal understandably wished to express its disapproval of split custody orders, but in order to do this, analysed the law as follows: 1. "It used to be considered that the parent having custody had the right to control the children's education, and in the past their religion. This is a misunderstanding"(Ormrod L J); 2. Whatever the parent's "custodial status" (Cumming-Bruce L J) "neither parent has any pre-emptive right over the other" (Ormrod L J) with respect to "education or any other serious matter" (Ormrod L J) or "any other major matters" (Cumming-Bruce L J); 3. Both parents are "entitled to know and be consulted" on these matters (Cumming-Bruce L J); 4. In the case of disagreement either parent has "the right to come to the court in order that the difference may be determined" (Cumming-Bruce L J). Without doubt the judgement is both unorthodox and confused. The current orthodoxy, in Hewer v Bryant (1970) and the Children Act 1975, is that "custody" does not simply mean actual care and possession, but refers to parental rights over children, including education, religion and other major matters; yet Cumming-Bruce L J calls this "a fallacy which continues to rear its ugly head". The confusion is evident in the final order made which belies the internal contradictions in the judgement. The court approved an agreed joint custody order with care and control to the mother: "In this case a joint custody order seems to me entirely right because this is a case where the father has an intent to play an active part in his children's lives" (Ormrod L J). One wonders what is the purpose of a joint custody order when no custody order at all achieved, according to the judges themselves, the same position under the Guardianship Act 1973, s 1; but, more importantly, what does "joint custody" mean when their Lordships have already explained that "custody" only amounts to care and does not entail rights of decision-making for the child's upbringing, and how then is it possible to separate "custody" from "care and control" if "custody" means merely "care and control" anyway? The explanation must be that in their conclusions the judges are reverting to the orthodox wider view of custody. This is the internal inconsistency: the new definition is dropped midway for the old; there is no way of understanding Dipper v Dipper (1980) on its own terms.

It is too early to foresee the implications of the attempt to canvass a reformulation of the concept of custody in Dipper v Dipper (1980), and since its analysis departs from the usual understanding, the term "custody" will be used here to entail full parental rights. The issue to be addressed next is the fragmentation of parental rights which occurs when a custody order is made.

CUSTODY ORDERS AND THE FRAGMENTATION OF PARENTAL RIGHTS

The fragmentation of parental rights which takes place on the breakdown of marriage depends on the type of order which the court makes. There is a variety of ways in which the courts can distribute parental rights and duties between natural parents.

No custody order

Neither spouse need apply for custody, in which case the court cannot make an order. The statutory equal parental rights created by the Guardianship Act 1973 will continue to be exercised.

No custody order; care and control to one parent

The court may be asked to make a care and control order (Re M (1967)) (called alternatively "actual custody"). The effect is that the spouse with care and control gets the right to actual physical possession. All other parental rights remain equal and separate.

Sole custody order to one parent

This is the most common type of order applied for and made (Maidment, 1976). It had been suggested that after the Guardianship Act 1973 joint custody orders would normally be made (Justice, 1975; Law Commission, 1973), but there appears to be no evidence of that. The effect of a sole custody order is to give parental rights generally to one parent, not just those which relate to the person of the child. It is therefore not possible to substitute the statutory term "legal custody" for this type of matrimonial custody order, although to the parent who gets custody it matters little whether he gets "custody" or "legal custody", since whatever rights he does not get by virtue of the custody order, he retains in any case qua natural guardian of his child.

It is open to a divorce court to grant "legal custody" to one parent; whether such is the practice of any divorce court judges is unknown. Under the Domestic Proceedings and Magistrates' Courts Act 1978, a magistrates' court must make a "legal custody" order under s 8 if it wants to make a sole custody order. As explained, this limits the parent to personal rights over the child qua custodian.

The legal position of the non-custodian parent who loses custody, but who remains, as does the custodian, the "natural guardian", of the child will be considered later.

Joint custody order - type 1

An order for joint exercise of parental rights will only be made where the court is satisfied that there is "a reasonable prospect that the parents would co-operate for the well-being of the children" (Jussa v Jussa (1972)). The first joint custody order appears to have been made in Clissold v Clissold (1964) and joint orders are now being sought more often than formerly (Practice Direction (Joint Custody) (1980)). While legal parental rights are shared, a care and control order to one parent is in addition necessary. It is unclear whether a joint custody order differs from the pre-order statutory position of equal parental rights. The Children Act 1975, s 85(3) provides:

> Where two or more persons have a parental right or duty jointly, any one of them may exercise or perform it in any manner without the other or others if the other or, as the case may be, one or more of the others have not signified disapproval of its exercise or performance in that manner.

While this sub-section does not require consultation or notification, it does suggest that signification of disapproval prevents the exercise of the joint right. In this respect separate equal rights allow more freedom of action. It may be that the courts should consider the alternative of no custody order rather than a joint custody order if this distinction is correct.

Joint custody order - type 2

This type of joint custody is probably rare in this country although there is an unusual reference to it in the Marriage Act 1949, schedule 2, but in the United States joint custody has provided for the care and control of the child to be actually physically shared between the two parents. This means that the child has de jure two homes, for example, the

29

child spending "2 days a week, and alternative 3-day weekends with each parent", or summers with the father, the rest of the year with the mother. The success of such arrangements will be considered subsequently. Analytically such a joint custody order differs from a joint custody order with care and control to one parent and staying access to the other, though in actual practice the difference may be minimal.

Split custody order

This order grants custody (or legal custody) to one parent, care and control (or actual custody) to the other. Thus the right of physical possession is split from the other custodial rights which remain with the other parent. The parent with care and control must therefore act subject to the other parent's right to make decisions regarding the child's upbringing. The advisability of split custody orders has been often questioned for the practical burden it puts on the parent with care and control. Moreover, its original rationale, to provide for the need of a young child for the care of its "guilty" mother but leaving the parental rights with the "innocent" and "unimpeachable" father at a time when divorce law was permeated by considerations of matrimonial fault, has now disappeared. The Law Commission has officially frowned upon split orders (Law Commission, 1977), and they may now give way to the next type of order.

Custody order on the formula of section 8(4) Domestic Proceedings and Magistrates' Courts Act 1978

Although this Act governs magistrates' court custody orders only, there is no reason why divorce courts should not adopt the formula in s 8(4):

> An order shall not be made under this section giving the legal custody of a child to more than one person; but where the court makes an order giving the legal custody of a child to any person under this section, it may order that a party to the marriage in question who is not given the legal custody of the child shall retain all or such as the court may specify of the parental rights and duties comprised in legal custody (other than the right to the actual custody of the child) and shall have those rights and duties jointly with the person who is given the legal custody of the child.

This order gives full legal and actual custody to one parent, but the other parent retains "all or such as the court may specify of the parental rights and duties comprised in legal custody (other than the right to the actual custody of the

child) and shall have those rights and duties jointly with the
person who is given the legal custody of the child". This
convoluted formula can result in a joint legal custody order,
with actual custody to one parent (who is also granted legal
custody), although the court is free to limit the rights of
the parent without actual custody.

Two points need to be noted about s 8(4). Firstly, legal
and actual custody are not defined in the Act; thus the Interpretation Act 1978 applies. This illustrates that the Children Act 1975, s 89, intended the definitions to be universal.
Secondly, the grant of legal custody does not touch the non-
personal parental rights in relation to the child. Under the
s 8(4) formula both parents must retain these non-personal
parental rights equally, under the Guardianship Act 1973,
since the court has not made any order concerning them.

Unfitness to have custody

The Matrimonial Causes Act 1973, s 42(3) empowers a court to
make "a declaration that either party to the marriage in question is unfit to have the custody of the children of the family". This power is used sparingly only in very exceptional
circumstances, such as incest by the father with his daughter
(ACB v JLB (1980)). Its purpose is not punitive to the parent
but to protect the child. It ensures that custody cannot
automatically revert to the "unfit" parent on the death of the
custodian (Matrimonial Causes Act 1973, s 42(4)). In the absence of a declaration, this result can only be achieved by
the custodian appointing a testamentary guardian (Guardianship
of Minors Act 1971, s 4) to act jointly with the surviving
parent, and if necessary the testamentary guardian applying to
court for removal of the surviving parent (Guardianship of
Minors Act 1971, s 6).

Wardship

As an alternative to making a custody order, the divorce court
may "direct that proper proceedings be taken for making the
child a ward of court" (Matrimonial Causes Act 1973, s 42(1)).
Parents may themselves initiate wardship proceedings in order
to resolve questions of care of their child, and this is a
particularly useful procedure where an emergency order is required, for example, where one parent has or is threatening to
remove the child out of the jurisdiction.

A wardship order is not easily analysed in terms of the
fragmentation of parental rights. The courts in the last century took the view that wardship vested the guardianship of
the child in the court (Eekelaar, 1973). In Re Gyngall (1893)
the effect of wardship was said to be that the court displaced
the parent as the natural guardian of the child. Nowadays
judges consider that the custody of the child vests in the

court; so the better view now is that a wardship court cannot make a custody order as such but merely a care and control order (Lowe and White, 1979). The result is that the natural parents remain natural guardians with such rights as natural guardians always retain, the court has custody, and some other named person who may be the parent has care and control. Nevertheless, wardship cannot be analysed that simply. It has been said that the effect of a wardship order is that the child comes under the court's "control", that the court becomes the child's "legal protector and guardian and is thereby vested with special control over both the ward's person and property"; that such an order avails against the whole world; that "a ring of care is thrown immediately around the ward" (Lowe and White, 1979); so that "no important step in the child's life can be taken without the court's consent" (Re S (1967)).

The analogy between a parent with custody and the wardship court is appropriate in many respects. Custody entails the right of the court as custodian to give consent to the child's marriage between the ages of sixteen and eighteen (Marriage Act 1949, schedule 2); the court's power to consent to the child's removal out of the jurisdiction (Matrimonial Causes Rules 1977, rule 94(2)); the court's right to determine "important steps" in the child's life (including giving consent to medical treatment); the court's right to veto the issue of a passport. Presumably also the wardship court has the power to determine the child's religion. It seems, then, that the wardship court has by virtue of its custody of the child all the parental rights which a custodian parent has. But the wardship court may also have in addition some of the rights of the non-custodial parent who remains natural guardian of the child. Thus pre-eminently the wardship court takes control of the child's property, to the exclusion of both parents; the court's consent is required before adoption proceedings can be initiated (F v S (1973)), though parental agreement is still normally necessary for the application to succeed: in this sense the parental right is not actually displaced, but significantly modified; finally, the parental right to object to a Child Care Act 1980, s 3 resolution is abrogated by the very nature of the wardship order.

In other respects, it appears that parents, apart from having care and control, may retain some parental rights over their warded child who is under the custody of the court. The wardship order does not seem to affect the parents' right to succeed on intestacy, nor to appoint a testamentary guardian (although the testamentary guardian will be in no better position vis-a-vis the court than the parent was). It seems, therefore, in conclusion, that while a wardship order does not vest full guardianship, it does appear to vest more than just custody in the court. The analogy with custody is imperfect to the extent, as will be seen, that the non-custodian retains more rights on a custody order than parents do on a wardship order.

Committal into local authority care

The court, instead of making a custody or care and control order, may "in exceptional circumstances making it impracticable or undesirable" for the child to be entrusted to either parent or any other person, commit the child into local authority care. It was held in Monk v Monk (1979) that where a divorce court wishes to commit a child to care, the local authority must be given an opportunity to make representations according to the Matrimonial Causes Rules 1977, rule 93. The legal effect of such a committal is that the local authority must treat the child "as if" he had been received into care under the Child Care Act 1980, s 2: it also has "a similar effect to a (s 3) resolution under the (1980) Act in so far as a parent cannot require the child to be returned", but "the order cannot be regarded as its equivalent in that the local authority will not be vested with parental rights and duties" (Lowe and White, 1979). To remove the child from care, therefore, the parents must seek a discharge from the court which made the committal order.

According to Re Y (1975) the effect of a divorce court committal to care is not "to make the child into a (s 2) child", but merely to allow the powers and duties of the local authority under Part III of the Child Care Act 1980 to operate "as if the local authority had taken the child into care under (s 2) no more". In addition, the exercise by the local authority of their powers under Part III are subject to any directions given by the court (Matrimonial Causes Act 1973, s 43 (5)). In one very important respect also a child committed to care in divorce proceedings is not to be considered as a child in s 2 care. The child is not actually in s 2 care since the parents did not consent to the child being "received into care", but is in care only "as if" received under s 2. Therefore in respect of such a child, the local authority could not pass a s 3 resolution.

The non-custodial parent

It is necessary to consider the legal rights of the parent to whom custody or legal custody has not been granted. Since it is the practice of the courts, usually with the consent of the parties to make sole custody orders, the assumption henceforth will be that this is the type of order made unless the contrary is indicated.

(a) Custody. In Jussa v Jussa (1972) the reason for granting joint custody to both parents was so that the husband "should not be cut out altogether from a voice in his children's

future; that he should be recognised still as their parent".
On this view a sole custody order to the mother would have
excluded the father's parental rights, although it is not
clear whether all parental rights (relating to the person and
property of the child) or just those parental rights relating
to the person of the child were excluded. Re T (1963), the
first known English case to consider the right of a mother
with custody to change a child's name, however, took a contrary view.

> An order for custody ... does not deprive a father,
> who is not given custody of the child, of all his
> rights and obligations in respect of his child. He
> remains, subject to the rights conferred on the per-
> son to whom custody is given by the court, the natu-
> ral guardian of the child, and among the residual
> rights which remain to him are any rights which he
> may have at law with regard to the name of the child
> (Buckley J).

Leaving aside for the moment the father's right to have a
child known by his name, the general analysis seems correct.
Both parents are also natural guardians of their child and although custody is granted to one parent there are residual
rights which remain to the other as natural guardian. Pre-
eminently he has the right to apply to court for a variation
of the custody order. He also has at least a right to access
(Children Act 1975, s 85) (despite judicial reformulations of
access as the right of the child to the companionship of his
parents: M v M (1973)), subject to the welfare principle; he
has the right to veto the child's adoption, and object to a
s 3 resolution vesting parental rights in the local authority
under the Child Care Act 1980; he has the right to appoint a
testamentary guardian and a right to exercise his surviving
guardianship on the custodian's death, and he has the right to
succeed to the child's property on intestacy. Finally, a non-
custodian parent has at least a right not to have a child's
name changed unilaterally by the custodian or without a
court's permission.
Re T was decided before the father's common law rights
over his children were replaced by statutory equal parental
rights. There is no reason to suppose that the Guardianship
Act 1973 has changed the non-custodian parent's position. The
effect of the Guardianship Act 1973 was in fact on the contrary to create both mother and father as natural guardians
of their child. The non-custodian does therefore retain some
residual legal rights, the rights of a parent as natural
guardian. Whether these residual rights equate with the parental rights which relate not to the person of the child is
more problematic. It is not clear that these residual rights
which remain to the non-custodian represent only the

34

non-personal parental rights which are excluded from the statutory definition of legal custody in the Children Act 1975, s 86. Thus, for example, access is a personal right (Bevan and Parry, 1979).

(b) Legal custody. As has been seen, the effect of a legal custody order is to give personal parental rights to the custodial parent and leave the non-personal rights equally and separately with both parents qua guardians. On this formula the non-custodian, as also the custodian, will retain the right to veto the child's adoption, the right to appoint a testamentary guardian and to exercise his guardianship. The right to object to a s 3 resolution is also expressly included in the Children Act 1975 among the personal rights, so that this may exclude the right from a non-custodial parent. If it is excluded this would appear to be one right where the difference between a custody and a legal custody order is critical. It must, however, be added that it is also an absurd difference which should not exist. There is no doubt in addition that the right to apply for a variation of the legal custody order and the right of access vest in the non-legal custodian, but it is not clear how this can be explained in terms of the statutory formula in the Children Act 1975, s 86.

It may at this stage be helpful to summarise the foregoing discussion. What the new definition of legal custody has done is to make apparent the analytic distinction between the rights of a parent qua custodian and his rights qua guardian, i.e. between the parental rights relating to the person of the child and those relating to his property. Where only one parent has custody he thus has both custodial and guardianship rights. For the parent with custody, the particular form of analysis of his parental rights makes no difference to the sum total, i.e. he retains all parental rights. To the non-custodian it is the difference between custody rights and personal rights which matters. The non-custodian remains natural guardian of his child, but the content of that natural guardianship may vary according to which parental rights have been given exclusively to the custodian.

The problem of the definition of legal custody exists because the context of the Children Act 1975 in which legal custody was created is quite different from the present considerations. Legal custody was created to provide a new form of custody for non-parents, for example, foster parents, step-parents, or relatives. Thus the reference in section 86 to the non-parental legal custodian not having the right (which otherwise is a personal parental right) to effect or arrange for the child's emigration from the U.K. The contrast between the legal custodian's rights and parent-qua-guardian's rights achieves a logic, although one which might be disputed on policy grounds. But to transport the definition of legal custody to another context, of matrimonial proceedings between two parents, and thus natural guardians, of the child, as did the Domestic Proceedings and Magistrates' Courts Act 1978, s 8, begins to stretch the definition in a way which is inappropriate and unworkable.

It will be unfortunate if the legal effect of a divorce court custody order differs from a magistrates' court legal custody order under the 1978 Act. The need for clarification and harmonisation is evident.

The death of the custodian

If it is correct that the non-custodian parent retains certain parental rights qua guardian of his child, what is the position of the non-custodian on the death of the custodian? This issue may arise where another person, for example, a relative or step-parent, has had actual "care" of the child and wishes to establish a legal basis for such "care".

The question is whether the non-custodian's position as surviving natural guardian (Guardianship of Minors Act 1971, s 3), with such residual parental rights as remain to him despite a custody order, entitles him to automatic custody of the child. This issue arises whether or not the custodian has appointed a testamentary guardian to act jointly with the surviving parent. The question is not whether the non-custodian loses his rights as natural guardian, for there is no way that this can legally occur except through an adoption or possibly through an exclusion order on the application of the testamentary guardian under the Guardianship of Minors Act 1971, s 4(4). The question is whether natural guardianship carries with it a "surviving" right to automatic custody of the child. The non-custodian certainly has the residual right to apply for a variation of the custody order, but once the custodian is dead there is no longer any jurisdiction in the matrimonial court to deal with the matter. The one circumstance where it is clear that custody cannot revert to the non-custodian is where the divorce court (the magistrates do not have such a power) has made a declaration that one parent is "unfit" to have custody (Matrimonial Causes Act 1973, s 42(3)). Otherwise the answer to the question is unclear. Historically when the father had at common law absolute rights of custody even as against the mother, on his death the mother did become entitled to custody. Further, although a court may appoint a guardian where a deceased parent has not done so under the Guardianship of Minors Act 1971, s 3, this power is rarely exercised so that "on the death of one parent the other will become solely entitled to custody if the deceased appointed no testamentary guardian" (Bromley, 1981). Why should it make a difference that a testamentary guardian has been appointed?

Re C (1978) suggests that custody reverts to the non-custodian. After the custodian mother had died in the U.S.A.

and the step-father had applied for custody in the local courts, the father kidnapped the children back to the U.K. The step-father then applied in the U.K. to make the children wards of court. The father opposed. The Court of Appeal took the view that the father "left England with tickets to bring the children back to England at a time when there was no order of any court in existence which prevented him as their father from doing exactly that". The legal position of the father was not analysed further but the reference to "him as their father" suggests a reversion of custody to him.

Further support for this view is the Guardianship of Minors Act 1971, s 4(4). Where a testamentary guardian has been appointed by the deceased parent (in the example, the custodian), that testamentary guardian may apply to the court to have the surviving parent removed as guardian and himself appointed as sole guardian on the grounds that the surviving parent "is unfit to have custody of the minor". The assumption behind this machinery must be that the surviving parent in the absence of such exclusion does have custody of the child in the sense of "the bundle of rights and powers". It is worth noting what the effect of such an exclusion order might be. The implication is that by the court appointing a sole guardian the surviving parent is no longer even guardian of the child. (The most that a court can do when making an exclusion order under s 4(4) is to grant a right of access to the parent (s 10). It can also make a custody order - by implication this cannot be to the excluded parent - and a maintenance order against the parent). Does this mean that, for example, he can no longer veto an adoption, or succeed to the child's property on intestacy? If so, this particular type of termination of parental rights is as far-reaching as an adoption order, and certainly more extensive than a Child Care Act 1980, s 3 resolution whereby a local authority assumes parental rights.

A more guarded view of the problem is that on the death of the custodian "the natural guardian of the child could claim it" (my emphasis; is it necessary to get a court order to enforce the claim or is self-help appropriate?) but only where the deceased custodian has not appointed a testamentary guardian (Hall, 1972).

The position of the non-parent with actual "care" of the child is that he has no parental rights in relation to the child (Re N (1974); Maidment, 1976a) unless either the deceased parent has appointed the non-parent as a testamentary guardian under the Guardianship of Minors Act 1971, s 4; or the court has appointed him guardian (presumably on his own application) under section 3 (where there is a surviving parent) or section 5 (where there is no person exercising parental rights at all), in each of which cases he exercises the guardianship jointly with the surviving parent (ss 3 and 4).

It is at this point that a distinction between the

natural guardianship of a parent and the guardianship of a non-parent by appointment becomes apparent. It has already been suggested that a parent's guardianship encompasses custody, in the full sense of legal rights and actual custody (unless a court order has deprived a parent of any such rights). The Guardianship of Minors Act is, however, silent on whether the non-parent's guardianship includes custody, or care and control. The most that the Guardianship of Minors Act does is to provide a procedure for removal of one guardian at the request of the non-parent (s 4(4)) or for the resolution by the court of "any question affecting the welfare of the minor" in the event that the joint guardians are unable to agree (s 7). The content of sole non-parental guardianship may therefore include the prima facie right to care and control, which may be enforced through court proceedings, but "when a guardian is acting with a surviving parent, it will obviously usually be the latter who will be entitled to care and control" (Bromley, 1981). The word "usually" suggests that there may be circumstances when the parent will not have custody: for example, when that parent has previously had a custody order made against him in matrimonial proceedings.

The strongest statement on this question appears in Re N (1974) on an application by a step-parent for guardianship of the child, both of whose parents had died, and so had no surviving parent/guardian. The court held that such an application was entirely proper. But "the consequence of a guardianship order ... is not in fact going to achieve much practical utility in relation to the custody and care of these children ... (it) would leave him in the position of having a status, but not having the children unless he took some other step to enforce it", i.e. invoking the wardship jurisdiction and asking for the appropriate directions, as the only way of obtaining actual control or even access. Ormrod J pointed out that guardians who are appointed under any provision cannot under the Guardianship of Minors Act "apply for custody or any other order" because no procedure for enforcing "any of the powers or rights of a guardian" is provided in the Act. The court thus advised the step-father to institute wardship proceedings and thereby get a care and control order.

This view of guardianship seems strange. A guardian once appointed, whether by a court or a will, is in loco parentis to his ward. Thus:

> a guardian has custody of his ward and therefore, broadly speaking, has the same rights and duties with respect to his person as a parent has with respect to his legitimate child ... Where there is only one guardian, he will prima facie have the right to the care and control of his ward, a right which he may enforce by habeas corpus, or alternatively by proceedings ... (to make the child) a

ward of court (Bromley, 1981).

Why therefore need a sole guardian, any more than a natural
guardian, i.e. a parent, enforce his guardianship? Custody,
care and control are surely concomitants of the guardianship
(Levin, 1974) unless there is some reason why this should not
be, such as that there is a surviving parent whose right to
custody takes prima facie precedence. This then makes a distinction between the position of a sole guardian, as in Re N
(1974), and a non-parental guardian who must act jointly with
a surviving parent. The surviving parent will have custody
prima facie until and unless the non-parental guardian challenges it under the Guardianship of Minors Act 1971, s 4 or 7.
The success of such a challenge will depend solely on the welfare of the child.

To return to the original issue of the immediate effect
on parental rights of custody of the custodian's death: it is
exactly custody which has been removed previously from the
surviving parent by a court order, and therefore is not one of
the residual rights which the surviving parent retains qua
natural guardian. How can it be, then, that the surviving
parent regains custody? The answer may be that he does not,
i.e. that there is a hiatus in the ownership of parental
rights and in particular of custody. For even if there is a
testamentary guardian it is law that he will not have custody
unless steps, presumably wardship, are taken to enforce his
guardianship (Re N (1974)). It might be in the better interests of the child if no such hiatus occurred; and that until
someone else challenges the surviving parent through legal
proceedings such as a guardianship or wardship action, custody
ought to revert to the parent. The need for speed in a case
where the surviving parent is considered to be unfit to have
custody of the child is provided for by issuing a wardship
originating summons. One is still left with the case of a
parent having been declared unfit for custody by the divorce
court, then becoming the surviving parent. Of legal necessity
in this case there must be a hiatus in the parental right of
custody.

There is clearly a need for a statutory solution.
"Ideally it should be ensured that the case is automatically
referred back to the court for a further order in such an
eventuality, but the actual machinery to achieve this might
prove very difficult to devise" (Hall, 1972). In Australia
such an attempt was made in the Family Law Act 1975, s 61(4):

> On the death of a party to a marriage in whose favour
> a custody order has been made in respect of a child
> of the marriage, the other party to the marriage is
> entitled to the custody of the child only if the court
> so orders on application by that other party and, upon
> such an application, any other person who has the care

and control of the child at the time of the application is entitled to be a party to the proceedings.

ACCESS

Access is the contact which the non-custodial parent with whom
the child is not living has with his child. Issues concerning
access are governed by the same welfare of the child principle
as governs custody (Matrimonial Causes Act 1973, s 52). The
judges therefore have an unlimited discretion to make access
orders for the child's welfare. Orders are often made rou-
tinely for "reasonable" or "liberal" access, unless particular
circumstances suggest more specific terms, such as for staying
access, or specified as to the day or hours and frequency (for
example, Saturday afternoons, from 2 - 6pm). Access may also
be ordered to be supervised, in the presence of a third party
such as a relative, or in extreme circumstances a divorce
court welfare officer (but only with the officer's agreement:
Practice Direction (1980)(a)).

In the divorce courts other persons, such as grandparents,
may apply for access to the child, though the court's leave is
required to intervene in the proceedings (Matrimonial Causes
Rules 1977, rule 92(3)). In magistrates' matrimonial proceedings grandparents have now been given a statutory right to
apply for access (Domestic Proceedings and Magistrates' Courts
Act 1978, s 14); and where a parent has died, his parents may
also apply for access (Guardianship of Minors Act 1971, s 14A).

There is a very strong presumption in English law that
access to a non-custodian parent is in the child's interests,
and access will not be refused unless there are exceptional
circumstances justifying it. In M v M (1973) the parental
right of access was elevated into a "basic right of the child":

> The companionship of a parent is in any ordinary
> circumstances of such immense value to the child
> that there is a basic right in him to such compan-
> ionship. I for my part would prefer to call it a
> basic right in the child rather than a basic right
> in the parent. That only means this, that no court
> should deprive a child of access to either parent
> unless it is wholly satisfied that it is in the
> interests of that child that access should cease,
> and that is a conclusion at which a court should
> be extremely slow to arrive (Wrangham J).

Despite this formulation of the child's right, judges
generally treat access as a parental right, albeit subject to
the overriding welfare principle; but the view that the child
has a right "not to be deprived of an important contribution
to his emotional and material growing-up in the long-term" has
been widely accepted. "Where parents are separated, there is

a heavy duty on the one with whom the children are living to encourage them to see the other" (Wood v Wood (1974)). In D v B (1977) a father who had never seen his one year old child, born after the mother had left him, was granted reasonable access:

> The view of the courts is that unless there be good reason to the contrary it is in a child's interests to be brought up to know the truth of his parentage and to know both his parents. In the absence of such a reason, it is undesirable that a child should believe that his own father had displayed no interest in him, but had abandoned him. Such a belief would be far from the truth of this case. The father has done all he could to ensure that he had an appropriate link with the child, including offering to pay maintenance for the child, which incidentally the mother refused while reserving the right to make claim for it in the future. In my judgment this father has much to offer the child in the way of affection, companionship and guidance. The mother and the co-respondent have each had one unsuccessful marriage already ... Were difficulties in their marriage to arise, it would be an advantage for the child to have his father's care available to him. However, this is not to say that at the present time there is any indication that the marriage of the mother and the co-respondent will not last. The child has received, and is receiving, affection and good care from the mother and the co-respondent, and it is to be hoped that they will manage to master the resentment which I have no doubt they will feel at the order I am about to make (Lane J).

In recent years the right of the child to "know" both his parents has also been extended to illegitimate children (S v O (1978)).

Access may be refused on the ground of the child's welfare, not as a reward or punishment to parents (C v C (1971)). Thus, for example, a mentally ill mother was refused access (C v C (1971)); a father was refused access because his 16 year old son refused to see him and psychiatric evidence was that it would harm the boy to force him against his will (B v B (1971)); a mother was refused access on evidence that access was unsettling her son (M v M (1973)); a father who on an access occasion had taken the children out of the jurisdiction and might have done so again lost access (Rashid v Rashid (1979)).

As will be seen in the next chapter, most orders are for "reasonable access". When difficulties arise over access, as they often do, there are procedures available to the non-custodial parent to return to the court which made the order to enforce it. The divorce courts have the power to impose a fine or to imprison (including suspending sentence) for a period of up to two years for contempt of court for failure to obey a court order (Contempt of Court Act 1981, s 14; County Courts (Penalties for Contempt) Act 1983), but "whether it is wise to /enforce access by committal to prison/ of course is a very different matter" (Re K (1977)(a); R v R (1980)). The non-custodial parent could apply to vary the custody order to give custody to himself, although that may not be the solution desired; or to vary the access order so that it is defined more specifically, or even supervised. The wardship jurisdiction could also be used for these purposes. The non-custodian parent, as an alternative to legal processes, could simply ask for the court to refer the matter informally to the court welfare service for counselling. The custodian parent may use these same procedures, for example in an attempt to have an access order revoked.

Finally, a custodian parent who wished to live abroad with her child has been required to pay money into court which would be forfeited if she failed to return the child to England for access visits (Bond v Bickerdike (1979)). And a mother's persistent refusal of access to her husband of her daughter was held to be unreasonable behaviour giving grounds for divorce (Shears v Shears (1973)).

It may be concluded that despite available legal procedures, access raises social and emotional issues which are fairly intractable to legal compulsion. Alternative methods of resolution of access difficulties will be considered later.

STEP-PARENTS

In English law a step parent qua step-parent has no legal relationship with his step-child. This is so whether the step-parent has married the custodian or not. He may have rights and/or duties by virtue of having de facto care of the child either at common law or by statute. But

> ... neither as a matter of status stemming from the
> position of being a step-father as such, nor as a
> matter of rights or obligations stemming from the
> result that under particular Acts particular rights
> and obligations are granted to or imposed on step-
> fathers who in fact take children into their family,
> or perhaps become adoptive parents, do any of those
> matters, in my judgment, result in a person in the
> position of the step-father in this case having
> parental rights (Re N (1974)).

The step-parent has no duties either qua step-parent, not even a duty to maintain; with one exception on the dissolution of

42

his marriage if he has voluntarily assumed the maintenance of a step-child.

If the child's parent dies, the non-custodian parent who remains the surviving natural guardian of the child can claim the child, as in Re N (1974). If the child's parent appoints the step-parent as a testamentary guardian the natural parent and step-parent must then act as joint guardians. In case of disagreement between them, a court may remove one of them. The step-parent may in this way become sole guardian, for the court will decide the matter according to the child's welfare. It is important then that the step-parent is appointed a guardian of his step-child by the child's parent; the parent can do this whether he has married or is cohabiting with the step-parent. If the step-parent has not been appointed guardian, he will have to use the wardship jurisdiction.

Apart from on the death of the custodian, the step-parent may acquire parental rights in respect of his step-child (Maidment, 1980) by making the child a ward of court and asking for care and control, jointly with the parent. More commonly, however, a divorce court application would be appropriate. The possibility of a step-parent applying for custody of his step-child or more normally for joint custody with the child's parent, i.e. his spouse, has always existed where the child's parent was divorced. The Children Act 1975 however specifically provides for the right of step-parents to apply for "custodianship" (i.e. non-parental custody) of a step-child (after three months actual custody where the person with legal custody, i.e. the child's parent, consents, or after three years without consent) (s 33(3)(a)(c)). The custodianship application will be decided according to the child's welfare (s 33(9)); and a custodianship order will give "legal custody" as defined in s 86 of the Act to the applicant. The custodianship provisions are not yet in force; but in any event the Act also provides, in order to prevent a conflict of jurisdiction, that the custodianship procedure cannot be used by a step-parent where the child has been named in his parents' divorce for the purposes of a judicial declaration of satisfaction about the arrangements for the children, made before the decree nisi can be made absolute (Matrimonial Causes Act 1973, s 41), and the other parent is still alive and "can be found" (Children Act 1975, s 33(5)(8)). Instead he must apply to the divorce court for a custody or joint custody order, and he may intervene in the divorce proceedings as of right (Matrimonial Causes Rules 1977, Rule 92(3)).

Apart from custody, step-parent adoption had become an increasingly popular method of cementing the new family created through remarriage, by creating legal rights over the step-child for the step-parent. In 1976 out of 17,621 adoptions in England and Wales, 67% (11,827) were by parent and step-parent, of which almost half (7,838 or 44.5%) were of legitimate children adopted by parent and step-parent following divorce or death in the child's family. This trend had been increasing for many years. In 1961 only 9.7% of children adopted were legitimate children adopted by a parent and step-parent. By 1971 the figure was 25.5% (Social Trends, 1976).

The desirability of adoption by mother and step-father had been considered by the Houghton Committee on Adoption (1972). The problem was that adoption "severs in law, but not in fact, an existing relationship of blood or of affinity". The Committee concluded that "legal extinguishment by adoption of a legitimate child's links with one half of his own family was inappropriate and could be damaging", and therefore recommended that although adoption by natural parent and step-parent should not be prohibited, relatives (including a step-parent applying jointly with his spouse) caring for a child should be given a new right to apply for guardianship.

The Children Act 1975 gave effect to these proposals by creating the custodianship procedure (not yet in force) or alternatively the possibility of the step-parent applying for custody of his step-child. More importantly the Children Act 1975 attempted to reverse a major popular trend, by limiting step-parent adoption of a legitimate child. The Act provides that where an adoption application is made by a parent and step-parent of the child (s 10(3)) or a step-parent alone (s 11(4)), "the court shall dismiss the application if it considers the matter would be better dealt with under section 42 (order for custody etc) of the Matrimonial Causes Act 1973". This provision does not affect the step-parent of an illegitimate child or of a legitimate child whose natural parent has died, because the matter cannot be dealt with by a divorce court. However, even these step-parents may not succeed in their adoption application, because the court making the adoption decision must give "first consideration to the need to safeguard and promote the welfare of the child throughout his childhood" (s 3).

At least in the higher courts, the judges have displayed an unwillingness to allow step-parent adoptions. The issue often arises on an application by the parent and step-parent to dispense with the natural father's agreement to the adoption either on the grounds of his unresonableness in withholding agreement, or on the grounds of his persistent failure without reasonable cause to discharge the parental duties in relation to the child (Adoption Act 1958, s 5; Children Act 1975, s 12(2)). The courts have been reluctant to find a divorced father guilty of such persistent failure. Re D (1973) held that the father's failure "must be culpable and culpable to a high degree ... In all too many cases there is a temporary drifting apart and a withdrawal by the husband father, when a marriage is breaking up". Where the father seeks renewed contact with his children, such failure cannot be called permanent or persistent. Re H (1974), affirming Re D (1973), held that the persistent failure must be such

44

that

there could be no advantage to the children in keeping continuous contact with him ... The test was not whether a parent was irresponsible, feckless or casual in his care or concern for his children, or over-reliant on others for financial support of his children, and for their care, though those were factors to be taken into account. Nor would the bare fact that a father was a criminal or in prison be justification for dispensing with his consent.

Similarly, in refusing to dispense with the natural father's agreement on the grounds of unreasonableness, Re B (1975) held:

it is only where the welfare of the child so overwhelmingly requires adoption, that the father can and should be deprived of his parental status ... The right question was, not how sincere the father was as to his future role in the upbringing of the child, but whether his decision that he wished his own son to remain in law his son was honest.

The court also expressed its disapproval of step-parent adoptions following divorce and remarriage.

I appreciate that in this case, as in many, it is strongly in the child's interest that he should be settled in the family life of the mother and her second husband; that he should form a close relationship with the father-figure represented in that husband. I also appreciate that in this case, as in many, the fact that the child continues to have a relationship with his natural father is a source of practical inconvenience and irritation to the mother, who wishes to put her first husband out of her life as completely as possible ... It is quite wrong to use the adoption law to extinguish the relationship between the protesting father and the child, unless there is some really serious factor which justifies the use of the statutory guillotine. The courts should not encourage the idea that after the divorce the children of the family can be reshuffled and dealt out like a pack of cards in a second rubber of bridge. Often a parent who has remarried and has custody of the children from the first family is eager to achieve just that result, but such parents, often faced with very grave practical problems, are frequently blind to the real long-term interest of their children.

The courts now take the view that not only is it wrong to cut off the legal relationship with the natural father, but they must also be satisfied that adoption will in some material way, other than legal, contribute to the child's welfare. In Re S (1977) Ormrod L J in the Court of Appeal argued both sides of the case, but his views are clear:

It is a condition precedent to an adoption order that the making of it will 'safeguard and promote the welfare of the child throughout his childhood': s 3 of the 1975 Act. So, in all cases the court must consider whether and to what extent an adoption order will achieve these objectives; this means comparing the position of the child, assuming an adoption order is made, with the existing situation. The question, in other words, is 'will adoption safeguard and promote the welfare of this child better than the existing arrangements?' In the normal class of adoption where the adopters are strangers and the child is a small baby, and usually illegitimate, the answer to this question, once the adopters are shown to be suitable parents, is so obvious that it is taken for granted, and the question scarcely even asked. But in the class of case with which we are concerned the welfare of the child is likely to raise very real and difficult issues. The situation is, in fact, the reverse of the normal class. The children are legitimate, they have usually spent some part of their lives with their fathers and will have established some kind of relationship with them; they will remain after adoption in the same physical environment; and they will have acquired, as children of the family of the natural parent and step-parent, all the material advantages which adoption can provide (leaving aside the very rare case where succession rights may be involved). The advantages of adoption in these cases will, therefore, have to be found, if at all, in the intangible results which may flow from it. The effect of s 10(3), in our judgment, is to require the court, even in a case where adoption would safeguard and promote the welfare of the child, to consider the specific question whether, even so, the case might be 'better dealt with' under s 42(1) of the Matrimonial Causes Act 1973, presumably by a joint custody order in favour of the natural parent and the step-parent, or by leaving the child in the custody of the natural parent. In cases like the present one the question becomes: 'will adoption safeguard and promote the welfare of the child better than either the existing arrangements or a joint custody order under s 42?' ... Looking at the other side of the picture, the advantages

of adoption are vague and uncertain. It was suggested that the children would feel more secure if they
were adopted, and wanted to 'belong' to Mr R. They
had said they wanted to be adopted and, like so many
children, wanted to be known by the same surname as
their mother and step-father. /I/ did not think that
adoption would increase their sense of security or
make them feel more 'integrated' into the new family
unit.

In the final analysis he agreed with the trial judge: "To me
it seems that custody recognises the reality of the situation,
whereas adoption imposes an artificial status. Whatever order
the court makes, it cannot alter the fact that Mr R is their
step-father and Mrs R their real mother and Mr S their real
father".
    Adoption will therefore be allowed where it makes some
material difference to the child's welfare: for example, the
absence of the natural father from the child's life where the
step-father had been the "father figure in the child's life"
from an early age (Re S (1975)). In Re D (1977) the House of
Lords allowed adoption after dispensing with a natural
father's agreement on the grounds of unreasonableness because
he was a self-confessed practising homosexual. The court held
that a reasonable father in the circumstances would want to
protect his child from his proclivities "even if it meant
parting from the child forever so that he could be free from
this danger of homosexuality", and the father had nothing to
offer the child at any time in the future (see also Re D
(1980)).
    While dispensing with parental agreement is therefore
difficult in step-parent adoptions, adoption may not be allowed even where the natural parent does actually agree. The
general policy is against step-parent adoptions unless they
are of clear benefit to the child, and this is so regardless
of parental agreement. In Re S (1977) the natural father had
actually agreed to the adoption. He had "access to the boys
regularly, but the maintenance was paid irregularly and in
diminishing amounts. He lives only a few miles away from the
children's present home, but has taken little interest in
them." Nevertheless the adoption application by the mother
and step-father was refused on the grounds of the general welfare principle (s 3). It seems therefore that questions of
parental agreement only arise once the court has already
decided that a step-parent adoption is appropriate.
    Similar considerations arose regarding adoption of a
child whose natural father had died. In Re L A (1978) an
adoption order was refused at the request of the paternal
grandparents. They "and other close relatives had always been
attached to the boy. The grandparents had set up a trust fund
for him hoping that he would join the family business". It

was for the boy's welfare not to be severed from his grand-parents now or in the future. In any case "the child was al-ready integrated within his new family and making an adoption order added nothing to his welfare".

In law therefore an adoption order may be refused where (a) the father, or if he is dead his family, opposes the severing of their legal links, or (b) in any case where it cannot be shown that the adoption will in any material way, except the purely legal, add to the child's welfare. Whether custodianship or custody orders will replace step-parent adoptions of legitimate children is not known. But clearly the numbers of legitimate step-parent adoptions has fallen, from 45% of all adoptions in 1976 to 32% in 1981 (OPCS, 1983). It has also been revealed that within the sharp national reduction, there are "dramatic differences" in the number of applications received by courts in different areas, and in the success rate of such applications (from 96% of cases in one area to 9% in another)(Masson and Norbury, 1982). The guide-lines developed in the higher courts clearly do not appear to have restricted the wide discretion given to judges in the Children Act 1975, s 10(3) and s 3.

THE LEGAL CONSEQUENCES OF A CUSTODY ORDER

Enforcement

The custodian can attempt to enforce his rights against a per-son who has unlawfully removed the child from his custody in three ways. Habeas Corpus proceedings are no longer approved for resolving disputes over children (Re K (1978)); and ward-ship proceedings are nowadays considered more appropriate. The divorce court may also fine or imprison for contempt of court order, as for breach of an access order. Finally, injunctions may be granted by a divorce court (as by the High Court in wardship proceedings) from before the commencement of divorce proceedings to any time thereafter to order that the child not be removed from or be returned to the de facto or legal custodian.

Removal out of the jurisdiction

Divorce court custody orders have a standard condition that the child must not be

removed out of England and Wales without leave /of the court/ ... but provided that if either parent do give a general written undertaking to the court to return the children to England and Wales when called upon to do so, and unless otherwise directed with the written consent of the other parent, that parent may remove the children for any period specified in such written consent (Matrimonial Causes Rules 1977, rule 94(2)).

The court also has the power to grant injunctions to order that the child be not removed out of the jurisdiction; it may order the court enforcement officer (tipstaff or bailiff) or the police and government departments to assist in tracing the child; it may order the Passport Office not to issue a passport for the child; and it can request the Home Office to use its "stop list" to try to prevent the child leaving major sea and airports in England and Wales. Once the child is out of the jurisdiction, wardship is the only possible legal procedure in respect of the child. The wardship court may exercise its jurisdiction in respect of any child who is a British national or is ordinarily resident in England and Wales but presently outside the jurisdiction; and will act according to the criterion of the child's welfare both as regards the question of jurisdiction, whether to make the child a ward, and on the merits of the case, so that the kidnapping of a child by a parent will not necessarily be punished (Re C (1978)).

The child's surname

The custody order also contains a standard provision that

> no step (other than the institution of proceedings in any court) be taken by the /custodian/ which would result in any child being known by a new surname ... except with the leave of the judge or the consent in writing of the other parent (Matrimonial Causes Rules 1977, rule 94(2)).

Two issues arise: what is meant by "no step", and on what criterion does a judge give leave for a change of surname?
Names have no legal significance in English law. A person may call himself by any name he chooses, and equally change it. By making a statutory declaration or enrolling a deed poll he merely gives legal evidential validity to it. A child's surname is therefore not a matter of law, but of social practice which in England is to call a wife and children by the husband's surname. This is the surname which is usually entered on the child's birth certificate. When the marriage ends, the wife may choose to change her own surname to that of her subsequent partner, whether she marries him or not. If, most commonly, she has custody of the children, she may wish to change the children's name also. Her partner, the step-parent, has an obvious direct interest in this: for both of them jointly the new family name has symbolic significance. More practically, the mother (and step-father, step-children and half-siblings) may find it inconvenient and awkward to

have to explain to persons in authority, for example, doctors, schools, etc., why her children bear a different surname from her own. Yet change of the child's name hides both from the child himself and from the world at large the truth of his parentage (see chapter 9).

In recent years, as a result of the increase in divorce and re-marriage, this problem has confronted the courts. Re T (1963), the first reported case, held that a mother had no right to change the child's name unilaterally on her remarriage, since one of the father's residual rights as natural guardian of the child, even though he had lost custody, was to have the child known by his name. This case was decided eleven years before the father's common law rights over his children were replaced by statutory equal parental rights, which explains the terminology used. But the decision was in terms of the child's welfare.

In the case of a divided family of this sort it is always one of the aims of the court to maintain the child's contact, respect and affection for both of its parents, so far as the circumstances will permit. But to deprive the child of her father's surname, in my judgment, is not in the best interests of the child, because it is injurious to the link between the father and the child to suggest to the child that there is some reason why it is desirable that she should be called by some name other than her father's. The fact that there has been a divorce and that the father was the person against whom the decree was granted are insufficient grounds for such a view (Buckley J).

It is clear that the child's welfare is overriding. In Y v Y (1973) the mother on remarriage had arranged for the children to be known at school by her new surname. Four years later the father discovered this and came to court to change the name back. Latey J approved Re T (1963) adding that equally the custodian father had no right to unilaterally change the child's name. But in the circumstances he considered that the surname should be left for the time being. "Whatever the court's decision might have been in 1965, the matter had, after a lapse of four years, to be decided in a way which best served the interests of the children". He also held that it was important that the two sisters have the same surname; and that a change of name should only occur with the consent of the father, or by decision of the court. The rule in Y v Y (1973) was subsequently written into the Matrimonial Causes Rules 1977, rule 92(8).

The courts have still not resolved the meaning of "no steps". Formal legal procedures to change a name may not be taken, but whether an informal change of name, which in law is equally valid, is allowed is still ambiguous. In R(BM) v R(DN)

(1978) the mother had taken the surname of her cohabitee. The father asked the court not to grant her custody of one child on the ground that the three other children whose custody she already had were being known by her new surname. It was held that the change of name of the three children itself was no reason for refusing her custody of the fourth. The change of name was regarded as of little significance: "It was merely more convenient that they should be known by W's name in the (army) camp in which they were being brought up where he was head of the family". It was also significant that W "would always be ready to remind the children that he was not their real father, but their real father was live and well and very fond of them ... He would make it a point of honour to ensure that any of the children that were with him continued to remember and respect their father". According to Stamp L J: "I think that too much attention is paid to these matters of names, the names by which they are known". Ormrod L J went further:

> It may be, I say no more than that, that the new rule about changing names, has been drawn in a wider sense than the draftsman intended. I remember that at the time it was directed to preventing parents with custody or care and control orders changing children's names by deed poll or by some other formal means, but, unfortunately, it now seems to be causing a great deal of trouble and difficulty to school authorities and to children, and the very last thing that any rule of this court is intended to do is to embarrass children. It should not be beyond our capacity as adults to cope with the problem of dealing with children who naturally do not want to be picked out and distinguished by their friends and known by a surname other than their mother's, if they are thinking about it at all. It is very embarrassing for school authorities and indeed to the court if efforts have to be made to stop a little girl signing her name "W" when it really is "R". We are in danger of losing our sense of proportion. All one can say in this particular case is that one can understand the situation, which is not at all unusual, and I just hope that no one is going to make a point about this name business, in other words, to treat it as a symbol of something which it is not. There is nothing in this case that suggests that the mother or W want to make a takeover bid for this family from the father and turn these children into their own children, nothing at all.

R(BM) v R(DN) (1978) was followed in both Crick v Crick (1977) and D v B (1979), Court of Appeal decisions and in both of which Stamp L J sat. In D v B (1979) the father had never seen his baby. Ormrod L J, finally achieving an order by consent (of the father) that the child be known by the surname of his mother's cohabitee, insisted that the parents behave sensibly about the child and not fight over what he called "formalistic things that do not much matter":

> What is real is that the father and the child should know one another, that the child should, in the course of time, come to recognise the fact that D is his natural father, and so long as that is understood names are really of little importance, and they only become important when they become a casus belli between the parents.

Further

> I am sure everyone understands that the question of the surname of a child is a matter of great emotional significance, particularly to fathers. If the name is lost, in a sense, the child is lost. That strong patrilineal feeling we all to some extent share. But this has to be kept within the bounds of common sense, in my judgment. It is not very realistic to be litigating over how a child of 2½ should be called, so far as its surname is concerned. A child at that age is quite unaware of its surname, even though it will acquire later on, fairly quickly perhaps, some idea of what his name or her name is. But what matters is whether the child identifies with the father in human terms. I suspect that children are much better at distinguishing between reality and formality than adults. If the child knows that D is his father, he may be confused later on if he is known by the name B, but I would doubt it. He is certain to be confused if everybody insists on calling him D when very nearly all the people he lives with are called B. But this is, as one appreciates all too clearly, a very sensitive issue. Fathers feel very sensitive about it. Mothers feel that it is a plague on a day-to-day basis; they have to explain to schools, people have to make special notes in records, and so on, about the name. The matter is one which, in my judgment, ought to be capable of being resolved by two sensible adults who bear in mind that they are dealing with a child, and a child who sooner or later, and probably sooner, will make some decisions for himself in the matter. Pressure, I would have thought, is more likely to produce unwanted results than anything else.

Ormrod L J recognises the conflicting issues, but there is another line of cases which emphasises the social significance of names. Re W G (1976) held that the mother's change of her daughter's name following her remarriage, at the request of the school headmistress for reasons of administrative convenience, was not in the long-term interests of the child.

It is important that it should be realised that the mere fact that there has been a divorce, that the mother had remarried and had custody of the child, was not a sufficient reason for changing the child's surname. The courts recognised the importance of maintaining a link with the father, unless he had ceased to have an interest in the child or there were some grounds - having regard to his character and behaviour - which made it undesirable for him to have access to the child at all (Cairns L J).

A similar view was taken in L v F (1978):

A marriage could be dissolved but not parenthood. The parents in most cases continued to play an important role in their children's emotional lives and development. From the point of view of the children's best interests it was essential that the parents' feelings should be taken very carefully and anxiously into consideration ... A very distinguished child psychiatrist had given evidence that, when they grew older, children were often greatly concerned with their biological origin. How then could one accept that a change of name was of little importance to the children? His lordship could not. In one case a change might be of benefit to them. In another it might injure them. Surely it was an important decision? The mother had said that a change of surname would add to the children's sense of security. Today divorce was commonplace. The fact that the children's surname was different from that of the mother and their half-sister would not cause embarrassment. The children would have a better sense of security if there was co-operation between the parents and the step-father. In the particular circumstances of the case the children should retain their father's name (Latey, J).

The issue of whether informal steps to change a name are allowed remains unresolved, since the Court of Appeal in W v A (1981) has now approved Re W G (1976) and L v F (1978). There are therefore conflicting decisions of the Court of Appeal. But W v A did resolve the other question, of the criterion to be used by the court in deciding whether to consent to a change of name. Refusing to allow a change of name for two children of ten and twelve who were emigrating with their

mother and step-father to Australia, Dunn L J ruled that the
welfare of the child was:

> the first and paramount consideration which must
> be in the judge's mind. When considering the
> question of a change of name, that is to be re-
> garded as an important matter (see Cairns L J in
> Re W G). It is a matter for the discretion of
> the individual judge hearing the case, seeing the
> witnesses, seeing the parents, possibly seeing
> the children, to decide whether or not it is in
> the interests of the child in the particular
> circumstances of the case that his surname should
> or should not be changed; and the judge will take
> into account all the circumstances of the case,
> including no doubt where appropriate any embarrass-
> ment which may be caused to the child by not chang-
> ing his name and, on the other hand, the long-
> term interests of the child, the importance of
> maintaining the child's links with his paternal
> family, and the stability or otherwise of the
> mother's remarriage.

While applications to court must be subject to the
judge's discretion, it is unfortunate that the rule governing
change of names in the absence of litigation is unclear.
Divorcees need to know what they may do. Further, although
surnames have no legal significance, they do have great social
significance, and whichever way the rule goes, in favour of
the father or step-father, there will be dissatisfaction. It
is all the more surprising that an important issue of social
policy, symbolising as it does the whole process of family
restructuring following divorce, should be left to judges.
Popular feelings, indeed, are not even known: how many fathers
do actually consent to a child's change of name, or consent in
return for release from maintenance? Does consent coincide
with non-exercise of access? How often do changes of names
occur in practice without the father knowing or without him
challenging it in court?

APPEALS

There has also been for a long time and still is disagreement
in the Court of Appeal over the grounds on which an appeal
court can reverse a lower court's discretionary decision on
child custody. On one view, recently endorsed by the Court of
Appeal in Clarke-Hunt v Newcombe (1983), the court is only entitled to intervene "if it was shown that the judge was plain-
ly wrong", that the lower court must have acted outside the
ambit of its discretion, or was what might be called "wrong in

principle". These circumstances were elaborated upon in
Clode v Clode (1982): "if the judge has taken into account an
irrelevant matter ... if the judge has failed to take into account a relevant matter ... if the judge's decision is so outrageous that, somewhere along the line, he must have been
guilty of error of method, even if the court cannot identify
it" (Sir J Arnold P).

The competing approach is most recently expressed in
D v M (1982):

> In cases concerning the custody of children there is
> a statutory right of appeal without leave, and the
> appellate courts had a statutory duty to rehear such
> appeals ... It is the duty of the appellate court
> in these cases to review the way in which the court
> below has conducted the 'balancing exercise' and if
> satisfied that it has erred, to correct it (Ormrod L J).

This "error of balance" approach has a distinguished history,
receiving majority support in the Court of Appeal in Re F
(1976). Browne L J accepted that an appellate court could not
substitute its own discretion for the discretion of the trial
court, but insisted that it could interfere where "the lower
court has gone wrong in the balancing operation implicit in
such phrases as (failing to give) 'due weight', (or giving)
'no sufficient weight', or 'too much weight' (to the considerations which ought to have weighed with him)." Bridge L J
agreed:

> It is impossible to say that (the judge) considered
> any irrelevant matter, left out of account any rele-
> vant matter, erred in law, or applied any wrong prin-
> ciple. On the view I take, his error was in the bal-
> ancing exercise. He either gave too little weight
> to the factors favourable, or too much weight to the
> factors adverse, to the father's claim.

The two principles for intervention, the "wrong in principle" and "error of balance" approaches, are thus juxtaposed
as two opposing methods. Certainly the latter approach allows
the appeal court more freedom to review the exercise of the
discretion, and theoretically may lead to a greater chance of
overruling the trial court. It is less likely that a court
espousing the "error of balance" view would say, as Sir John
Arnold (as so many other judges) felt driven to offer apolo-
getically after having taken a "wrong in principle" line:
"Taking the matter in the round, I am not sure by any means
that I would have come to the conclusions these magistrates
reached, but I can find nothing in their decision or the
reasons for it which would justify reversing their conclusion
in the matter" (Faulkner v Faulkner (1981)). Nevertheless,

even on an "error of balance" approach, appellate courts are loath to interfere with the discretion of trial court. Cairns L J, dismissing a custody appeal, said: "It was a difficult case, and it was impossible to say that the discretion has been wrongly exercised or that the decision was against the weight of the evidence" (Re B (1971)).

The difference between the two tests is therefore more a question of degree, and on the facts of a particular case one test may not necessarily produce a different result from the other. Indeed, the general impression is that there is widespread reluctance to interfere with the discretion of the lower court, whichever approach is adopted, or whether any particular approach is articulated at all. An appeal court which chooses to interfere will often do so simply by stating that the lower court was wrong, without explaining the basis to justify interference. A not uncommon type of case is M v M (1980) where a county court judge had in a custody dispute given custody of a young girl to her father. He gave two reasons for his decision: firstly he was very impressed with the father, and believed that he would put the child first at all times, and secondly, the father was more likely to allow the mother access than vice versa. Stamp L J held that the judge was simply "wrong", that "the reasoning in the judgment does not bear examination": "this little girl of 4½ years ought to be brought up by her mother who is the person that nature has ordained should look after her own little girl". Ormrod L J agreed: there was no good reason to remove custody from the mother, the order was "unpractical in the highest degree and I cannot understand why he made it". The Court of Appeal in this case could no doubt have provided some theoretical justification for interfering. It chose not to and blatantly substituted its own discretion for that of the trial judge. Did the Court of Appeal find him to have erred in the balance of considerations, or did they find his carefully argued reasons for giving custody to a father antithetical to their social conception of the family and child-rearing?

Custody decisions are pre-eminently exercises of discretion. Since there are no rules for the exercise of the discretion other than that "the welfare of the child is the first and paramount consideration" (Guardianship of Minors Act 1971, s 1), decisions must be person-based rather than rule-based. Appeals against a discretion unlike appeals on law or on facts, are therefore by nature problematic, for the essence of the case is that the judge was "wrong" in the way he exercised his discretion. In custody cases, there are no rules to guide that discretion so that it is difficult to even construct in theory the grounds on which a discretionary decision might be "wrong in principle". How can a judge be "wrong" to take into account facts which he considers relevant, but which the appeal court thinks are "irrelevant"? The concept of irrelevance seems to have little place in custody decision-making.

All matters are relevant if the judge thinks they are. The only clear ground for interfering with the judge's discretion is when he actually mis-states the law, i.e. he makes an "error of law", such as when he believes there to be a rule (for example, the maternal preference) guiding his discretion when in fact there is none (as in Faulkner v Faulkner (1981)). Since most judges know that there are no rules, and would not speak in such terms, the "wrong in principle" criterion for interference by the appellate court turns out to be simply a more stringent version of the "error of balance" view. Indeed the difference between the tests now appears to be one of wording and of degree, but not of essential quality.

The distinction between the two tests is therefore more apparent than real in theory, though in practice a court which espouses the "error of balance" approach is probably more willing to interfere. The underlying conceptual similarity is the reluctance to substitute one discretion for another, i.e. for the appellate court to merely substitute its own discretion for that of the trial court. In this sense appeals from discretionary decisions are not simply appeals on the merits, but more in the nature of a review, on the grounds that the decision was "wrong in principle" or in "error of balance".

Whichever formulation of the appellate power to interfere is used, there is an evident unease at overruling the trial court. When it is overruled, it is because the appeal court cannot subjectively accept that the exercise of the discretion was "reasonable". The justification for intervention on the grounds of an "error of balance" derives from a desire to enlarge the circumstances in which such interference can occur. As Ormrod L J says in D v M (1982), the stricter test of "wrong in principle" renders the statutory right of appeal "nugatory". The attraction of the lesser "balance" test is that it appears to allow the appeal court more freedom of action to overrule the trial court, and is therefore more likely to be espoused by an appeal court which indeed wishes to make such an overruling. Not all appeal courts, however, (M v M (1980)) seek to justify their action on this theoretical level so that the chances of success on appeal are largely unpredictable, both as to outcome and as to reasoning.

The reason why appeal courts are reluctant to overrule custody decisions lies in the argument that the trial court sees and hears the parties and witnesses, and that its subjective impressions are matters which the appeal court is in no position to gainsay. There are two objections to this. Firstly, the ultimate logic of the argument would be that an appeal court is never in a position to overrule a trial court, because by definition it does not hear the evidence at first hand. Secondly, the argument may not be as strong as is made out:

In my own experience, I have found it difficult enough

57

to decide from seeing and hearing witnesses whether or not they are telling the truth at that moment. I should find it even more difficult to form any reliable view of how their characters were going to develop over, say, the next five years. I am inclined to agree with what Donovan L J said in his dissenting judgment in Re B (1962), "In matters where credibility is an issue, of course that consideration /that being seeing and hearing the witnesses/ is of great weight. I do not think it is of such weight when one is assessing a person's character and ability to look after a child. The encounter is too brief for any reliable conclusion" (Broome L J in Re F (1976)).

The fact is that appeal courts do overrule exercises of discretion on grounds little stronger than that they do not agree with the trial court (as in M v M (1980)). Arguments about seeing and hearing the evidence appear to amount to little more than a form of etiquette, that the court which was given the statutory discretion ought not in general be interfered with.

For the appellant, the nature of custody appeals is not satisfactory. He wants an appeal on the merits, a second opinion from a higher court, with more experienced judges who sit two or usually three together and who can share the benefit of their experience and wisdom. But the appellant is not allowed a second opinion; he gets a review which only results in an overruling where the appeal court finds the trial decision "wrong" on what are to the appellant extremely technical grounds. It is no comfort to him when an appeal judge states in his judgment that he would not have come to the same decision as the trial court but that that is not sufficient reason for overruling it.

The function of custody appeals may need reconsideration. Appeals squarely on the merits are what litigants want. If that is undesirable for policy or practical reasons, then the true nature of custody appeals as reviews ought to be made clear, so that litigants and their advisers understand better the nature of the appeal process, and not expect a substitution of discretion, of which fact Cumming-Bruce L J felt compelled to remind practitioners in Clarke-Hunt v Newcombe (1983).

It may be that custody appeals are being used to rectify the inadequacies of the custody decision-making process at trial level. A custody dispute between two adequate parents, requires, as the judges frequently comment, an agonising decision; there may be "little to choose between the parents", it may be "transparent that there is a strong bond between the child and each of the parents" (M v M (1980)). Whatever the judge decides will be imperfect, because that is in the very nature of the decision at stake. Much of the dissatisfaction with trial court decisions might be dissipated if such "agonising" decisions were not made by a sole, usually male and past middle-age judge, but by a panel of judges sitting in a specialised family court, which would thus be accorded greater respect and receive greater acceptance than the present procedure, and thereby reduce the demand for appeals.

Chapter 3

THE LAW IN PRACTICE

THE REALITY OF CHILD CUSTODY DECISION-MAKING

The reality of child custody decisions is rather different
from the technical details of the law or the difficulties in
interpretation of the welfare principle. Official statistics
relating to custody decisions do not exist, and, prior to recent empirical studies, systematic information about the outcome of custody decisions was not available. Research has now
modified the impressions gained from a purely legal perspective and the media and public obsession with custody disputes
over children. The Keele study (Maidment, 1976) was based on
the 1973 court records of one Midlands court with a sample of
95 cases, being one in five of divorce petitions with dependent children presented in that year. The Oxford study
(Eekelaar et al, 1977) was a larger sample of 652 cases selected from the records of ten courts in England and Wales, representing regional variations and a cross-section of the
divorcing population, being one in twenty of divorce petitions
with dependent children filed in 1974. The results of the two
studies were remarkably consistent.

The Keele study found that it was mainly wives who claimed and got custody, regardless of their status in the divorce
petition. In 89% of the total sample, the wife claimed custody. Where custody was awarded to one parent only (in 90% of
the sample) whether by the divorce court itself or by allowing
a magistrates' court order to stand, 77 wives out of 89 parents (87%) got sole custody, and husbands got sole custody in
13% of the cases. In the Oxford study sole custody was
ordered or allowed to stand in 83.2% of the sample representing 496 wives (91.3% of sole custody orders) and 47 husbands
(8.7% of sole custody orders). To this extent the claim that
"nine out of ten children end up in the sole custody of the
mother" is roughly true (Families Need Fathers, 1974). But
these simple statistics hide more important facts. In the
Keele study only 12% of the custody cases were contested
initially, i.e. as indicated in the petition and the

respondent's acknowledgement of service. Six of these initially contested cases resulted in custody orders by consent or by agreement, so at some point in the legal process they became uncontested. On this basis the percentage of fully contested cases drops to 6%. The Oxford study made the same finding: "6.0% of the sample were classified as being contested on the custody issue at hearing" (paragraph 6.1), though others were contested on access.

Contrary to impressions then, fully contested custody cases are rare. Few fathers choose, for reasons of money, time, energy, will-power, or commitment, to pursue a custody contest to the final hearing (Maidment, 1981). Moreover, the small percentage (6%) of contested custody cases probably represents a self-selected sample of very determined fathers, or fathers who in the assessment of lawyers (Gersick, 1979) and perhaps society had such a good case that they had a chance of winning in the end. With changing attitudes towards men's social role, more fathers may also perhaps pursue their custody claims to a contest, so that the 6% contested cases of 1973/74 will increase. This may have already happened: no official statistics are kept.

Six percent contested cases is clearly a very small percentage but in human terms it is a serious social issue. Of decrees absolute of divorce granted in England and Wales the percentage in which there are one or more dependent children is about 60% (OPCS, 1983). In 1981 145,713 divorce decrees were made absolute. If 60% of these divorces involved dependent children (86,838 divorces) and 6% of these resulted in contested custody suits, in 1981 there were 5,210 custody cases contested through to hearing, involving possibly two or three times that number of children. In absolute numbers that is a lot of contested custody cases in one year. It is perhaps not surprising then that custody contests hit the headlines or the public consciousness.

The uncontested cases

The most consistently significant factor in uncontested cases in determining who gets custody or care of the children, is the "residential status quo" i.e. the residence of the child at the time of the petition as indicated in the petitioner's Statement as to Arrangements for the children. In the Keele study there was a 99% confirmation of the status quo in contested cases. The living arrangements of the child(ren) at the time of the petition were: 80% solely with the wife, 11% solely with the husband, 9% other arrangements (for example, local authority care, joint residence, split siblings). In the Oxford study, similar findings emerged: in uncontested cases, the child(ren) was living solely with the wife in 76%, solely with the husband in 9.1% and in other arrangements in 14.9% of the cases. The authors comment: "If the children are living with the husband, they are more likely to be older children and less likely to be under four (especially if they are girls). But the differences are not striking" (para 2.2). Their main finding, however, was that "this de facto situation was crucial to the outcome of the custody issue" (para 2.2): "in uncontested cases the court's intervention resulted in a change in the child's residential status quo only in 0.6% cases" (para 13.13); i.e. the status quo was maintained in 99.4% of cases (representing eight in number). Indeed, in the 0.6% cases where the status quo did change, only in two cases was the change as a result of a clear choice made by the court between the mother and father as such. In the other six cases, the change resulted from other special circumstances (para 5.2 - 5.4).

The overwhelming paramountcy of the status quo in uncontested cases suggests this as the factor to consider in contested cases as well.

The contested cases

In the Keele study there were 13 cases classified as contested, i.e. defined as contested at the time of the petition. In no case did the residential status quo immediately before the court hearing change as a result of the court order (i.e. 100% confirmation of status quo). But in two of the 13 cases the previous court order did change as a result of a subsequent hearing, in both cases by consent: (in one, children in care were returned by ultimate consent to their mother; in the other, children were given to the mother but voluntarily handed back to the father, which was then confirmed by the court order in favour of the father by consent.

In the other 11 cases where the court confirmed the petition's status quo, the child's residence at the time of the petition was with the wife in four cases (two by consent, two by court order), with the husband in four cases (one by consent, three by court order), in care in two cases (both by court order), split siblings in one case (by consent). It is significant that the percentage of children living with the father in contested cases (36% or five out of thirteen) is much higher than the percentage in uncontested cases.

The status quo then was clearly the single most significant factor in even the most difficult custody disputes. Neither the ground of divorce, nor the existence of a welfare officer's report was at all significant. The age of the children also seemed to be irrelevant although in the Keele sample all the children except for one were above school age. Neither sex nor size of family seemed relevant. One factor which may be significant, however, is the mother's failure to provide adequate accommodation. In two cases, both involving four children each, where the children were living with and thus given to the father, it was specifically mentioned that the mother could not provide suitable accommodation.

The Oxford study confirms many of these findings: firstly, there was a much higher percentage of children resident with their father at the time of the petition in contested cases than in uncontested ones (Table 8 and para 6.2); in contested cases, the child(ren) was living with the husband in 26.7% (compared with 9.1% in uncontested cases), and with the wife in 37.7% (compared with 76.0% in uncontested cases). Secondly, residence with the wife was more likely to go unchallenged than was residence with the husband. This has already been indicated by the fact that most children live with their mothers by agreement and this arrangement is then merely confirmed by the court. According to the Oxford study: "Husbands expressed an initial intention to apply for custody of children currently in their wife's care only in 10.3% (49) of such cases, whereas in 34.3% of cases (23) where the children were living with the husband, the wife expressed an initial intention to seek custody herself" (para 13.7). In the event, however, only a few cases became contested at the hearing: where the child(ren) were living with the wife, 12 out of 49 were finally contested (24%), and the outcome resulted in no change of status quo from wife to husband; where the child(ren) were living with the husband, 11 out of 23 cases became clearly contested (48%), resulting in only one order transferring the status quo from husband to wife (para 3.2, 3.3). The authors conclude: "This evidence shows that wives are more tenacious than husbands in their attempts to obtain possession of the children" (para 3.6). There is no doubt that social attitudes largely explain this differential behaviour. Nevertheless the courts' response to wives' challenges is perhaps the most significant:

> The very low success rate of wives where they did challenge their husbands' possession of the children shows that the courts do not necessarily share that assumption (that the wife is seen as prima facie the proper person to have care of the children) or, if they do, they have regard to other factors in making their decisions. This point is of extreme importance (para 3.6).

The Oxford study discusses at great length the contested custody cases. It found that 6% of custody cases were contested at hearing (39 cases). The outcome resulted in the husband getting sole custody or care and control in six cases, the wife in 20 cases (and other arrangements in the rest). But the most significant finding was that in only five out of the 39 cases did the court outcome result in a change of status quo. Moreover, a close study of those five cases where the status quo did actually change shows that in one case the child had already voluntarily moved to the father prior to the father getting custody; in one case the child had already been moved to the mother by agreement; in one case the wife got custody on a welfare report recommendation after having abducted the children so that they were already living with her at the time of the hearing. In only two cases was there a real change of status quo: in one case a move from husband to wife although the children of five and 11 had been living with their father for six months prior to the petition, and in the other case a split status quo was altered to custody of the two children to the wife (the report expresses concern that in these two cases, the first change occurred against a welfare report recommendation, and in the second no welfare report was called for at all (para 6.5)).

From these two cases where a real change of status quo in the mother's favour occurred (and there were no changes made in the father's favour) the study admits that there is "evidence of a certain judicial caution about allowing husbands to look after children" (para 6.5). But these were only two out of 39 (5%) contested custody cases. The paramountcy of the status quo even in contested cases appears to be much the more significant finding overall:

> Our study confirms that the major factor taken into account by courts in deciding where a child is to live is the avoidance of disruption of the child's present residence. We could find no significant relationship between the outcome of the residence issue and factors such as the age of the children, the sex of the custodian or the separation of siblings. However, it is of interest that in the only cases we did find where a court moved children from one parent to another, it was from the husband to the wife and that wives succeeded in two of the twelve cases where they contested their husband's possession of the children at the hearing. Occasional instances of 'favouritism' for the wife may still, therefore, be found, but they are quite uncharacteristic of the general practice (para 13.14) (my emphasis).

Other studies

Similar findings to the British studies emerged in a custody study conducted in the Family Court of Australia (Horwill, 1979). In a sample of 430 divorce cases opened in the first half of 1977, most children were living with their mothers at the time of application (71.8% with mothers, 15.3% with fathers); the success rate in custody orders was greater for wives in that where the child was living with the mother, 94.8% of mothers got custody or care and control (and only 1.3% of fathers), but where the child was living with the father only 74.2% of fathers got custody or care and control (and 24.2% of mothers). As in Britain, however, most (64% and probably more) custody orders were "by consent"; more mothers applied for custody (mother was applicant in 83% of cases, father in 24%) and as expected there was a preponderance of custody orders (78%) in favour of the mother. The most prominent finding was the maintenance of the status quo: "In only 10% of cases was it disturbed and in many of these it was a 'status quo' of only a few days' or weeks' duration" (para 3.2).

In 11% of cases (48) both parties did apply for custody. But the report indicates that only eight cases were identified as "fully defended". If this is so, the true contested custody percentage drops to 1.9% (eight out of 430). No clear findings emerged regarding defended custody cases, except the limited comment that in Melbourne, one of the seven registries of the Family Court, only six out of 105 cases were fully defended (6%) and in three custody went to father and in three to mother (para 3.3).

In California (Weitzman and Dixon, 1979) a similar picture emerged from a study of child custody awards after the introduction of no-fault divorce in 1970 and after the repeal in 1973 of the statutory preference for the mother as the post-divorce custodian of young children. It found that only 13% of men actually requested custody in the divorce petition (and these were not necessarily contested by their wives). More men had considered custody but had rejected it on practical grounds, or were dissuaded by their wives or lawyers. The study concludes:

It is the claims of this minority of about 13 fathers in a hundred, or one out of every eight fathers, that are processed by the legal system. About three of these men will have worked out their custodial arrangements with their wives, and want the court to sanction their agreement. One or two of the others will eventually settle their cases and obtain joint custody or liberal visitation. The remaining 8 or 9 men will proceed with a fully contested custody battle and their claims will be heard in court. Eventually, the court will award sole physical custody of the children to about 3 men, one third of those who actually contested custody in court... Today the vast majority of divorced fathers are not really interested in obtaining custody of their children after divorce, while the vast majority of divorced women are. And until these preferences and the social patterns on which these preferences are based change, mothers will continue to have custody of most children after divorce. Thus the legal system serves primarily as a means of formalizing the custodial arrangements that have already been agreed upon by divorcing fathers and mothers.

Reported appeal cases

The British custody studies disclosed that in uncontested (as
expected) but also in contested cases (which may be more surprising) the single most important indicator of the custody
outcome is the residential status quo of the child immediately
before the hearing. There is however evidence that in a very
small number of cases some judges attach great importance to
the need of young children for their mothers, so that in the
Oxford study in two cases children were transferred from husband to wife for apparently no other reason than the judge's
predilection for the mother's role. Some slight preference
for the mother is also indicated in the Keele study where justification for the mother not getting custody in two cases was
that she could not provide suitable accommodation for the children.

The Oxford report however pointed out the discrepancy between their findings regarding custody orders at first instance
and the reported cases that go on appeal:

> We do not suggest that cases do not occur in which judges
> assess the relative merits of parents and dispose of the
> issues accordingly, and such cases are to be found in re-
> ported appellate judgments. But our data (which confirms
> that obtained in the Keele study) shows that the general
> pattern of decisions is to leave the children where they
> are (para 13.29).

At first instance both the Keele and Oxford studies have shown
that the maintenance of the status quo was the most 'normal'
result of a custody order. But in a study of reported cases
(Maidment, 1981) it appeared that some 37% (14 out of 38) of
reported appellate cases did not maintain the status quo, and
children were moved by court order from their father to their
mother after a status quo of between one and five years, on
grounds such as maternal preference, reuniting siblings,
assessment of a parent's personality, and punishment for refusing or obstructing access.

It seems then that in the ordinary routine custody case
there is evidence of some very slight favouritism towards
mothers, but not enough to support any claims of substantial
bias on the part of the judges. The odd cases of favouritism
could be explained in terms of judicial idiosyncracies but not
of such a level as to cause real concern. On appeal cases do
provide evidence of real, even widespread bias. Why there
should be such a discrepancy between the ordinary cases and
the appealed cases is not clear - unless it is simply a re-
flection of the idiosyncratic attitudes of the very small
number of 22 appeal judges. Furthermore, these appeal cases
have presumably on paper the best chance of success for fathers,
since the father has the most important factor, the status quo,

on his side.

Access

Sociologists had previously indicated that access visits tended to become less frequent and regular over time after the
marriage breakdown (Marsden, 1973; Goode, 1956; George and
Wilding, 1972; Maidment, 1975), but the British custody studies
have shown that even at the time of the divorce petition, when
information about access is provided by the petitioner in the
Statement as to Arrangements for the children, access is often
not exercised. In the Keele study access was not even claimed
by the non-custodian in 28% of the cases. and the court finally granted access in 68% of the cases; in the Oxford study
access was granted in 55% of the cases. Where access was refused in the Keele study, it was usually to a husband; wives
who did not get custody were usually granted access whether
they asked for it or not. The order was for "reasonable
access" in 89% of the Keele cases, and in 95.5% of the Oxford
cases.
      The most significant finding however was that the access
order appeared to bear no relation to the actual factual situation. Thus access orders are made by judges even where
access is not taking place, and access orders are not made because they were not asked for even though access is taking
place (Davis et al, 1983). In the Keele study access was not
taking place at all, according to the Statement as to Arrangements, in 34% of cases (in the Oxford study 32%, of which only
2.6% were cases where the custodian refused to allow access);
regular access was taking place in 29% of cases, irregular
access in 14%, and in 23% no information appeared in the document. Regular access tended to be frequent, irregular access
infrequent. The main finding therefore was that in the majority of cases even at this early stage of the proceedings access
was not taking place regularly. Wives as well as husbands were
failing to see their children. Similar findings have been reported elsewhere (Willmott and Willmott, 1982; Fulton, 1979).

THE LAW AS SHADOW FOR PRIVATE ORDERING

The British studies have produced three major findings.
Firstly, about 94% of divorcing parents agree between themselves the arrangements for the care of their children after
the divorce. Secondly, about 90% of these arrangements provide for the mother being the main caretaker in that the children live with her. Thirdly, the court, which need not but
usually is asked to confirm the private consensual arrangement, rarely disturbs parents' agreements and almost invariably preserves the residential status quo of the child (in
the Keele study in uncontested cases this was in 99.4% of the

cases, in contested cases in over 95% of the cases).

The phenomenon of private ordering in the legal process of divorce has only recently begun to be explored (Mnookin, 1979), but its prevalence cannot be doubted. Apart from custody agreements, divorce petitions themselves are also overwhelmingly consensual at least in the technical sense; in 1980, 99.4% of divorce decrees made absolute were undefended (Judicial Statistics, 1980). There are no similar statistics available for financial arrangements after divorce.

The reality then is that most decisions arising out of marriage breakdown are negotiated between the parties themselves, with or without the aid or intervention of lawyers. The appropriateness of <u>judicial</u> procedures for supervising this private ordering has been questioned (Elston et al, 1975), although the residual role of the law and the judges in guarding the public interest in a fair and just legal framework or in protecting individuals against their own follies (in particular in protecting women in their economically weaker position) remains unresolved (Mnookin, 1983).

In England recognition of the prevalence of private ordering has combined with a new attitude to family life which values personal autonomy, to produce a process of dejuridification of family law. Pre-eminently this has occurred in the substantive law by the partial removal of a fault-based divorce law (Matrimonial Causes Act 1973). Procedurally the judicial decision-making function of family law which embodies the retrospective, punitive and normative perspective of adversary procedure is giving way to administrative decision-making with a prospective, preventive and instrumental perspective, whereby courts 'rubber-stamp' privately negotiated settlements while at the same time professing an investigative role for the protection of the individuals involved (such as the children or the economically weaker party). The Special Procedure for undefended divorce introduced in 1977 whereby divorce petitioners are processed administratively by a Registrar is an outstanding example of procedural dejuridification, although the requirement that the judge still pronounces the decree nisi of divorce in open court is a meek attempt to preserve a facade of a public interest in marital status. Nor should it be forgotten that the introduction of the Special Procedure owed more to a government attempt to save money than to any coherent social philosophy concerning divorce (Bradley, 1976).

For children of divorce one of the consequences of the shift to administrative and investigative procedures is the s 41 declaration of satisfaction about the arrangements for the children without which his parents cannot normally be divorced. The private ordering of arrangements for children has however made even that into a rubber-stamping procedure as has already been seen (Davis et al, 1983).

The virtues of private ordering in creating "participant

justice" (Murch, 1980), arrangements which are made by the parties themselves and thus acceptable to them in a way that court-imposed settlements are not, have also given rise to new procedures for facilitating out-of-court agreements. Divorce conciliation services have been established, often with the primary aim of encouraging private agreements concerning the children of the marriage. The first of two models presently operating involves out-of-court conciliation, whereby parties refer themselves or are referred by solicitors to an independent conciliator, whose role is to assist the parties to reach an "emotional" divorce and thus explore possibilities of reaching agreements concerning their post-divorce relationships (Parkinson, 1983). Indeed the experience of the only fulltime conciliation service in Bristol suggests that conciliation, encompassing "emotional, practical and legal aspects" of the divorce, helps in reducing confusion, clarifying issues, opening a door to reconciliation, settling disputes out of court, accepting mutual responsibility for decisions, protecting against marital violence, and containing crisis. "Early and skilled intervention" by a conciliator can also reduce children's adverse reactions to and fears surrounding the divorce, prevent continuing the conflict through the children, and achieve agreements for custody and access (Parkinson, 1983). The features of out-of-court conciliation are that it is available early in the marriage breakdown process, when intervention is considered to be most effective before attitudes harden, and that it allows for self-referral. The second model involves in-court conciliation, pioneered in the Avon area county court (Parmiter, 1981). The Principal Registry of the Family Division in London in January 1983 put into operation a pilot scheme of conciliation for contested custody and access applications (Practice Direction (1982); Matrimonial Causes Rules 1977, rule 92(7)) and this model is being copied in other provincial courts. The registrar will now hold a conciliation conference in all contested children's cases at which the parties and their legal advisers, all children over 11 years of age, and a court welfare officer, are present. At the conference the parties may adjourn with the welfare officer in an attempt to reach agreement. If agreement is not reached, the appointment may be adjourned to enable further conciliation to take place or a welfare report will be ordered. If custody or the principle of access is still in dispute, the matter will finally go to the judge. Early reports suggest that agreement results from the procedure either at the appointment itself (50% of access disputes) or at some later date, possibly with the benefit of a welfare report (more commonly in custody or care and control cases) (Davis and Bader, 1983). The cost however appears to be a slight increase in the ordering of welfare reports, since all cases not actually agreed at the appointment now attract a report (Davis and Bader, 1983) which was not previously true of contested children's cases (Maidment, 1976; Eekelaar et al, 1977).

The encouragement of private ordering, and the very virtues which are claimed for it nevertheless raises difficult philosophic issues for the professed concern of the law to protect the welfare of the child, which is embodied in the s 41 declaration procedure. The question remains unresolved as to the extent of the power of a court to refuse to accept the agreement made between the parties themselves, or the grounds on which the supervisory protective jurisdiction ought to be exercised. These important issues about the limits of family autonomy and the justification for state intervention in the divorce process will be addressed subsequently (chapter 6).

The existence of private ordering does not however detract from consideration of the substantive law. The law of custody has been made through the minority of "hard" cases which have reached the courts, but many cases are not litigated, either from ignorance of the legal system, from lack of financial resources, or from a disbelief in the efficacy of the law to resolve emotionally charged issues. Other cases, perhaps most, may be genuinely agreed by the parties. In all events only about 6% of custody cases are disputed, and it is in those cases that the judges make the law. In the vast majority of divorces, arrangements are made which may or may not follow the rulings of the judges. In one sense then the law of custody is largely bypassed or ignored and the guidelines created by the judges, for example rejecting a maternal preference, may be in the majority of cases irrelevant.

Nevertheless private ordering does not operate outside of a legal framework. It takes place against a background of legal rules, what Mnookin (1979) has called "bargaining in the shadow of the law". Most importantly the legal rules form part of the "bargaining endowments" of each party. The knowledge that if he went to court for resolution of the dispute he would get a particular result is part of and is used in his bargaining out of court. The more uncertain the rules are however, as the law of custody is now becoming, the more difficult such out-of-court bargaining becomes. In theory then one might expect more disputes referred to court for settlement where rules are uncertain or indeterminate. This ignores however other equally important factors influencing the decision to negotiate or to litigate, such as the transaction costs, the parties' preferences, and strategic behaviour (Mnookin, 1979).

Current exhortations to private ordering through the use of divorce conciliation or mediation procedures, and the interest in reform of procedural law, do not therefore detract from the importance of the substantive law being "seen to be securely founded on principles which are generally thought to be just and equitable" (Law Commission, 1981). The substantive law has many roles to perform: it symbolises societal beliefs about justice and fairness between individuals; its principles govern the settlement of disputes; it reduces the exercise of naked judicial discretion; it provides the shadow of legal certainty against which bargaining and private ordering can take place; and it, arguably, provides principles for a supervisory function over private ordering in order to protect weaker parties.

The substantive law of custody will be considered in subsequent chapters in the light of available social science knowledge.

PROCEDURES FOR DETERMINING WELFARE

At the Children's Appointment, the judge may make a declaration of satisfaction about the arrangements for the children which is the precondition to the divorce decree being made absolute. He may make a s 41 declaration even though custody is going to be contested in order that the divorce is not delayed (Ashley v Ashley (1979)). The judge may also make a custody or access order (unless this has already occurred at the in-court conciliation conference). Such orders would necessarily only be made by consent of both parties. If orders are not made at this stage but at some other stage in the proceedings (either earlier at the conciliation conference, or later after an adjournment), the registrar also has jurisdiction to make agreed custody orders or orders where the principle of access is agreed to but the extent of access is in dispute (Matrimonial Causes Rules 1977, rule 92(2); Practice Direction (1980)).

At the Children's Appointment the judge may not be satisfied with the arrangements or there may be some contested issues. In these cases the judge may refuse to make orders and instead adjourn the children's issues to a later date in his chambers. In particular the judge may wish to have fuller information about the children than is available from the Statement as to Arrangements or the interview with the petitioner at the Children's Appointment. In contested cases also, although the parties will present evidence and may even introduce expert witnesses, the judge may wish to undertake his own investigations. There are therefore two mechanisms for providing fuller information: adding to the existing adversarial system by the introduction of expert evidence, or separate representation of the child; or promoting the investigatory role of the court by welfare reports or judicial interviews. Each seeks to enhance the protection of the child's welfare in otherwise adversary proceedings between adults.

Welfare reports

"A judge or registrar may at any time refer to a court welfare officer for investigation and report any matter which concerns the welfare of the child"; the parties themselves may also request the registrar to order a report (Matrimonial Causes Rules 1977, rule 95). Court welfare officers are probation officers, but increasingly individuals are specialising in divorce court work. Their statutory role is to investigate and report, but in the nature of the task they are increasingly becoming involved informally in conciliation and counselling (Murch, 1980).

The judicial discretion to order welfare reports is unlimited and there appears to be a sharp variation in their use between courts of between 3 and 20% of custody cases (Eekelaar et al, 1977; Murch, 1975). Furthermore, until the recent practice of in-court conciliation (supra), it was by no means certain that a report would be ordered in all contested cases. In the custody studies (Maidment, 1976; Eekelaar et al, 1977) in only 50% and 53% respectively of contested custody or access cases were welfare reports available. Of uncontested cases, in 8.2% of the Oxford cases there was a welfare report, presumably following a finding by the judge that he was not satisfied with the arrangements for the children.

The probation service itself recognises three categories of welfare reports (for example, North West Regional Divorce Court Welfare Officers, 1976; Wilkinson, 1981): (i) "Satisfaction" reports (i.e. in uncontested cases) "usually called for because the judge does not feel he has sufficient independent knowledge of the well-being of a child to say that he is satisfied that the arrangements are made and are satisfactory"; (ii) contested custody disputes; (iii) access disputes.

But both the Keele and Oxford custody studies found it difficult to discern clear criteria on which welfare reports were ordered. The Oxford study suggested that "factors associated with a tendency to seek welfare reports" included "the number of children in the family; whether the child had moved between separation and petition; where it was proposed that the child's residence should be changed; if non-relatives (other than a cohabitee) were present in the same household; where the children were living with persons other than a parent. It was not more common to find a welfare report where the children were with the husband rather than the wife" (para 4.7 and 13.10). The Keele study found the factual backgrounds to the cases in which welfare reports were called as: difficulties over access; simple contested custody; child(ren) already in care; mother in prison; split custody arrangements; quality of mother's care in question.

The Oxford study looked at eight cases, all uncontested, where the residential status quo of the child was different after the conclusion of the proceedings from that at the time of the petition. In only two of these cases were welfare reports ordered. The important factor however is that only two of these eight changes in residential status quo represented court intervention as opposed to voluntary switches by the parents. It concludes: "In only ... two cases did the court appear to make a qualitative judgment between the two households, but in neither was the matter thoroughly investigated nor the advice of a welfare officer sought" (para 5.3, 5.4). There were five contested cases where the residential status quo changed. Even in these circumstances in one case out of the five a welfare report was not called for (para 6.4), (and in one other case a report was called for but its recommendation not followed). The Keele study was less specific in its findings:

> There were cases where a reading of the papers would have suggested that a welfare report might have been appropriate, e.g. two cases of contested custody, in one of which the W could not provide suitable accommodation and therefore lost custody, and one in which the divorce court varied the magistrates' court order to give custody to the H, with whom the children were then living rather than the W.

The development of in-court conciliation may alter the use of welfare reports significantly. All cases which remain contested after the registrar's conciliation conference will now probably attract a report; "satisfaction" reports in uncontested cases may still be ordered.

There are no statutory or legal guidelines as to how the welfare officer should prepare the report. This is a matter of good practice for the probation service. It has been suggested (Wilkinson, 1981) that both parents, custodial and absent, should be interviewed and visited at home, probably more than once; the role of second partners needs to be considered; the children themselves must be seen, the reason for the enquiry explained, and an attempt made to establish their views; other relatives, other agencies involved with the family, schools, day nurseries and play groups, medical profession, health visitors etc, may need to be interviewed. Welfare reports are clearly time-consuming; indeed one of their disadvantages is the delay caused to the decision-making process. Further, the judges have repeatedly voiced a preference for one welfare officer seeing both parents and producing one composite report despite the distance involved in seeing the non-custodian parent (W v W (1971); Anon (1971); B v B (1973)). A recent attempt to make more efficient use of welfare officers' services suggests that the court specifies those matters on which the report ought to be made (Practice Direction (1981)).

The report itself will contain facts as well as opinion,

74

and it is good practice to differentiate the two (Sutton, 1981). Hearsay evidence is allowed, in the interests of the investigation (Official Solicitor v K (1965)) but the nature of the evidence as second-hand (or opinion) should be made explicit (Thompson v Thompson (1975)). The parties, and their lawyers, are entitled to a copy of the report which is the court's property, despite the fact that it may contain sensitive information about the parents (Matrimonial Causes Rules 1977, rule 95(3)(b); Murch, 1975, 1980). Recommendations by the welfare officer may be made, and indeed may be positively encouraged (Wilkinson, 1981). The responsibility of welfare officers in making recommendations is increased in view of the apparent reliance of the judges on them. In the Keele study in every case where a welfare report was made, the existing residential status quo was recommended by the welfare report and confirmed by the court. This is not saying that the court accepted the recommendations in every case, for in fact the court accepted the specific recommendations or general intimations in only 71% of welfare report cases. In the other 29% the court deviated from the recommendations, but always on issues other than the residential status quo (for example, the court ordered access in three cases though the welfare report had recommended against it; the court granted joint custody but gave care and control to the wife respondent as the welfare report had recommended; the court granted custody to the husband, but gave care and control to the local authority as the welfare report had recommended).

Nevertheless welfare reports clearly can be very influential and may result in children being returned to their mother after a period with their fathers (P v McK (1973); Re C 1973 (1979)); other judges are confident enough to disturb the father's status quo without the benefit of any welfare report (Maidment, 1981).

Where a judge differs from a welfare report recommendation, he is required to make clear his reasons for doing so, in case of an appeal (Re C 1973 (1979); Re T (1980)).

In principle the welfare officer ought to be available in court for cross-examination on his report; in practice cases are settled out of court on the basis of the report, or the parties may not intend to challenge the welfare report. In the interests of efficiency therefore, parties are now requested to notify the registrar or the welfare officer himself whether his attendance will be necessary (Practice Direction (1981)).

There are many concerns about the use of welfare reports by divorce courts. The first raises practical questions about the efficient use of resources:

Where judges follow the suggestions of welfare officers, it is not clear what functions they are performing; where, as occasionally happens, they depart from the suggestions, it may be asked whether they are better able to make the judgment than the officer. In uncontested cases ... it is not clear what the courts achieve in practice by attempting to exercise the supervisory function. A "satisfaction" report by a welfare officer, when sought, may indeed more fully inform the judge of the situation, but it is very unlikely to lead him to make an order which alters the existing situation. One obvious reason for this is the limited range of alternatives open to a judge. Even assuming the conditions in which the child is living are not very satisfactory, it would seldom be practicable or even sensible to transfer the child to the other parent (who may not want the child) ... There would seem to be a case for the view that the needs of the children in families recently broken down through divorce would be better met by improving the awareness of the custodian parents of the available resources than by compiling reports to judges which rarely influence their actions /e.g. information and advice about welfare rights available to one-parent families/. Further, it might be considered whether a screening mechanism could be devised which would identify those families to which a visit from a member of the welfare services would be advisable. The purpose of the visit would not be the compilation of a report for the use of the judge, but to see that the family is receiving proper social assistance and whether any further intervention is necessary in the children's interests (Eekelaar et al, 1977: paras 13.25 - 13.27).

Most important may be the need to identify potential conflicts over custody or access which are hidden from the court in an apparently uncontested case.

In contested custody cases, the Oxford study suggests: "If there is a dispute between the parties over custody and the outcome is to leave the children where they are, it would seem that there is room for the provision of a counselling service which will assist the parties in adjusting to this situation" (para 13.29). In access cases, the Oxford study comments that "it is unlikely that the orders made have much impact on the practices of the parties". But where access is contested "these are perhaps among the most difficult cases to come before the courts ... we believe there is room for adapting our procedures to the urgency of these situations in fuller recognition of the importance of their resolution in the interests of the children concerned" (para 13.30).

The second area of concern is the issue of welfare officers' expertise. Attention has already been drawn to the problems of social science knowledge about child development; there is the related problem of the assumed scientific base and professionalism of social workers:

When evidence is presented to the courts about 'the needs of children' everyone involved in the proceedings should clearly recognise that expertise does not equal science. They should realise that the evidence presented by experts in child care represents a conglomeration of a number of factors, some favourable, some not, with science making little or no contribution in most instances. The favourable factors involved will probably include relevant experience, judgment and good sense, and personal sensitivities to the feelings, etc. of others. Many social workers and other professionals make significant contributions to the decisions of the court on such a basis. Less favourable factors include prejudices, rationalizations to justify the needs of the institution, and willingness to improvise rather than say 'I don't know' (Sutton, 1981).

A study of the opinions of welfare officers on the effect of divorce on children, varying on particular issues between 51% and 91% agreement, concluded that their opinions were no more valuable than those of "the man in the street" (McLoughlin, 1980). In the United States where courts more often than here appoint child psychologists as consultants to report in custody cases, it has been found

In general, the courtworkers considered the most practical and reality-based criteria for their custody decisions. Instead of evaluating parents as functioning adults and projecting the possible future adult-child psychological adjustment, the workers were relatively more concerned about who was currently available, capable, and willing to take physical charge of the child (McDermott et al, 1978).

Thirdly, welfare officer investigations highlight the philosophical problems of state intervention in the divorce process. The nature and development of custody investigations has been likened (Levy, 1982) to the child-saving interventionist policies of the juvenile court movement, which now attract much scepticism. The juvenile court was based on the same ideas of non-adversary investigation in the interests of the child's welfare, specialised courts and judges, with "expert" assistance for diagnosis and treatment. The child protection role of the divorce court is therefore now equally being attacked as a form of social control (Levy, 1982). It has been noted in the United States that judicial discretion has been exercised to control the lives and behaviour of divorced parents through custody and access orders, more commonly in lower class divorces (Levy, 1982). Similar impressions were gained in Britain from a study of s 41 Children's Appointments (Davis et al, 1983).

The parens patriae role of the divorce court in children's cases, of which welfare reports are an important part, requires careful consideration, and is returned to in chapter 6.

Judicial interviews

A judicial interview of a child to seek his views or feelings on the custody or access issue, or even an interview with parents as sometimes recommended (Andry, 1968), represents the apogee of an investigatory stance. It was a long-established practice of the Court of Chancery (Ex p Hopkins (1732); Re O'Hara (1900); Re Gyngall (1893); Official Solicitor v K (1965)); but there is no statutory provision for such a procedure by judges (magistrates may not see children in private: Re T (1974)), and judicial views and practice differ on its desirability. The holding of an interview is in the discretion of the judge, and to decline an invitation by counsel to do so cannot be a ground for appeal (D v D (1980)). A questionnaire to 98 judges in 1968 elicited a response from 49 (50%) (including the majority of High Court judges) that they did interview children, but 21 of the 49 only did so where the issue was contested (Hall, 1968). The minimum age at which interviews were considered appropriate differed from six to 13. (The new in-court conciliation procedure requires children of 11 and above to be present at the registrar's conference). The circumstances in which judges might interview children include:

> where it is suggested that the child should leave the country permanently; where there is a controversy regarding education; where the child is living with a mentally disturbed parent; where the child is unwilling to see a parent who has rights of access; where the child is alleged to have an invincible repugnance to one parent; where one parent alleges violence against the child by the other; where the welfare officer is puzzled; and where the judge feels he can help a child who is subject to the pull of conflicting loyalties (Hall, 1968).

Although the main purpose of a judicial interview would be to elicit the child's own viewpoint, the procedure is not unproblematic. Firstly, while in law the child's wishes are relevant, they are not presently deemed to be determinative of the issue (Bersoff, 1976). A judge may therefore find himself in the "embarrassing" position of wishing to decide contrary to the expressed wishes of the child (D v D (1980)) on the basis of other considerations. Secondly, there is serious judicial doubt about the weight to be given to the child's expressed wishes. Judges are sceptical about the influence that parents can have on a child, so his views may not be "an independent exercise of his own will". They also make a distinction between the child's current views and their own considered opinion of the child's long-term interests (Re S (1967)). Finally, there is the issue of whether a judge can communicate effectively with a child in the strange surroundings of a court building. If the aim is to elicit the child's wishes as part of the evidence, it may be that a welfare officer is a more suitable person to achieve it.

Despite the adult orientation of the adversary legal process, there can be no doubt that the child's views are at the least a relevant consideration to be weighed by the judge in the balance. The child may even provide confirmation of allegations of parental conduct (S v S (1971)). The issue here is not whether the child ought to be interviewed, but who is the most appropriate person to conduct it.

Finally there is the issue of confidentiality. In an attempt to encourage a child to "speak freely and frankly and without fear" a judge promised the child that "in no circumstances would anything he said be made known to anyone else". The Court of Appeal considered this to be wrong, since an appeal on the merits was impossible without full possession of the evidence on which the judge came to his decision (H v H (1974)). The decision highlights the delicate nature of the interview, and raises again whether a judge is necessarily skilled in communicating with a child. The decision however is in line with welfare report procedure, the most common alternative method of seeking the child's views, which provides that the parties and their lawyers are entitled to acquire a copy of the welfare report on payment (Matrimonial Causes Rules 1977, rule 95(3)(c)).

Expert evidence

Divorce court welfare officers are officers of the court and appointed to assist the court; they are social workers seconded only from the probation service. There is no power in this country, unlike Australia (Watson, 1980) or parts of the United States (McDermott et al, 1978) to appoint psychologists or psychiatrists as court welfare officers or consultants; and it appears that the court has no jurisdiction to appoint any other person, such as another social worker or a child psychologist or other medical expert, to prepare a report for the court (Children Bill 1973, cl. 53; Cadman v Cadman (1982)). Divorce court welfare officers could not therefore be expected to administer "parent-child interaction tests" of the type recommended by McDermott et al (1978). The welfare officer is however entitled to collect any evidence relevant to the case, and this might include the opinion of a child psychologist, psychiatrist or paediatrician etc, who may be called to give oral evidence and be cross-examined. In cases where the court appoints a separate representative for the child (infra), most commonly the Official Solicitor in wardship proceedings,

however, that representative also may instruct an expert; such
a procedure is preferable to an expert instructed by one of
the parties unilaterally (Re S (1967)).
   The most common way that independent expert evidence is
introduced in court is by the parties calling expert witnesses.
Traditionally such witnesses have been psychologists or psychiatrists, but more recently independent social workers have
emerged (Cadman v Cadman (1982)). The court cannot require
another adult party to co-operate with the opposing party's
expert witness; and otherwise healthy children involved in a
parental dispute should probably not be examined by a psychiatrist (or other expert) without the consent of both parents
or leave of the court (Re S (1967); A-W v E (1974)).
   A psychiatric examination of an otherwise healthy child
is considered undesirable therefore in principle. This view
implicitly suggests that children from "the perfectly ordinary case of a broken home" (Re S (1967)), as opposed to a "not
ordinary" case, need not necessarily be psychiatrically disturbed by their parents' divorce; the alternative interpretation that all children of divorce are vulnerable, thus they
all ought to be professionally examined, which given present
resources is not practicable, has not been judicially
sanctioned (Re S (1967)). The debate on the effects of
divorce on children will be returned to in chapter 6.
   Expert medical evidence began to be introduced into court
by parties in children cases in the early 1960s, but this most
commonly occurred in adoption or fostering cases where the
parent, usually the mother, had changed her mind or wished to
recover her child from the applicants. Experts have also been
used in wardship cases, where disputes between estranged parents have led to the child being warded; and less commonly in
ordinary custody cases (B(M) v B(R) (1960)). The attitude of
the judges in these cases to expert evidence has been ambivalent (Michaels, 1967; Bates, 1976). On the one hand they
deny that they "live in the past and have no time for psychiatrists and such new-fangled nonsense", and to the contrary
enthusiastically welcome such expert opinions (Re S (1967));
in some cases strong, uncontradicted medical evidence of the
dangers of moving a child from one set of adults to another,
has been determinative of the decision (Re C (1964)); and
psychiatric evidence based on observing the child with the
adults has been welcomed (Re E (1964)). On the other hand
views on the weight to be given to medical evidence differ.
The classic statement of judicial scepticism of expert evidence appears in J v C (1970) in the House of Lords, a fostering case, where nevertheless the court did accept the evidence
of the dangers of a change of home

      where the infant is under some treatment or requires some
      treatment for some physical, neurological or psychologi-
      cal malady or condition. In such cases medical evidence

if accepted must weight heavily with the court.
Secondly, ... one has the case of a happy and normal
infant in no need of medical care and attention for any
malady or condition who is sent to a psychiatrist or
other medical practitioner for the sole purpose of calling the practitioner to give quite general evidence on
the dangers of taking this, that or the other course in
the relevant proceedings ... Such evidence may be valuable if accepted but it can only be as an element to
support the general knowledge and experience of the judge
in infancy matters, and a judge in exercising his discretion should not hesitate to take risks ... and go against
such medical evidence if on a consideration of all the
circumstances the judge considers that the paramount welfare of the infant on the balance of probablities ...
points to a particular course as being the proper one.

There is also an aversion to allowing the decision-making
power to be transferred to the experts (Re C (1964)); dangers
of abuse exist between an unscrupulous expert and the party
who has instructed him (Bevan, 1973); and most crucially, the
evidence may be indecisive (Re W (1963)) as where two paedia-
tricians called by opposing parties disagree (Re EO (1973)),
or it may be speculative, confusing, based on general principles rather than the particular circumstances of the case
(Re C (MA) (1966)), or based on experience in problem cases
without any evidence of the chances of successful adjustment
(J v C (1970)). Instruction of the expert by one party,
resulting in no knowledge of the other party, is considered
"unfortunate" and disputing parents have been urged to co-
operate in giving joint instructions (B(M) v B(R) (1968)).
An attempt by a solicitor to delete a section of a psychiatrist's report on access which he considered prejudicial to
his client's (the mother) case was defeated conclusively by
the court (Noble v Thompson (1979)).

     In general there is a sympathetic judicial reception of
expert witnesses, but their evidence is treated with suspicion.
This contrasts with the benevolent attitude towards divorce
court welfare reports. This contrast may be a function of the
fact that the welfare officer is largely unchallenged professionally (and this is why independent social workers are now
being introduced), whereas expert witnesses appearing on behalf of one party are cross-examined, and can be challenged by
experts for the other side, so that the unscientific nature of
their opinions is exposed.

     In some ways judicial scepticism of expert evidence epi-
tomises the major issue which this book attempts to address:
that a desire to incorporate current social science understandings about children and families into legal decision-
making founders on a recognition that such understandings may
be incomplete, controversial, speculative or time- and

culture-bound. At present the "general knowledge and experience" of the judge is set against possibly conflicting prognostications of experts; in this situation it is not apparent
why the judge should not fall back onto his own intuition and
common-sense. But there may be a case for the judge (as well
as other participants in the process, adult parties, lawyers,
welfare officers), to inform his general knowledge with social
science, so that when he makes a choice, perhaps between experts, he does so in full understanding of its context and
significance. The following criticism would thereby be de-
stroyed:

> Can legally trained judges be expected to know that the
> level of diagnostic opinion among the so-called experts
> can range from a skilful barrister presenting for one
> parent a psychiatric "maternal-deprivation theorist",
> and the barrister for the other parent calling upon an
> expert who is less committed to the maternal-deprivation
> theory, but more to the "duo-parental" theory which would
> give both parents at least an equal chance to claim their
> child? And how can judges take these "expert" opinions
> seriously when some barristers set out to play off one
> theorist against another in order to reveal their lack
> of unanimity (Andry, 1968).

Separate representation

By court order. Similar to calls for expert evidence in all
contested custody cases (Children Bill 1973, cl. 53; Bevan,
1973) is the concurrent call for separate representation of
the child (Children Bill 1973, cl. 52; Justice, 1975). At
present divorce courts may order representation by the Official Solicitor or any other proper person, of its own motion
or of that person, whenever "it appears to the court that any
child ought to be separately represented" (Matrimonial Causes
Rules 1977, rule 115). The cost will be borne by the Legal
Aid Scheme subject to a means test. There is no power to
appoint a non-lawyer guardian ad litem in matrimonial cases,
as there is in care proceedings (Children Act 1975, ss 58,64).
    A survey of 98 judges in 1968 disclosed that 75 (77%) had
never ordered separate representation, but 60% of the High
Court judges had done so, compared to only 16% of county court
judges (who dealt with undefended divorces). The most common
reason for doing so was a paternity issue; also mentioned were
where the child was living with a mentally ill mother, or a
request to take the child abroad, or a "bitter fight" over
custody (Hall, 1968). The appointment of the Official Solicitor even in contested custody cases is not common.
    The purpose of separate legal representation is to over-
come the fact that the child is not a party to the case. Separate representation therefore creates a status for the child

in the proceedings, in recognition that the child's interests
may not coincide with his parents',either as individuals (in
contested cases) or even jointly (in uncontested cases). Separate representation of the child as a party to the proceedings is therefore an attempt to make the "object" of the proceedings, the child and his welfare, into a legal "subject"
with procedural rights.

Despite widespread and increasing support for the idea of
separate representation (Justice, 1975; Foster and Freed,
1972), not only in divorce but in all children's proceedings
(Giller and Maidment, 1983), in the belief that this will ensure that decision-making by and between adults will more
effectively protect the interests of the child in question,
both in principle and in practice it is a complex issue. The
issue of principle is whether the representative is an officer
of the court, "amicus curiae", as the Official Solicitor is,
whether representation is of the child and his wishes (assuming he is old enough to articulate them) i.e. an "advocacy"
role which assumes that the lawyer takes instruction from his
client, or whether representation is of the child's interests
as defined by adults, whether his parents, lawyer, social
worker or the court, i.e. a "guardianship" role. While that
issue remains unresolved, the practice of separate representation will remain confused. At present separate representative lawyers display a confusion as to purpose, choose a
stance according to their own preferences, and most commonly
adopt a "guardianship" role (Hilgendorf, 1981). Separate
representation does not always produce a fuller hearing in
court, but often leads to compromise and negotiated outcome
out-of-court (Giller and Morris, 1982). Separate representation may then result in no more than a manipulation of procedure, which does not fundamentally alter the nature of the
decision-making process as an adult form of child conflict
resolution. In other words, procedural reform cannot create
substantive justice (Giller and Maidment, 1983).

The practice of separate representation is also complex.
Various models exist for the filling of the separate representative's role: an officer of the court (Justice, 1975), a
specially designated independent representative (for example,
the Official Solicitor or the Australian Legal Aid Office
lawyers), or private lawyers (the New York Law Guardian)
(Dickens, 1978). The efficacy of representation depends on
many factors, in particular the extent to which the court
allows representation to operate on an adversary model
(Stapleton and Teitelbaum, 1972); the quality of the separate
representatives (in Australia separate representatives provided under the Family Law Act 1975 from the Legal Aid Office
were initially too young and inexperienced); and undue delay
in the resolution of the case may result (Stone, 1982).

The case for separate representation in proceedings by a
local authority to remove parental rights (care proceedings)

is strong in that the parents are in a weak position to challenge social work findings by the applicant. In custody disputes, the assumption is that both parents will present the
viable alternative dispositions from a position of rough
equality. The case for separate representation in contested
cases is nevertheless strong since in the heat of the battle
the parents may fail to pay sufficient regard to the child,
his wishes or his interests. The same claim for uncontested
cases (Justice, 1975) however is subject to considerations of
family autonomy where there is no issue to be tried (Bersoff,
1976) and practical use of resources.

The issue of representation cannot be isolated from other
mechanisms for providing a "guardianship" protection for the
child. The courts have recently pointed out that "in most
cases the child's interest will be sufficiently protected by a
welfare report" so that separate representation should not be
necessary except in special circumstances (Practice Direction
(1982)(a)). (The implication that welfare reports are intended to protect the child specifically, rather than the interests of the family, has however never been explicitly enunciated). Indeed, one of the strongest criticisms of the separate representation approach has been that it obfuscates the
real issue in children's cases which is that the judiciary
needs to be more specialised and expert, and should adopt a
more inquisitorial procedure (King, 1975).

The introduction of in-court conciliation conferences in
all contested children's cases may also have a profound effect
on the development of separate representation. All disputes
not agreed will be subject automatically to a welfare report;
by the time the few cases contested to the bitter end reach
court there will have already been extensive welfare intervention. In these circumstances, court-ordered separate representation may add nothing to the proceedings.

Independent social workers. While separate legal representatives are clearly under a duty to conduct their own investigations in order to inform the court on the child's needs, and
to present this if appropriate in opposition to the parents'
evidence, there remains the problem of effectively challenging
social work evidence. In care proceedings this results from
the fact that the local authority applicant has social work
expertise and information which is not available to the parents, their lawyers, or any representative of the child. In
custody cases it may be the welfare officer, as officer of the
court, whose opinions ought to be challenged by the parents
or the child. The practice has therefore recently arisen of
an independent social worker or reporter being appointed by
the parties (the court itself cannot do so: Cadman v Cadman
(1982)). The Legal Aid scheme has approved payment for such
independent reporters in certain circumstances. The purpose
of the appointment is to allow an independent social worker

to investigate the case, and present a "second opinion" on the welfare report. Given the scepticism now being expressed of social work expertise (Sutton, 1981), the independent social work assessment is a natural corollary to adversarial legal presentations.

The position of the "independent" reporter is in many ways analogous to the expert witness, despite the title; he is instructed by one of the parties, but his role in custody cases will usually be to challenge the officer of the court. A recent ruling from the Family Division confirms this view: while the court may entertain the evidence of an "independent" reporter, no person is under any obligation to discuss the case with or to be interviewed by him; the "independent" reporter may not see the welfare report which is confidential to the court and the parties; the welfare officer may not discuss the case with the "independent" reporter without leave of the court; and the courts will not depart from "the usual practice" of relying on that report or of ordering a further report by a different welfare officer (Practice Direction (1983)).

Conclusions

The purpose of all the mechanisms discussed here, whether superimposed on the adversarial or investigatory role of the court, is to introduce extra-legal information about the child and the family, or information which the parents themselves cannot be relied upon to provide. The recognition that children cases involve person-based rather than rule- or law-based decisions has produced alternative ways of providing the court with social and social science information. It is difficult to assess the efficacy of the different procedures, since all have virtues as well as faults. Nor is it easy to assess the desirability of having more than one procedure operating in one case, since to a large extent their findings will overlap; yet the more individuals concerned in the case the fuller might be the airing of the issues. What is clear is that to date the divorce court welfare service has provided the main extra-legal input in most cases. In uncontested cases this will remain the case; and the development of in-court conciliation procedures in contested cases may increase the involvement of welfare officers, since all cases not settled successfully by the registrar will be referred to a welfare officer for conciliation or report. The aim of in-court conciliation is indeed to prevent contested cases coming before the judge for trial, both on the grounds of cost and of reducing the effects on the child of parental hostility and litigation. The expected reduction of contested trials therefore will also reduce the use of procedures for judicial interview, expert witnesses and separate representation.

SUPERVISION ORDERS

The only power that a court has when it is concerned to keep
post-divorce arrangements for children under review is to make
a supervision order. These can only be made "if there are exceptional circumstances making it desirable that the child
shall be under the supervision of an independent person" (Matrimonial Causes Act 1973, s 44).

    In practice supervision orders are made in between 3.5%
(Eekelaar et al, 1977) and 8% (Maidment, 1976) of custody
cases, most commonly though not necessarily on the recommendation of a divorce court welfare report. Indeed, in 1981
there were 16,000 children supervised by local authorities
under orders made in divorce proceedings (Social Services for
Children in England and Wales 1979-81, 1982-83). The circumstances in which supervision is considered appropriate include
family or parental instability, handicapped or truant children,
poor housing, poor maternal care, children in local authority
care, and difficulties over access (Griew and Bissett-Johnson,
1975; Maidment, 1976); the purpose of the order is variously
to check how arrangements are working out, to try to establish
proper access, or to provide help and advice to an inadequate
custodian. Supervision orders are more likely to be made when
the father is granted custody or on a lower-class family
(Southwell, 1982). A supervision order is considered preferable to a matrimonial care order if the local authority in-
tends to leave the child at home (C v C (1981)).

    Orders may be for an unlimited or fixed period; they may
be allocated to the Probation Service or to local authority
social workers, depending on availability of resources, any
current or previous involvement of the family with either service, the age of the child (younger children to Social Services), and the nature of the concern (for example, suspected
child abuse to Social Services). Supervised access is clearly
time-consuming for the supervisor; the courts now encourage
"mutual friends, unprejudiced relatives, god-parents" with
their consent to be approached to supervise, and welfare
officers only as a last resort, preferably not for supervision
at weekends, the number of occasions for supervision to be
specified in the order, and the place of access not to cause
the officer undue travelling difficulties (Practice Direction
(1980)(a)).

    The duties of the supervisor are undefined. Generally
the Probation Service's duty is to "advise, assist and be-
friend" its clients. How that is carried out in matrimonial
cases depends on probation service practice; officers vary
considerably in frequency of visits, in their involvement with
the family and in their perceptions of what supervision entails (Southwell, 1982). Differences in attitudes towards the
value of access with a non-custodian parent is also apparent;
as is confusion over the purpose of the order (Southwell, 1982).

In practice, supervisors assume that orders are made because parenting is in question or the child is considered to be "at risk" in some way, neither reason specifically related to the divorce nor warranting legal intervention under other legislation. Generally, social workers may operate less effectively as supervisors; they are less aware than probation officers of the legal context in which the order operates, and more confused as to its purpose and their role (Southwell, 1983; Wilkinson, 1981). There is a general lack of understanding that the supervision arises out of the marriage breakdown, and that the purpose is to assist in the post-divorce reconstruction of the family. The extent to which the child should be actively involved in the process of supervision is also unclear, or whether the child and/or the family is the client.

The supervisor has no legal rights of entry, of enforcement, or of securing co-operation from the family. Legally he can only return to the court which made the order for "directions as to the exercise of his powers" (Matrimonial Causes Rules 1977, rule 93(4), to vary the court orders, or to seek a matrimonial care order (rule 92(3)); or he might instigate alternative legal proceedings, for example, for emergency care. Many supervisors would not want legal powers, since the nature of their role is seen as "persuasion and influence" not policing. The supervisor finally may apply for discharge of the order if its purpose has been fulfilled (rule 93(4)), but in practice many orders simply expire on the child reaching 18.

The confusion over the purpose of orders among supervisors is mirrored by the confusion among the families. It is a measure of the supervisor's success whether his intervention is appreciated or resented.

The creation of guidelines for supervision orders would help to reduce many of the difficulties presently surrounding their operation. New terminology such as "parental guidance order" (Hall, 1968), or "family court order" (North West Regional Divorce Court Welfare Officers, 1976) might also indicate better the purpose of the order, as well as reducing the confusion with juvenile court supervision orders under the Children and Young Persons Act 1969. But most importantly the criteria for making orders need to be debated; permanent, long-term intervention in family life on the grounds of divorce needs justification, if the circumstances do not otherwise warrant state intervention under child care legislation.

Chapter 4

THE LAW IN HISTORICAL PERSPECTIVE:
JUDICIAL CREATION OF THE WELFARE PRINCIPLE

THE PRESENT LAW

In 1925 the Guardianship of Infants Act, section 1, established the legal principle which still governs all judicial decisions concerned with custody of or access to children (and now
codified in the Guardianship of Minors Act 1971, s 1) (see
chapter 2).

Section 1 represents the culmination of a long process
involving two very different problems and purposes. The first
was the elevation of the child's welfare into the central position in child custody litigation by creating a statutory rule
out of a principle of Equity originating and developed in the
courts of Chancery. The history of the welfare principle is
the subject matter of this chapter. The second element in
section 1 was the creation of a neutral principle as between
fathers and mothers in relation to the custody of their children. But the principle of neutrality only operated when a
custody case was brought to court, for until that occurred the
"sacred rights" of the father at common law remained intact.
Furthermore, the wording of section 1 indicates that in any
case the neutrality principle as between fathers and mothers
was to be subordinated to the "first and paramount consideration" of the child's welfare. The history of women's struggle
for equal parental rights over their children, and the explanation for the supremacy of the welfare principle over that
struggle is the subject matter of the next chapter.

In many ways it is difficult to separate the two strands,
although for purposes of exposition it becomes necessary (and
also results in repetition). This is because, as will be seen,
women and children were both denied legal personality and competence under the common law patriarchy, and indeed the social
changes in the family in the eighteenth century resulted in
the emancipation of both women and children in the nineteenth
century. More specifically, however, in practice, both historically and at the present time, the legal position concerning
parental rights has influenced enormously the judicial

interpretation of the welfare principle; and conversely it was the welfare principle which was developed by the judges to justify eroding the sacred rights of fathers over their children. The reason why this could be so is that the welfare principle is essentially indeterminate. Neither in 1839 (Serjeant Talfourd's Infants' Custody Act) which is taken as the starting point for a statement of the legal position as it was at the beginning of the modern period, nor today, does the "welfare of the child" have any objective reality or definitive meaning. It has always been and still is essentially a value-laden tool for focussing on the child in an attempt to resolve disputes between its parents (or their representatives). As will be seen, neither in 1839, 1886 nor 1925, which are the legislative landmarks, was there any essential understanding of what the welfare principle meant other than as a reference to existing judicial values as expressed through judicial decision-making. Nor was the welfare principle related to extra-legal knowledge or understandings. That is as true today as it was in the earlier period, for the achievements of the twentieth century in the scientific study of the child have largely passed by the legal system, so that the legal system appears to be operating on little more or better extra-legal knowledge than it did at the turn of the century: there are merely many more cases arriving in the courts. The history of child custody therefore demonstrates that the welfare principle was never much more than a code for resolving disputes between adults over children, in which the adults' interests were a central focus. This may be inevitable for one of the problems of appearing to focus solely on the child is that it ignores the interaction of parents with children, the family as a social unit, and that identifying a child's interests will inevitably in most cases involve making invidious choices between its parents, whose interests in the matter can only with difficulty, and perhaps wrongly, be ignored.

To understand, therefore, how the welfare principle in the custody process operates today, it is necessary to trace how the present legal position of equality of parental rights and of the welfare of the child as "the first and paramount consideration" in custody cases was reached.

THE PROTECTION OF CHILDREN

Changes in the nature of the family from the seventeenth century onwards had important implications for the concept of childhood (Aries, 1962). The more egalitarian and "companionate" nuclear family of the eighteenth century (Stone, 1977; Shorter, 1975) was characterised by affective bonds between husband and wife, and parents and children. The social status of both women and children benefited from these changes; the rise in women's status will be traced in the next chapter, but the implications of the greater child-orientation of families is the subject matter of this chapter.

One of the keys to the social changes in the family in this period is the "revolution of sentiment" (Shorter, 1975). While some have emphasised the growth of sentiment between husband and wife (Stone, 1975), Shorter (1975) argues that until the turn of the nineteenth century ordinary parents were indifferent to their children and that "the nuclear family would take form about the mother-infant relationship", that the "revolution in maternal love" preceded "romantic love" i.e. sentiment between husband and wife, and that Stone's emphasis on the "companionate" marriage of equals omits children from the "sentimental unit". One of the other changes in the family involved a concept of "individualism within the bosom of the family" (Flandrin, 1979), of "privacy" and "domesticity" (Shorter, 1975). Indeed the sanctity of the family itself became the justification for non-interference despite the child's need for protection throughout the nineteenth century (Pinchbeck and Hewitt, 1973).

Like women, children benefited from the growth in sentiment and individualism. Aries (1962) has shown that the concept of childhood did not exist until the seventeenth century, from which time there developed specifically children's dress, toys, games, sexual mores, literature, in the portrayal of children in art, and new attitudes to education, that increasingly separated children from adults. Attitudes to children changed too:

> They were seen more and more as small human beings whose feelings could and should be understood, who were to be played with like toys or pets, and above all to be enjoyed. Along with this went a second new theme, that children were a responsibility, fragile beings who needed to be understood and safeguarded, creatures with potential for good and evil who needed discipline to ensure that the innate evil was suppressed and the good fostered. The modern concept of parenthood, with its duties and obligations to child and society, was thus born (Anderson, 1980: 59-60).

Aries' concern was with the idea of childhood, not with whether there was affection for children, but Shorter (1975) believes that before this development of concern for children's welfare mothers were indifferent to their children's happiness: "these mothers did not care /about the dangers of wet-nursing/, and this is why their children vanished in the ghastly slaughter of the innocents that was traditional child-rearing" (Shorter, 1975). Shorter's view is disputed, but this need not concern us here. Aries' evidence has also been criticised, for using highly selective historical documents, mainly emanating from the higher and literate classes, and for his excessive and literal emphasis on artistic representations (Lloyd de Mause, 1974). But Aries' main theme of the emergence of a concept of the child as a child at this time in history is largely undisputed.

The welfare of children at this period was manifested by concern for education (moral welfare) and for hygiene and health (physical welfare) (Aries, 1962). In England the first manual of childhood diseases had been published in 1545 (Lloyd de Mause, 1974) and throughout this period there were published child care manuals, and calls for the ending of child-care practices such as swaddling and wet-nursing which were seen to be detrimental to the child's physical welfare. Indeed, it may have been only when the middle-classes ceased wet-nursing and swaddling from the mid-eighteenth century onwards (earlier in England than on the Continent) that concern for the child's welfare and mother-child interaction became possible (Shorter, 1975).

There is no doubt that in the eighteenth century concern for the emotional welfare of children, their happiness, became firmly rooted. Although the concern was already current (Shorter, 1975), J J Rousseau's educational tract Emile (1762) was an important influence. At the same time the "Romantic revival" in sensibility and thought at the end of the eighteenth century brought with it an unprecedented literary interest in "the child" as the focus and theme of English literature (Coveney, 1967). The poetry of the late eighteenth century of Blake and Wordsworth glorified Rousseau's innocence of the child, but the child was still at this stage a vehicle for symbolising the artist's dissatisfaction with society. By the early nineteenth century Dickens had created the novel, for example, Oliver Twist (1839), in which the child became the central concern and vehicle for psychological analysis. By the turn of the nineteenth century too the significance of childhood experience for adult life had also received wide currency. Wordsworth wrote in The Prelude (1802): "The Child is father of the man", and Wordsworth's influence in the scientific study of the child at the turn of the twentieth century was recognised (Coveney, 1967).

By the early nineteenth century then, when the physical survival of children was no longer quite so precarious and perhaps because of this (Kessen, 1965), children and their welfare were culturally valued. It was perhaps the cruel conditions of child labour, especially in the factories, which finally brought the welfare of the child to the political foreground. Beginning feebly in 1819 but with growing pace over the century legislation was passed to regulate the number of hours per day and the ages at which children might work in factories and mines. In 1833 the first minimal requirement for compulsory education was introduced in the Factory Act; by 1870 the Education Act made state provision for compulsory public schooling available for all.

There were those who were opposed to the humanitarian intervention of the state in the employment of children: "The
new industrial middle-class ... were quite happy to see the
new industrial labour force, of whom children were the most
exposed, become the sacrificial offering to the gods of economic progress" (Walvin, 1982). There were however also those
who, reflecting contemporary views of parental responsibilities, were opposed to any interference with the patriarchal
authority of the father in the family:

> The children ... were not pauper apprentices, but child-
> ren of parents who were free to send them to the factory
> or not as they pleased. They were the natural guardians
> of their children and to interfere was to imply that they
> were unfit to exercise their parental responsibilities.
> Surely this, it was argued, must lessen the bond between
> parent and child and lead to filial disrespect (Marshall,
> 1973: 208).

Indeed Lord Shaftesbury himself believed that "to undermine
parental responsibility was to undermine family stability and
thus the stability of society itself" (Pinchbeck and Hewitt,
1973).
    State intervention in the family for the protection of
delinquent children nevertheless also dates from this time.
The origin of the current Children and Young Persons Act 1969
lies in the Infant Felons Act 1840, by which the Court of
Chancery could grant "care and custody" of an infant convicted
of a felony to a person other than the father or guardian.
    By the beginning of the Victorian period therefore the
concept of childhood was firmly rooted, and childhood was
valued and glorified even though at the same time children
were subjected to what is to modern eyes, horrifying cruelty
both from their parents and employers. The beginning of the
child protection movement had already taken place in the realm
of child labour, and control of delinquency, although protection from parents was not introduced until the very end of the
century.

THE COURT OF CHANCERY

There were before 1875 two court procedures for resolving disputes over the custody of children. At common law a writ of
habeas corpus could be sought from the Court of King's Bench
by the person with the right to legal custody, i.e. the father
or the guardian appointed by him, to recover the child from
the person who was keeping him without legal cause. The other
procedure was in the Court of Chancery, which anyone could invoke on behalf of the ward child's interests.
    The Court of King's Bench would usually enforce the
father's right to custody regardless of his behaviour or of

the child's age. In R v De Manneville (1804) a baby girl of
eight months old still breast-fed was ordered to be returned
by the mother to the father whom she had left because of his
violence, though in theory the common law displayed some concern for the child's welfare, for Lord Ellenborough added that
the court would protect the child on proof that the child was
injured "for want of nurture" or in any other respect. In
R v Greenhill (1836) three young girls were ordered back to
the father who had committed adultery and was refusing to pay
alimony; Lord Denman ruled that the father would retain custody at common law unless there was danger to the child, for
example, "the apprehension of cruelty, or contamination by
some exhibition of gross profligacy or corruption". /See also
Whitfield v Hales (1806) (father deprived of custody because
of his ill-treatment); R v Dobbyn (1818) (father lost custody
because of his profligacy and cruelty); and Ex p Bailey (1838)
(father convicted of felony lost custody)./ But in practice
the father's rights were near absolute, and even after his
death. In R v Isley (1836) testamentary guardians appointed
by the father recovered orphan children from the maternal
grandparents.
     While the common law courts would almost never in theory,
and probably never ever in practice, give custody to the
mother, it did make an inroad into the father's absolute legal
position, as regards access. In Ex p Lytton (1781) Lord Mans-
field bound a father to a voluntary deed of separation in
which he had allowed the mother to have access to her child.
     The near absolute character of the common law could only
withstand the pressure of the social changes in the family already described because Equity, the system of justice dispen-
sed in the Court of Chancery on behalf of the Monarch as the
parens patriae, had already by the middle of the eighteenth
century come to recognise the need for a jurisdiction which
would protect the child's welfare (Lowe and White, 1979). The
Court of Chancery was originally intended to protect the property of infant wards and indeed it was mainly the propertied
classes who used the court up to its abolition in 1875. By
1745, however, the court had begun to remove this precondition
for the exercise of its jurisdiction. In Smith v Smith (1745)
the Court entertained a petition from a mother simply to prevent her daughter marrying: "It is not a profitable jurisdiction of the Crown, but for the benefit of infants themselves,
who must have some common parent".
     The court's jurisdiction, for the benefit of the child,
then, originated in the protection of the ward's property, but
long before the turn of the nineteenth century it had begun to
protect the child for the child's sake. Indeed a remarkably
modern-looking decision was made in Ex p Hopkins (1732) in
which the father claimed custody of his 13 year old daughter
who had been living with her now deceased uncle. Lord Chancellor King held that had the father claimed habeas corpus the

94

court would have had to hand over the girl. But, since the case was in the Court of Chancery, he asked the girl her opinion, which was that she wished to stay in her uncle's house. He therefore made an order for custody to the deceased uncle's cousin, with reasonable access to the father and mother.

Where the dispute was between the father and mother of a child, however, at the early part of the nineteenth century, the Court of Chancery tended to follow the practice of the common law courts in refusing to disturb the absolute rights of the father unless he had by his behaviour forfeited his rights. The conceptual contribution of Equity was however of the greatest significance. The justification developed by the Court of Chancery for interfering with the father's rights was that it was in the interests of the child (De Manneville v De Manneville (1804)). Thus in Wellesley v Duke of Beaufort (1827) the father lost custody because of his immoral and adulterous conduct, although it was still in the "interest and happiness" of the children for their caretakers to allow "filial affection and duty towards their father to operate to the utmost". This case appears to be the first in which the reason for the decision is in modern terminology: "The court has authority to control the legal rights of the father, if the welfare of the infant renders its interference necessary".

JUDICIAL DEVELOPMENT OF THE WELFARE PRINCIPLE

In 1857 the Matrimonial Causes Act created a secular jurisdiction over divorce and the other matrimonial causes of judicial separation and nullity. The new 'divorce court' was required to make custody orders "as it thinks fit" (section 35), but in the years after 1857 these courts were much influenced by the attitude of the Courts of King's Bench and of Chancery which were in practice still upholding the absolute rights of the father. A mother who was guilty of adultery could never get custody of and access to her children (Clout v Clout (1861); Codrington v Codrington (1864)).

At this stage, disputes between mothers and fathers were treated by the judges on the basis of the father's common law rights, or the mother's guilt. Consideration of the interests of the child was largely absent from the judgments, but gradually the judges began to justify their decisions by reference to the welfare of the child. In a leading case, Symington v Symington (1875) a father who had committed adultery but was no longer "continuing his immorality" was allowed to keep custody of his three sons. After referring to the father's right of guardianship as "high and sacred", Lord Chancellor Selbourne added that it was in "the material and moral interest of the boys to leave them in the care of their natural and legal guardian". In access cases too, the judges began to talk of the parents' claims in terms of the child's welfare. The result, however, was often to deny a mother access to her

children. In Heathcoat v Heathcoat (1864) a drunken, violent,
disorderly etc., mother was denied access on the ground that
the real object of her application was said not to be love and
affection for the child, but also because the effect of access
on the child was considered to be injurious to her physical
health. In Philip v Philip (1872) an excitable, violent
mother accused of cruelty was denied access to her seven year
old daughter on the ground that the child's recovery to health
would be retarded. In a sophisticated and well-argued judgment, based centrally on the question of the child's welfare,
and supported by two medical affidavits, it was held that to
deny access there must be evidence of "real and serious
injury":

> It has always been a leading principle of the court to
> consider the welfare of the child before the indulgence
> of the parents. However natural the affection of the
> parents may be, and however reasonable its indulgence
> might be in a proper case, yet whenever the welfare of
> the children is likely to be seriously jeopardised by
> that indulgence, the court gives precedence to the
> interest of the children.

It was however in the Chancery and common law courts
where the main development of the welfare principle took place
at this time. After the Custody of Infants Act 1839 (infra)
a mother could apply to the Court of Chancery for custody of
and access to her children. If less usually the father or a
testamentary guardian wanted to regain possession of the child,
then the appropriate proceedings were by habeas corpus. At
first the father's rights and wishes were upheld as against
the mother or any third party, regardless of his behaviour or
of the age of the child. By 1848 however the judges had established criteria for interfering with the father's rights. In
Re Fynn (1848) the principle for interference was stated to be
the welfare of the child:

> The acknowledged rights of a father with respect to the
> custody and guardianship of his infant children are con-
> ferred by the law, it may be with a view to the perform-
> ance by him of duties towards the children, and, in a
> sense, on condition of performing those duties ... Be-
> fore this jurisdiction can be called into action it must
> be satisfied, not only that it has the means of acting
> safely and efficiently, but also that the father has so
> conducted himself, or has shown himself to be a person
> of such a description, or is placed in such a position,
> as to render it not merely better for the children, but
> essential to their safety or to their welfare, in some
> very serious and important respect, that his rights
> should be treated as lost or suspended - should be super-
> seded or interfered with.

96

Although the court could in principle interfere with the father's rights, on the facts of the case however the father did not lose custody, despite his not being considered "fit parent". In practice therefore the test for losing custody was extremely strict. The significance of the case however is the statement that erosion of the father's parental rights, until now near absolute, could be justified by the competing principle which recognised legal protection of the child.

Later cases developed the principle in Re Fynn. It was held in Re Curtis (1859) that there was no jurisdiction to remove the child from the father merely because it was for the benefit of the child; it had to be shown that the father's custody was injurious to the child "either physically, intellectually or morally". In this case a passionate man with peculiar notions about religion and the upbringing of children did not lose custody. Only behaviour of the most extremely anti-social nature to Victorian society would lose a father the custody of his children (infra).

While passing reference was made to the interests of the child, it was a rare judge who dealt with these interests sensitively. Warde v Warde (1849) is a rare earlier example. Lord Chancellor Cottenham insisted on keeping all four children together with the mother "so as not to create factions in the family", although had the issue concerned the boy of nine alone, he said there might have been a different result. He was also unhappy about making a compulsory order for custody; he wanted the children to have "respect for both parents", and an order would "suggest that one parent was not considered fit to be entrusted with them" (although note that the one parent in question here happened to be the father). But the Lord Chancellor saw his task to be "to do the best one can for the interests of those who are the objects of the protection of the court".

> Children are by nature entitled to the care of both of their parents, but when the conduct of one or both of the parents has been such as to render it impossible that they can live together, and the court has, therefore, the painful duty cast upon it of deciding whether the children shall be brought up by one parent or the other, all that it can do is to adopt that course which seems best for the interests of the children, without regard, so far as it interferes with that object, to the pain which may be inflicted on those who are the authors of the difficulty.

In 1873 the Judicature Act finally merged the systems of common law and Equity, both as regards the courts and the principles to be applied in them. Section 25(10) of the Act specifically provided that "In questions relating to the custody and education of infants, the rules of equity shall prevail". In cases after this date, it is clear that the

attitude of the courts, including the divorce courts, was becoming more child-centred. In Re Taylor (1876) a father who
abandoned his home, later kidnapped his son of three, and was
cited as co-respondent in a divorce case lost custody. Jess-
ell M R emphasised as considerations in his decision firstly
the breach of marital duty (first raised in Re Halliday's Estate (1852)), which entailed more than the husband's misconduct,
and secondly the interest of the child: "Here what is the interest of the child? Who is likely to take the most care of
him - the mother or the father?". In Re Elderton (1883) a husband who was violent and mentally cruel to his wife lost custody. He had committed a breach of the marital duty, i.e. the
duty of husband and wife to each other, and "the responsibility
of each to the child so that the child has the benefit of the
joint care and affection of his father and mother". Similarly
in Re Goldsworthy (1876) the father's "intemperate and vicious
life", his use of "gross and insulting language", "cannot but
be seriously prejudicial to the moral safety and welfare of
the child".

The judicial development of the welfare principle received
its first statutory recognition in 1873. The refusal of the
courts to allow the voluntary transfer of custody by the father
to the mother in a separation deed (Hamilton v Hector (1872))
led to the Custody of Infants Act 1873, which made three
changes in the law. Firstly it raised the age at which a
mother could be granted custody of her child under the 1839
Act from seven to 16; secondly and most significantly it removed her adultery as a bar; and thirdly it provided that separation deeds in which custody was given to the mother were
not invalid, but were unenforceable "if the court shall be of
the opinion that it will not be for the benefit of the infant".
The elevation of the "benefit" of the child into a statutory
principle confirmed its importance, and led to later judicial
and statutory refinements. But in practice the old attitudes
to separation deeds continued: fathers' rights were usually
upheld and adulterous mothers lost their claims (for example,
Re Besant (1879); Jump v Jump (1883)).

The highpoint of the "sacred rights of the father" was
reached in Re Agar-Ellis (1883). In the judges' view, the interests of the child meant upholding the "natural law" which
gave the father rights:

> When by birth a child is subject to a father, it is for
> the general interest of families, and for the general in-
> terest of children, and really for the interest of the
> particular infant, that the Court should not except in
> very extreme cases, interfere with the discretion of the
> father but leave to him the responsibility of exercising
> that power which nature has given him by the birth of the
> child (Cotton L J) ... It is not the benefit of the in-
> fant as conceived by the court, but it must be for the

benefit to the infant having regard to the natural law which points out that the father knows far better as a rule what is good for his children than a court of justice can (Bowen L J).

THE GUARDIANSHIP OF INFANTS ACT 1886

The injustice of the decision in Re Agar-Ellis in 1883 prompted women's groups to seek joint guardianship (parental rights) over their children through legislation. The legislative respone was a proposal that where the marriage was in difficulties, the mother could apply for custody of her children, even during the father's lifetime. The result was section 5 of the Act which elevated the child's welfare to a new ascendancy, as the first of three considerations which the court had to take into account in deciding on the mother's claim:

> The court may, upon the application of the mother of any infant (who may apply without next friend), make such order as it may think fit regarding the custody of such infant and the right of access thereto of either parent, having regard to the welfare of the infant, and to the conduct of the parents, and to the wishes as well of the mother as of the father.

The Guardianship of Infants Act 1886 was by the turn of the century clearly being interpreted as having made two important changes in the law. As between husband and wife in custody or access disputes considerations of their conduct and wishes were in principle equal (Re A and B (1897)), although in practice it took a long time for the adulterous wife to be treated with full equality (infra), but "paramount" above these was the court's understanding of the welfare of the child. There was however another type of custody case where disputes arose between a parent and a third party or between third party and third party (for example, foster parents, relatives, or a children's institution). Most of the cases in this period in this category were essentially disputes about the religious upbringing of the child in mixed Catholic/Protestant marriages. At first the courts held that the 1886 Act had made no change in the law of paternal rights; in these cases the courts, whether in habeas corpus or wardship proceedings, espoused the common law rule that the father's wishes regarding the religion of his children were absolute unless he had forfeited them by his misconduct (Re Scanlan (1888); Re Plomley (1888)). By 1893 however a change of attitude had occurred. The father's wishes would stand but only if there was no case based on the "dominant" consideration of the child's welfare, for overriding them. Re McGrath (1893) was one of the two cases in that year which elevated the welfare of the child to a new importance by explaining what

"welfare" meant, and in particular stressing the importance of
what would now be called "attachment" or "bonding":

> The duty of the court is to leave the child alone, unless
> the court is satisfied that it is for the welfare of the
> child that some other course should be taken. The domi-
> nant matter for the consideration of the court is the
> welfare of the child. But the welfare of the child is
> not to be measured by money only, nor by physical comfort
> only. The word welfare must be taken in its widest sense.
> The moral and religious welfare of the child must be con-
> sidered as well as its physical well-being, nor can the
> ties of affection be disregarded (Lindley L J).

It may have been easier for the court to take this approach in a case where the dispute over the control of the
children's religious education was not between the parents but
was between the father's aunt and the testamentary guardian
appointed by the mother who had been caring for the children
since her death. But the court showed sensitivity: the relatives must not be allowed to play "battledore and shuttlecock"
with the religious training of the children.

In the same year in Re Gyngall (1893) a mother sought unsuccessfully to recover her daughter of 15 from a foster-home
where she had been happily settled for four years. Lord
Fisher M R pointed out that to deprive a parent of custody
when the parent was actually caring for a child would need a
very strong case. But in this case the problem was whether
the child should be forced after a long time to go back, involving "a very serious dislocation of an existing tie".
Again, as a rule of law, the parents' rights could only be
interfered with if it could be shown to be for the welfare of
the child "and for her happiness, what her prospects are if
not interfered with, the fact that in a short time she will be
able to choose for herself, and what her position will be if
taken by her mother to live with her". The court may have
been influenced by the fact that the mother was a poor domestic servant, while the foster-home was comfortable and religious. But the court saw itself as deciding according to the
child's interests. The court was "the supreme parent of children" exercising its jurisdiction in the manner in which "a
wise, affectionate and careful parent would act for the welfare of the child"; a parent may intend to act for the child's
welfare, but may not be doing what a "wise and high-minded"
parent would do.

By 1896 the judges were speaking of the welfare of the
child as "the main and paramount consideration" (Re Newton
(1896); although the word "paramount" in this context seems
first to have been used in D'Alton v D'Alton (1878)). The
father's misconduct began to be interpreted as making his
wishes or custody inimical to the child's welfare, especially

where the child was already in the care of others who were
providing adequately for him. A subtle change of emphasis was
taking place around the turn of the century, so that children
would not be returned to their parent(s) simply because the
parent wished it. The court would consider the child's "best
interests", which often dictated that the child remained where
it was. In some cases medical evidence on the effects of a
move on the child's health was introduced (Re Mathieson
(1918)).

THE CHILD AND VICTORIAN SOCIETY

As 1839 had been a turning point in the law by making the
first legislative inroad on behalf of a mother into the absolute common law rights of a father over his children, so too
the 1886 Act represented a milestone in recognising for the
first time in legislation that questions of custody might turn
on the "welfare of the child". The courts gradually came to
take the view that the appearance of the welfare of the child
in section 5 of the Act as the first of the three considerations which they were required to take into account was deliberate.
    Why it was at this time that the welfare of the child
assumed a predominant position must be related to wider developments in society. While the eighteenth century had created
the concept of childhood, the nineteenth century had become
the child's century, in providing first voluntary and philanthropic and later legal protection for children. By the turn
of the twentieth century there was hardly an area of children's lives about which there had not been legislation. The
changes in society's conception and treatment of children under
the Victorians have been described fully elsewhere (Pinchbeck
and Hewitt, 1973; Walvin, 1982). The origins of this concern
may not have been wholly philosophic, but also practical, i.e.
the vast numbers of children in an expanding population and an
emergent consensus that they were in need of protection
(Walvin, 1982). The concern for the unprotected, of whom
children were the largest number, was allied to a revulsion
against cruelty in all its forms. The religious revival and
the importance of discipline in the home and in school were
part of the concern for moral welfare (although religion and
discipline were also used to justify enormous cruelty to
children (Pinchbeck and Hewitt, 1973)). Concern for physical
health led to the growth of paediatrics as a specialism within
medicine in the mid-century and to the establishment of hospi-
tals for children (the first in 1852 was the Great Ormond
Street Hospital for Sick Children). By the end of the century
child health centres were founded in local areas and the cam-
paigns of the Women's Co-operative Guild for better maternity
conditions led in 1918 to the Maternity and Child Welfare Act
requiring the setting up of welfare clinics. In 1902 the

Midwives Act regulated the training required for the safe delivery of babies. Smaller family size resulted from a recognition by parents that they could not provide adequately for
too many children. Philanthropic societies for destitute
children were set up (there were said to be 50 in London alone
in 1878), and Dr. Barnardo set up his first home for boys in
1870. The most remarkable response to this new sensibility
was however the largely ad hoc but extremely complex structure
of legal protection which aimed to safeguard the interests of
the young: there were some 90 Acts passed between 1780 and
1914. Legislative restrictions on the employment of children
had begun feebly in 1802 (Apprentices Act), but by 1867 were
extended to control the hours of employment in all industries,
and in 1873 was extended to agricultural work. In 1870 education became the right of every child through the compulsory
provision of a public school system. By 1906 school meals,
and by 1907 compulsory physical examinations of schoolchildren
were provided for by legislation. By 1871 moral concern over
child prostitution led to raising the age of sexual consent
from 12 to 13, and in 1885 again to 16, with parents being
made responsible for the moral danger to their children. Protective legislation for orphaned, deserted, neglected or destitute children in the Poor Law Amendment Act 1889 allowed the
Poor Law Guardians to assume parental rights. By the Custody
of Children Act 1891 the courts were empowered to refuse
habeas corpus to parents who were deemed on various grounds to
have forfeited their right to custody. This provision was
seen as providing protection for poor children in the same way
that the Court of Chancery did for wealthier children (Pinchbeck and Hewitt, 1973). In 1889 the Prevention of Cruelty to
Children Act was passed, in the same year as the National
Society for Prevention of Cruelty to Children was founded;
protection of children from their own parents developed relatively late because it was par excellence an interference with
the absolute rights of parents (Pinchbeck and Hewitt, 1973).
The scandal of poor mothers leaving their children in "baby
farms" led to the Infant Life Preservation Act 1872 which required foster-mothers to register, but it was not until after
the First World War that the legal adoption of orphan and
unwanted children was allowed (Adoption Act 1926).

    While philanthropic concern for children displayed pity
for the unprotected, it is in relation to juvenile delinquency
that one discerns the growing view that children were different from adults, so that their treatment ought to be differen-
tiated, and that juvenile crime might have social causes
(Platt, 1969). From 1788 philanthropic societies espoused
these views, such as the Society for Investigating the Causes
of the Alarming Increase in Juvenile Delinquency set up in
1815. In 1847 juvenile offenders could be tried summarily by
magistrates for petty larceny; in 1854 reformatory schools and
in 1857 industrial schools, still run by voluntary efforts,

were allowed as an alternative to prison; and in 1908 juvenile courts were set up throughout the country (Children Act 1908).

In this climate of opinion it is understandable how the courts, whether divorce, common law (in habeas corpus proceedings) or Chancery (in wardship proceedings), dealing with questions of child custody, were able to build on the time-honoured Equitable concept of the parens patriae, of the duty to protect the interests of children. By 1878 the Court of Appeal in a divorce case was speaking of the interests of the children as being "paramount" (D'Alton v D'Alton (1878), though this did not constitute a complete revolution in judicial thinking, and for at least another seventy years the interests of children were interpreted in accordance with other social values). Only five years later the "sacred rights of the father" were held to be near absolute by the same Court of Appeal on a question of religion (Re Agar-Ellis (1883)), and "guilty" spouses continued to be punished until after the Second World War.

Many of the appeals to the "interests of the child" throughout the nineteenth century (perhaps even in the twentieth) may appear to have been hollow sentiments, with the purpose of justifying a judicial choice between two competing adults. Certainly until 1893 no content to the "welfare of the child" was elucidated. But in Re McGrath (1893) for the first time the Court of Appeal spelt out the concept. The welfare of the child, in its widest sense, included considerations of not only money, and physical comfort and well-being, but also moral and religious welfare, and also "the ties of affection". Physical care, moral and religious welfare had all been prime concerns in the ethos of Victorian society. But the expression of concern for the ties of affection was a new feature.

It is not easy to locate the source of this newly expressed understanding of the attachment that children develop with their caretakers. It may have been a matter of common-sense both then and even now, for scientific interest in or understanding of children's experiences and development was still in its infancy at the turn of the century. The child's attachment to its adult caretakers had not always been recognised, thus earlier practices of wet-nursing or the sending away of children at an early age to apprenticeships, domestic service or to schools. Even in the nineteenth century when the mother's roles as child-carer and housemaker were extolled, middle and upper-class women were likely to leave a large part of child-caring to governesses and nannies, and lower-class working women to child-minders.

In the mid-nineteenth century the development of babies and children began to be a source of scientific study. Previously interest in the child directed towards its control and discipline, had been the source of speculative literature by philosophers (for example, John Locke in the seventeenth century, and Jean Jacques Rousseau in the eighteenth), clergymen, physicians, educators, humanitarians, and reformers (Kessen, 1965). The origins of scientific study of the child is ascribed to Charles Darwin who began a biography of his baby in 1840, which when published in 1877 excited widespread interest. In Darwin's theory of evolution of the species also, childhood assumed a scientific importance, for man could only be understood by his origins in nature and in the child; and the development of children was mirrored in the natural world. Darwin's theories stimulated the "father of the child study movement" in the United States, G Stanley Hall, in 1880 to investigate "the content of children's minds" by using questionnaires to elicit children's feelings and thoughts. Other scientific approaches to children's development followed: the first intelligence tests were devised by Alfred Binet in France in 1905 to assist in the education of mentally retarded children; John B Watson began to observe and measure the behaviour of rats and children in the early years of the twentieth century; child guidance clinics for delinquents, and clinical psychology for the educationally retarded and handicapped child started at the same period.

At the same period, Freud, a neurologist by profession, was treating adults with neurotic symptoms. His experiences led him to a theory of personality development in which childhood experiences, in particular infantile sexuality, played a crucial role in adult neuroses. Freud's work was first known in 1894 in the United States, although Freud did not lecture there himself until 1909 at the invitation of G Stanley Hall. In this country Freud's theories were not influential until 1916 when some of his concepts were applied in cases of battle neurosis (Brown, 1961). Subsequently psychoanalysts of the Freudian school, both British and in the 1930s emigres from Europe (including Freud himself, his daughter Anna Freud, and Melanie Klein), were working and writing here. Dr. Ian Suttie (1935) shared Freud's interest in the psychology of the child, but emphasised more the importance of love, and particularly in the mother-child relationship: "the child's basic need is for mother-love, his basic fear is loss of such love, and all his later social and cultural attitudes depend on the nature of this relationship" (Brown, 1961). Freud's influence was to "redirect, clarify, sometimes enrich, and in part, perhaps, explain an interest which was already very clearly there" (Coveney, 1967). Freud's followers were particularly influential in the United States, where child psychologists took their unscientific insights as starting points for research by clinical verification. In particular, Freud's theories created interest in the effects on adult life of child-training practices, and parent-child relationships. Serious interest in maternal deprivation did not really exist until John Bowlby's classic work in 1951 which was written as a

contribution to the United Nations programme for the welfare
of homeless children (Lomax et al, 1978). Since then, popular
and psychological interest in attachment and bonding, and separation anxiety, has grown at an enormous and overwhelming
rate.

Those Court of Appeal judges who in 1893 expressed beliefs about "the ties of affection" were voicing ideas which
may have been deemed to be common-sense, popular or intuitive
understanding, but in many ways they were ahead of their time
in terms of social science knowledge. Where their beliefs
came from and why they were suddenly expressed in 1893 is unanswerable, except that a more sensitive approach to children
and their needs was generally evident at that time. But the
child-centred expression of their concern should not be over-
emphasised, for "the welfare of the child" would for many more
decades be interpreted in accordance with social and cultural
values about the family and marriage.

THE GUARDIANSHIP OF INFANTS ACT 1925

The Guardianship of Infants Act 1925 is hailed as a landmark
in the legal protection of children. "The welfare of the
child" was elevated to "the first and paramount consideration"
in all cases concerning children which came before the courts.
Further, any rights of the father at common law were to be
subordinated to the statutory equality of mother and father.
Yet as will be seen in the next chapter the origins of the
Guardianship of Infants Act 1925 betray political purposes
far removed from its apparent child-centred orientation.
The bill's final version, introduced by the Government, succeeded in appeasing the women's organisations' attempts to
achieve legislative recognition of joint rights of guardianship, by introducing the welfare principle whereby the claims
of a mother to the custody of her child could only be recognised as a "spin-off" from judicial protection of the child's
interests. The promoters of the bill had two purposes in mind
in proposing the child's welfare as a statutory principle.
The first was to shift the debate away from the issue of
women's rights. The second was to merely codify the welfare
principle already developed and operated by the judges. Despite doubts cast on this in J v C (1970), it is clear from
the debates in Parliament on the Guardianship of Infants Bill
that the Government did not believe they were materially
changing the substance of the law. The welfare of the child
was already the standard by which in principle claims to the
custody of children whether between parents or third parties
were decided. The welfare of the child was also a very convenient principle, because it allowed social and cultural
values and beliefs about the family and marriage to inform the
interpretation that the judges gave to it.

There can be no doubt that the Guardianship of Infants

Act 1925, section 1, owes more to the fight of women for joint guardianship over their children during marriage, than to any child protection philosophy. The welfare principle nevertheless, despite its dishonourable origins, displays a child-centred concern which was at the time and still is socially approved. How the interpretation of the "indeterminate" welfare principle has been moulded to incorporate changing ideologies of the family and marriage since 1925 is the subject matter of chapter 6.

Chapter 5

THE LAW IN HISTORICAL PERSPECTIVE:
WOMEN AND THE REFORM OF CUSTODY LAW 1839-1973:
FROM SACRED RIGHTS OF FATHERS TO EQUALITY OF PARENTAL RIGHTS

THE PRESENT LAW

The Guardianship of Infants Act 1925, section 1, as has been
seen, created two new statutory principles: the first elevating
the welfare of the child to "the first and paramount consideration in custody" cases, the other imposing a role of neutrality
as between mothers' and fathers' claims to their children.
This neutrality principle was only intended to operate when a
custody issue came before a court. It in no way affected the
law as it applied to the parental rights of fathers and mothers
during the marriage or in the absence of litigation. In particular it did not affect the basic rule of common law that the
father had absolute rights over his children. The 1925 Act
merely provided in section 2 that the mother now had the unlimited right to apply to court for custody and access, and in section 1 that the child's welfare should govern the decision of
the court. Section 1 was the culmination of a long process,
whereby the courts of Equity and later from 1839 onwards the
legislature had allowed inroads into the father's absolute
rights by permitting the courts to make custody or access
orders in favour of the mother. Only in 1973 did the Guardianship Act finally embody complete equality of parental rights
between mother and father (see chapter 2).
     The relationship between the welfare principle and the
equality of parental rights principle is complex. In theory
the welfare principle applies in all court cases concerning
children, while the equality of parental rights principle operates within marriage before a court is seized of any dispute.
But in practice the law on parental rights has influenced enormously the interpretation of which parent ought to have the custody of the child in cases of conflict. The welfare of the
child principle was thus used in the nineteenth century to deny
a mother any right to custody, or even access, because the
judges deemed the welfare of the child to be best served by upholding the "sacred rights of the father" to his children.
Conversely the welfare principle was used at this time to dilute

women's demands for equal parental rights to their children. Indeed the 1925 Act was a political device to actually deny women equality of parental rights. The traditional approval of the "welfare principle" as a highpoint in the legal protection of children must therefore be diluted by a recognition that had it not been for the women's struggle for equal parental rights, it is most probable that the Guardianship of Infants Act would never have reached the statute book at all.

The historical process whereby the common law patriarchal rights were eventually superseded in 1973 by statutory equality of parental rights will be traced in this chapter. This account will demonstrate again how the welfare principle, in essence indeterminate, has been informed by the dominant social and political values of the time, and in particular how the very existence of the principle owes as much to the Victorian women's movements as to any child protection humanitarian philosophy. A recognition of the welfare principle's origins, it is hoped, will again put modern controversies in perspective.

THE COMMON LAW PATRIARCHY IN SOCIAL CONTEXT

The father's absolute parental rights at common law, dating from Edward I's reign at the end of the thirteenth century, were well-established by the mid-eighteenth century, when Blackstone in his Commentaries on the Laws of England (1765-69) encapsulated the legal incapacity of a married woman:

> By marriage the husband and wife are one person in law: that is the very being or legal existence of the woman is suspended during the marriage, or at least is incorporated and consolidated into that of the husband: under whose wing, protection, and cover, she performs everything: and is therefore called in our law-french a feme-covert ... is said to be covert-baron, or under the protection and influence of her husband, baron, or lord; and her condition during her marriage is called her coverture (Holdsworth, 1922-72: 526).

The most important consequences of coverture were that the married woman could own no property of her own, and that the mother had no parental rights in relation to her own children. The common law's recognition of the husband and father as the only subject of legal rights within the family reflected a male patriarchy which had always dominated Western civilisation. The New Testament proclamation that "A man shall cleave to his wife, and they twain shall be one flesh" (Matthew 19:15) was translated into the husband's legal superiority and the wife's legal inferiority in Church doctrine (O'Faolain and Martines, 1974), and in the Roman Law paterfamilias whereby at least in the earlier period of the Roman Empire, a woman was always in legal subjection, first to her father, then to her husband.

The social position of women began to change in the six-teenth and seventeenth centuries when, according to social historians, the modern nuclear family began to develop in place of kinship and community as the main organising prin-ciple of society (Anderson, 1980). In England (Anderson, 1980) the nuclear family of parents and children has always largely been the normal form of residential arrangement (with perhaps relatives, servants, or lodgers living in (Laslett, 1972)), but within the nuclear family "power flowed increas-ingly to the husband over the wife and to the father over the children" (Stone, 1975).

Until the middle of the seventeenth century, the nuclear family actually became more patriarchal and more authoritarian, mirroring the growth of the State, and the political and legal authority of the King as the <u>parens patriae</u>. Indeed the State was supportive of the patriarchal nuclear family in order to buttress its own increasing power (Stone, 1975), and the house-hold with the male at its head was valued as an institution for social control (Stone, 1977). Beginning in the eighteenth century however, the patriarchal family was becoming a more egalitarian and companionate nuclear family, characterised by affective bonds between husband and wife, and parents and children, tying the conjugal group together.

> The four key features of the modern family - intensified affective bonding of the nuclear core at the expense of neighbours and king; a strong sense of individual auton-omy and the right to personal freedom in the pursuit of happiness; a weakening of the association of sexual pleasure with sin and guilt; and a growing desire for physical privacy - were all well established in 1750 in the key middle and upper sectors of English society (Stone, 1977:22).

This new family type of "Affective Individualism" (Stone, 1977), was manifested by strong bonds between close relatives, the decline of the husband's authority, and was more child-oriented and permissive in its attitudes to child-rearing.

The key to the changes in the family in this period lies in two ideas. One was the "revolution of sentiment" (Shorter, 1975) by which there was a growth of romantic love between husband and wife (Stone, 1977) and of maternal love between mothers and their children (Shorter, 1975). The other was the idea of "domesticity" i.e. "the family's awareness of itself as a precious emotional unit that must be protected with pri-vacy and isolation from outside intrusion (Shorter, 1975:412).

Social historians have also shown how the habits and cus-toms of the new middle classes, who were acquiring wealth from the growth of industrialisation and capitalism, only later percolated upwards to the aristocracy and downwards to the poorer sections of society (Shorter, 1975). In the

eighteenth century it was the greater material prosperity of
the new middle classes which allowed the wife freedom from
work. This had two important consequences: "Although the economic dependence of these women on their husbands increased,
they were granted greater status and decision-making power
within the family, and they became increasingly preoccupied
with the nurturing and raising of children" (Stone, 1977:412).
Social historians are not agreed about how or why these
changes in the family occurred. "We still lack any really
satisfactory account of the relationship between the emergence
of ideas like privacy, domesticity and of any change in emotion
on the one hand, and the economic transformations of the period
1700 to 1870 on the other" (Anderson, 1980: 64). But it is
apparent that two of the great changes, brought about by the
development of the modern nuclear family beginning in the
eighteenth and continuing into the nineteenth century, relate
to the position of women and children in society. The position
of women changed through the decline in patriarchal authority,
but at the same time through the rising emphasis on "domesticity".

> In the bourgeoisie /the family/ became associated with a
> new set of sex-role ideologies involving the strict seg-
> regation of work (performed by men away from home) from
> domestic concerns (ideally performed in the home by ser-
> vants under the supervision of women). The home came to
> be seen as a haven, or retreat from the pressures of a
> capitalistically oriented competitive world
> (Anderson, 1980: 47).

Changing attitudes allowing a reciprocal basis to interpersonal
relationships thus had important implications for women's
rights. Prompted no doubt by the political beliefs of the
French Revolution, women at this time too were beginning to become aware of their limited social status. Early feminist
writing was concerned with the education of women, and indeed
Mary Wollstonecraft, the first great feminist, who published
her Vindication of the Rights of Women in 1792, made a "genuine
breakthrough" in feminist thinking when she called for the
exercise of the rights of man to include woman, principally
through the better education of girls (Walters, 1976).

THE LAW IN 1839

By 1839 important social changes had taken place in and around
the family. Relations between husband and wife, and parents
and children, were based on affection; the belief in individualism had led to growing calls for women's rights in the
political, social, educational and legal fields. Indeed Mary
Wollstonecraft had wanted to write a tract on the laws relating
to women but was only prevented from doing so by premature death.

110

Long before 1839, the English common law had been formed at the stage of the patriarchal family. The common law was concerned to ensure patriarchal authority as a form of social control of the family, in particular over "the accumulation, control and orderly devolution of property and its accompanying status" (Hoggett, 1982). Paternal power over children was necessary therefore for the identification of legitimate heirs, and their marriage. This legal structure, fortified by the Church, withstood the social changes in the family. At common law the husband and father had absolute legal rights, both over his wife and children and their property. As a married woman, his wife could own no property, and the father's authority over the children was absolute both during the marriage, and in the event of the marriage ending by divorce, separation, or most commonly at this time by death. "In the seventeenth century the remarriage rate, made possible by death, was not far off that in our own day, made possible by divorce" (Stone, 1977). A law (4 & 5 Ph & M. c 8, s 4) allowing the mother guardianship and custody of her child after her husband's death had been repealed in 1660 (Tenures Abolition Act) where the father had himself appointed a testamentary guardian. If the marriage was terminated by Parliamentary divorce, as it was in an exceptionally few cases (McGregor, 1957), the common law position was in no way affected. The Bill of Divorcement made no reference at all to any children of the marriage. Indeed it was argued before the Royal Commission on the Law of Divorce in 1853 that divorce should not be allowed because it would cause "extreme injustice to the wife" since she had the "right as well as the father, to the gratitude of her children, and the comfort of their society, of both of which she is almost necessarily deprived by her dismissal from her husband's family". If the husband and wife separated, the husband could not legally give up his parental rights to his wife even by a voluntary separation deed (Westneath v Westneath (1821)).

It has already been seen how the Court of King's Bench upheld the rights of fathers to the custody of their children, except in very rare cases where the father's behaviour was considered to be outrageous. In practice before 1839 it was almost impossible for a mother to get custody of her child, or even access to her child from the courts, although one exception to this was where the father voluntarily allowed access (Ex p Lytton (1781)). The Court of Chancery at this period mainly followed the common law, but had begun to develop the Equitable principle that the father's absolute rights could be forfeited by considerations of the welfare of the child. Indeed Equity had also intervened to remove the wife's inability at common law to own property. By the end of the sixteenth century it had developed the concept of the wife's separate estate, and by 1800 the concept of the restraint upon anticipation. These allowed a married woman to use her own property but only if the property was conveyed to her by proper legal

111

procedures, i.e. a settlement. Equity therefore only came to the rescue of the rich who needed to and knew how to use the legal process.

Equity at first provided relief to the mother only where the father had not appointed a testamentary guardian on his death. In Villareal v Mellish (1737) the court recognised that on the death of the father the mother had a right, "from nature", notwithstanding her remarriage, to the custody of the persons and care of the education of her children, which guardianship she could not as the maternal grandfather was claiming, assign to another even by deed (similarly in Roach v Garvan (1784)). But where there was a testamentary guardian the common law did not allow the mother any rights, and Equity did not intervene (Eyre v Shaftesbury (1722)).

Gradually however Equity began to make inroads into the common law position regarding custody while both parents were alive. After the habeas corpus proceedings in R v De Manneville (1804) in which the court had ordered custody to the father, the mother then petitioned the Court of Chancery. While not actually delivering the child to the mother, but merely ordering the father not to remove the child out of the country, Lord Chancellor Eldon in De Manneville v De Manneville (1804) espoused three principles. First, he was concerned with the child's welfare: "It has been truly observed, that the court will do what is for the benefit of the infant, without regard to the prayer". Second, he favoured access: "I shall take care that the intercourse of both father and mother with the child, as far as is consistent with its happiness, shall be unrestrained". And third, he enunciated criteria for removing the child from its father's custody if the father was abusing it, for example, if he was not maintaining the child, or because of his insolvency, or his character, or for espousing a non-established religion, or that he was in prison. A few years later in a rare example the poet Shelley lost custody to the maternal grandmother for his "vicious and immoral" conduct, i.e. being an avowed atheist (Shelley v Westbrooke (1817)).

Despite these inroads however, in practice Equity would usually only intervene if the father had acted so as to forfeit his right to custody, on similar grounds as at common law. The father's behaviour had to be considered exceptionally culpable; his adultery did not come into that category. The adulterous father would therefore never be deprived of custody, nor would he be required by any court, common law or Chancery, to allow the mother access to her children. By 1827 this legal situation was unacceptable to some of the legal profession, let alone women. In Ball v Ball (1827) a mother who had a divorce a mensa et thoro from the Ecclesiastical court (a legal separation) for her husband's adultery was denied access to her 14 year old daughter by her husband. In the Court of Chancery, the Vice-Chancellor Sir Anthony Hart said: "The question is whether a child of 14 years old is to be deprived by the brutal conduct of the father, of the company, advice and protection of a mother, against whom no imputation can be raised". Although by precedent he was bound to rule that he could not order access unless the father was culpable (in the accepted sense), he complained: "I do not know that I have any authority to interfere ... if any could be found, I would most gladly adopt it; for in a moral point of view, I know of no act more harsh or cruel than depriving the mother of proper intercourse with her child".

In 1836 the problem arose again. Mrs Greenhill, who already had a divorce a mensa et thoro and an order for alimony from the Ecclesiastical Court, lost her case for custody of her three young girls of 5½, 4½ and 2½ in habeas corpus proceedings (R v Greenhill (1836)). She then petitioned the Court of Chancery which in December 1836 again found itself unable to interfere with her husband's custody merely on the ground of his adultery (Greenhill v Greenhill (1836)). Mrs Greenhill then simply hid with the children and subsequently left the country. Even the Ecclesiastical courts were unhappy with the legal position. Dr Lushington refused to reverse his order for the payment of alimony because of the wife's behaviour: "... in this case I am at a loss to know why I should, by starving an innocent wife, compel obedience to the order of other tribunals to render up to the guilty husband the offspring of that union, the obligations of which he has grossly violated". In April 1837 Serjeant Talfourd, a lawyer and Member of Parliament, first moved for leave to bring in the Custody of Infants Bill in the House of Commons. Mrs Greenhill's case was mentioned in the debates on the Bill and was in one sense the forerunner of the Act, for Serjeant Talfourd had acted as a lawyer in Mrs Greenhill's case.

The immediate cause of the 1837 Bill was however the case of Mrs Caroline Norton (Perkins, 1909; Pinchbeck and Hewitt, 1973). Mrs Norton, a beautiful granddaughter of Richard Brinsley Sheridan, a well-known novelist and poet, "one of the most fashionable London hostesses" (Strachey, 1928:36), had married a man who, as a younger son, needed her influence to get him "lucrative promotion in his profession" (O'Faolain and Martines, 1974:334). With the help of Lord Melbourne, then Home Secretary, she secured her husband a police magistracy. In 1836 Norton quarrelled with his wife, and was violent to her. When she separated from him, he sued Lord Melbourne for criminal conversation (i.e. for damages for adultery for "converting" Mrs Norton to his own use), but was unsuccessful. Norton nevertheless claimed with success a legacy left by her father. Mrs Norton was finally moved into political action when she discovered that he could not only take her three children away from her care, but also refuse to allow her to see them. Indeed only after the death of one of her children in 1842 did Norton allow her full access (Hollis, 1979). In

February 1837 Mrs Norton asked a Mr Hayward to ask Mr Talfourd to introduce a bill to change the law.

The first Custody of Infants Bill, introduced by Serjeant Talfourd in April 1837, sought to give jurisdiction to both the common law and Chancery courts to make an order for access to the mother of a child under the age of 12 "as shall seem meet". The bill was withdrawn when the Nortons appeared to be reconciled (Hollis, 1979), but was introduced again in December. In the debates in the House of Commons, Serjeant Talfourd made it clear that he was only asking for "a simple palliation" i.e. access for an innocent, separated mother: he had no intention of disturbing the common law right of the father to the custody of his children. He would have liked "to effect the transfer of the right of custody of children in their earliest infancy, especially female children from the father to the mother", but he did not seek that in view of "the length of time during which the father's paramount right has been recognised by our law, the various fibres by which that power is entwined with our social system".

Others would have gone further than Serjeant Talfourd. Many speeches spoke of the injustice of the law to mothers: "One of the finest principles of human nature was the attachment of a mother to her child" (Mr V Smith); "In nine cases out of ten, especially when the children were of tender years, the mother was the better guardian, and this no-one would deny" (Mr Praed). There was nevertheless enormous opposition to the bill because it would encourage mothers to separate from their husbands and so undermine the stability of the family. It was also argued that access to a mother was positively injurious to children since it provided an opportunity for both parents to poison the child's mind against the other (Sir E Sugden). The parameters of the debate were essentially about the needs and rights of mothers. Alone, Mr J T Leader saw the bill as protecting the interests of children.

The second Custody of Infants Bill passed the House of Commons, but failed in the House of Lords. Serjeant Talfourd introduced a third bill in 1838, which was to become law. This bill was much bolder but passed with little debate. It empowered the Court of Chancery on the petition of the mother to order her access up to full age, and custody of the child under the age of seven, except where she was adjudged guilty of adultery. The argument in relation to children under the age of seven was that the bill merely sought to put the mother of the legitimate child in the same position as the mother of the illegitimate child, who under the Poor Law was deemed to have the right to its custody until that age. In De Manneville v De Manneville (1804) it had been stated that a child could not be removed from its mother before seven years under the Poor Law. And under the Poor Law Amendment Act 1834 the parish could claim against the putative father for the support of the illegitimate child until the age of seven only. Seven was therefore considered at this time to be the "age of nurture".

The bill's passage was secured by the "vehemence, indignation and sense of outrage" with which Caroline Norton made out her case. In 1837 she wrote and circulated privately two pamphlets, The Natural Claim of a Mother to the Custody of her Child as affected by the Common Law Rights of the Father and Illustrated by Cases of Peculiar Hardship, and Separation of the Mother and Child by the law of Custody of Infants Considered. In 1838 she wrote under the pseudonym, Pearce Stevenson, A Plain letter to the Lord Chancellor on the Infant Custody Bill, in which she found "incomprehensible" a law which could deprive an innocent wife of her children while allowing the sinful father the freedom to do as he pleased with them (Bauer and Ritt, 1979:182).

Caroline Norton was not a feminist. Indeed real feminists such as Harriet Martineau viewed her with suspicion (Hollis, 1979:167). She was however attacked virulently in the British and Foreign Review 1838 (Bauer and Ritt, 1979:239), for among other things, attempting to invade the legal rights of fathers. She replied in a letter to The Times (29 August 1838) that she firmly believed in the "religious duty a woman owes her husband" and "the inferiority of the position she is intended to occupy". She declared that feminist theories of "equal rights" and "equal intelligence" were "wild and stupid theories". "I (with millions more), believe in the natural superiority of man, as I do in the existence of God" (Neff, 1929:239). Indeed Caroline Norton never became a feminist nor a reformer; what she wanted was simply protection from her husband's arbitrary power over her children and her property. It was only her personal problems which led her into radical positions on the law concerning married women, and later in 1855 on the question of divorce reform.

1839 represents a turning point in English family law. For the first time the legislature, though not of its own initiative, had made an inroad into the father's absolute common law rights, by allowing the mother to apply for custody or access. The enormity of this step can only be judged by the prevailing views of parental responsibility and the privacy of the family.

> Traditionally both the legal and the social structure of the family in England expressed the principle of paternal domination which religious sanctions had long supported. To propose that the State should restrict the exercise of parental authority was thus not merely to propose a restriction of parental rights which had long been established at law, but to propose a modification of a family pattern which had been held to be the will of God (Pinchbeck and Hewitt, 1973).

The 1839 Act was a response to an obvious injustice to innocent wives, a humanitarian intervention for the benefit of mothers. There was at this stage only a mere undercurrent of concern for what was best for the children, mirroring perhaps the nascent concern for children in other areas of social life. The Act was also, one may presume, a palliative change in the law for the rich, and for those in conflict. It is difficult to document the methods of family rearrangement following the breakup of marriage at this date for the vast majority, not rich enough to invoke the help of the courts. The law appeared to be an insoluble obstacle to the uninfluential Miss Weeton whose marriage in 1814 to Mr Stock was an early disaster, and who finally got a deed of separation from him only to find that he allowed her to see her young daughter only three times a year (Weeton, 1939).

The vast majority did not invoke the help of the courts. Many marriages ended in death, a few ended in Parliamentary divorce, others ended in factual separation, and others still ended through the institution of "wife-sale", a social custom whereby the husband sold for a price his wife, who had usually committed adultery, to another man, usually her lover, often in a market place (Menefee, 1981). Women have probably always fulfilled the nurturing role (Mead, 1949) (and have always been subordinated to men in this role), and it is quite likely that at the turn of the nineteenth century, most women kept their children, and took them into any remarriage, despite the common law patriarchal rule, since they were the childcarers in practice (Anderson, 1971). This would probably have always been true at any time in history, since the law was concerned with the legal authority of the head of the household, rules of inheritance and kinship, not with the actual day to day care of the child, unless that day to day care was in dispute. One may presume that, as today, also in those days in most cases the issue of the child's residence was not in dispute. Thus Anna Wheeler, a feminist and co-author with William Thompson in 1825 of An Appeal of One Half of The Human Race, Women, a strident call for rights for women, took her two daughters with her when her marriage broke up (Pankhurst, 1954:72). The 1839 Act was therefore a limited legislative recognition of existing social arrangements for child care.

THE LEGAL EMANCIPATION OF WOMEN

Caroline Norton and the Custody of Infants Act 1839 were an early and isolated inroad into the law as it affected married women. The issue of rights for women was at this time very much only the concern of intellectuals, and socialists. William Thompson, an early British socialist, had written in 1825 his Appeal of One Half of The Human Race, Women, and his influence on the Chartist movement in the 1830s has been noted (Pankhurst, 1954). Married women were heavily involved in the working-class Chartist movement (Thompson, 1976), which in its

116

earlier stages had considered including women in their claims for the vote (Strachey, 1928). Indeed throughout the nineteenth century the fight for political rights for women competed with the fight for the legal emancipation of married women, although there were those women and men who were involved at various stages with both fights. For example, the fight for political rights, the vote, consumed the energies of middle-class and working-class women from about 1865, when the Society for the Promotion of Women's Suffrage was set up in Manchester (Pankhurst, 1931; Bauer and Ritt, 1979). The honorary secretary of the Manchester Suffrage Society, Elizabeth Wolstenholme, later Mrs Elmy, a Macclesfield school headmistress, was also involved in the fight for better education for girls (Bauer and Ritt, 1979), and was also a main activist in reform of the law of property for married women and of guardianship and custody. Elizabeth Wolstenholme was also a member of the Kensington Society, a ladies' discussion group set up in 1865, led by Emily Davies who in 1849 had founded the second school for women, Bedford College (after Queen's College in 1848) (McWilliams-Tullberg, 1977:122).

Another member of the Kensington Society was Barbara Leigh-Smith. In 1854 influenced by Caroline Norton's case, she had published her first pamphlet, A Brief Summary, in Plain Language of the Most Important Laws Concerning Women. Her views on property law reform prompted Lord Brougham, the former Lord Chancellor, and president of the new Law Amendment Society, to set up a Committee to review the law for married women. Barbara Leigh-Smith herself organised petitions with 26,000 signatures calling for property rights for married women. In 1856 the first resolution to change the law was introduced into the House of Commons. Between then and 1882 when the law finally allowed married women to own their separate property, eighteen Married Women's Property Bills were introduced in Parliament, all private members' bills depending for their fate on the attitude of the Government.

The first delay to the cause of Married Women's Property Law reform, but also the first legislative inroad into this law, arose out of the controversial divorce reform bill which was by 1854 before Parliament. Divorce reform was initiated as a matter of judicial administration, in order to remove the ecclesiastical matrimonial jurisdiction to a new civil court, and to allow to this new court jurisdiction over the substance of Parliamentary divorce.

> Halfway through its legislative consideration feminists sparked a controversy over two of its features. They denounced the sexual double standards implicit in the differing grounds of divorce for men and women, and they deplored the inability of married women - including wives who were separated but not divorced from their husbands - to hold property in their own names (Shanley, 1982:355).

Caroline Norton's own personal problems with her husband, who had been successfully claiming the right to her property and earnings, prompted her to publish in 1854 her English Laws for Women in the Nineteenth Century. In 1855 she published A Letter to the Queen on Lord Chancellor Cranworth's Marriage Bill (in fact the 'divorce' bill) complaining on the two grounds already mentioned. The joint efforts of Caroline Norton, the Law Amendment Society, and Barbara Leigh-Smith however only achieved one minor though significant result. The sexual double standard remained in the ground of divorce, for until 1923 whereas a husband could divorce his wife for adultery, a wife had to prove unnatural offences in addition to adultery; but the new law allowed married women to control their own property if divorced, judicially separated from or deserted by their husbands (in the case of desertion through a court protection order). This first concession was important because it "undercut the hierarchical conception of marriage perpetuated by the doctrine of coverture" (Shanley, 1982). But it also took "the wind out of the sails" of the married women's property law reform movement. For a while the activists were subdued, partly also because Barbara Leigh-Smith married a Frenchman, Bodichon, and left England temporarily, and the movement only revived after 1865 when J S Mill was elected to Parliament.

In 1867 after J S Mill's amendment to the Reform Bill failed to get women the Parliamentary vote (although in 1869 women were given the municipal vote), a Married Women's Property Committee was formed under the leadership of Mrs Ursula Bright, whose husband Jacob Bright was a radical MP, and an original member of the Manchester Suffrage Society, and Elizabeth Wolstenholme, later Mrs Elmy. This committee finally achieved the passing of the Married Women's Property Act of 1870. This was no doubt aided by the publication in 1869 of J S Mill's Subjection of Women, which likened the legal position of women to that of slaves, and argued that the "moral regeneration of mankind" would only come through the legal and political equality of husband and wife. It is also likely that the Prime Minister Gladstone was sympathetic: he had in 1857 supported equality between men and women as regards the ground of divorce (Hollis, 1979:68). The 1870 Act allowed a married woman to own as separate property in Equity her earnings, money invested in specified ways, and in some cases property devolving upon her on intestacy, thus providing some limited exceptions to the common law. The Married Women's Property Committee pledged to continue their fight for full legal equality. Amendments were passed in 1874 and 1877 but the Conservative Lord Chancellor, Lord Cairns, refused to be moved to full rights. After the Liberal Government came to power in 1880, and with the Lord Chancellor Selbourne's blessing, the Married Women's Property Act 1882 became law "quietly and almost without debate" (Holcombe, 1977:24). This Act which is still law today allowed

118

a married woman to own and deal with her "separate property" (the concept of Equity) as if she was unmarried, whatever the source of the property, or whether acquired before or after the marriage.

Mrs Elmy had been a leading member of the Married Women's Property Committee throughout. She was also at this time involved in the fight for women's suffrage, and it is clear that her and others' experience of the difficulties in achieving reforms in the legal status of women through a Parliament elected solely by men contributed to their belief that only political emancipation would finally bring equality to women (Vicinus, 1977:26).

At this same period the Law Courts were being faced with claims by women to be treated in the same way as men, at first in the context of the vote, then in education and entry to the professions. These "person" cases (i.e. whether the statutory use of the word "man" "person" could include by interpretation "women") began in 1868 with a claim to be entitled to vote (Charlton v Lings (1868)), later on the question of the right to be registered as a medical student (Sophia Jex-Blake 1873) and continued into the twentieth century, until finally women were allowed the vote (1918) and to enter the professions and hold public office (Sex Disqualification Removal Act 1919) (Sachs and Wilson, 1978).

There appears to have been a drift in the early suffragette movement after 1869 when Mill's attempt to include women's suffrage in the Third Reform Act failed. There were also those women who wanted to campaign for the vote for unmarried women only, for a very strong undercurrent in feminist thinking from the early part of the century had been anti-marriage (Thompson, 1825), and early organised feminism had arisen out of lack of opportunities for the unmarried middle-class woman, of whom there were very many in the mid-century (Rosen, 1974:5). But when in 1889 Mrs Pankhurst and her husband Dr Richard Pankhurst, formed the Women's Franchise League, which directly led to the main violent suffragette fight culminating in 1918 in the change in the law to allow women the vote, rights for married women were the main platform of the League, including the vote for married women, and also equal rights in divorce, inheritance, custody and guardianship (Pankhurst, 1931:96; Rowbotham, 1973:50). This concern for the married woman was a reaction to the established suffrage societies' concerns with widows and spinsters (Rosen, 1974:17).

At the same time as the fight for the vote and for married women's property rights, other legislative changes concerning parents and children were also occurring. The Matrimonial Causes Act 1857, which introduced judicial divorce, provided in section 35 for the court to make orders for custody of the children of the marriage "as it thinks fit". This was a matter for which provision had to be made; (Bentham (1747-1832) in his Theory of Legislation had proposed judicial divorce with custody of boys to their father, girls to their mother; Graveson (1948) comments that this proposal "bears the touch of its bachelor authorship"). But in the debates on the bill in Parliament there was hardly a mention of children, other than to argue that it was in their interests not to allow divorce at all.

The revelations of Frances Power Cobbe's Wife Torture in England led to the first legislation in 1878 giving magistrates jurisdiction to make separation orders for women whose husbands were guilty of aggravated assault upon them and who could not afford divorce. The magistrates were also empowered to make custody orders in their favour in respect of children under ten. This was raised to 16 in Summary Jurisdiction (Married Women) Act 1895. But women could only make these applications if they had first separated from their husbands, and they could not take their children with them (Brophy, 1982).

JUDICIAL INTERPRETATION AND THE VISTORIAN FAMILY 1839-1885

Divorce

After 1857 it was not only the cost of divorce or the ground which made it difficult for women to divorce their husbands: "The implicit threat of the loss of her children was probably a potent deterrent to divorce on a wife's petition for many years after 1857" (Graveson, 1958:17). There was nevertheless an immediate increase in the number of divorces after 1857 (1860-70, annual average 148; 1890-1900, annual average 582 (McGregor, 1958:79)).

The new "divorce court" always emphasised its discretion in the matter of custody and access (Spratt v Spratt (1858)); but in practice the judges throughout this period interpreted their powers restrictively, and upheld the father's common law rights and punished an erring mother. In 1862 a father was allowed to keep custody pending suit of a seven month old baby, on the grounds that the court must exercise its discretion under the Matrimonial Causes Act 1857, S 35, in accordance with the common law right of the father; to displace this, the mother must show "more than the mere natural desire of the mother to have custody of the child" (Cartlidge v Cartlidge (1862)). There were rare cases where the mother did get custody; where the father himself did not wish to actually care for two children under the age of four himself, but had already put them with a stranger, the mother, whose health was suffering from the separation, was allowed custody (Barnes v Barnes (1867)). But she was not allowed custody where the father wanted the child to live with the paternal grandmother (Boynton v Boynton (1858). Where the mother had herself committed or was accused of adultery she would be denied custody and also access (Clout v Clout (1861); Codrington v Codrington (1864); as also under the Custody of Infants Act 1839). Where the mother had taken away the children "improperly by violence" she

120

was also denied custody (<u>Allen v Allen</u> (1859)).

An adulterous husband might lose custody (in <u>Hyde v Hyde</u> (1859) custody of a boy of 13 was given to an innocent wife until he reached 14, the age of nurture, when at common law he could exercise his own choice); but the leading statement appears in <u>Symington v Symington</u> (1875). A husband who had committed adultery, but who was not "continuing his immorality", was allowed to keep custody of his three elder sons who were away at school.

> The father's right to the guardianship of his child is high and sacred. Our law holds it in much reverence, and it should not be taken from him without gross misconduct on his part and danger of injury to the health or morals of the children. Bad as the offence of adultery may be, there may be considerations of convenience and advantage to the children which, if injury to them be not likely to arise, should forbid their withdrawal from the father's care (Lord O'Hagan).

Three points emerge from this decision. Firstly, a clear discrimination is made between an adulterous husband and an adulterous wife. Secondly, the mother, against whom there were no allegations, was allowed her daughters for she was "the natural person to have their custody". This device of allowing an innocent mother to keep her daughters, while sons stayed with their father was quite common at this time, although in other cases judges were concerned to keep siblings together (<u>Warde v Warde</u> (1849)). Thirdly, there is a reference to the welfare of the child, though as justification for upholding the father's rights.

The judicial recognition of the child's welfare as a justification for the decision was also apparent in access disputes. A mother was denied access on the ground that "the indulgence" of the parents must be subordinated "whenever the welfare of the children is likely to be seriously prejudiced by that indulgence" (<u>Philip v Philip</u> (1872)).

Separation deeds

An issue which exercised the courts in this period was whether it was against public policy to enforce a separation deed in which a father agreed to his wife having custody of the children. In 1865 such a deed was enforced on the ground that the father himself was guilty of "gross misconduct" (indecent conduct) towards his daughter (<u>Swift v Swift</u> (1865)). But generally such deeds would be considered void as contrary to public policy as an attempt by the father to abandon his parental duties (<u>Vansittart v Vansittart</u> (1858)). This question arose again in <u>Hamilton v Hector</u> (1872). The father was refusing to abide by a separation deed, drawn up as a compromise to a divorce suit, which gave custody of two children under seven to the mother, with reasonable access and shared holidays of two older children to the mother. The court held that the agreements concerning the holidays were proper and should be enforced but cast doubt on whether the agreement, which was not actually in dispute, to give custody of the younger children to the mother was legal.

It appears that this case led to the statutory amendment of the law. The Custody of Infants Act 1873 made three changes. Firstly it amended the 1839 Act by raising the age at which the court could grant custody to the mother from seven to sixteen. It was said in the Second Reading of the bill that the 1839 Act "had been found to act so beneficially" that it would be extended to the age of sixteen which was the legal "age of nurture" at which children could choose their own guardian. Secondly, it removed the rule that the mother's adultery was a bar to her custody (in the same way that the father's adultery was not a bar). Thirdly, it provided that separation deeds whereby the father gave up "custody or control" of children to the mother were not invalid, but that they would not be enforced "if the court shall be of the opinion that it will not be for the benefit of the infant or infants to give effect thereto". The court would therefore retain discretion to enforce a custody agreement if it was for the welfare of the child (Hart v Hart (1881)). Nevertheless Annie Besant lost custody of her daughter to her clergyman husband, despite a custody agreement in a deed of separation (Re Besant (1879)); a court still refused to enforce a custody agreement in a separation deed where subsequent to the deed the husband divorced his wife for adultery, for it was held that his agreement ought not to be enforced in the circumstances (Jump v Jump (1883)); nor was a husband required to keep his children in England so that the separation deed providing for a right of access to the mother could be enforced (Hunt v Hunt (1884)).

Separation

As in the divorce court, the Chancery and common law courts faced with claims to custody or access arising out of the separation or death of the parents, struggled with developing the criteria on which they could interfere with the father's common law right to guardianship of his children. In general however the father's wishes concerning custody were upheld, both vis-a-vis his wife (in Re Bartlett (1846) a father guilty of one act of violence gave his wife the youngest girl, but was allowed by the court to "decline to give up the youngest boy") and vis-a-vis others (in R v Smith in re Boreham (1853) a father's agreement to allow his six year old daughter to live with her uncle was not enforced). The father's rights were upheld regardless of the child being under seven years of age (Ex p Young (1855)); and the father's right to control the mother's access was

upheld, because, it was said in Re Winsom (1865), he was denying access not in order to hurt his wife but so that he could
bring up the child in the way he thought best. The father's
rights vis-a-vis the mother were transferred on his death to
his testamentary guardians (Shillito v Collett (1860)), and in
Re Andrews (1873) the court "with great regret" because of the
"apparent harshness to the grandmother" who had been caring
for the child for eight years since the father's death, ruled
that it could not refuse habeas corpus to the testamentary
guardians if they were "fit persons".

Nevertheless quite early on the courts did establish criteria for interfering with the father's rights. The leading
statement, cited throughout this period, occurred in Re Fynn
(1848). A father, who had neglected the care of his two sons,
had been imprisoned on suspicion of theft, and had no means of
providing for them, was nevertheless allowed to keep custody
of them as against the maternal grandmother. The youngest
daughter aged 14 months remained by his consent in her custody.
The court did not believe the father to be a fit person to be
guardian of the children, but nevertheless felt bound to defer
to the father's common law rights:

> Of the present case, I may say that, were I at liberty,
> as I am not, to act on the view which out of court I
> should, as a private person, take of the course likely to
> be most beneficial for the infants, I should have no doubt
> whatever upon the question of interfering with the father's
> power. Without any hesitation I should do so.

The father in Re Fynn kept custody, but the importance of the
case is the principle that the father's rights could be eroded,
but only where he had forfeited them by his conduct, so that
the welfare of his children was prejudiced:

> The acknowledged rights of a father with respect to the
> custody and guardianship of his infant children are con-
> ferred by the law, it may be with a view to the perform-
> ance by him of duties towards the children, and, in a
> sense, on condition of performing those duties ... Before
> this jurisdiction can be called into action it must be
> satisfied, not only that it has the means of acting safely
> and efficiently, but also that the father has so conducted
> himself, or has shown himself to be a person of such a
> description, or is placed in such a a position, as to
> render it not merely better for the children, but essen-
> tial to their safety or to their welfare, in some very
> serious and important respect, that his rights should be
> treated as lost or suspended - should be superseded or
> interfered with.

Though the principle was now established that the father's parental rights could be forfeited, the justification for this was that the welfare of the child demanded it, rather than any reference to recognition of the rights of mothers. In this period in practice it was clear that the judges took the view that it was usually in the interests of children to remain with their father. Thus it was decided that interference with the father's rights was not justified by cruel discipline (Blake v Wallscourt (1846), comparative destitution (Ex p Pulbrook (1847)), or "mere incontinence or habits of intemperance" (Re Goldsworthy (1876)). The rare husband who lost custody had grievously abused and illtreated his wife (Warde v Warde (1849), had anti-religious views which were "pernicious, noxious to society, adverse to civilisation" (Thomas v Roberts (1850)), was accused of an unnatural crime (homosexuality) so that he might "morally contaminate" his children, or so that others would "shun their society" (Anon (1851)), or was a labouring man who deserted his wife (Re Halliday's Estate ex p Woodward (1852)). It is clear that only behaviour which was unacceptable to Victorian society would lose a father custody of his children.

The Victorian family

It is not surprising that the judges of this period agonised over the extent of their discretion to interfere with the paternal right of custody. "The nub of the problem surrounding the role of women was to be found in the Victorian definition of the family" (Black, 1973). "The family was indeed a kind of estate, like say, the British Empire, and subject like it to the benevolent despotism of its lord and master. For it had a lord and master, and his ways were expected to be authoritarian" (Beales, 1966:343).

The Victorian idealisation of women as "The Angel in the House" (Christ, 1977) and her "genial influence" complemented the husband's authority as "the two domestic pillars" of Victorian society (Wohl, 1978:19). "One can discern the three features most common to the early Victorian paterfamilias, namely remoteness, sovereignty and benevolence" (Roberts, 1978). Whether this was true of the working-class family too in which the women, unlike leisured middle-class wives, worked in factories and in jobs related to sewing and cleaning such as laundry work, charring, seamstressing, tailoring, glove-making, and lace-making (Vicinus, 1977:xv; Alexander, 1976), the fact is that the judges by virtue of their social position, held middle-class patriarchal values. For them the "home" was a "moral force" with the "male head of this natural hierarchy (who) took care of and protected his dependents". In the mythology of the home and the "cult of domesticity", it was the "house mistress, ideally the wife" whose "special task was the creation of order in her household" (Davidoff et al, 1976).

124

Indeed despite the growth of affection in the family before the nineteenth century, in some ways the patriarchal nature of the family became strengthened with greater material prosperity, and bolstered by the temperance movement and religious revival of the same time (Davidoff et al, 1976:152). One of the transforming forces of the nineteenth century was evangelicalism, "centring the family around prayers, bible readings and serious morality", creating "seriously religious fathers" for whom "raising children became part of one's duty to God". He might delegate his functions and duties, for example to governesses or to the boarding school, but he never abdicated them (Roberts, 1978:68-74).

It is no coincidence then that many of the custody disputes in the later nineteenth century about the care of the child turned on the control of religious education or upbringing. By the 1880s, the courts had accepted that granting "custody or control" of the child implied giving all the rights which a father had over his child at common law including the right to determine the religious upbringing of the child. The courts recognised that any other order would have been "futile" (Condom v Vollum (1887)).

In 1879 Annie Besant lost custody of and even access to her child, despite a separation deed giving her custody, to her husband the Reverend Besant, because of her Atheism and Malthusianism (i.e. publishing an obscene libel by advocating birth control). Lord Justice James said: "It is the duty of the court to see that the child is brought up in the religion of the father". No attacks on her personal character, nor on her care of the child were made (Re Besant (1879); Besant, 1893). In 1873 testamentary guardians appointed by a father successfully recovered the child from her grandmother after eight years, because they wished to carry out the wishes of the father that the child be brought up as a Roman Catholic (Re Andrews (1873)).

In 1883 the "sacred rights of the father over his children" reached its highpoint. In Re Agar-Ellis (1883), a Catholic mother and her daughter now over the age of 16 both wanted the court to remove the Protestant father's rights which he was exercising both as regards her religious upbringing and by restricting access and correspondence with her mother. The Court of Appeal held that the father's rights over his children lasted until they were 21, and rehearsed the "extreme" grounds on which the court might interfere, i.e. for immoral or capricious conduct, or extreme cruelty or "pitiless spitefulness". But the thrust of the judgment was to uphold "the general trust which the law reposes in the natural affection of the father".

> When by birth a child is subject to a father, it is for the general interest of families, and for the general interest of children, and really for the interest of the

particular infant, that the Court should not except in very extreme cases, interfere with the discretion of the father but leave to him the responsibility of exercising that power which nature has given him by the birth of the child (Cotton L J).

In passing condescension to the interests of the child, Lord Justice Bowen explained: "It is not the benefit of the infant as conceived by the court, but it must be for the benefit to the infant having regard to the natural law which points out that the father knows far better as a rule what is good for his children than a court of justice can".

THE GUARDIANSHIP OF INFANTS ACT 1886

In the years before 1886 the courts were grappling with two principles, the father's rights and the interest of the child. From time to time, and depending on the particular judge, one principle might gain ascendancy over the other, and more often in the Court of Chancery the interests of the child did so. But in general the father's rights were sacred, unless he could be shown to have forfeited them by some extremely improper conduct. The father's rights were sacred even after his death if he had appointed testamentary guardians. It was only where he had not done so that the mother was entitled to legal custody up to the age of nurture (14 for boys, 16 for girls) (R v Clarke (1857)), and even then she might not be granted habeas corpus to recover the child if it was considered to be injurious to the child's health (Re Turner (1872)), nor could she appoint a testamentary guardian to act after her own death. But Re Agar-Ellis in 1883 "excited strong feeling at the time owing to the rival claims of father and mother" and became the immediate cause of the claim for a change in the law (Scrutton L J in Re Carroll (1931)).

The Married Women's Property Act had been passed in 1882 and women now turned their demands to equal rights to custody and control of their children. John Stuart Mill had already laid the theoretical arguments for such equality between husband and wife. In The Subjection of Women (1869) he had written of the family as "a school of obedience for children, of command for parents" but that between the parents there must be "a school of sympathy in equality". Likening marriage to a partnership, he argued:

> It is quite true that things which have to be decided every day, and cannot adjust themselves gradually, or wait for a compromise, ought to depend on one will; one person must have their sole control. But it does not follow that this should always be the same person. The natural arrangement is a division of powers between the two; each being absolute in the executive branch of their

own department, and any change of system and principle requiring the consent of both. The division neither can nor should be pre-established by the law, since it must depend on individual capacities and suitabilities ... There would seldom be any difficulty in deciding such things by mutual consent, unless the marriage was one of those unhappy ones in which all other things, as well as this, become subjects of bickering and dispute. The division of rights would naturally follow the division of duties and functions; and that is already made by consent, or at all events not by law, but by general custom; modified and modifiable at the pleasure of the persons concerned (Mill, 1883:75-6).

By early 1884 "outside Parliament there was great activity; lectures were delivered, petitions drawn up, members bombarded, funds appealed for" (Reiss, 1934:98), and Mrs Elmy had succeeded in getting a bill introduced into the House of Commons (Reiss, 1934; Pankhurst, 1931:31). Clause 2 of the bill sought to create joint guardianship between mother and father over their children, and clause 5 provided that where parents were separated and disputes arose over control of the child or its religious training the court should have power to make orders as it thought fit.
Mr Bryce, the promoter of the bill, though a self-declared opponent of women's suffrage, argued that there was enormous public support for the principle of equal rights: 150 petitions with 15,000 signatures had been presented to Parliament supporting it. He talked of the "terrible engine of oppression which (a husband) could bring to bear upon his wife". He urged:

Some might hold it a graver objection to the Bill that where two people lived together one must rule; that the father ought to be at the head and have control of his family, the wife yielding to him; and the usual illustration was given that if two people rode together one must ride behind. But this answer was that the old system of giving the husband supreme power over the child had not worked well in the past; and he believed that nothing could be more conducive to harmony than that husband and wife should be placed in a position of perfect equality before the law, the former recognizing and respecting the rights of the latter. When women had had the power over their children, they generally used that power well - as well, on the whole, as fathers did. So far from his proposal being likely to breed discord in families, he was sure it would improve the relations between husband and wife, by removing from him an engine of tyranny, and from her a motive for attaining her ends by indirect methods ... It must be remembered that the

provisions of this measure would only be needed where the
parties did not agree. Where they lived together and
loved one another, all would go smoothly; where affection
had ceased, the Bill would apply the principles of justice
(House of Commons, Vol 286, 1884, c 817-8).

There was much debate about "women's rights", "the great cruelty to women" caused by the present law, "the mother's natural
and moral rights" to her children. But the majority of Members
of Parliament (all men) were still not prepared to countenance
a law whereby a mother could share rights of custody of her
children during the father's lifetime.

The main objection to joint guardianship was that it was
undesirable to allow the possibility of disputes between husband and wife. Mr Ince replying in the Second Reading debate
said:

> If he might epitomize his argument in a somewhat personal
> manner, he would venture to say that he was a married man
> himself, and that he was deeply sensible of the advantages
> of being so; but he did not covet the further distinction
> of being one of the last of the species. For if this Bill
> should ever become law, it would ... make the position of
> married men one which called for such great sympathy that
> he thought few would be found to follow their inauspicious
> example ... The great objection that he had to the Bill
> under consideration was that it would establish duality of
> control in the household - a thing to be avoided. Because
> husbands and wives occasionally quarrelled his hon. Friend
> would introduce into every household a most fertile source
> of dispute. Duality of control and of leadership was
> often to be regretted in other matters; but it would be
> especially bad within the domestic circle ... For the
> sake of some fancied philosophical uniformity they were
> asked to pass a Bill which would lead to constant disputes
> (House of Commons, Vol 286, 1884, c 824).

The clause for joint guardianship was dropped in the committee stage in the House of Commons. The other provisions to
allow the mother the right of guardianship on the father's
death, jointly with any testamentary guardians appointed by him,
though uncontroversial, also failed to pass before the end of
the session.

In 1885 a second Guardianship of Infants Bill was introduced. Joint guardianship again failed, but a new clause
appeared which would allow a court on the mother's application
to make an order for custody "having regard to the welfare of
the infant", during the father's lifetime. This was a compromise aimed at the wife who was separated from her husband, although that was not stated as a condition for the application.
The concession was acceptable because while it recognised the

right of the mother to apply where the marriage was de facto ended, it did not alter the father's absolute rights while the marriage subsisted.

In 1885 an incident occurred which so highlighted the problem of the mother's rights that the passing of the bill became inevitable. Attempts to reform the law concerning child prostitution, in particular to raise the age of consent to sexual intercourse from 13, were at this time unsuccessful. Mrs Josephine Butler, one of the leaders of the movement, asked W T Stead, editor of the Pall Mall Gazette, to publicise the urgency of the situation. He chose to use a dramatic journalistic attack, finding a mother who was willing to sell him for £5 her daughter, just over 13, and then taking the girl to a brothel for a night. His exposé, The Maiden Tribute to Modern Babylon, caused a public storm, and led to the passing of the Criminal Law Amendment Act, which among other things raised the age of consent to 16. Stead himself remained the object of virulent attack, and was subsequently arrested, convicted and imprisoned for three months for abducting the girl, fraudulently taking the child without her parents' permission, and making a contract with the mother which was illegal because "in law the mother was not a legal parent and it was the father alone who was legally entitled to negotiate such a sale". (It emerged later that the girl was indeed illegitimate and therefore in her mother's custody). It was "this technical fault" for which Stead was convicted that gave prominence to the law in regard to mothers, and led to the 1886 Act (Strachey, 1928: 222).

In 1886 the Government finally introduced the Guardianship of Infants Bill. The battle for joint guardianship was already lost, and the Act passed with little opposition. It gave mothers the right to the guardianship of their children after the father's death, either alone or jointly with any testamentary guardians he or the court might appoint: and though the mother herself could provisionally appoint a testamentary guardian the court could annul her appointment if the father was fit to be sole guardian. Section 5 however introduced a new procedure whereby a mother could apply for custody or of access to her child, regardless of age, and the court could make "such order as it may think fit ... having regard to the welfare of the infant, and to the conduct of the parents, and to the wishes as well of the mother as of the father".

Mrs Elmy graciously wrote that "the Bill, though it will not establish the rights of parents, will do much to remedy the injustice of the present law"(Elmy, 1886:221). Others were not so charitable:

> Our country is to be congratulated on this achievement and
> on the liberality of our law, which discerned ... that a
> child generally has two parents, and that one of them,
> though comparatively unimportant - even verging on the

superfluous - might feel hurt if her existence and wishes
were altogether ignored ... Yet even now their position
is subordinate. The woman who bears, suffers, risks her
life, rears, trains, watches - of whom, indeed, public
opinion demands these things ... has still only secondary
rights to her children ... Father and mother are to share
pleasantly between them the rights and duties of parenthood - the father having the rights, the mother the duties
(Caird, 1890:56-7).

THE ASCENDANCY OF THE WELFARE PRINCIPLE: 1886-1925

Although the common law doctrine of the father's absolute
rights of custody (which entailed the determination of the religious, educational and general upbringing of the children)
had not been abolished, there was no doubt that the 1886 Act
had been intended to and did materially alter the law as between the husband and wife in relation to their children. In
1897 the Court of Appeal spoke of it as "essentially a Mother's
Act ... it was to increase her rights ... it is remarkable how
the word 'mother' pervades this Act". These "new and important
rights - I will not say equal rights" were clearly intended to
diminish the father's rights. But, according to section 5, in
exercising discretion on a mother's application for custody the
first consideration was the welfare of the infant; the second
was the conduct of both parents, not merely the kind of misconduct that would previously have forfeited the father's rights,
and when considering the whole of their conduct the parents
were not to be treated in an unequal manner; the third was the
wishes of both parents, so that the father's wishes would not
override the mother's. In one case the court took the law
literally and ordered that the children should be in the custody of each parent for half the year; the parents were both
of good position and means, and equally adulterous (Re A and B
(1897)).
    Under the Act a father's misconduct might lose him custody
to his innocent wife (Re Witten (1887)); for the father's
rights at common law were said to be controlled by both his
marital duty and the welfare of the children, both being described in Re Smart (1892) as "the welfare of the family". The
changes in the law by the courts and Parliament since 1839, it
was said, "showed a growing sense that the power formerly
accorded by law to fathers of families was excessive, and that
the welfare of children required that it should be cut down".
    The Guardianship of Infants Act 1886 was clearly by the
turn of the century being interpreted as having made two important changes in the law. As between husband and wife in custody or access disputes considerations of their conduct and
wishes were in principle equal, although the adulterous wife
was still not treated with full equality, but "paramount" above
these was the court's understanding of the welfare of the child.

As has been seen where the custody dispute was not between father and mother, the courts began to develop quite sophisticated understandings of the need to maintain "the ties of affection" (Re McGrath (1893)) that the child had developed with its caretaker, but the child's welfare in this psychological sense was given as the reason for refusing a parent custody only as against a third party. In the divorce courts, although the father's rights were no longer "sacred", beliefs about the sanctity of marriage required that an adulterous mother be punished, and guided the judicial interpretation of the child's interests.

The divorce courts claimed to operate on the same principles as embodied in the Guardianship of Infants Act 1886 (B v B (1924)) i.e. that the question of custody and access was to be determined by the test of the "best interests" of the child (Witt v Witt (1891)) which was the "paramount" consideration (Stark v Stark and Hitchins (1910)). Nevertheless in the early days the child's welfare was deemed to require that a mother who was living in adultery would still lose custody (Witt v Witt (1891); in Re G (1899) at the request of her late husband's trustees), and a mother who had committed adultery even though now remarried to the co-respondent would be denied access, unless there were "very exceptional circumstances" for allowing it (for example, the husband's consent) (Handley v Handley (1891)). By 1910 the courts were prepared to countenance in the interests of the child giving access, or even custody, to an adulterous wife, depending on the particular circumstances of the case, for example, where the daughter of 16 (i.e. the age of discretion) had by her own choice gone to live with her mother: "The benefit and interest of the infant is the paramount consideration, and not the punishment of the guilty spouse" (Stark v Stark and Hitchins (1910)). Nevertheless in 1924 it was argued that an adulterous mother should not have access to her 11 year old daughter; the court was prepared to grant her limited access because "although her mother has fallen she remains her mother" and it was in the paramount interests of the child for the mother to have access (B v B (1924)). In the case of younger children it was not until Allen v Allen (1948) that an adulterous mother was considered not "unfit" to have care and control, custody remaining with the father, on the ground that a bad wife did not necessarily make a bad mother.

THE GUARDIANSHIP OF INFANTS ACT 1925

The failure of the women's organisations to achieve equality of parental rights for mothers in 1886 did not remove the issue. In 1889 Dr Richard Pankhurst, who had been for many years involved in the fight for the legal rights of women to the vote, to medical education, and married women's property, with his wife Emmeline, founded the Women's Franchise League. Initially rights for <u>married</u> women, including equal rights to the vote, in divorce, inheritance, custody and guardianship, were the main platform. By 1903 it had become clear to them that en-franchisement of women was a precondition to achieving equality of rights in other areas. It was also clear that no political party would achieve that position for women, and the Pankhursts broke away from the Labour Party. The Women's Social and Poli-tical Union was founded by the Pankhursts in 1903, adopting in-creasingly militant tactics to further their single aim of achieving the suffrage. Their willingness to use violence and non-constitutional methods alienated large sections of the gen-eral public, but also many women who had been part of the earlier movement. In particular the National Union of Women's Suffrage Societies, whose President from 1897 to 1919 was Millicent Garrett Fawcett, committed itself to democratic organ-isation and constitutional, non-violent methods of achieving the vote. It was the NUWSS which continued the tradition of campaigning for equal legal rights for women in addition to the vote.

In 1906 Sir Gorell Barnes, as he then was, had given a judgment in <u>Dodd v Dodd</u> (1906), which had highlighted the in-equity of the differential grounds of divorce under the Matri-monial Causes Act 1857, whereby the husband could sue his wife for adultery alone while the wife had to prove her husband's adultery in addition to cruelty, desertion for two years, or rape, sodomy, bestiality, bigamy or incest. A wife who had left her husband was refused a divorce on the grounds of his adultery because she could not also prove that he was in deser-tion. Her husband had no intention to end the cohabitation, and in any case it was held that her separation order from the magistrates' court for his wilful neglect to maintain her and her child (under the Summary Jurisdiction (Married Women) Act 1895) had in law terminated his desertion. Sir Gorell Barnes expressed great concern at both the differential grounds of divorce, and the lack of grounds other than adultery. In re-sponse the Government set up in 1909 the Royal Commission on Divorce and Matrimonial Causes (Gorell Committee, Cd 6480, 1912) to consider, among other things, the need for equality between the sexes in the grounds of divorce. The original jus-tification in 1857 for maintaining the difference in grounds, which already existed for Parliamentary divorce, had been that the wife's adultery was more unacceptable socially, and could "palm spurious offspring upon the husband" which clearly the husband's adultery could not. Lord Lyndhurst's attempt to in-troduce equality in the grounds in 1857 had thus failed. By the early twentieth century "such arguments appeared irrelevant and even dangerous to morality" (McGregor, 1957). Mrs Fawcett gave evidence to the Gorell Committee:

> I hold it to be highly injurious to the moral sense of men
> and a real degradation to them, to put them on a lower

132

plane than women as regards marital fidelity ... In a
very large number of matters it begins to be thought that
what is good enough for men is good enough for women, and
vice versa. If in matters of morality you do not level
up, you will almost certainly level down ... If the law
were equalised as between men and women in the matter of
divorce, it would tell in the direction of levelling up
(Minutes of Evidence, Cd 6480, Vol II:371).

The Gorell Report recommended that the sole ground of
divorce should be adultery for both husband and wife. Pre-
occupation with Germany and Home Rule for Ireland, and Lord
Gorell's death in 1913, prevented the Government from introducing legislation, and Lord Gorell's son's bill introduced in
1913 failed for lack of discussion by the end of the session.
After the war, recognition of the contribution of women in mun-
itions manufacture and the armed services led to a climate of
opinion where not only was the Parliamentary vote granted to
women in 1918, but also, with the fourfold increase in the number of divorces as a result of the social upheaval caused by
the war, the reform of the law of divorce in 1923 by establish-
ing a sole ground of adultery.

Divorce reform was only a diversion. The main fight in
the early years of the century was for the vote. Only after
this was achieved in 1918 for women over 30 (only reduced to
21 as for men in 1928), could women turn to other issues. In
1919 the Sex Disqualification Removal Act declared that no one
was disqualified from holding any public office or civil and
judicial post by reason of sex or marriage. In 1919 too the
NUWSS was renamed the National Union of Societies for Equal
Citizenship, presided over by Eleanor Rathbone. It decided to
take up again the question of equal rights of guardianship.
NUSEC argued that the present law did not make it possible for
women to apply for custody of their children. Under the
Summary Jurisdiction (Married Women) Act 1895 the magistrates
could grant custody to a woman whose husband was found guilty
of a matrimonial offence against her, but to make an application
she first had to separate from him without taking her children
with her. For the vast majority of women such applications
were inappropriate: they could neither establish a separate
residence, nor were they willing to go without their children.
The Guardianship of Infants Act 1886 also allowed the court to
make a custody order in favour of the wife, but, although separation was not stated to be a pre-condition as in the magistrates' court, they risked being held to be in desertion, and
suffered from the same practical difficulties as under the 1895
Act (Brophy, 1982:152).

NUSEC proposed that even during marriage, mother and
father should be treated equally. In 1920 a private member's
bill was introduced in the House of Commons to make husband and
wife "joint guardians" with "joint custody ... and ... equal

authority, rights and responsibility" over their legitimate children; they would also be jointly liable for the costs of maintenance and education of their children; the right of the mother to apply for custody under the 1886 Act, s 5 was also extended to the father; and they would both have equal rights to appoint testamentary guardians, thus removing the 1886 limitation of the wife's ability to do so. This first Guardianship of Infants Bill passed its second reading early in 1921 but the Government refused to find time for it beyond the Committee stage. The bill was introduced again in the same form in 1922, but by now the Government and Members of Parliament had been "persecuted" (according to one MP) by a bombardment of resolutions from women's organisations, (these included NUSEC, Women's Co-operative Guild, National Union of Trained Nurses, National Council of Women, Church Army, Association of Moral and Social Hygiene, National League for Health Maternity and Child Welfare, Catholic Women's Suffrage Society, British Women's Patriotic League, Women's International League, Federation of Women Civil Servants, State Children's Association, Women's Local Government Society, Union of Jewish Women, Conservative Women's Reform Association, Young Women's Christian Association, Women's National Liberal Association, Scottish Mothers' Union, Standing Joint Committee of Industrial Workers, National Women Citizens' Association, Scottish Christian Social Union).

A joint committee of the Lords and Commons was set up to consider joint guardianship. The committee failed to report before the end of the session, and the bill died when Parliament was dissolved. In 1923, with a new Government in power, a third attempt was made to introduce the same bill by Lord Askwith in the House of Lords. Again the Government got agreement to the setting up of a joint select committee to consider the matter. It was however already clear that the Government opposed the principle of the bill, in Lord Askwith's words, "of improving the status of women". The Lord Chancellor in the second reading debate in the House of Lords warned against "the tremendous change" being proposed. He summed up the arguments against the proposal in a speech reminiscent of the debates on the 1886 legislation: the principle would encourage disputes between husband and wife, would damage the disciplining of the child, would increase the burden on the courts in resolving such disputes, and finally but probably most importantly would derogate from the father's position as head of the household:

> I look upon it with some misgiving not only with regard
> to its effect upon the harmony of many thousands of homes
> where perfect harmony now prevails, but also with regard
> to its possible effect upon the discipline of the child-
> ren, who may find a divided authority in the home and may
> perhaps as children will, take advantage of it. There is

also the objection that it may possibly throw a very
great burden upon our courts ... There is much to be
said for the view that somebody in the household must
decide, and if you must have somebody to decide you
naturally give the decision to the head of the home, who
in nine cases out of ten, or perhaps more, provides the
means out of which the children are maintained and educated (House of Lords, Vol 53, 1923, cc 632-633).

In the House of Commons debates, Sir Charles Wilson MP renamed
the bill "The Promotion of Domestic Strife Bill". Some believed that the principle would discourage men from marrying;
others described the effects on children:

We are talking of ordinary family life, in which one must
be the master. I am quite prepared to say it should be
the woman, but I prefer it should be the man ... To say
that this bill would make the child in any way happy -
why it simply means that the poor child would be the
shuttlecock of its father's and mother's idiosyncracies
(Major Sir B Falle, House of Commons, Vol 141, 1921,
c 1407).

Mr Jameson warned against women, described mockingly as
"suffragettes out of a job", lifting themselves up into a sort
of trade union (c 1410), but he did concede that the bill was
to be welcomed for allowing the courts to recognise the "particular sphere" of women which was by nature "the superinten-
dance and the guidance of the young". Lieut-Colonel Hurst
wondered how a court could compromise between husband and wife
on a question of religion where they held different views:
both in principle and in practice the bill was impossible.
The arguments in favour of joint guardianship had been
largely rehearsed in the second reading of the first 1921 bill.
Viscountess Astor's main thrust was that the current law which
"made possible the existence of autocrats" in the marriage,
i.e. fathers, was outdated: "People nowadays are beginning to
look upon marriage as a sort of co-partnership" with "equality
of conditions". Disputes could be resolved by the courts in
the same way as disputes between business partners "judged not
from the point of view of a particular partner, but on the
facts of the case". She disagreed that the law was good enough
as it stood. "It may be good enough for the men, but it is not
good enough for the women ... In practice, also the administration is sometimes worse than the law. The court tends naturally to look upon the case from the father's side, and is
biased in favour of the father, which is not at all unnatural,
because the law has been made by man for man, and it is quite
natural, therefore, for it to be biased" (House of Commons,
Vol 141, 1921, c 1403).
Viscountess Astor rejected the argument that the principle

would lead to more disputes, or that they would be brought to the courts. She believed husbands would be more reasonable if they knew the courts would not automatically back their authority. The House was told that 28 states of the USA, Queensland, New Zealand, and British Columbia had all introduced laws for equal guardianship. The Agent-General for British Columbia had written to The Times (5 May 1921) that their law of 1917 "wiping out one of the most abominable anomalies of British law" had been a "complete success". Viscountess Astor reminded the Government that the bill would "not cost the country a penny", and that it might at some future date need the votes of women. But finally she sought to persuade the House of the merits of the bill by appealing to the interests of the children. The bill, she claimed, "only asks for equality of men and women ... and it is really passed in the interests of children ... It takes nothing away from the men, but it really gives a great deal to the children."

Nevertheless the parameters of the debates were largely concerned with equality of rights between husband and wife.

> It is utterly unfair and illogical for the woman, who has the pain and responsibility of bringing the children into the world and looking after them in their early days, particularly the working woman, who has everything to do for the child and is nurse and governess, domestic servant and everything, that she should not have equal rights as well as equal responsibilities (Miss Jewson, House of Commons, Vol 171, 1924, c 2668).

Some Parliamentarians did see the interests of the children as coterminous with the interests of the mothers: "To give the woman equality would be to assist in the right upbringing of the child" (Mr J Brown, c 1429). But equally concern for the interests of the child could also lead to a lack of sympathy for the woman's rights, and there is no doubt that there was much resentment of and opposition to the women's organisations.

> I think it is clear that the one /the sentimental and natural care of children/ must not be mixed up with the other /the advancement of women's rights/ - that this whole problem of the guardianship of infants must not be in any way damaged by any suggestion that in this way we are deciding for women's rights as apart from the right of the infant. That is the danger which I seen in Clause 3 /joint guardianship/ (Lieut-Colonel Fremantle, House of Commons, Vol 171, 1924, c 1420).

And so a compromise position began to emerge: full equality for women was not necessary to protect the child in cases where the welfare of that child dictated the care of the

mother. Indeed the House was reminded several times that the
courts already interpreted the law not merely to give the
mother equality but even in some cases preference: "In all
cases the courts have always leant in favour of giving the
mother the custody and the care of children of tender age. I
cannot recall, for my own part, a single case in which violence has been done to those sentiments, which accord both
with our feelings and our wishes" (Solicitor-General Sir
Ernest Pollock, House of Commons, Vol 171, 1924, c 1433).

> I have always found ... the judge gives the custody of
> small children and of girls to the mother, unless it is
> proved that she is not fit to have the custody of the
> children. The only time when the father stands any sort
> of chance of having the custody of his children is in the
> case of boys growing up and of school age (Mr Storry-
> Deans, House of Commons, Vol 171, 1924, c 2711).

The joint select committee could not, predictably, reach
agreement. The undesirability and unenforceability of joint
guardianship remained the major source of disagreement, but a
subtle change of emphasis away from women's rights to the welfare of the child also emerged. When Mrs Wintringham introduced the fourth Guardianship of Infants Bill in early 1924,
clause 3 of which provided for joint guardianship and custody
etc., the tactics of the promoters changed. Mrs Wintringham
herself opened the debate: "Not only do the women of the country want this Bill themselves, but they want it essentially
for the welfare of the children" (House of Commons, Vol 171,
1924, c 2659). The motion was seconded by Mr R Murray:

> The chief reason, and the reason which moves me and many
> of the supporters of the Bill most of all, is not that it
> is an extension of recent movements towards equality be-
> tween the sexes, but that it is the extension of an idea
> which is essentially a modern idea, namely, the necessity
> of utilising all the powers of our social organisation
> for the care and well being of the child. Primarily,
> this is a Bill for the protection of the child, and only
> incidentally, is it a Bill for dealing with certain legal
> anomalies in the position of fathers and mothers. There
> have been civilisations and generations which have exact-
> ed the absolute rights of parents over children, but it
> has been left to the 19th and 20th centuries to exalt the
> rights of the child. I think that is the right and
> proper way in which to regard human life (House of Comm-
> ons, Vol 171, 1924, c 2664).

The Government's position regarding clause 3 (joint guardianship) emerged during the debate. It was announced that a
new bill would be introduced which would have as its "main

object the welfare of the child". According to the Government "from the point of view of the children of the future, today will be regarded as a redletter day in the history of our country" (Vol 171, c 2693).

The bill that was introduced in the House of Lords on behalf of the Labour Government in June 1924 was in the terms that remain to this day (as s 1 of the Guardianship of Minors Act 1971). The 'clause 3 compromise' had resulted in no provision for joint guardianship, but contained a statement of the general principle on which questions relating to the custody or upbringing of infants were to be decided. The welfare of the infant was to be the "sole" consideration, and "the claims of the father, or any right at common law proposed by the father, in respect of such custody, upbringing ..." was not to be considered "superior to that of the mother" or vice versa. In the committee stage the word "sole" became "the first and paramount consideration". It was argued that "after all, the infant is a member of a social unit, the family", and there were other relevant considerations, as the Guardianship of Infants Act 1886 had recognised, which judges ought to be allowed to take into consideration. These included "the conduct of the parents", "the wishes of the parents", "the responsibilities of the father for his children", "the special suitability of a mother to have charge of young children, questions of religion, and matters of that kind" (Viscount Cave, House of Lords, Vol 58, 1924, c 349). The main virtue of this new proposal was that it merely codified "that parental jurisdiction over the children which the Chancery Courts have always carried on" (The Earl of Wemyss, House of Lords, Vol 57, 1924, c 796). According to Lord Phillimore, who had sat as a judge in the King's Bench Division, the clause was "only stating the law as it at present stands" (House of Lords, Vol 57, 1924, c 802).

The women's organisations were unhappy at the compromise, but they had no choice but to accept it. It was quite clear that their attempt to create equal rights within marriage, to erode the legal position of the father as head of the household, had failed. The Lord Chancellor, Viscount Haldane, had opened the second reading debate on the bill, with the clearest expression of this policy:

> The status of women has very much changed in the last twenty-five years. Recently it has been so changed that the woman has almost the same status as the man. She has not altogether the same status, because it is necessary to preserve the position of the family as a unit, and if you have a unit there must be a head to that unit (House of Lords, Vol 57, 1924, c 792).

When the unit had broken down, however, it was accepted that the mother's position ought to be equal to that of the father, according to the welfare of the child. "When you come to the interest of the child it is recognised as most important that the mother should be able to intervene and take care of the child with a power of doing good and preventing evil equal to that possessed by the father" (Viscount Haldane, House of Lords, Vol 57, 1924, c 792).

Although this fourth bill again failed when Parliament was dissolved in 1924, Baldwin's Conservative Government pledged in its address to the new Parliament to reintroduce it. There was one more abortive attempt by women to introduce a clause for equal rights at the committee stage, but finally the women's organisations were resigned to the Government view that this went further than "general public opinion would accept". With some bitterness Miss Wilkinson put this on record: "We welcome it as an instalment of the time when there shall be many more women sitting on these benches, and when it will not be completely taken for granted that women have to be satisfied with crumbs that fall from the table of the right hon. Gentlemen on both sides" (House of Commons, Vol 181, 1925, c 523).

The Guardianship of Infants Act 1925 remains the law to the present day. It was at the time and still is today hailed as a landmark in the development of the law's protection of children's welfare. The sentiments behind this view need not be belittled, but it is also necessary to remember that the origins and social interests which shaped the law were part of a quite different debate. There is no doubt that the Act would not have been passed had it not been for the fight of women to try to establish equal rights for mothers with fathers over their children. It is equally apparent that the governments and Parliaments seized of the matter were not prepared to entertain any principle which was "subversive for family life".

> The feminists' original demands had sought to attack the unequal distribution of power between mothers and fathers, husbands and wives within marriage. The Government's chief justification for its own Bill was that it was superior to the feminists' proposals precisely because it did not interfere with the status quo of normal family life (Brophy, 1982).

The Government's disingenuity is all the more obvious in the preamble to the bill, which clearly demonstrates its origin:

> Parliament by the Sex Disqualification (Removal) Act 1919 and various other enactments has sought to establish equality in law between the sexes and it is expedient that this principle should obtain with respect to the Guardianship of Infants the rights and responsibilities conferred thereby.

The Act did not achieve full "equality in law between the sexes", but it did nevertheless make some fundamental changes. For women, the claims of the mother to custody or upbringing were equal to that of the father (section 1); the mother was given an equal right with the father to apply to court on any matter affecting their child (section 2); the consent of both parents (or the parent with custody) was required to the marriage of the child unless it was unreasonably withheld (section 9); and each parent had the equal right as surviving parent to guardianship and to appoint testamentary guardians (sections 4 and 5). The Act also made an important provision for women who did not wish or could not afford to separate, and thus leave their children, before applying for a custody order (either in the magistrates' courts, or in the High Court under the 1886 Act). At this period the number of separation orders granted by magistrates had escalated. In the year before the Summary Jurisdiction (Married Women) Act 1895 came into force there were 1035 magistrates' court orders; in 1896, the first year of operation, it had risen to 5399 and in 1903 was 7292 (Sir Gorell Barnes in <u>Dodd v Dodd</u> (1906)). The number of divorces at this time was low by comparison: in 1903 there were 743 (Sir Gorell Barnes in <u>Dodd v Dodd</u> (1906)); by 1925 the annual average of divorces was about 2848 compared with 9101 magistrates' maintenance orders (McGregor, 1957:36, 51). Section 3 of the 1925 Act therefore provided that a wife could apply for custody under the Guardianship of Infants Act 1886, s 5, even though she was residing with the father, i.e. before leaving home, and she could also get a maintenance order, except that it was not enforceable while they cohabited and lapsed if they were still cohabiting after three months (the women's organisations had wanted six months) from the date of the order. (The right of the father to apply under section 3 was not added until the Administration of Justice Act 1928, s 16). The Act also allowed applications for custody to be made not only to the High Court as under the 1886 Act, but also now to the county courts and magistrates' courts, thus making the law more accessible to a larger section of the population.

As far as children were concerned, the supporters of the bill believed that section 1 had merely codified in legislation the existing practice of the courts, that the welfare of the child was the "first and paramount consideration" but not the "sole" one. The judicial interpretation to be given to this indeterminate principle of the child's welfare would depend largely on the judge's perceptions, but these would of necessity be of a changing nature and reflect wider societal values and understandings. The judicial interpretation of the child's welfare in the period after 1925 is discussed in chapter 6.

The absence of equal parental rights within marriage was largely forgotten for the next forty years. In 1934 Dr Erna

Reiss, a barrister and feminist, could write that the 1925 Act
had swept away "the remaining vestiges of inequality" (Reiss,
1934:103).

THE GUARDIANSHIP ACT 1973

It took another fifty years before the law finally recognised
mothers and fathers as equals with respect to their children
within marriage. When it came it was not as a result of the
revived women's movement of the 1970s, nor did they even
appear to welcome it (David Weitzman MP, House of Commons,
Vol 856, 1973, c 446).

In 1949 a committee of Conservative women under the chair-
manship of Lord McCorquodale reported on the continuing disadvantages of women, including the legal questions of domicile,
equal pay and guardianship of infants. Subsequently the Labour Party also produced a report, Discrimination against Women.
In 1962 Miss Joan Vickers, Labour MP, was granted leave to introduce a bill in the House of Commons which would have created equal rights to custody and guardianship and their joint
exercise. But the nature of the debate had altered. In her
speech she emphasised the practical problems of the deserted
woman who could not act as legal guardian of her children, for
example, in relation to passports, and the undesirability of
having to go to court as the only way of enforcing her rights
under the 1925 legislation. When this bill failed for lack of
support, she introduced an amended version in 1963 in which
she quoted 14 countries where equal guardianship was law and
operated successfully. At this stage the Government was still
maintaining the view that there was no practical alternative
to the father's common law rights. The Joint Under-Secretary
for the Home Department, Mr Charles Fletcher-Cooke argued
that "certainty" was more important than "equity"; it was important that third parties knew where guardianship lay; and in
any disputes between the mother and father, the mother's right
to challenge the father's position was already provided for by
law.

> It is a pity that there has to be this inequality. But
> the best efforts of reformers over the past forty years
> have so far failed to find a practical and workable way
> of putting the child's parents on equal footing in this
> respect. As a practical matter one parent or the other
> must be the guardian of the child during their lifetime
> (House of Commons, Vol 671, 1962-63, c 893).

Undeterred, Joan Vickers tried again unsuccessfully in
1964. This time she appealed to the new Labour Government to
honour its election pledge to give women equal pay by also
giving them equal rights to their children. Again she emphasised the practical problems of deserted wives, and the

141

injustice of equal responsibilities under the law without any rights.

In 1968 the Conservative Party set up a committee under Sir Anthony Cripps to inquire into the law relating to women. Its report Fair Share for the Fair Sex (1969) reviewed the whole area of legal discrimination against women. Concern for the deserted woman was no longer the issue. A more fundamental change of attitude had taken place on the question of women's rights, and in particular in relation to the family. The Committee premissed its recommendation on this new concept: "The role of women in society has changed enormously since the beginning of the century. Today a woman is not only accepted as an equal partner in marriage, but as an important member of the economic life of the family and of society ... But the law has often trailed behind" (Cripps, 1969). Amongst many other recommendations the Cripps Committee proposed equal rights of guardianship, exercisable by each without the other, rather than jointly which could give rise to practical difficulties: the present law did provide equality, for the father could exercise his rights as he pleased whereas the mother had to go to court to challenge her husband's decision, "a course which may be neither practicable nor desirable". The report was welcomed by the Conservative Party Conference. Mr Edward Heath described it in 1971 as "one of the most striking of our policy initiatives during the years of Opposition". Thus the same Conservative Government which introduced the Sex Discrimination Act 1975 also introduced a bill in 1973 to establish equal parental rights (although they may have been prompted into doing so by the success of Dame Irene Ward in the private members' ballot with the intention of introducing a similar bill).

The debates on the bill in 1973 in both the Lords, where it was introduced, and the Commons, are outstanding in the unanimous support and approval from all sides given to the principle of equal parental rights. Lord Colville proposing the bill admitted that women's organisations had "not surprisingly" never been satisfied with the 1925 compromise. The purpose of this Bill was:

> to remove from the law the outdated assumption that it is the husband who takes the decisions about the children, and instead to base it on the concept of marriage as a joint venture ... The Bill recognises at long last that the law should be based on the equal responsibilities of husband and wife in relation to their children and not on an assumption which, if valid in the Middle Ages or since, has long become outdated. We all know that in practice the bringing up of children is a joint responsibility between husband and wife (Lord Colville, House of Lords, Vol 339, 1973, c 22).

But just in case this new concept of marriage be interpreted too radically, Lord Simon of Glaisdale warned:

> The background to this Bill, as I see it, is that there is in the bearing and upbringing of children, a necessary division of labour between men and women which we should accept, and not ... try to put both sexes in the same position. What we should do ... is to see that the economic and other disadvantages which are inherent in the division of labour are mitigated so far as women are concerned (House of Lords, Vol 339, 1973, c 39).

Equal parental rights were seen by all to be an important change of principle, reflecting this new concept of marriage, rather than as having enormous practical effects. Fears that the principle would encourage litigation were said to be unfounded; it was thought to be "quite unusual", not "likely to become a common situation", for parents to take their disagreements to court, although this was provided for in section 1(2). The bill was intended to establish as a principle of law that within marriage both parents had equal rights. As long as the marriage was happy, the new law would have almost no practical impact; if the marriage was not happy, the law already amply provided for the resolution of disputes on a basis of equality between husband and wife (i.e. section 1 of the 1925 Act).

> I have no doubt that parents, particularly where they are living together, almost invariably agree about the upbringing of their children. They bring into the world and bring up the child as a joint enterprise, and it is not surprising that normally they agree in decisions about the child. But the Bill provides for the case where the parents might disagree by giving them equal rights (Mark Carlisle, House of Commons, Vol 856, 1973, c 428).

CONCLUSION

This historical account of the erosion of the "sacred right of the father" to the guardianship and custody of his children to the exclusion of the mother has been a formal analysis, which has concentrated on the resolution of disputes and the attempts to challenge the common law patriarchal position through appeal to the courts and the legislature. It must be left to sociologists and social historians to fill in the details of family organisation both within the subsisting marriage, and on its breakdown. It would seem, however, that there has never been much coincidence between the legal rights of parents and the social organisation of child-rearing and child-care, in other words between form and content.

The sexual division of labour and male patriarchy, by which is meant the social control of women by men which is reflected in the legal rules, may be universal phenomena. All known societies are patriarchal in form in that they "associate hierarchical authority and leadership ... with men", have expectations of male dominance on a personal level, and the social roles relevant to those expectations (Goldberg, 1977). /Anthropologists in the early twentieth century did produce evolutionary theories stating that matriarchal societies did precede patriarchal societies but these it seems were totally discredited, although they have been resurrected recently by feminists. There are also of course matrilineal societies which follow matrilineal descent and inheritance but even there "power tends to be held by males in the female lineage" for example the mother's brother (Goldberg, 1977)./ In some societies the woman's maternal role, i.e. a role only a woman can play, may be given high status, women may be given equal rights with men, or accorded great respect; but, a woman's status "derives from her lineage or her husband" (Goldberg, 1977), and men's occupations are considered more important than if performed by women (Mead, 1949). Moreover there is in all societies, a sexual division of labour, by which "the care of infants is believed to be more women's work than men's" (Mead, 1949). Mead offers a psychological explanation that whereas women achieve by fulfilling their biological role, men need to define a role for themselves, to find achievement in something that women do not or cannot do.

Certainly in the period under review here it is clear that the law was concerned with the enforcement of patriarchal authority and not with the practice of child-care. The common law which gave father absolute rights over wife and children was concerned with the social control of the family and its stability, and with the orderly devolution of property. This is why the Court of Chancery originated in and was limited to the protection of the child ward's property. It was only in the late eighteenth century when the idea of childhood had emerged that the wardship jurisdiction could be exercised for the protection of children whether they had property or not. But it took a long time for the Court of Chancery, and almost until this century for the common law courts in habeas corpus proceedings to allow that it might be in the interests of the child to erode the father's rights where he had by his own conduct forfeited them. Historically then throughout the whole period of this study legal recognition of the mother's child-rearing role was only incidental to the legal protection of the child. The interaction between the claim for mothers' rights and the child's welfare is essential then to the understanding of this area of law. Yet the irony is that although the slow and gradual recognition that legal rights should attach to the ideological role of mothers in Victorian society was presented formally by the legal system (in the courts and in Parliament) as emerging from the concern for the interests of that mother's child, in actual fact it was the political

144

claims of mothers to gain those rights which focussed the legal concern and which gave rise to the principle that now dominates the law, that the welfare of the child is in all cases "the first and paramount consideration".

That the law's insistence on the sacred rights of fathers had nothing to do with the practice of child-care which remained a maternal role, is apparent from the sorts of disputes in which the issues of guardianship and custody arose. Mrs Norton's husband was doubtless jealous of his wife's social success; many of the early nineteenth century cases concerned men against whom their wives had sought an Ecclesiastical divorce a mensa et thoro (the modern judicial separation); from the mid-century onwards the cases all involved fathers who were insistent on controlling the discipline or religious upbringing of the children, which in Victorian society was socially approved behaviour. The courts were not in the slightest concerned with the proper care of the children. Nor were the fathers; they were fighting for higher principles. They were also fighting for control of their sons. It was a quite common arrangement for the husband to allow his wife custody of the daughters, and it was rare for a court to give a mother custody of her sons contrary to the father's wishes (unless he had so outrageously conducted himself as to forfeit them).

The Victorian concepts of marriage and womanhood which idolised the maternal role as child-carer and housekeeper themselves created the ethos out of which women fought for legal rights of guardianship. In 1839 Parliament recognised the maternal role for children under the age of seven, and although probably few fathers wanted custody of these young children anyway, this was a vitally important breakthrough for women's rights. Throughout the century and into the first quarter of the twentieth century, women's organisations sought reforms of the law, in divorce only partially successfully, on the question of married women's property rights completely successfully by 1882, for protection from violent and deserting husbands, and for guardianship of their children. But each time the question of guardianship arose, the women's rights issue became "muddied" by the child's welfare issue.

The child's welfare issue is of course tenable in its own right, certainly to modern eyes, and it is appropriate, in the century which above everything else displayed a growing concern for the protection of children in every aspect of their lives, that the courts and Parliament who took their cue from the courts should have wished to extol the virtues of embodying in the law the principle that the interests of the child should be the first consideration (as in the Guardianship of Infants Act 1886) and later "the first and paramount consideration" (as in the 1925 Act). But the political machinations which led to the legislative principle must be remembered. Each time that women's organisations sought to achieve joint guardianship between wife and husband, Parliament extracted a compromise, in order to quieten them, which allowed women rights only incidentally to extending the principle of the child's welfare. This is not to dispute that the underlying rationale of the women's claims was that the current law did not consider the child's interests because it respected the father's rights absolutely regardless of the consequences of that for the children: women's rights were being claimed in order to protect their children. But the claim for women's rights tended to take on a rationale and life of its own, as a claim for equality between the sexes which a male dominated society and Parliament was denying them. And they were right, for the origins of the Guardianship of Infants Act 1925, section 1, illustrates that the fundamental objection to allowing equality for mothers in guardianship and custody was that: "The prime concern was what was desirable for the family in terms of the state's relationship to the family as a unit of consumption and distribution" (Brophy, 1982). In this view the history of the nineteenth century fight for equal guardianship can therefore only be understood by considering "the role that the State plays in sustaining a particular family structure. This structure is one in which women's subordination to men has been perpetuated, sustained, and often secured through an assumption that women's main responsibility is towards their children" (Brophy, 1982). The women's claim for equal rights of guardianship was premised on their maternal role by which society gave them responsibilities without rights, and qualified them to provide care for their children; the state claimed that the stability of the family required that there be one head of the family with authority over the unit, and that head was not appropriately the parent (who happened to be the woman) who exercised the maternal role. The women's argument was initially about proper childcare: the state's argument was about power within the family and it is not surprising then that women got drawn into the debate on these terms, i.e. equality for mothers as women per se. Seen in this light, it appears somewhat disingenuous for the true parameters of the debate to have been portrayed and then resolved as a question of promoting the child's welfare.

This historical perspective has attempted to trace the origins of the two basic principles of English custody law, equal parental rights during marriage, and the child's welfare as the first and paramount consideration in custody cases between parents (or parents and third parties), to show that the two are inextricably linked, and that the child's welfare may not have developed as it did over the nineteenth and into the twentieth century had it not been for the fight which women made against the father's common law absolute patriarchal authority. The rise of the welfare principle could only come in proportion to the fall in the sacred rights of fathers, but this fall did not come essentially out of concern for the interest of the child but out of the fight of women's groups for

equality of legal rights. This is not to dismiss the Victorian concern for the welfare of children as hollow or empty,
but to say that in this particular context it was in fact a by-
product of the women's movement. It may have happened anyway,
because other developments in society emphasised the child as
a centre of concern (in the nineteenth century largely philanthropic, and in the twentieth largely social and scientific).
But as historical fact the emergence of the Guardianship of
Infants Act 1925 owes far more to the women's movement than to
the child protection movement. Indeed if this had not been
the case it is highly likely that neither the 1886 nor the
1925 Acts would have ever reached the statute books at all,
for it was the view of the Governments of both periods that
the legislation was merely a codification of the practice of
the Chancery courts and the rules of Equity as they had already
developed and were being already applied. On this view legislation was redundant.

And yet, the historical origins of an event do not prevent it taking on a life of its own. And this is true of the
legislation being considered here. For one thing the Acts
created new procedures whereby mothers could now challenge the
common law position, and procedures once created come to be
used. More importantly however legislation has influence over
social attitudes which judicial decision-making does not
achieve. The statement of public policy which legislation is
seen to make has implications far beyond the intentions of the
legislators. The 1925 Act clearly placed mothers and fathers
as equals whenever disputes over their children came before
the courts. The achievement of equality before the court essentially dissipated the claims for equality within marriage,
and this is one reason why the Guardianship Act 1973 could
pass almost unnoticed.

Of much greater significance in the 1925 Act however was
the elevation of the child's welfare to the "first and paramount consideration". Despite its origins as a rather disingenuous political compromise, this standard has become the
most important principle of English law, pervading all discussions of children, their legal rights and status. The welfare
principle has taken on new meanings and interpretations as
social values and social and psychological understandings of
child development and needs have changed through this century.
This is the subject matter of the next chapter.

Finally, however, one must briefly comment on the Guardianship Act 1973 which ultimately and rather flatly achieved
the full equality of parents over their children within the
marriage. What had happened to the family and marriage between
1925 and 1973, that what were seen as fundamental objections to
eroding the position of the father as head of the household in
1925 could by 1973 not even be mentioned? The 1973 debates
were unanimously in favour of the principle; even the practical
difficulties of joint control had been overcome by the

acceptance of equal rights which could be exercised separately without having to consult the other. There would seem to be two explanations. Firstly, in 1925 the Victorian ideal of the family was still widely held whereas by 1973, according to the Parliamentarians, marriage was more of a "joint venture", a "joint enterprise", with "joint responsibilities". Secondly, in 1925 the stability of the family was a matter of concern, despite the increasing number of divorces and separations resulting from the social upheaval of World War I, and that stability was thought to need an authoritative head in the person of the husband and father. By 1973 divorce had become socially acceptable amongst all classes of society, a new divorce law in 1971 had liberalised the grounds of divorce considerably, in theory even abolishing the matrimonial offence and introducing separation per se as a ground for divorce. In this climate of opinion the need for authority and legal rights to ensure the stability of the family must have seemed somewhat irrelevant. Perhaps also in 1925 the possibility of disputes over children where husband and wife had separated, but where no legal proceedings (in the magistrates' or divorce courts) were possible or would not for social reasons have been taken, seemed threatening. By 1973 it was apparent that disputes over children would almost always take place in the context of legal proceedings arising out of the breakdown of the marriage, for which the law in 1925 had already amply provided. The principle of equal parental rights in the Guardianship Act 1973 does have important practical consequences for mothers. But the reason why the principle of equal parental rights within marriage could pass into law without a murmur of opposition in 1973 was because the ideology of the family and marriage had already recognised the existence of divorce.

Chapter 6

THE LAW IN SOCIAL PERSPECTIVE: THE WELFARE PRINCIPLE

THE NATURE OF THE WELFARE PRINCIPLE

The law that all custody decisions are governed by the simply
stated principle that "the welfare of the child is the first
and paramount consideration", represents a clear invitation to
an indeterminate standard for judicial interpretation of the
needs of children (Mnookin, 1975). Historically it is apparent that judicial interpretation has changed according to
social and cultural values and beliefs about the basic social
institutions of the family and of marriage. The judges on behalf of the state are concerned to uphold social stability;
when adultery was legally and socially unacceptable, the denial
of custody to an adulterous mother upheld the institution of
marriage, though could simultaneously also be claimed to conduce the child's welfare in protecting the child against damaging influences.

It is the lack of essential meaning in the welfare principle which allows the relativity of interpretation. At first
glance, the principle is wholly child-centred: the child's welfare depends entirely on current understandings of what is best
for children. If the Victorians believed that strict paternal
discipline was essential for a child's upbringing then it is
difficult to argue with them, other than from hindsight, and
greater knowledge and understanding of child development.

But the welfare principle, ostensibly child-centred, has
also been and probably always will be a code for decisions
based on religious, moral, social and perhaps now social sci-
ence-based beliefs about child-rearing. Not only will these
beliefs inform the decisions which will thus change according
to the change in beliefs, but these decisions were in the past
and are for the present made by adults for adults about adults.
When a court makes a custody decision it may attempt to heed
the child's needs, but it is essentially making a decision
about which available adult (usually a parent, or in an unusual
case a third party) is to care for the child (Richards, 1982;
Mnookin, 1975). What the child needs is inevitably limited by

149

and subordinated to a choice by and between adults. Though this appears to be treating children as if they were property, this is the reality of the structure of the family and of the custody decision-making process, and a denial of it only obfuscates the issue. This is not to deny that a child's feelings and wishes ought to be respected, or that separate representation of the child may be beneficial where the adults are failing to represent the child's point of view. But even the separate representative is an adult, who in turn may seek to impose his adult beliefs about what is best for the child (Giller and Maidment, 1983).

Whatever may emerge in the future, it is true to say that so far custody decisions have been made for and by adults, despite the apparent child-centred direction in the law. The origins of the statutory principle themselves belie the child-centred orientation, for the women who fought for a change in parental rights law were more concerned with their own rights, although they did believe that their own enhanced rights would be in their children's interests too. The judges in the Court of Chancery who created the welfare principle were exercising a clearly paternalistic jurisdiction as parens patriae, imposing their views of what was best for the child. It is only in recent years that the rights of children to protection or "nurturance" have been challenged by the rights to self-determination (Rogers and Wrightsman, 1978). As yet however the welfare principle in custody decisions despite the phraseology can still be said to import rights of protection, subject to paternalistic discretion.

The modern child-centred approach in divorce may amount to little more than requiring the adults to attempt to see the issues from the child's point of view. Whether even this is possible in the context of the adversarial process where opposing parents, and possibly their lawyers, are concerned to represent their own interests, is questionable, although this view would not receive universal support (Bersoff, 1976). Separate representation of the child, currently in favour, will not necessarily enhance the child's position. The record of separate representation in juvenile crime or care cases does not augur well for its use in custody cases (Giller and Maidment, 1983). But in addition the child-centred approach may no longer be an appropriate stance to adopt in these cases at all. Interest in the family as a group is now being offered by sociologists as a more balanced perspective in which to consider social policy and family restructuring following divorce:

> Parents' needs and children's needs are not always coterminous ... In most families, arrangements have to be worked out to arrive at a tolerable mixture so that neither of the parties concerned will suffer unduly, and these arrangements are subject to change as the individuals develop and the family structure changes (Rapoport et al, 1977).

Psychologists are also currently interested in parent-child interaction (Henderson, 1981). On the one hand, within the family unit the welfare and needs of the child have a symbiotic relationship with the welfare and needs of the parent(s). On the other hand, however, "the needs of children and parents are not always congruent - a solution that contributes to the well-being of one may have disastrous outcomes for the other" (Hetherington, 1981). In the United States family therapy is being applied to the resolution of child custody disputes (Beal, 1979). This family systems theory approach attempts to understand individual development and adaptation

> through a study of the entire family and its multi-generational antecedents ... No single principle or finding concerning an individual family member can determine a "best" resolution to a custody conflict, since that principle or finding generally turns out to be only a part of the matrix of the whole family (Group for the Advancement of Psychiatry, 1981).

The importance of kinship networks (Bohannan, 1972; Lamb, 1982) and sibling relationships (Lamb, 1982a) is being rediscovered, and may have a future impact on custody decisions. Grandparents have already been given a statutory right to apply for access to their grandchildren in certain circumstances of marriage breakdown (Domestic Proceedings and Magistrates' Courts Act 1978, s 14).

It is interesting that this family approach to child custody determination is now being articulated as an antidote to the earlier individualistic child-centred orientation of psychiatry, and based on knowledge and experience of treating persons damaged by family conflict. Indeed it would be open to the judges now, quite justifiably, to interpret the welfare of the child as depending on the welfare of the family. A prescient judge in 1892 justified removing custody from the father on the grounds that "the welfare of the family" required it (Re Smart (1892); the father in this case was guilty of habitual drunkenness, making false allegations against his wife, and was financially worse off than his wife, all of which conduced to his losing custody in view of his wife's rights, financial position, and children's welfare).

It is being argued that the child-centred emphasis of the welfare principle has masked the reality of child custody decision-making, for the late nineteenth century right to protection or nurturance which it embodies is a right bestowed by adults on children according to an adult version of what is best for children, and convenient and acceptable to adults. The continued individualistic approach of the law to the exclusion of a family approach may also be questioned. The second feature of the welfare principle which needs to be explored is the way in which it allows judges to respond to social change

151

by recognising litigants' claims which reflect changing social
values. The Victorian judges, faced with mothers who in claiming access and custody of their children were seeking recognition for their social roles of child-rearing and home-making,
responded by reflecting the dominant patriarchal ideology and
subordination of women in their reluctance to interfere with
the sacred rights of the father. The judges did finally recognise the social forces for the emancipation of women, and were
accepting the special claims of (even adulterous) mothers to
their children by the first decade of this century (Stark v
Stark and Hitchins (1910)), long before Parliament put mothers
and fathers in an equal position in custody cases in the Guardianship of Infants Act 1925. These changes in social values
which present judges with new types of disputes, also influence the subject matter of research in the social sciences.
The greater equality of husbands and wives within marriage,
the greater participation of men in housework and child-rearing, and of women in work outside the home (Change in Marriage,
1982) have given rise on the one hand to claims by fathers for
custody and access to their children, and on the other hand to
a new research interest in father-child relationships (Stevens
and Matthews, 1978). There is indeed a symbiotic relationship
between social attitudes and social science research: new research is suggested by nascent social attitudes, while research
findings then influence social policy-makers, as well as ordinary people or parents through popularisation. Indeed nowadays
it is impossible for the ordinary person to avoid expert advice
on child-rearing, although the quality and sophistication of
explanation may suffer in the popularisation. Whether people
follow experts is debateable: middle-class parents are more
likely to seek out and follow experts, yet even they may search
for confirmation of their existing beliefs and practices (Kohn,
1971). The omnipresence of social science knowledge, which is
seen to legitimate social beliefs and values, also filters
through ordinary litigants into the courts. The judges may be
professionally unaware of social science research findings but
as individuals they must be subject to the same influences of
the mass media as anyone else, and in the same age-, sex- and
class-bound way. Yet in their professional capacity they must
respond to the ad hoc claims of litigants. Faced with arguments by litigants or by experts employed by them, about the
effect on children of being brought up by a lesbian mother or
an unemployed father, or on the psychological importance of
maintaining the residential status quo of the child, judges
respond not with social science knowledge, but with personal
sensibilities and values. Social scientists may say that social science is no more ultimately than "humanity and common
sense" (Newson and Newson, 1963), but intuition must be ground-
ed in a context of empirical and theoretical knowledge (Rutter,
1975). It is on this level that judges may be failing in their
judicial role. It is no longer acceptable that professionals

who are required to take critical decisions affecting families and the individuals who constitute them have no professional knowledge of the growing social science understandings surrounding marriage breakdown and its effects on children. The interpretation of the welfare of the child can nowadays be informed by social science understandings relating to the physical, emotional, cognitive, sexual etc., development of children. The charge is that judges act as if no knowledge other than the law exists or is relevant to the fundamental issues of family reorganisation that they deal with.

Nevertheless the social sciences are not prescriptive; they do not lay down rules, nor even claim to be predictive, but their descriptions can provide theoretical and empirical understanding. Judges may have problems in understanding social science findings (Andry, 1968); or they may, as is not uncommon, use expert knowledge in order to confirm existing beliefs (Kohn, 1971); or they may find that the social sciences do not indeed elucidate the issues in question. They must also be aware of the dangers of blind acceptance of social science knowledge, as explained in chapter 1. Social commentators nevertheless argue that despite the recognised imperfections of social science knowledge, it is sufficient to base action on (Kellmer-Pringle, 1974) and preferable to uninformed belief. It may be that judges need special training and a specialist role in a family court in order to widen their perspectives to take in the social science context of the legal process they operate. Yet even so, social science knowledge will still be no substitute for empathy and intuition. It is the personal quality of the judges as well as their training which matters.

THE NATURE OF JUDICIAL DISCRETION

The charge that judicial interpretation of the welfare principle ought nowadays to be informed by social science knowledge derives from a belief that a knowledge of the social sciences is today in itself a social expectation. The twentieth century development of child psychology, and the influence of Freudian psychoanalysis with its central concern with earliest childhood experiences, have introduced new dimensions in understandings about emotional health. Indeed the Victorian judges in some ways pre-empted the experts when they talked of the child's "happiness" as a consideration in making a custody decision (R v Gyngall (1893)), but their understanding of what "happiness" was may have been both uninformed and unsophisticated by present day standards; at that time moral, religious, social and cultural beliefs were acceptable as the determinants of the demands made on judges as well as of their responses.

It has already been seen that the welfare principle was a judicial creation by the courts of Equity for protecting children's property (Lowe and White, 1979). Until the mid-nineteenth century property was a precondition for the court

exercising this paternalistic jurisdiction, but even after
this precondition was removed (Re Spence (1847)) the jurisdiction remained essentially property-based, presumably because
only the rich needed to or could afford to use this expensive
and complicated court procedure. When divorce became a secular jurisdiction in 1857 the welfare principle was taken over
by the divorce courts as the criterion for deciding custody
questions (Matrimonial Causes Act 1857, s 35). Throughout the
nineteenth century, whenever the care of a child was in dispute, the courts, ostensibly deciding according to the welfare
of the child, grappled with the conflict between paternal
rights and authority in marriage and maternal claims to child
care, and later with a conflict between fathers' rights and
mothers' claims, and the child protection humanitarianism of
the late Victorians, which sought to place the child's interests above either of its parents or any other caretaker.
These powerful social forces were in constant tension, but until the end of the century the judges tended to uphold the
sacred rights of the father to the exclusion of almost all
other claims.

The other very powerful force in cases of marriage breakdown was the concept of matrimonial guilt. Throughout the
nineteenth century there were very few divorces anyway
(McGregor, 1957) and innocent wives petitioning for divorce
must have been an extreme rarity because the grounds to be
proved were extremely onerous (her husband's adultery together
with his desertion, cruelty, incest, rape, sodomy or bestiality, in contrast to the sole ground of adultery for a husband's
petition), apart from the prohibitive financial cost. Wives
whose husbands deserted them or were violent without committ-
ing adultery could not petition for divorce, and the Matrimonial Causes Act 1878 which created a magistrates' court jurisdiction for wives who were assaulted by their husbands was intended to be a working-class remedy. Social historians recognise the paucity of information about the family lives of all
classes of society even in the nineteenth century (Laslett,
1977; Hewitt, 1958) but it can be assumed that custody disputes between separated couples which came to the courts must
have been the very tip of an enormous iceberg. Wife sale
occurred, and desertion of wives may have been widespread, as
may have been wives voluntarily leaving violent husbands. The
actual number of marriage breakdowns is therefore likely to
have been far greater than the number of divorces, magistrates'
court orders or custody cases would indicate. And the Victorian ideal of wifely domesticity would probably have resulted
'n most women taking their children with them, despite the
 official and legal recognition of paternal rights to custody.
? conflict then between patriarchal rights and mothers'
ims to care of children would probably not arise often in
ictice, even perhaps where the wife was guilty of adultery.
cases where the courts were called upon to settle custody

disputes arose where the father chose to insist upon his
"sacred rights" to custody of his children, probably in order
to control the child's property, or out of malice or spite
(as in Caroline Norton's case in 1837), or later in the century for religious reasons (as in Re Agar-Ellis (1883)).

The response of the judges to the mother's claims were in
the last century guided by the two principles of paternal
rights and of matrimonial guilt. An innocent wife could still
lose custody to an adulterous husband in 1891 (Witt v Witt
(1891)), for it still had to be proved that the father had
forfeited his position and was unfit to retain his common law
right of custody (Re Fynn (1848) affirmed in Re Goldsworthy
(1876)). The Guardianship of Infants Act 1886 was clearly influential in the judges rejecting a prima facie preference for
the father's rights (Re A and B (1897)) and this was followed
in the divorce courts (B v B (1924)). In this country, unlike
the United States (Ullman v Ullman (1912); Kram and Frank,
1982), a maternal preference rule was never created by the
judges, but in practice the prima facie right of the father
gave way to the prima facie right of the mother from the early
part of this century. Innocent wives would now certainly expect to get custody, but the real test of the maternal preference or presumption arose in those cases where the wife was
the guilty party. In Re A and B (1897) where both parents had
committed adultery, it was held that in a proper case a court
could still grant the mother custody. But in 1891 an adulterous mother was refused access (Handley v Handley (1891)) and
in 1899 lost custody to her deceased husband's trustees (Re G
(1899)). The turning point came in 1910 with the beginning of
the demise of the matrimonial offence in Stark v Stark and
Hitchins (1910): "The matrimonial offence which justified the
divorce ought not to be regarded for all time and under all
circumstances as sufficient to disentitle the mother to access
to her daughter, or even to (her) custody ... The benefit and
interest of the infant is the paramount consideration and not
the punishment of the guilty spouse". The policy was expanded
to take in the maternal presumption in B v B (1924), to allow
access to an adulterous mother: "Although her mother has fallen
she remains her mother ... The whole of her childhood has been
under the substantial and sole charge and nurture of her mother,
so that it is not in her interest to be deprived at that age
(eleven years) of all association with her mother".

It is also significant that about this time (in the 1930s
according to Re W (JC)(1963)) the divorce court developed a
practice of making split or divided custody orders whereby the
innocent father kept custody, while the guilty mother was
allowed care and control of the child. These split orders
were a unique compromise between the sanctity of marriage ideal
and the mother's child-rearing role, and were a device frequently resorted to in the 1950s (Wakeham v Wakeham (1954)) and into
the 1960s. Adultery was no longer deemed to make a mother

unfit to have care of a child on moral grounds, but her matrimonial guilt had to be punished and the husband's claims of justice could not be overridden (Re L (1962)). During this period therefore adultery did not disqualify a mother from care and control of her children (Allen v Allen (1948); Willoughby v Willoughby (1951)).

The arguments about whether there was a maternal presumption and whether there ought to be did not arise until the 1960s. A clear judicial statement of the maternal preference appears in Re S (1958): "The prima facie rule (which is now quite clearly settled) is that other things being equal, children of this tender age /a boy of under 5/ should be with their mother". By 1962 the Court of Appeal had produced two opposite views on the existence of a rule. In Re L (1962) Lord Denning said that as "a general rule it was better for little girls to be brought up by their mothers", but in Re B (1962) all three judges, Evershed, Harman and Donovan L JJ, agreed that there was no such rule, although Donovan L J said that: "prima facie a child of this age ought to remain with his mother and strong grounds are required to justify taking him away. I agree there is no rule of law to that effect but certainly it is the natural law". By 1970 Harman L J was confident that the principle "that a girl of under three should, as a matter of principle, be with her mother ... has altogether been abandoned" (Re C(A) (1970)). But the view that the maternal preference, although not a rule of law, was "the natural law" was still echoed in judicial pronouncements (Goodfellow v Goodfellow (1968)). There are still in the 1980s judges who, embracing the ethos of the maternal deprivation theories of psychology of the 1950s and 1960s, consider that "however good a sort of man /the father/ may be, he cannot perform the functions which a mother performs by nature in relation to a little girl" (Stamp L J in M v M (1980)). Many judges choose nowadays to avoid such "loaded" comments, but it is nevertheless the case that the maternal presumption is still current, though to a far lesser extent than previously.

Similarly, the punishment of a guilty wife may no longer be foremost in the judges' minds, but the context and consequences of her adultery may on occasion still be adjudged to disqualify her from custody. In B v B (1975) Cairns L J granting custody to a clergyman father said: "It was still the law that where a mother disrupted the home and committed adultery, the wishes of the father could rightly be taken into account in deciding what was best for the children /two boys aged 8 and 6/". The father in Re K (1977) was also a clergyman, but despite the wife's adultery, the Court of Appeal agreed with the trial judge that custody of a boy of 5½ and a girl of 2½ ought to go to the mother. According to Stamp L J, "the dictates of nature that the mother is the natural guardian, protector and comforter of very young children, and in particular of a very little girl, had not been displaced". In this case

the welfare of the child was reasserted as the first and paramount consideration overriding any questions of "justice" as
between the parents, and in the judges' view the welfare of
the child was served by recognising the maternal role.

The emergence of the maternal presumption at the beginning of the century and its tenacity until today reflects a
historical reality which was idealised in the Victorian ideology of the family. If wives were to be home-makers and
child-carers, then the courts would be pressured into giving
legal recognition to this role. The courts in allowing a maternal preference were finally recognising a social fact, that
most mothers with young children probably always did, and still
do, remain at home to care for them. Despite the enormous
rise in women's employment in the 1970s, in 1978 only 14% of
mothers with children under the age of 16 worked full-time, 35%
worked part-time and 51% did not work at all (Nissel, 1982).
In Victorian times despite the enormous scale of women's employment in industry and in home-based activities, the proportion
of married women employed may have been usually about 27%, and
probably mainly women who did not have young children (Hewitt,
1958).

The maternal preference was therefore a belated recognition of the social facts of child-rearing, in which fathers did
not participate. This judicial recognition however could only
really come to predominate when other competing principles,
such as patriarchal authority and then the sanctity of marriage, lost some of their force. Another way of looking at the
maternal preference is to see it in terms of maintaining the
"status quo", i.e. continuity and stability in the child's
care. By allowing the mother custody, or physical care and
control, the courts were continuing the prevailing social reality. The child would stay in his mother's care, as he had
always done, despite the circumstances of his parents' marriage breakdown. This rationale for the maternal preference was
evident throughout its ascendancy. In B v B (1924) the reason
for allowing an adulterous wife access to her 11 year old
daughter was that "the whole of her childhood she had been
under the substantial and sole charge of her mother. It was
therefore not in her interest to be deprived at that age of
all association with her mother". This desire to preserve the
status quo is referred to in many of the decisions giving a
mother custody (Laxton v Laxton (1966)) or care and control
(Re M (1967)).

The status quo principle was far more developed and openly
asserted in cases where the custody of a child was in dispute
between his parent(s) and others or between third parties. In
Re Gyngall (1893) the court refused to return a child from a
foster-home to her mother on the grounds that it would be "a
very serious dislocation of an existing tie". In Re McGrath
(1893) the paternal aunt sought to remove the child from the
guardian appointed by the mother in order to ensure that she

157

was brought up in her father's Catholicism. The court refused: "The duty of the court is to leave the child alone, unless the court is satisfied that it is for the welfare of the child that some other course should be taken ... nor can the ties of affection be disregarded" (Lindley L J).

The balance between maintaining the status quo and recognising parental rights shifted from time to time, at times emphasising the latter. In Re O'Hara (1900) a mother succeeded on appeal in getting custody of her daughter from a previous employee who had with her consent de facto adopted the girl.

> No doubt, the period during which a child has been in the care of the stranger is always an important element in considering what is best for the child's welfare. If a boy has been brought up from infancy by a person who has won his love and confidence, who is training him to earn his livelihood, and separation from whom would break up all the association of his life, no Court ought to sanction in his case a change of custody. But I never heard of this principle being acted on where a boy or girl under the age of eleven has spent less than two years with the person who resists the parent's application. It is one of the advantages of youth that it can adapt itself to altered circumstances with a facility which disappears with advancing years (Holmes L J).

The courts were also exercised by arguments concerning the transient as opposed to long-term effects of a change of custody. In Re Thain (1926) a father also succeeded in regaining from relatives custody of his daughter after seven years. It was held to be for the child's welfare

> to have an opportunity of winning the affection of its parent, and be brought for that purpose into intimate relation with the parent (Warrington L J) ... It was said that the little girl would be greatly distressed at parting from (her aunt and uncle). I can quite understand it may be so, but, at her age, one knows how mercifully transient are the effects of partings and other sorrows and how soon the novelty of fresh surroundings and new associations effaces the recollections of former days and kind friends, and I cannot attach much weight to this aspect of the case (Eve J).

The importance of the status quo, the dangers of a change of custody, and the significance of "transient" unhappiness in the child, were particularly relevant to children living with foster-parents, or children who had been placed for adoption but whose parent(s) subsequently withdrew consent to the adoption. In the 1960s medical and psychiatric evidence began to be introduced in court, warning of the long-term dangers of a

158

change in the child's caretaker (Michaels, 1967), and the courts responded by ruling that the child's long-term welfare was served by not disturbing the status quo and thus allowing the adoption (for example, Re Adoption Application No 41/61 (No 2) (1963); Re W (1965), or by allowing the child to stay in the foster-home (Re E (1967)). The Re Thain approach was not however entirely discredited even in the 1960s (Re R (M) (1966)) until the leading decision of J v C in 1969 (1970). This House of Lords judgment not only reinterpreted "the welfare of the child" principle as "of first importance and the paramount consideration because it rules on or determines the course to be followed", but also asserted that parents' rights and wishes must be subordinated to the needs of the child for psychological parenthood (to use Goldstein, Freud and Solnit's terminology (1973)). The "serious harm" that can be caused by a change of custody required that it was for the boy's welfare to stay in the care of foster parents with whom he had lived for 8½ of his 11 years of age.

Throughout this century then, the status quo principle had been a very powerful consideration in third party custody disputes (although not always the determining factor (Re C(A) (1970)). The application of the principle to marriage breakdown is less clear because until the marriage breaks down the child usually lives physically with both parents, even if cared for substantially by the mother. This explains why the principle did not assume the importance in divorce cases that it did in third party custody disputes. But there were cases arising out of marriage breakdown where the principle was applied. In W v W (1926) the child of a broken marriage had lived all his life with his grandparents. The mother's application for custody of her five year old son was refused: "The well-being of the child while it is of tender age requires peremptorily that the child should remain ordinarily in the care in which since its birth it has been". The status quo was also upheld when interim custody orders were applied for pending the outcome of divorce (Boyt v Boyt (1948)), and to stay the execution of a custody order when an appeal was expected (Re S (1958)).

Despite the rather different application of the status quo principle in the context of marriage breakdown, nevertheless, as has been shown, the rationale of the maternal presumption was preservation of the social reality of maternal child-care. In most cases the two principles coincided. In cases where the father had in fact cared for the child however, the conflict between the status quo principle and the maternal presumption required resolution. The father may have cared for the child during the marriage, or more likely perhaps he may have had the care of the child following the marriage breakdown. The ascendancy of the status quo principle in the 1960s in third party disputes appears to have emerged at the same period as forceful opposition to any maternal preference. Thus in Re O (1964): "In all the circumstances of the case and bearing all these matters in mind, I think the infant's best interests will be served by leaving him where he is with his father". By the 1970s a mother who had left the home and her children on the breakdown of her marriage was likely to lose custody to the father. Although lip-service was still paid to the maternal presumption, for example, by holding that the wife had "abandoned" her child over a period of 20 months when she had no contact with the boy, raising "doubts as to the strength of her affection and real consideration for the child's welfare" (H v H and C (1969)), the reality of custody decision-making nowadays is that in 99% of disputed cases the courts, whatever they say they are doing, in fact allow the residential status quo of the child to stand (Eekelaar et al, 1977; Maidment, 1976; Maidment, 1981). Popular divorce advice books therefore alert parents to the significance of the earliest arrangements for the children, since these are likely to be confirmed by the court in the eventual order (Hooper, 1981). And this appears to be so whether the custody is disputed or not.

The maternal presumption has thus largely given way to the status quo principle in practice, and the law is described in neutral terms (J v C (1970)) as depending solely on the child's welfare. From a social point of view however while the maternal presumption was located in a social reality in which mothers cared for children, the status quo principle is more problematic. It is based on particular theories of child development which may be disputed. This issue will be returned to in chapter 8.

This historical review was intended to illuminate the nature of judicial interpretation as firmly located in the social structure. The late nineteenth century understanding of a child's welfare as involving the maintenance of "ties of affection" (Re McGrath (1893)) operated within the context of custody disputes between a parent and a third party, or between third parties, for example relatives arguing over an orphaned child. This increased sensitivity to the needs of children, which may have predated expert opinion, was at this time missing from the divorce courts' treatment of custody cases. As between husband and wife, patriarchal authority and the sanctity of marriage operated as overriding considerations, although couched in terms of the child's welfare. The maternal deprivation theories of the late 1940s and 1950s and the impetus they gave to psychological research into child development finally entered legal consciousness in the 1960s at the same time as the matrimonial fault theory was rapidly losing favour. From the mid 1960s onwards courts dealing with custody cases were confronted with medical and psychiatric experts arguing for custody decisions based on theories of child developmental needs and in particular warning of the dangers of a change in custody (for example, Official Solicitor v K (1965); Re W

(1965); Re C(MA) (1966)).

It is the social changes in the family and marriage, which have displaced patriarchal authority and the matrimonial offence, that have now allowed sociological and psychological considerations, such as the sexual division of labour, continuity and stability, or of maternal preference, to enter into the custody decision-making process. How this takes place within a legal criterion which makes the welfare of the child the central concern is not difficult to appreciate given an historical approach to the subject. The criticism that the welfare principle is "indeterminate" is not a new problem, and is not related to the deficiencies in social science knowledge of child development. The welfare principle is by its very nature indeterminate and always will be. What is new is that the dominant beliefs about the family and marriage which not so long ago laid down clear criteria for the exercise of judicial discretion no longer exist. The newly accepted diversity of family forms, and self-critical stance of the social sciences, have opened the way for a multitude of interpretations. The judges, like society, lack a clear structure for the exercise of their discretion, in addition to the vastly increased number of occasions on which they are required to exercise it.

THE RATIONALE FOR THE WELFARE PRINCIPLE: ARE CHILDREN OF DIVORCE "AT RISK"?

The welfare of the child is placed in two central positions in the modern divorce process. As has been seen the welfare of the child holds the central position in the resolution of custody cases. Whatever the practice, the law places the child protection or nurturance philosophy at the centre of the decision-making process, and whatever interpretations are given to the welfare principle, nowadays the pre-eminence of the child-centred approach receives universal support. The second provision, dating from 1958, makes the very divorce itself dependent on the arrangements that the parents have made for their children's welfare. According to the Matrimonial Causes Act 1973, s 41, no decree of divorce may be made absolute until the court has made a declaration of satisfaction about arrangements for the welfare of the children (see chapter 3). Under the Special Procedure for divorce since 1977, the purpose of the Children's Appointment at which the petitioner must attend before the judge, is to enable this declaration to be made, although this purpose is not however always appreciated by litigants (Davis et al, 1983); and the child protection philosophy embodied in this provision is subverted in practice in two ways:

> The switch of the court's attention from the divorce itself to the children of the family is explicable in terms of a socially punitive response to divorcing couples

161

because of their deviance and the threat which they are seen to pose to the stability of marriage and the family. One form of punishment might be to require them to submit to a humbling process of investigation (Davis et al, 1983: 142).

In addition the cursory nature of the appointments belies their avowed purpose; in the way they are arranged and conducted "it can be argued that the courts have never accepted it wholeheartedly, particularly when applied to middle-class families" (Davis et al, 1983).

The centrality of the child's welfare in divorce and custody decisions as understood nowadays continues the child protection tradition of the nineteenth century. The concern for the interests and well-being of children of broken marriages is held out as justification for far-reaching intervention in private family lives. Yet it has been claimed that humanitarian and philanthropic intervention on behalf of children can mask a multitude of purposes: for example the identification and treatment of juvenile delinquency at the turn of the century owed as much to child protection ideals as to the imposition of social order, and even to the worthwhile occupation of middle-class women (Humphries, 1981; Platt, 1969). Similarly the Children's Appointment procedure has been identified above as a socially punitive response to the deviance of divorce (Davis et al, 1983).

It is similarly not possible to take a uni-dimensional approach to the welfare principle. On the one hand, society is obsessed with the protection of future generations. Concern for the socialisation of children, with the mechanisms of child development, with education and training for the young, all derive from a desire to satisfy the needs of children so that they grow into adequate adults. Socialisation is defined by a psychologist as "the process whereby children acquire habits, values, goals and knowledge that will enable them to function satisfactorily when they become adults members of society" (Maccoby, 1980); by a sociologist as "organised by adults in order that successive generations shall learn the blue print for living that we call culture ... to ensure that children grow up with the ability to communicate, to play their parts in adult society and to play them in ways that are approved" (Shipman, 1972). Emotional health too is an essential ingredient of adequate socialisation.

Concern for the future generation, evident in the emerging idea of childhood from the sixteenth century (Aries, 1962), has taken on a new dimension with the development of the social sciences. Society now places the responsibility upon parents not only to provide physical and moral upbringing, but also "to recognise the child's emotional and egotistical needs as valid while still giving him a moral framework of principle" (Newson and Newson, 1976). Despite the feelings of inadequacy

162

that this responsibility may engender, "society requires (parents) to see the job through, and judges them accordingly" (Newson and Newson, 1976). The law plays a part in making this judgment, for example, in the laws against child abuse. But in the context of marriage breakdown also, the law at least in theory expects parents to judge and be judged according to the implications of their behaviour for their children. The law thus justifies state intervention in private family life on the grounds of the interests of the children because the parents have chosen to end their marriage. But since upholding the sanctity of marriage is officially no longer a stated purpose of the law (as perceived in the Divorce Reform Act 1969, now Matrimonial Causes Act 1973, which abolished the matrimonial offence theory and introduced irretrievable breakdown of marriage as the sole ground of divorce evidenced if desired through a period of separation), the justification for state intervention must lie in other than the divorce itself. Indeed, it is difficult to construct an argument for state intervention for the protection of children merely by reason of the parents' divorce, for it is not clear what distinguishes this circumstance from another family circumstance which does not present itself to a court for divorce but which in the privacy of its own home creates emotional conflict and disharmony. The balance between family or parental autonomy and state intervention on behalf of children is a constant source of tension (Dickens, 1981; Dingwall and Eekelaar, 1981), and bedevils many social and legal policies such as intervention on grounds of child abuse and neglect (Dingwall et al, 1983; Goldstein et al, 1979), and judicial control of parental consent to (sometimes irreversible) medical treatment or mental health/psychiatric care (Dickens, 1981). It has been suggested that

> the modern function of parental rights /autonomy/ is to permit parents to discharge their duties to their children ... The issue to be critically addressed is the point at which an exercise of parental choice over a child's management and future is so potentially harmful to the welfare or interests of the child as to require state intervention and possibly a countermanding of parental choice ... This indicates another means of expressing the modern function of parental rights. They exist to preserve and to prepare children for adulthood and emerging autonomy (Dickens, 1981).

On this view current legal intervention on behalf of the children of divorce must be justified by the premise that the children may be denied by their parents the opportunity of optimal socialisation to prepare them for adulthood. It is this premise, that children of divorce are "at risk", which needs elucidation. From a sociological point of view, the premise

that children of divorce are by definition "at risk" introduces assumptions about divorce as a deviant form of behaviour,
and judgments about children of divorced parents not being
reared in a "normal" family structure. From a psychological
point of view, one needs to ask whether there is evidence that
children of divorce are more "at risk" than children in other
family circumstances in respect of which the state does not
at present intervene, or that children of divorce suffer
emotional consequences which have long-term rather than transient consequences for their "proper" socialisation. None of
these issues is easy to address, and attempts at providing
answers present theoretical and methodological problems.

The idea of the "conventional family, the nuclear family
composed of two legally married persons "voluntarily choosing
the parenthood of one or more (but not too many) children"
(Oakley, 1982) is enormously powerful. Yet it was probably
never the most common family form (Eversley and Bonnerjea,
1982), and certainly today "judged by statistical criteria
alone, the conventional family is no longer 'normal'" (Oakley,
1982). On recent calculations, 14% of families with children
in Britain are headed by a single parent (NCOPF, 1983). Over
the past decade the number of families headed by two married
parents has decreased, while the number of families headed by
a lone parent has proportionally increased by about 6% a year
(Rimmer, 1981). The most important cause of these changes is
clearly the rise in the divorce rate, although cohabitation
and voluntary lone motherhood are also evident. The statistics however only indicate the situation at any one time, and
therefore underestimate the number of families and of children
who at some time during their life-cycle will live in a one-
parent family. Since 34% of new marriages involve remarriage
for one or both spouses, there is likely to be considerable
movement in and out of the one-parent family situations
(Rimmer, 1981). The number of children therefore who might
live at any one stage of their lives with one parent, or with
a step-parent, must be higher than the static figures suggest.
No accurate statistics exist on this number (or as a percentage
of all children), nor on how long a period is spent in the one-
parent family situation.

The "idea" of the "normal" family is therefore more widespread than its actual existence. Yet it is the ideology
which underlies much state provision of services, in particular health and social welfare legislation. Sociologists have
however called attention to the reality:

> Families in Britain today are in a transition from coping
> in a society in which there was a single overriding norm
> of what family life should be like to a society in which
> a plurality of norms are recognised as legitimate and,
> indeed desirable ... There is not only a greater range
> of recognised patterns, but a greater acceptance of the

value of enhancing personal freedom to choose the desired
pattern (Rapoport and Rapoport, 1982:476).

Whether divorce will continue to be treated as deviant behaviour, illustrating Mead's contrast between societal ideal and
practice (Mead, 1970), or whether the statistical incidence
will be translated into a social norm about what constitutes
the "normal" (Burgoyne, 1982) is impossible to predict. But
sufficient evidence of the diversity of family forms now
exists (Rapoport et al, 1982) for recognition in more flexible
and pragmatic official policies (Eversley and Bonnerjea,
1982). The courts too need to question the "widely held
assumption ... that in order to obtain a favourable decision
about the custody of children after marital breakdown, to be
seen to be once more involved in an apparently stable and
paired relationship is vastly superior than to have single
parent status" (Cooper, 1982:47).

Even if divorce and one-parent families were no longer
treated as deviant, the issue remains whether the consequences
for the children of a broken home puts them "at risk". There
is extensive literature indicating that children brought up in
one-parent families are disadvantaged and more likely to have
behavioural or delinquency problems (Rutter, 1975). The Finer
Committee, specifically asked to report on the problems of
one-parent families, concluded: "We believe that the facts
show that one-parent families are, as a group, subject to special disadvantages" (Finer Report, 1974), including financial,
housing, employment, and in child-rearing. On this latter
point the Finer Committee, after making an extensive review of
the social science literature (Finer Report, Volume 2, Appen-
dix 12) concluded that further research was necessary.

> The Appendix suggests that among children in one-parent
> families there may be proportionately more who show signs
> of disturbed or delinquent behaviour than among children
> in two-parent families and that these are less likely to
> do well at school, which they tend to leave earlier, from
> which they play truant more often, and at which they tend
> to achieve a lower level of attainment than children from
> two-parent families ... (Nevertheless) the studies sug-
> gest that the effects on children of being in a one-parent
> family are very complex and not well understood (Finer
> Report, 1974).

Much research on one-parent families has sought to identify the effect on children of being brought up in a "broken"
home. These studies tend to have methodological flaws. Firstly they often do not differentiate the cause of the broken
home, whether it was due to death, divorce, single motherhood
or other reasons, or whether it was a temporary or permanent
situation. Secondly, the studies tend to seek a single, global

variable, i.e. single-parent status, to explain the child's behaviour, such as delinquency. Mediating factors or possible multiple and related causes, such as social class or education, or the effects of poverty are ignored. Thirdly, in assuming one-parent families to be deviations from the traditional two-parent family, they have tended to assume that children will necessarily be affected adversely: "The views that single parent families are deviant forms, that they are homogeneous, and that they invariably cause disfunctioning in children have led to biases and problems in the choice of samples, designs, instruments and procedures" (Levitin, 1979).

One of the most important variables affecting children in one-parent families is poverty. Since 90% of single-parent families are headed by women, it is most likely that the family will suffer a drop in living standards, either because of reliance on state benefits, or because of the mother's lower (and possibly part-time) pay. According to the Finer Report "it has consistently been shown that, with only a few individual exceptions, fatherless families are considerably worse off than two-parent families ... the lone father will normally be better off than the lone mother" (Finer Report, 1974). Poverty itself, in whatever type of family, can cause stress, housing problems, unemployment, illness both physical and mental, and multiple deprivation (Wilson, 1982). It is therefore necessary in understanding the consequences of divorce for children to differentiate between the effect of living in a one-parent family from the effects of poverty.

Other factors associated with one-parent families can also be damaging to children:

> First there is the effect on the remaining parent who will lack the emotional, social and material support usually provided by the spouse. When things go wrong, the single parent will have to look outside the immediate family for advice and help. Society too puts special pressures and stresses on the unmarried mother and on the separated parent. Second, the child is himself subject to the social discriminations associated with the lack of a parent. Third, the child lacks the opportunity of seeing how two adults live together in a close and harmonious relationship - a lack which may make marital relationships more difficult for him later. Fourth, if the same-sexed parent is missing from the home, the child will lack an important model of sex-appropriate behaviour and the opportunity parents provide for same-sexed identification (Rutter, 1975:173).

Nevertheless, Rutter warns against too great an emphasis on "the ill-effects stemming from being brought up in a one-parent family":

... the effects are probably less uniform and less severe
than is widely assumed. In general the number of parents
in the home is probably less crucial to the child's development than the relationship and behaviour provided by
whoever is present. Furthermore family life is determined not only by the particular characteristics of the individual family member but also by the social circumstances
and environment within which the family live (Rutter,
1975:174).

The same is probably true of any other non traditional family
type (Lamb, 1982). And indeed the removal of the label "deviant" from family forms other than the traditional two-parent
family is likely to reduce still further an disadvantages
that presently exist.
    More important than whether the divorce results in a one-
parent family, for it would not be seriously argued nowadays
that divorce should be refused to the parents because of the
disruption in the family life of the children, is the question
to what extent the marriage breakdown and divorce in themselves
have adverse consequences for children which justify court
intervention of behalf of the child's welfare. Earlier research suggested that separation of a child from a parent,
with whom he had developed attachment bonds, could cause acute
distress reactions of "protest, despair and detachment" lasting up to a few months. Long-term emotional or behavioural
disorders were also cited. But Rutter (1975), a leading child
psychiatrist, has shown conclusively that it is not the separation itself, but the circumstances of the separation which
is the cause of the disturbance. While children from broken
homes "have an increased risk of anti-social problems and delinquency" (Rutter, 1975), not of neurosis or emotional disorders, Rutter argues that "it is the distortion in relationships (caused by family discord and disharmony) rather than
bond disruption as such which causes the damage" (Rutter,
1973), because children from homes broken by death display only
about half the rate of delinquency of children from homes
broken by divorce or separation. He suggests, given the present inadequate state of knowledge, that the main mechanisms by
which family discord leads to disorder in children are:

    First, children need to have stable, warm, intimate fami-
    ly relationships upon which to build their own social be-
    haviour and relationships outside the home. Discord and
    quarrelling interfere with the development of such family
    relationships ... Second, quarrelling parents provide a
    deviant model of interpersonal behaviour and in so far as
    the child follows this model his own behaviour may become
    disturbed ... Third, it might be supposed that where
    there is severe marital discord the child is likely to
    find it more difficult to learn how he is expected to

behave ... Finally, when parents are in dispute, the
child may have conflicting loyalties which give rise
to strain and anxiety (Rutter, 1975:171-2).

Other clinicians (for example, McDermott, 1970) have reported
the feelings and problems that children of divorce experience,
including: "denial, guilt, depression, fears of abandonment,
loss of self-esteem, feelings of blame, guilt, shame, anger,
sexual and oedipal difficulties, acting out and withdrawal,
immaturity and hyper-maturity, and other pathological sequelae"
(Levitin, 1979). These outcomes are no doubt related to the
parents' divorce, but those children who present for treatment
are most probably the worst affected, and most highly distressed. These findings cannot be generalised to all children of
divorce.

Children of divorce studies

Only recently researchers in the United States have begun to
study the impact of divorce on ordinary, rather than atypical
or clinical, samples of children and to provide wider understandings of the effects on children of the divorce process.
The two major studies (Hetherington, Cox and Cox, 1982;
Wallerstein and Kelly, 1980) are of children being brought up
in mother-custody families, since, as here, most children of
divorce live with their mothers. These studies have exposed
certain effects of divorce which are probably not gender-specific, i.e. they would apply whichever parent had custody;
other effects seem to be specific to mother-headed one-parent
families, and will be addressed in detail in chapter 7.
    Hetherington et al (1982) in Virginia, USA, studied a
sample of white, middle-class, pre-school children and their
divorced parents where the mother had custody, and compared
them with a similar number of non-divorced families, over a
period of two years from the divorce (in total 102 families).
Three major findings have emerged; the first concerns the significance of continuing marital conflict:

    In the first year following divorce, children in the
    divorced families were functioning less well... than were
    children in non-divorced families with high rates of mari-
    tal discord. By two years following divorce the pattern
    of differences between children from stressed non-divorc-
    ed and low-conflict divorced families was reversed
    (Hetherington et al, 1982:261).

The second concerns the greater suffering of boys: "The impact
of both discord and divorce seems more pervasive and long lasting for boys than for girls". The third concerns divorce as a
"process". By the end of the second year of divorce

a process of re-equilibration in the divorced families
seemed to be taking place ... particularly in mother/
child relationships. However ... on many dimensions
parent-child relations in divorced and intact families
still differed ... In this study, we found that families
in which the parents had divorced encountered many more
stresses and difficulties in coping, which were reflected
in disturbances in personal and social adjustments and
family relations, than did non-divorced families. (In
the families we studied) we did not encounter a victim-
less divorce, that is, a divorce in which at least one
family member did not report distress or exhibit disrupted behaviour. However, if these effects were not compounded by continued severe stress and adversity, most
parents and children adapted to their new family situation within 2 years and certainly within 6 years
(Hetherington et al, 1982:285).

Hetherington et al do not generalise their findings to
different populations: "There is already considerable evidence
that such factors as age of the child, sex of the custodial
parent, socio-economic status, culture, and ethnicity shape
the responses to and outcomes of divorce". But, despite the
very different methodological and professional background, it
is remarkable how similar their findings are to Wallerstein
and Kelly's (1980). This was a study of 60 divorced families
headed by a custodial mother (in all except one case), with
131 children aged initially between 3 and 18 years of age, who
were referred to a clinic for the purposes of the research as
well as for the offer of divorce counselling. The study took
place in Marin County, California, which has one of the highest divorce rates in the USA, and followed the families over
a five year period from separation. Wallerstein and Kelly
also found acute distress in the first year after separation,
but by two to three years later "many children recovered their
usual functioning (although) girls recovered faster than boys".
The most useful findings of this study relate to the different
impact of divorce according to the age or developmental level
of the child. In the first year after separation pre-school
children were not psychologically disturbed but responding to
a severe stress in their lives which left them unprepared and
bewildered; they made extensive use of fantasy to deny the
separation and loss, and continued to believe that someday
their family would be reunited. The most striking response
of six to eight year olds was "their pervasive sadness" and
difficulty in obtaining relief from it. The nine to twelve
year olds however showed great perception of the realities of
the divorce and actively struggled to give coherence and continuity to the disorder in their lives; the distinguishing
feature of this group was "a fully conscious, intense anger"
rather than sadness or helplessness. The thirteen to eighteen

169

year olds experienced anguish and fear at parents leaving them at a time when as adolescents they needed a stable family structure from which they could make their own spring-board into adulthood. At three years after separation almost half of all the children had resumed expectable developmental progress, but a quarter had suffered a moderate or severe developmental inhibition or regression, with the main psychopathological finding being depression which manifested itself in sadness, poor self-esteem, impaired school performance, social withdrawal, petty stealing, obesity, sexual promiscuity etc. Another quarter (mainly with psychiatrically disturbed fathers) experienced a significant developmental spurt after the divorce. At five years, one third of the children were well-adjusted, but one third were still unhappy, angry, yearning for the absent parent, feeling deprived and rejected.

Wallerstein and Kelly's conclusion is largely in agreement with Hetherington et al:

> Although the initial breakup of the family is profoundly stressful, the eventual outcome depends, in large measure, not only on what has been lost, but on what has been created to take the place of the failed marriage ... A major conclusion ... is that the relationships within the post-divorce family are likely to govern long-range outcomes for children. /If these relationships are successful/ children are not likely to suffer developmental interference or enduring psychological distress as a consequence of the divorce (Wallerstein and Kelly, 1980:316).

It is also widely believed that the effects of divorce on children are mediated by two major factors, firstly, the continuance of marital discord. Luepnitz's study of custody arrangements after divorce found that only eight out of 91 children studied were psychologically impaired and all eight had a history of problems preceding the divorce. There were no differences in the children's psychological adjustment according to whether the father or mother had custody. "The only variable that predicted poorer adjustment in children was parental conflict" (Luepnitz, 1982). "It is the current conflict rather than the past conflict that is associated with most emotional and behavioural problems in children. Children who find themselves in a stable, conflict-free situation recovered within a two year period from the hostility and dissensions associated with the separation and divorce" (Hetherington, 1981).

The second mediating factor concerns upbringing in a one-parent family: "the longer-term adjustment of the child is related to more sustained or concurrent conditions associated with growing up in a one-parent household" (Hetherington, 1981: 36) (see chapter 7).

The most important finding for future policy is that the effects of divorce on children need not be damaging. The weight of opinion (see also Hess and Camara, 1979; Weiss, 1979; Santrock and Warshak, 1979; Benedek and Benedek, 1979) now emphasises the quality of the post-divorce experience for the successful adjustment of children to divorce, and that all noted consequences of divorce for children are moderated or mediated by other factors. Factors considered particularly significant are the quality of the child's relationships with both parents, custodial and non-custodial (Wallerstein and Kelly, 1980), the child-rearing practices of the custodian parent (Santrock et al, 1982), and the availability of support systems to the custodial parent (Hetherington et al, 1982; Santrock et al 1982).

Intergenerational effects of divorce

While researchers are now investigating the short-term and longer-term responses of children to divorce, in some cases seeking to measure the impact of different custodians (Santrock and Warshak, 1979; Luepnitz, 1982) less is understood about the inter-generational effects of divorce. Clinical impressions are that childhood experiences such as institutional care or cold relationships with parents can influence parenting skills in later life, and experimental studies have shown that monkeys isolated during infancy become incompetent parents (Rutter, 1975). Women whose parents had divorced or separated during their childhood may be more likely to have illegitimate children or a pre-marital conception (Illsley and Thompson, 1961), and to marry and give birth young (Rutter and Madge, 1976). Children from homes broken by divorce or separation may be more likely to show marital instability when adult (Rutter and Madge, 1976; Gurin et al, 1960; Langner and Michael, 1963) and to get divorced themselves (Mueller and Pope, 1977). In the most recently reported English study of 68 working-class women and their first-born babies, it is suggested that early life experiences influence later mothering behaviour. No distinction however is made between parental death or divorce and separation when considering the effect of a "disrupted family of origin" on later mother-baby interaction, and to that extent the findings are unsatisfactory. Nevertheless the study concludes that "(20 week old babies) of women from a disrupted family of origin received significantly less physical and social stimulation at the hands of their mothers in their early months ... (and) at 27 months (these) children were less advanced than other children in their language development" (Hall et al, 1979).

On the other hand there is little evidence that a parent's own experiences of child-rearing influence his or her own parenting behaviour (McGlaughlin, 1981). American research suggests that, after controlling for contemporary life circumstances and social background factors such as class, geographical location or religion, "there is little evidence for the existence of any long-term effects of coming from a home broken by parental divorce or separation" (Kulka and Weingarten, 1979). Kulka and Weingarten did note that adults from divorced homes still identify childhood as the most unhappy time of their lives (unless they themselves have been divorced), that men from broken homes report higher psychological anxiety when marital problems arise, and that married women from broken homes may consider the marital role as less important to them than women from intact homes. Nevertheless none of these findings are statistically large, and they conclude that "early experiences have at most a modest effect on adult adjustment" (Kulka and Weingarten, 1979; see also Ferri, 1976; Willmott and Willmott, 1982). An English review of the literature suggests that although there are "important and statistically significant continuities in terms of marital behaviour, intergenerational dis-continuity is more common" (Rutter and Madge, 1976).

These findings seem consistent with other research. Life crisis literature suggests that for most crises, including divorce, "its disruptive effects seem to wane over time as new modes of coping and adaptation are brought into play" (Kulka and Weingarten, 1979). Psychological research on the long-term effects of early experiences, such as maternal and social deprivation or institutionalisation now suggests that experiences in the early years of infant development are not critical to later adjustment, and "personal change" can be brought about by "environmental change" during the whole period of a child's development (Clarke and Clarke, 1976). Thus the effects of early misfortune and deprivation can be reversed by subsequent environmental changes, for example by the adoption of older children who have been brought up in an institution (Kadushin, 1976).

This belief that children's "resiliency and capacity for adaptation very often enable him to struggle effectively and successfully with the tragic circumstances of his life" (Kadushin, 1976) has been noted also in the context of divorce. In a study of 120 children from 82 one-parent families, 80% of which were the result of divorce or separation, attending a Gingerbread playschool for working lone parents, between one quarter and one half of the children showed "no sign of distress apparent to the staff" (Willmott and Willmott, 1982). The study concluded "that children can indeed come through such changes wholly or relatively unscathed ... although research suggests that there is probably a somewhat greater propensity to difficulties among people whose childhood was affected by parental separation, most children are probably more resilient (and adaptable) than it has been fashionable to admit" (Willmott and Willmott, 1982:345).

Conclusion

There are two major implications from current empirical research: that divorce is a process and the effects of divorce will vary over a period of time, and according to the individuals involved, and that effects are and can be mediated: divorce is "a sequence of events involving a transition in the lives of children", a "process" of "reorganisation to an eventual attainment of a new equilibrium" (Hetherington, 1981:34-5); and that "the eventual outcome depends, in large measure, not only on what has been lost, but on what has been created to take the place of the failed marriage" (Wallerstein and Kelly, 1980:316).

One of Wallerstein and Kelly's most interesting findings is "the significance of the relationships within the present in determining outcome at the time. The parent-child relationships of previous years appeared not to be sufficient to maintain good functioning within the present" (1980:208). They suggest that while pre-divorce relationships between parent and child are significant (indeed the stronger the relationship, the greater will be the child's difficulty in adjusting to the divorce (Wallerstein and Kelly, 1980:208)), the post-divorce relationship is a more important consideration. Relationships change, and pre-divorce relationships are unreliable indications of post-divorce relationships. Wallerstein and Kelly (1980:315, 258) found no correlation between the non-custodian father's post-divorce contact with the child and the pre-divorce relationship; and Hetherington noted the discontinuity between the quality of pre- and post-separation parent-child interaction, particularly for fathers: "A substantial number of fathers report that their relationship with their children improves following divorce, and many previously relatively uninvolved fathers became competent and concerned parents when confronted with becoming a custodial parent" (1982:49). There is indeed unanimous support for Wallerstein and Kelly's "major conclusion ... that the relationships within the post-divorce family are likely to govern long-range outcomes for children and adolescents" (1980:316), and for the view that the risks of divorce and of one-parent family upbringing can be mediated and moderated by factors not related to which parent is custodian, nor necessarily to pre-divorce parent-child relationships. It may be possible to identify risks normally associated with one-parent family upbringing, or with particular custodian and access arrangements, but these may not necessarily be consequent on the quality of pre-divorce or even trial-date parent-child relationships. Goldstein et al (1973:51) warned of the inability of the law (or social science knowledge) to predict "the unfolding development of a child and his family" and urged that the law be "less pretentious and ambitious in its aim". Indeed, despite recent increases in knowledge of the effects of divorce on children, both short-term and longer term, still for example, "we know nothing about the long-term effects of children growing up in mother-custody compared to father-custody families" (Santrock et al, 1982:303); and the full-term effects of divorce for children as adults or the inter-generational effects are barely beginning to be understood. In general, the long-term effects of early experience, and the influence of childhood experiences on parenting behaviour remain uncertain (Rutter, 1981).

The centrality of the child's welfare in the law as a precondition to his parents' divorce is based on the premise that children of divorce are necessarily "at risk". There are however dangers implicit in the premise: one is that intervention may occur on grounds which do not otherwise justify child care intervention under other legislation. Another danger lies in the absolute nature of the assumption which hides the relative basis of comparison: are children of divorce "at risk" as compared with children of some ideal model happy family, or as compared with children in pre-divorce unhappy families? The third danger concerns the empirical evidence for the premise.

There is no simple answer to whether and how divorce affects children. There is some evidence that growing up in a broken home, or a one-parent family resulting from divorce or separation, can cause educational retardation, antisocial behaviour such as delinquency, or impair later parenting. But most of these effects may be associated with other factors, such as poverty, class, occupational status etc; much research does not take a longitudinal approach but relies upon evidence at one point in time, rather than considering the family breakdown as a process over many years; it also fails to make comparisons with intact families in which there is parental disharmony; and earlier research fails to consider possible mitigating factors. The American research studies by Hetherington et al and Wallerstein and Kelly are likely to be much more reliable, and need to be replicated in this country.

It is possible that the damage to children caused by parental divorce has been overstated. With the increased rate of divorce, marriage breakdown is less likely to be treated as deviant, so that the social stigmatic effects of divorce on children will diminish. Short-term effects of divorce may also have been over-emphasised over longer-term resilience and adaptation by children to new family circumstances. One must also distinguish between the general pattern and individual differences, particularly by sex and age. Most importantly, mitigating factors in the post-divorce arrangements may be the most significant variables in the success of the family to restructure their relationships. In other words children of divorce need not be "at risk"; there is a potential danger of it, although the nature of that danger is not at all clear. After controlling for factors such as social and economic disadvantages, there is very little direct evidence that family breakdown itself is linked with any longer-term consequences (although this could be a result of lack of evidence rather than lack of effects), and certainly none that cannot be reversed by a satisfactory change in environment.

The issue here is whether there is any justification for making the welfare of the child central to the granting of divorce. Just as earlier experts found it necessary to distinguish between separation from a parent and the family discord which often surrounded the separation, and point to the latter as the mechanism resulting in childhood disorders, so it is now becoming apparent that it is not the divorce itself, but the circumstances in which the divorce takes place that have deleterious consequences for children.

It is clear from the research cited above, that in our present state of knowledge, the ill-effects for children of divorce may not be as widespread as have been believed, not as serious, and are certainly reversible, able to be mitigated, or even avoided altogether by satisfactory post-divorce arrangements. The justification for present legal intervention in the divorce process on behalf of children then is to identify those cases where children may be "at risk" and to provide for the introduction of mitigating circumstances. It may be that the "welfare of the family" rather than the "welfare of the child" is a more appropriate criterion for intervention in the light of psychological understandings of parent-child interaction and family processes. An important issue concerns whether the law should provide as it does that the divorce itself cannot be granted until the judge has declared his satisfaction for the arrangements for the children. The issues which are addressed in the Children's Appointment, i.e. the facts as stated in the petitioner's proposed (material) Arrangements for the Children relating to the child's residence, education, financial provision and access (Matrimonial Causes Rules 1977, Rule 8(2)), may only indirectly or partially bear on the circumstances which are now understood to conduce to the success or failure of the divorce process for the child. Nevertheless the Children's Appointment is the one stage in the present process when any potential difficulties can be detected. As the mechanisms of post-divorce problems are becoming better understood new assessment methods may be able to be devised which will enable a screening process to be operated to identify those families where children are likely to be "at risk" from their parents' divorce. Suggestions of this type have already been made in this country (Dodds, 1983), but the proposed criterion for assessment has usually been whether there are any contests between the parents over the children. Thus it has been suggested that welfare reports should not be used in uncontested custody cases (Eekelaar and Clive, 1976), and that judicial Children's Appointments should not take place where there is no "issue" between the parents (Davis et al, 1983). Certainly parental conflict has always

175

been understood to result in post-divorce problems of children, but it is questionable whether the presence of a formal issue or contest is an indication of whether parental conflict exists. Many conflicts, in particular over access, may not present themselves to the court at this stage or at any later stage (Southwell, 1982), and indeed the present law which makes the granting of a divorce conditional on the judge being satisfied about the arrangements for the children may actually conduce to the parents hiding any conflicts which may exist.

The purpose of the s 41 declaration of satisfaction must be as a screening procedure to identify cases (formally contested or not) in which there is the potentiality of damage to children. Criteria for consideration must include less the pre-divorce relationships, but more importantly prognostications of post-divorce relationships and arrangements. But the ability of courts to operate an effective screening procedure is severely limited in practical terms. The policing of arrangements once made is also both impractical and often objectionable (such as where supervision orders are made on grounds not otherwise justifying child care intervention (Southwell, 1982)). If the concern of the legal system is to minimise the known potential risks of divorce, then this concern and knowledge on which it is based ought to be embodied in the provision of facilities for advice and counselling on the material and psychological factors which can mediate and mitigate the effects of divorce. This is a task going well beyond present proposals for conciliation services which seek to address only one of the known mediating factors, i.e. family discord.

Most children of divorce probably emerge nowadays quite unscathed in any deeper or longer-lasting sense. Legal procedures must therefore be devised which can identify that minority of cases of potential damage to children. How such procedures can be devised needs consideration. But there can be no other justification for making the welfare of the child the linchpin of the legal process of divorce.

Chapter 7

CUSTODY CONSIDERATIONS: WHICH PARENT?

THE LAW

Most divorces result in one parent receiving custody, or care
and control, of the children of the family (Eekelaar et al, 1977
83.2%; Maidment, 1976 94%); the court is thus bound to make a
choice between parents as to the child's future caretaker.
Current judicial thinking displays a tension between the earlier
maternal preference and a less a priori, more open-minded approach of whatever is the best interests of the child. These two
views are encapsulated in the following recent comments:

/The judge/ looked, as he should, at the whole background
and considered where had the infant /a boy of 8/ better
be - and that is really the only question that the court
has to ask. I do not at all agree with expressions of
opinion which have fallen ... from judges that a boy
should, as a matter of principle, be with his father -
just as much as I disagree with the other 'principle',
which has altogether been abandoned, that a girl of under
three should, as a matter of principle, be with her
mother. Other things being equal, these things may be so,
but there is no principle involved in either. They are
merely considerations which may weigh with the judge where
the scales are nicely balanced (Harman L J in Re C(A)
(1970)).

There is no indication in this case at all that the mother
is not a suitable person to look after this little girl
/of 4½ years/, as she obviously is the appropriate person
to look after her unless there is some good reason to the
contrary (Ormrod L J in M v M (1980)).

The current view is therefore that the welfare of the
child no longer requires as a matter of principle that mothers
should have the care of their children, but judges still vary
in the significance they attach to the age or sex of the child -

177

some prefer maternal care for younger children, and for girls - and in their assessment of the extent to which other considerations are needed to or do displace the social expectation that the mother will care for the children. Since all custody decisions are in the discretion of the judge, idiosyncracies and personal prejudices may be expressed; and the appeal process will not necessarily provide a remedy (see chapter 2).

The posing of the issue as a choice between parents is itself problematic, since although the ultimate decision dictates such a choice, the process of decision-making involves other considerations which do not directly or explicitly address the issue in terms of a choice or "which parent?". In particular there may be considerations relating to the character, personality, life style or circumstances of one of the parents which it is alleged should disqualify that parent from having care of the children. Marital conduct, in the sense of responsibility for the breakdown of the marriage, may no longer be deemed to be a relevant consideration when assessing competence in child care (Re K (1977)), but such conduct may be considered illustrative of a general "irresponsibility" towards family life which may affect the court's judgment as to what is best for the children (B v B (1975)). Promiscuity or overt sexuality ("the girl told the father that she had been sleeping in the same room as her mother and another man who lived in the flat and that she had seen amorous exchanges between the mother and the other man": S v S (1971)) may lose a mother custody. Lesbianism has lost a mother custody (S v S (1980)), though not always (Guardian (1976)); homosexuality has lost a father his son through adoption (Re D (1977)); transvestism has almost lost a father access to his children (G v G (1981)). Religious beliefs which create social isolation for children such as Jehovah's Witnesses have influenced the court's view of what is in a child's best interests (Buckley v Buckley (1973) (mother lost custody); Re H (1980) (mother got custody)).

A practical consideration of great importance in custody decisions concerns the disposition of the matrimonial home. The practice of the divorce courts since 1973 has been to preserve the children's home until they have grown up, by allowing the custodian parent the use of the matrimonial home either through occupation or ownership rights (Smith v Smith (1975)). This applies to all forms of home, owner-occupied, privately or council rented. Since accommodation is an important part of the decision of what is in the material interests of the child, the decision on custody and the decision on the matrimonial home are inextricably linked. Indeed one cannot be made without the other, since both will be determined by the same considerations. Yet in practice the issue of the matrimonial home is often determined first; sometimes in domestic violence injunction proceedings, or in divorce. The judges have frowned upon this practice, indicating that the question of custody ought to precede the decision on the home, since the grant of custody will on present principles actually determine the use of the home (<u>Smith v Smith</u> (1980)). Indeed it has been alleged that some fathers contest custody solely for the ulterior purpose of retaining the matrimonial home. While this remains to be investigated, it is certainly the case that the social practice of allowing the mother to have custody has implications for the father's property rights and accommodation; and this is one facet of the complaint that husbands suffer more from divorce than wives.

Since it is normally expected, both socially and judicially, that mothers will have care of the children after the divorce, any deviation from the norm will usually turn on the "unfitness" of the mother, for any of the reasons discussed above. Where a father seeks custody these same grounds may apply, but there are in addition particular challenges that fathers in practice have to overcome. The quality of caretaking may not be questioned, but the suitability of a father to bring up a girl may be raised: "However good a sort of man he may be, he cannot perform the functions which a mother performs by nature in relation to a little girl /of 4½/" (Stamp L J in <u>M v M</u> (1980)). Even more commonly articulated is the question of how an employed father can provide full-time care for children, and after school hours or in school holidays:

> The father's proposals were that the child /aged 2½/ would be looked after on 3 days a week by a child-minder and on at least one day by /the step-mother's/ mother. We were told that the child would be with one or other from about 8 a.m. to 4.30 p.m. each day. The result, inevitably, would be that he would spend most of his waking hours away from his father and /step-mother/, and that his care would be divided between at least three, possibly four, adults. This is a situation which is to be avoided if it is possible to do so (Ormrod L J in <u>D v M</u> (1982)).

Men may, with some justification, feel aggrieved at such comments. It appears that judges are imposing a particular model of family life, where the wife stays at home to look after the children; and assuming that this is both the norm and also somehow "better" for children. The fact that a mother who works would make exactly the same arrangements for the care of her child is ignored; yet judges allow a contested custody case to turn on such issues, even though within marriage or in uncontested custody applications such arrangements are socially and legally approved. It is in cases such as these, that a judicial awareness of the social context of legal decisions, as described below, is overdue.

The final aspect of custody decision-making which needs to be explored is the most important determinant in practice (see chapter 3): the residential status quo of the child. A custody order in favour of a mother may be the result of a maternal preference or it may be the result of a preference for not changing the child's residence. Since most children from broken homes live with their mothers and most mothers claim custody (see chapter 3) it is not surprising that most mothers get custody. Indeed the child's residence at the time of the court hearing is the major factor in custody decisions at first instance (Eekelaar et al, 1977) and this is so even if other reasons are stated by the judges in their decisions:

> Our study confirms that the major factor taken into account by courts in deciding where a child is to live is the avoidance of disruption of the child's present residence. We could find no significant relationship between the outcome of the residence issue and factors such as the age of the children, the sex of the custodian or the separation of the siblings ... occasional instances of "favouritism" for the wife may still be found, but they are quite uncharacteristic of the general practice (Eekelaar et al, 1977).

When first instance decisions are appealed against, however, the picture changes. In appeal cases there is "real, even widespread bias" in favour of mothers, as evidenced by those cases where a status quo in the father's favour is overturned:

> Preference for the maternal role ... reuniting siblings ... a parent's personality, and punishment for refusing or obstructing access all seem weak reasons for disturbing a status quo of between one year at the least and five years at the most, and in some cases a status quo which began when the child was as young as two or three years old (Maidment, 1981).

Further, judges may be prepared to depart from a professional divorce court welfare officer recommendation supporting a father's status quo because of a personal preference for the maternal role (Maidment, 1981).

While examples of judicial favouritism may arouse public concern, they do not however explain the often quoted complaint that "nine out of ten children end up in the sole custody of the mother" (Families Need Fathers, 1974). The statistics quoted are correct, but the reason is that well over 90% of custody cases are uncontested, and that in 80% of divorce petitions children are stated to be living with their mother (Maidment, 1976). The almost total confirmation of the status quo in uncontested, as well as in contested cases, therefore results in children remaining with their mothers.

Apart from those appeal cases, where a father who has been caring for his children loses custody to their mother, the explanation then for the still widespread court practice of granting custody to the mother derives more from concern for upholding the status quo than from any maternal preference, though it is no doubt comforting to the judges that these two considerations usually coincide anyway. Apart from in contested cases where judicial choices have to be made, the outcome of custody decisions relates less to the judicial process than to judicial recognition of the social organisation of family life and of respect for private ordering. What remains uncertain is whether the divorce process does accurately reflect family organisation, or whether fathers are obstructed by lawyers and the legal process, or other agencies, from pursuing claims for custody (Gersick, 1979). The evidence that at first instance there is no judicial bias in favour of mothers, and that fathers who have had children living with them have as good a chance of getting custody as a mother in the same position, may merely prove that those fathers are a self-selected sample, who have enough money, time, energy, will-power or commitment to pursue a custody claim, if contested to a final hearing, or have such a good case (usually based on the status quo) that their chances of winning were high.

Parent homosexuality

An issue of particular topicality, and thus its separate treatment here, concerns the "fitness" for custody of the homosexual parent. Mothers specifically have claimed that judicial prejudice against lesbians has resulted in losing custody even though under normal circumstances they as mother would have been the preferred custodian.

In S v S (1980) a mother who had a lesbian relationship lost custody of her daughter aged 7½ and her son aged 6 because of "the risk of children, at critical ages, being exposed or introduced to ways of life which, as this case illustrates, may lead to severance from normal society, to psychological stresses and unhappiness and possibly even to physical experiences which may scar them for life" (quoting Re D (1977)). The welfare report had recommended custody to the mother on the grounds that the sexual identity of both children was well established, both children expressed wishes to be with their mother, and the mother could provide better material care for the children than the father. Both sides had called expert witnesses: for the mother it was said that "there was no danger in this case of the children being led into deviant sexual ways"; for the father the consultant psychiatrist agreed as regards sexual deviation, but considered that the "social embarrassment and hurt" resulting from local knowledge of their mother's lesbianism would be very harmful to the children. In other words the fears for the children were more concerned with social stigma than with sexual deviation.

In the United States research on the effects of being reared in lesbian-mother families is more advanced because the

issue has arisen more often than here in child custody litigation. Early reports comparing children in divorced or separated lesbian-mother and heterosexual-mother families find no
significant differences in children's sex-role behaviour as
measured by toy preference tests (Hoeffer, 1981), no difference
"in the type or frequency of pathology as evaluated by blind
psychological testing and a playroom evaluation", nor any differences in gender development "by evaluation of the sex of
first-drawn figure, the history of play preferences and sexual
interest, and behaviour exhibited in the playroom" (Kirkpatrick
et al, 1981).

THE SOCIAL CONTEXT

The judicial expectation that mothers will care for their children after divorce unless there is some good reason to the contrary will be examined in the light of psychological and sociological knowledge of parenting; and also of whether judges'
perceptions of family organisations and relationships are outdated. The aim is to explore whether social science understandings can answer the question: which parent? The earlier exclusive focus of social research on mothers has now been modified
considerably by the growing literature on fathers and their
children (see for example the special issue of the Infant Mental Health Journal (1981) and the 25 pages of bibliography
cited).

Mothers and children

A dominant conception in our society is that "parenting means
mothering" (Rapoport et al, 1977:35). While anthropologically
"in all societies the care of infants is believed to be more
women's work then men's" and men display "nurturing behaviour
(by) fending for females and their children" (Mead, 1962:149,
182), this universal sexual division of labour was interpreted
in the 1940s into theories of maternal deprivation. Studies of
the effects of early institutionalisation of children on their
mental and physical development had been reported in the 1940s,
but it was John Bowlby, reviewing these studies for the World
Health Organisation in 1951, whose theory of maternal deprivation became the most influential: "What is believed to be
essential for mental health is that an infant and young child
should experience a warm, intimate, and continuous relationship
with his mother (or permanent mother-substitute - one person
who steadily mothers him) in which both find satisfaction and
enjoyment" (Bowlby, 1972:13). Bowlby thus suggested three principles: (i) that the mother-child relationship was the crucial
one for the child's emotional development; other relationships
were very subsidiary, including the father's; (ii) that continuity of care was essential; and (iii) that early experience was
critical for adult mental health. The second principle will be

considered in the next chapter; and the third principle has already been discussed in chapter 6. It is the first principle which caught the imagination. For more than the next twenty years psychologists explored the mother-child dyad to the exclusion of all other relationships (Lamb, 1976), fathers were excluded from all aspects of their children's birth, a maternal preference prevailed in custody cases, mothers were discouraged from working and thus leaving their children, and policy-makers discouraged alternative care arrangements for children such as day nurseries (Pilling and Kellmer-Pringle, 1978:151).

The central focus of Bowlby and others (for example, Winnicott, 1957) on the mother-child "attachment" i.e. emotional tie between mother and child, has in the last ten years been discredited. The recognition of fathers' influence on their child's development specifically will be discussed in the next section. The main critique of Bowlby has come from psychological research which has shown that attachment bonds can and often do develop from a very early age between the child and both parents (and others) (Rutter, 1981). Bowlby believed a child was biased to attach himself initially to one person only, his mother ("monotropy"). A 1964 study however showed that as many as 29% of children directed their first specific attachments at several individuals, and that although the mother was often the initial attachment object, "in the first month after onset 27% selected (the father) and by eighteen months 75% of infants had formed an attachment with him" (Schaffer, 1971:134). It was also shown that the infant's primary need was not for proximity to other people, but for stimulation. Nor is there any evidence that the attachment to the mother, which is often the first, is different in kind from attachments to others (Schaffer, 1971; Rutter, 1981:19). More sophisticated research, measuring attachment by indexes of separation protest (crying, disuption of play) and frequency of interactive behaviour (smiling) has shown consistently that in the absence of stress "twelve to twenty-one-month-old children show no preference for either parent, whether observed at home or in unfamiliar laboratory sessions" (Kotelchuk, 1972; Lamb, 1978:89). Other research

> sharply suggested that seven-to thirteen-month olds were attached to both their mothers and their fathers. In the stress-free and undisturbed home environment, furthermore, there was no indication that either parent could be described as a primary or preferred attachment figure ... By the end of the second year, all but one of the boys in the sample were showing consistent preferences for their fathers over their mothers on our attachment behaviour measures. The girls by contrast, were much less consistent - some preferred their mothers, some their fathers, and some neither parent (Lamb, 1978:91).

When distressed, however, and both parents were available, while 8- and 24-month old children did not show preferences for their mothers, 12- and 18-month old infants did; for a short period then in the second year, mothers do appear to be primary attachment figures (Lamb, 1978:99). Although much research still focusses on the mechanisms of attachment, in particular on mother-child interaction from the moment of birth (Shaffer and Dunn, 1979; Ainsworth et al, 1976) and on the effect of the child's personality on the mother's response (Bell and Harper, 1977), and those of a psychoanalytic persuasion still attach much significance to the mother-figure particularly in the first three years (Pilling and Kellmer-Pringle, 1978; Erikson, 1950; Bowlby, 1969; Wolff, 1981), nevertheless Bowlby's view of the exclusivity of the mother-child bond has now been discredited in psychology. Bowlby's extrapolation from severely deprived children in institutions to normal children has also been shown to be inadequate (Morgan, 1975); the harmful implications of the maternal deprivation theory for the role of women as child-carers, their status in society and for social welfare policies, have been criticised (Wilson, 1977); and shared (day) care between a parent and other adults is no longer considered necessarily damaging: "If the child is provided with stable, good-quality care and is able to develop secure attachments to one or two adults there are unlikely to be adverse effects on his development" (Pilling and Kellmer-Pringle, 1978:160). Currently then the exclusive interest in the mother-child relationship has been replaced with a recognition that (a) the biological mother need not necessarily be the child's main attachment figure, and (b) that the child has attachments to other persons, in particular its father, and its siblings and wider family. Whether the nature of the child's bond with its main caretaker, often its biological mother, is different from its relationships with others remains unknown (Bernal, 1976).

The discussion so far has been concerned with the role of the mother in the psychological mechanisms in the child's emotional development. The judicial pronouncement that "young children need their mothers" cannot stand up to current psychological understandings that young children become attached to any adult with whom they have "day-to-day interaction, companionship and shared experiences" i.e. their "psychological parent" (Goldstein et al, 1973). Posed as a custody choice between father and mother, the mother cannot claim any special psychological consideration; in normal family life, attachment bonds with both parents will exist, although they may be of differing strength or intensity (and measurable by psychological testing).

Attachment or emotional ties do not depend on the physical care given by the caretaker, but on the quality of the interaction between the child and the caretaker. Attachment to a father may exist despite the fact that in many families the

184

father spends less time with the children. This leads to a consideration of the social role of mothers, for even if they have no special psychological role, nevertheless there may be social reasons why courts should prefer mothers as custodians.

In working-class families in the nineteenth century, the bonds of affection between mother and child were particularly strong (Anderson, 1971), and the mother is still "the one person on whom the whole household depends for succour and comfort; the sure anchor to which husband and children cling" (Newson and Newson, 1965:222). Mothers are regarded as publicly responsible for the upbringing of the child, his behaviour and appearance (Newson and Newson, 1978:439) and traditionally the care of the younger children is "a predominantly female occupation, and in most normal families the mother is necessarily the central figure in the child's early life" (Newson and Newson, 1965:133).

If it is not clear whether the quality of the mother's social role is changing, it is apparent that the conventional family in which the father worked full-time while the mother stayed at home to care for the home and the children is no longer the norm. In 1951 22% of married women were economically active, rising to 48% in 1975. Though many women drop out of all employment while their children are of pre-school age, in 1977 26% of them were working. These are mainly women from very low-income families or those with high commitment and qualifications. As children enter school, many women enter part-time employment (in 1977 43% of women with youngest child aged five); and shift to full-time employment as their children get older (Gowler and Legge, 1982:139-140).

Women's employment has been one of the most important catalysts for change in the power relationships between husband and wife, in the creation of marriage as a "partnership" in which decisions are taken jointly and activities shared (Newson and Newson, 1965:133). But although the family may have become more "symmetrical" (Young and Willmott, 1973), in the sense that gender roles in work and home are less segregated, nevertheless there is still a division of labour, partly determined by the age of the child, and the hours which the father works (Newson and Newson, 1965). There is no doubt that the domestic participation of the father has increased, particularly in the area of child care (Oakley, 1982; McGlaughlin, 1981) but fathers' participation is at the level of "helping out" rather than taking complete responsibility for traditionally female tasks (Gowler and Legge, 1982; Backett, 1982). The significance of this will be explored further in the next section.

While there may have been some movement towards "joint role families", there are nevertheless social class differences: working-class and managerial middle-class families are more likely to retain "traditional" gender roles (Oakley, 1982). Even where there is some acceptance of male domestic involvement however,

men are said to be "highly participant" when they do
things which are simply taken for granted in relation to
the mothering role ... what a highly participant father
contributes tends to be seen as an added bonus for the
children, rather than as a naturally expected nurturant
function of any father. Indeed a term like mother participation ... would seem almost nonsensical, reflecting
the fact that, in our culture, a mother's duties are presumed if not mandatory (Lewis et al, 1982:185).

Whether employed or not, then, women are still, both in
ideology and in practice, the main child-carers, in the sense
of having responsibility for the task, even if fathers "help
out" on a practical level. The fact that in the Keele custody
study (Maidment, 1976) 83% of wives (and only 22% of husbands)
asked for custody and that the children were living with the
mother in 80% of the cases is part of this picture. Indeed
the irony of the feminist claim for custody of their children
on divorce is that they rely on the very ideology of gender
which they claim is used by a patriarchal society in the social
control of women (Oakley, 1982:136).
The judges may then prefer mothers in custody cases, not
because the child has any special psychological relationship
with her, but because the practice of family life prior to the
divorce gave the mother the responsibility (and perhaps the
pleasure!) of caring for the children. The danger is that the
judges may assume that the form of family life where the father
participates not at all or only at the level of "helping out"
is present in every case. Levels of father-responsibility and
participation vary, and it would be wrong to impose a particular family form or ideology in the instant case. Most importantly, it is clear that the mother has no inherent qualifica-
tion for filling the child-care role, neither in terms of any
special psychological relationship, nor in terms of any
necessary social role.

Fathers and children

It has already been seen that children can become attached to
their father from a very early age (at least from seven months
old, which may be the earliest stage of neurological development at which attachments can form (Schaffer, 1971)), and that
this depends not on the amount of care (or father-participation)
that takes place, but on the quality of interaction when it
does occur. Bowlby's belief in the child's special relationship with the mother was not supported by research which failed to display any preference by young children between their
mother and father except for a very short period between 12
and 18 months. When a preference in two year old boys for
their fathers was demonstrated, the explanation offered was
that fathers were more active in their interaction with their

186

sons, so that the boys were responding to "the sex-differenti-ating behaviour of the fathers" (Lamb, 1978:92). The converse of demonstrating that attachment bonds between child and father exist, is to ask whether the father has any particular influ-ence on a child's development. Bowlby did not dismiss the father's role in the child's development totally, but he play-ed "second fiddle" and his main "use" was "as the economic and emotional support of the mother" so that she could "devote" herself unrestrictedly to the care of the child. This indirect role of the father was popularised in child care advice books, and remains an important consideration in the understanding of the family as a complex, multi-dimensional system.

To assess the father's direct influence on his child's de-velopment, one can consider his influence in the intact home, and the effect of his absence.

Father's influence in the intact family. The psychoanalytic tradition has always emphasised the unique contribution that fathers make to the psycho-sexual development of their sons, but "current evaluation ... ranges from the view that his role is not to disturb the successful work of the mother to the view that pre-oedipal father-child relationships are of consi-derable importance" (McGreal, 1981:223).

A review of the psychological literature (Pilling and Kellmer-Pringle, 1978) also reports that father-child inter-actions affect a child's intellectual or cognitive functioning from an early age (end of the first year), both in verbal and numerical and analytical abilities. The father's child-rearing practices and the warmth of the relationship are also important influences on the child's, particularly boy's, sex-role deve-lopment, and emotional and social adjustment: "Affection from the father has been found to be associated with good peer ad-justment, leadership qualities, personal adjustment and mascu-line sex-role orientation in boys, while inadequate affection is associated with delinquent behaviour" (Pilling and Kellmer-Pringle, 1978:218). Warmth may however be insufficient unless a certain minimum level of time is spent with the boy.

Father-absence studies (infra) support the finding that sex-role orientation (feelings of masculinity) and sex-role behaviour in boys (only - not girls) are most affected by the father's behaviour in the family; masculinity in boys' sex-role behaviour is also related to good personal and social adjust-ment in pre-school and adolescent boys. What is not known is whether low masculinity in boys is associated with adjustment difficulties in adult life. Indeed there is no conclusive evi-dence associating early experiences of any kind with later personality.

The most recent British research (Lewis et al, 1982) has attempted to measure the effect of father participation on the child's development, in respect of educational achievement and criminality. The researchers, having controlled for sex, class

and family size, found a definite correlation between father
participation and the child's educational/career aspirations
at age 11, and this remained significant at 16. Low father participation at age seven and 11 was also related to the child
having a criminal conviction by the time he was in his late
teens. These findings had been reported by others previously;
and although Lewis et al do not believe that there is a "simple
causal connection between parental involvement and later outcome in child ... our data indicate that the influences upon
the child are far more complex than these correlations would
suggest", nevertheless they conclude "that involved fatherhood
is an important predictor of the child's success at 16". They
suggest as an explanation however that high father participation relates to "cohesiveness and philosophy of the family", to
"marital satisfaction", creating a certain "style of family
interactions" which tends towards high aspirations and lower
criminality.

Effects of father absence. Father absence has been linked in
the literature with a host of life problems such as delinquency, underachievement, promiscuity, and confused sexual identity" (Luepnitz, 1982). Although there has been much more research on father-absent families than on fathers in intact
families, it is now clear that the effects of father absence
are also extremely complex and cannot be simply related to the
lack or decrease of interaction between father and child. The
father's absence will affect the response of other members of
the family, particularly the mother, and the wider family and
community response, towards the child, and the reason for the
absence, which in many of the earlier studies was not considered, may be critical. The age and sex of the child, social
class, ethnic group, presence of other males (for example,
step-father), degree and quality of contact with the father
where it exists may all be modifying factors (Herzog and Sudia,
1973). Most important indications however appear to be the
family discord preceding the absence (Rutter, 1981), the economic strains suffered by the father-absent family (Herzog and
Sudia, 1973; Marsden, 1973; Wynn, 1964), and the ability of
the mother to provide good parenting in the one-parent family
(Wallerstein and Kelly, 1980).
    Father absence due to divorce or separation is

    generally found to have some adverse effects on educatio-
    nal attainments particularly on boys, and this different-
    ial effect ... does suggest that the mother and other per-
    sons may not entirely be able to compensate for the lack
    of interaction with the father ... There is some evidence
    that father absence due to divorce, separation or desert-
    ion is more likely to produce exaggerated aggressiveness
    or sex-role deviancy ... There is some evidence of a
    sharper association between delinquency and broken homes

among the middle rather than the working class ... (which)
appears to be partly at least accounted for by the greater
economic disadvantage of the former situation. Tension
and discord in the family before its break-up and greater
difficulty for the mother in maintaining a harmonious
family atmosphere after the divorce may also be partly
responsible for the relationship ... On the whole the
studies of father absence suggest that lack of the father-
child relationship has relatively little effect on the
child's cognitive, emotional and social development, when
the material deprivations of father absence have been
taken into account. Where adverse effects do appear to be
the result of the family situation rather than of economic
circumstances, these are usually although not always,
found to be greater when father absence is due to divorce,
separation or desertion than when it is due to death ...
However there remain some adverse effects of father absence for which the most plausible explanation does appear
to be the lack of father-child relationship itself. The
greater effect of father absence on the educational attainment of boys than of girls, and the difficulties experienced in opposite sex relationships by girls whose fathers
have died, as well as those whose fathers have left the
family, are examples (Pilling and Kellmer-Pringle, 1978:
218-9).

The evidence that the known adverse effects of father
absence are slight, especially when other circumstances surrounding the family breakup are accounted for, does not necessarily indicate conversely that the father's influence on the
family is not significant. One explanation for the discrepancy is that the father's absence results in a "complex change
in relationships" whereby the mother, relatives, neighbours
and friends and the children themselves, take over some aspects
of the father's role (Pilling and Kellmer-Pringle, 1978:219).
Thus for example children in one-parent families "grow up a
little faster", having to share managerial responsibility for
the household (Weiss, 1979).
The weight of opinion now is that "fathers are important
contributors to child development ... in sex roles, cognitive
abilities and achievement motivation" (Weinraub, 1978). While
it is often argued that this is because fathers can provide a
different role model for the child (Andry, 1968:506-7), it is
now claimed that the contribution is not so much because
fathers participate and interact with children differently from
mothers, but rather because of the similarities (Lewis, 1982):

The warmer, more accepting and more involved the father is
toward his child, the more positive his contribution may
be ... Fathers ... are ... important ... because they act
as second (or one of two) co-equal parents in children's

social network ... Though second parents do not appear necessary for adequate child development, when they are present they exert significant effects ... Because parenting is a difficult and demanding profession, two caregivers may be better able than one to meet the economic, social and intellectual needs of children (Weinraub, 1978).

Apart from psychological aspects of the father's contribution, which emphasises the quality of his participation rather than its quantity, there is certainly a belief that fathers participate more now in their children's upbringing (as evidenced, for example, by the inclusion of the father's role in popular advice books). There is nevertheless some scepticism as to whether in practice this is so. Some discrepancy between attitude and behaviour has been noted: working-class fathers are more involved than they think proper, while middle-class fathers who believe in egalitarian attitudes concerning family responsibilities may not in practice demonstrate them (Richards, 1982:123). One serious criticism is the lack of historical evidence against which modern practices may be measured (McKee, 1982); another is of the indices of participation which are used by researchers: fathers may play with their infants rather than feed them, and they may be more involved in activities with older children. Nevertheless some researchers do claim clear evidence of increased father participation. Firstly it is undisputed that fathers are now more involved in their partner's pregnancy and delivery (Richards, 1982). Secondly, the Newsons' study of child-care in families in Nottingham has been updated (Lewis et al, 1982), and reports that "real change has taken place" over twenty years. More fathers now feed, put to sleep, take out, bath, change nappies, get up at night for one year olds; at age seven maternally-reported "father participation is higher in middle-class than in working-class families, is greater for boys than for girls and is higher in the case of small /working-class/ families". (Gavron (1966) did not agree that middle-class fathers participate more than working-class fathers). Nevertheless "many mothers ... claim that their husbands do not involve themselves extensively in their children's lives"; and "fathers' perception of their status as subsidiary caregivers persists throughout childhood." The conclusion has been suggested that "fathers are doing more with their children ... (but) while most men do some caretaking for their children, compared with their partners, their rates are low" (Richards, 1982:123). Others have commented that in the new acceptance of male domestic involvement, "playing with children seems to be the most popular" (Oakley, 1982:131).

Applying these findings to the issue of child custody raises some interesting questions. It is said that more fathers want custody of their children (though concrete evidence of this is lacking). These fathers may be the ones,

particularly middle-class men, who do participate more in
their children's upbringing. They may also be men who believe
that they are more involved, although in practice they are
still subsidiary caretakers (Backett, 1982). The belief itself is important since it suggests an emotional commitment to
children, which according to the psychologists is more significant for the quality of the relationship or attachment than
the actual quantity of care given. If the quality or quantity
of the parent-child relationship were to be determinants of a
particular custody decision, guidelines exist by which judges
could measure the degree of participation and attachment existing between each parent and child. There is however no evidence that in general one parent or the other is better qualified because of his or her sex to have primary caretaking.
Nevertheless socially mothers are still regarded both by
mothers and fathers as and in practice are the main caretakers.
The implications for custody decisions are that (i) measure-
ments of parent-child relationships might identify to which
parent the child is more attached; and this may be either
parent regardless of sex; but (ii) in a family which was intact
prior to its breakdown a child may have been attached to both
parents, despite differential participation. Unless custody
decisions are to be based solely on quality of participation
therefore, the legal construction of the question as a choice
between parents presents an unrealistic determination. Psychologically, while two parents are not necessary for successful
development, they are an advantage. How the divorce process
can recognise this fact, and a consideration of alternative
approaches, such as joint custody, will be addressed in chapter 11.

Mother-custody v father-custody

The material presented so far has sought to assess the competing mother-child and father-child relationships retroactively
in the intact family. It may be however that custody determinations based on prognostications of post-divorce relationships may be more appropriate in predicting the future welfare
of the child. One of the most interesting findings of Wallerstein and Kelly's study of children of divorce is "the significance of the relationships within the present in determining
outcome at the time. The parent-child relationships of previous years appeared not to be sufficient to maintain good
functioning within the present" (1980:208). The implications
for access and joint custody are obvious and will be dealt with
later. In the context of this chapter however the finding
suggests that while pre-divorce relationships between parent
and child are significant (indeed the stronger the relationship, the greater will be the child's difficulty in adjusting
to the divorce (Wallerstein and Kelly, 1980:208), the post-
divorce relationship may be a more important consideration.

While recognising the law's incapacity to predict how post-divorce arrangements will unfold (Goldstein et al, 1973) nevertheless there may be new understandings which indicate chances of success in post-divorce custody arrangements.

Mother-custody. Until recently there were few studies of children in homes broken specifically by divorce, rather than in one-parent families generally, and the studies which did exist were mainly of children in their mother's custody (Hetherington et al, 1982; Wallerstein and Kelly, 1980). Only now are studies of father-custody appearing, so for the first time it may be possible to make some assessment of alternative placements of children after divorce.

The American mother-custody studies have sought to provide wider understandings of the effects of the divorce process on children, since in the United States as here most children on divorce live with their mothers. Father-custody studies to the contrary have sought to identify the particular problems involved in motherless families as compared with fatherless families. Nevertheless the mother-custody studies have exposed certain features specific to mother-headed one-parent families created by divorce. Hetherington et al particularly noted the negative behaviour, harassment of and aggression to divorced mothers by their (pre-school) sons which persisted at two years after divorce (1978:170). A differential response to divorce according to sex has been often found (Hetherington, 1981), with higher rates for boys of behaviour disorders and problems in interpersonal relations at home and in school. Hetherington suggests that both mothers of sons and sons themselves find divorce more stressful compared with daughters:

> After divorce mothers of boys report feeling more stress
> and depression than do mothers of girls ... After div-
> orce, boys confront more inconsistency, negative sanc-
> tions, and opposition from parents, particularly from
> mothers. Divorced mothers are less sensitive to the
> needs of their sons, and are more likely to identify sons
> in a negative way as being similar to their fathers. In
> addition boys receive less positive support, solicitude,
> and nurturance and are viewed more negatively by mothers,
> teachers and peers in the period immediately following
> divorce than are girls (1981:42-3).

Mothers with custody may also confront particular changes in life experiences which create stress in the one-parent family. Divorce causes a drop in income for women but not for men (Finer Report, 1974), so that "children in homes in which the father has gained custody are exposed to less actual financial duress" (Hetherington, 1981:45). The employment of mothers is also problematic:

The economic problems of divorced mothers and their children are compounded by the fact that many divorced women do not have the education, job skills, or experience to permit them to obtain a well-paying position or to pay for high-quality child care. Divorced mothers are more likely to have low-paying, part-time jobs or positions of short duration. For the child this results in temporary, erratic, sometimes inadequate provisions for child-care, and if the mother feels forced to work in a dissatisfied, resentful mother ... If the divorced mother wishes to work and if adequate provisions are made for child-care and maintenance of childhood routines, maternal employment may have no adverse effects on children and positive effects of the mother such as increased self-esteem, less social isolation, and greater financial resources. However ... if the mother begins to work at the time of divorce or shortly thereafter, the pre-school child seems to experience the double loss of both parents, which is reflected in a higher rate of behaviour disorders ... Great task overload is experienced by working divorced mothers with young children (Hetherington, 1981:45).

In addition to "downward economic mobility", "increased task overload" and maternal employment, the mother-custody family may also move home, bringing further personal losses, disruption, and social isolation, at a time when "continuity of support systems and the environment can play an ameliorative role" (Hetherington, 1981:46). Indeed the British judicial practice of allowing the custodial parent to remain in the matrimonial home with the children appears to be supported by observations of the effect of relocation of the child's home. Finally, there is evidence that fathers are more important than mothers for children's sex-role modelling. "When the mother is hostile and critical of the father, the child begins to view the father in a more ambivalent or negative manner and as a less acceptable role model. For young boys /under five/ this is associated with disruption in sex typing. For girls it may be associated with disruptions in heterosexual relations at adolescence" (Hetherington, 1981:47). The explanation offered is that

> fathers usually are much more concerned than mothers about the maintenance of stereotype sex-role behaviour in their children and more likely to vary their role as they relate to male and female offspring ... By 2 years following divorce the only paternal variable related to sex typing in sons and daughters was paternal availability. If fathers maintained frequent contact with their children the children were more stereotypically sex-typed (Hetherington et al, 1982:276-7).

193

Apart from these particular effects of mother-custody, the much wider noted effects of divorce on children and parents in the mother-custody studies cannot be shown to be gender-specific to the custodian. Hetherington et al (1982) studied 96 white middle-class families with pre-school children in Virginia, USA, half of whom were divorced, half not divorced. In all the divorces, mothers had custody, fathers had access rights; and the families were studied for two years following divorce. [In the first year after divorce mothers displayed poor parenting particularly with sons, including lack of control; and children (especially sons) exhibited more negative behaviour in the presence of their mothers than their (visiting) fathers. The second year after divorce showed great improvement, however, although less so for boys than for girls (1982:252-8). As regards social development, in the first year, children from divorced families "were more oppositional, aggressive, lacking in self-control, distractible, and demanding of help and attention in both the home and school than were children of non-divorced families with high rates of marital discord" (1982:261). But at two years, both for boys' and girls' social and emotional development, the adverse factor was not whether the family was divorced, but whether there was still a high degree of conflict in the family whether divorced or not.] Nevertheless boys from high-conflict divorced families showed more problems than any other group (1982:261). This finding is therefore in line with Wallerstein and Kelly (1980) and Rutter (1981) [that children are affected more by the marital discord accompanying divorce.]

Hetherington et al also observed children at school. By two years after divorce differences in free-play behaviour between girls from divorced and intact families had disappeared, but boys still differed (1982:265). Similarly as regards social interactions in school with adults and peers; boys in particular seemed to be less helpful, played less with others and were becoming more socially isolated (1982:268). At two years, children in non-divorced families scored higher on some IQ tests, but not on verbal IQ (1982:273).

"Children of many divorced parents receive less adult attention and are more likely to have erratic mealtimes and bedtimes and to be late for school" (Hetherington et al, 1978), but the parent's "chaotic lifestyle" and "task overload" (child care, work and household responsibilities) makes coping difficult for custodians, whether mother or father (Hetherington, 1981:46). Certain changes in the parent-child relationships also affect the child (Hetherington, 1981): [family conflict may lead to hostile alliances with one parent against the other] to "dissonance, questioning and revision and de-idealisation of children's perceptions of their parents"; to an increased awareness in adolescents of their parents' sexuality, when parents begin new relationships or remarry. The contribution of a second parent to the family and the child's development is

194

lost, both as indirect support and as an agent of socialisation, and as a protective buffer between the child and one of the parents.

The custodian becomes an increasingly salient figure in the child's life, thus influencing the child's personality and social and cognitive development. Poor parenting in the first year dramatically improves in the second year, but "problems in parent-child relationships continue to be found more often with divorced mothers and children than with mothers and children in (intact) families" (Hetherington, 1981:51).

There are many other noted effects of divorce on children. Some emerge rapidly, some increase and then abate, some emerge subsequently. The child's response to divorce will also vary widely in quality and intensity according to his temperament, developmental age, sex, and cumulative stress already experienced. To summarise there are effects of short-term emotional distress, commonly anger, fear, depression and guilt; there may also be longer-term delays or deviations in "cognitive, personality, or social development such as disruptions in learning, peer relations, sex-typing, self-control, or affectionate relations" (Hetherington, 1981:36). The wider impact of divorce on children has already been considered (chapter 6) and will be returned to in the conclusion. The purpose of this section is to explore whether the finding that "the longer-term adjustment of the child is related to more sustained or concurrent conditions associated with growing up in a one-parent household" (Hetherington, 1981:36) has any particular implications for which parent should be sole custodian of the child.

It has been noted that there are certain gender-specific effects of mother-custody associated particularly with the lowered economic circumstances of divorced mothers, with difficulties in mother-son relationships, and with sex-role stereotyping in boys. Other effects do not appear to be gender-specific but are problems of marital discord or of mother-headed one-parent families: fathers report the same problems of being overburdened with tasks and of coping with emergencies as sole mothers (Ferri, 1973), of problems of "time, money and feelings" (Hipgrave, 1982; George and Wilding, 1972). Other problems may be associated with the custodian having to fill the practical and emotional roles of two parents: mothers have reported finding house maintenance and repair jobs difficult (Luepnitz, 1982), while fathers, although aided on a practical level by the mass technology of the household (Luepnitz, 1982) have difficulties associated with feelings of parental competence and community attitudes (Hipgrave, 1982).

Father-custody. The father-custody studies now emerging recognise that the families they are studying are a more unusual product of divorce, although they may have increased and may be predicted to increase even more. In 1978 12% of one-parent families were headed by men, and this was increasing at a rate of 6% a year (Leete, 1978). Just over half of the 100,000 one-parent families headed by men were the result of marital breakdown (OPCS, 1978). Three major areas of findings appear to have emerged from these studies to date. The first suggests that the reasons why the father has custody may be an important indicator of the success of the arrangement: Gersick (1979), comparing 20 custodial fathers with 20 non-custodial fathers, found that 18 of the 20 father custody cases (90%) were with the mother's pre-trial consent, either because the mother did not want custody, or it was agreed that the husband could offer the children a more secure home, or the husband's determination to fight for custody scared the wife out of a contest, or in seven of the cases (35%) the child was allowed to choose. Santrock et al (1982) also found "no differences between the father- and mother-custody groups in the number of custody decisions that had been reached by a court in a contested case" (1982:291). Luepnitz's study (1982) of 16 mother-custody, 16 father-custody, and 18 joint custody parents, however, found

> twice as many legal contests over custody among paternal as among maternal families (25% v 12%). In an additional 19% of paternal cases, there was a bitter struggle over custody, which was settled out of court. In nearly half of the paternal families, the children had been initially in the custody of the mother. Most of these children were turned over to their fathers explicitly because their mothers felt incompetent to care for them (1982:24).

Santrock et al suggest that ex-spouses relinquish custody either because they actively do not want it, or they do not care, or believe that the child is better off with the other parent (1982:292). They also indicate reasons why men seek custody: some genuinely want it, some feel wronged or sufficiently vindictive to use custody to intimidate or harass ex-wives; some believe they are the better parent, in some cases the mother does not want custody, and some "may seek custody as a means of economic gain if they believe their ex-wives would be willing to take less property or support in the divorce settlement" (Santrock and Warshak, 1979:113). Gersick (1979) also noted that nearly all the fathers with custody remained in the marital residence; he also found no greater interest in custody of sons (1979:313).

Mendes (1976) emphasises the process of becoming a custodial father as the predictor of the one-parent family's functioning. She identified four categories of men: aggressive seekers, conciliatory seekers, aggressive initiation by other spouse, conciliatory initiation by other spouse. O'Brien's study of 59 fathers with custody suggests that the success of the father's transition from joint to lone parenthood depends not only on choice (Mendes, 1976), but also other dimensions, such as "whether there was any discussion; the extent of hostility involved; the degree of abruptness in the transition; and whether the needs of the child were put before or after the needs of self" (O'Brien, 1982:186-8). Fathers who were conciliatory negotiators (one-third of the group) more often made joint decisions, were more concerned with what was the most suitable solution for the children, had more egalitarian marriages and participated extensively in child care, had mutually agreed separation, and were committed to and involved in parenthood. The "hostile seekers" (one-third of the group) made, intentionally or by default, the children "pawns" in the marital conflict, were "morally outraged" by their wife's conduct, and seeking custody was a symbolic way of punishing her. This group fought for custody, despite relatively lower levels of pre-separation child involvement. The third group (one-third) were "passive acceptors" who involuntarily became lone fathers after their wives' desertion; the absence of choice resulted in feelings of conflict about their new role and negative feelings about their own parenting abilities despite substantial child-care responsibility prior to the wife's desertion (O'Brien, 1982). Gersick (1979) found four variables affecting fathers with custody: relationships in their family of origin ("men with custody showed more closeness towards their mothers and less toward their fathers; they were more likely to be later-born children with both male and female siblings ... men from traditional families are more likely to make the extremely non-traditional decision to seek custody"); feelings about the departing wife ("The more wronged, betrayed or victimised that a man felt, the more likely he was to have sought custody ... Anger and revenge seemed to be components of many decisions to seek custody"); the wife's intentions about custody; and the attitudes of lawyers. There were however no differences between the custody or non-custody fathers on measures of participation in child-care prior to the divorce; all of the fathers were described as "active".

Each of these variables discussed may produce different outcomes for both custodial parent and children, in particular concerning male satisfaction with the new life-style and status, and motivation to succeed in parenting. "The child's adjustment is intimately connected with that of the father and the nature of the father's feelings towards his wife, his present role, and how the community views him" (Hipgrave, 1981:163). Hipgrave has identified a number of "risk factors" both institutional (such as material disadvantage, downward mobility associated with single parenthood, community responses) and interpersonal ("time, money and feelings" difficulties) which research suggests will affect father-custody families: that the father was rarely involved in care-taking activities prior to becoming a single parent (but see Wallerstein and Kelly); the family is isolated from the father's extended family; the father has to give up work; the family suffers a sudden drop in its standard of living; the father is generally unwilling to re-allocate his time commitments in favour of his children; the father or child has no psychosocial outlet, or the father has no relief from full-time work and care-taking activities; the child has no regular, enduring and close contact with a female adult; the father is still in aggressive dispute with the mother, or is in a state of prolonged grief; the child is customarily used as the focus or outlet of parental feelings; contact with the absent mother is irregular, or the issue of access remains unresolved or a source of conflict; and intra-familial roles become distorted to the extent that the parent-child distinction is lost.

The second major aspect of father-custody studies concerns the effects on the children. Santrock et al (1982) studied 60 white, middle-class families with children aged 6-11; in one-third the father had custody, one-third the mother, and one-third were intact families. Parents had been separated for 2¾ years on average. Two separate comparisons were made between divorced and intact families and between father-custody and mother-custody (Santrock and Warshak, 1979). Father-custody boys were <u>more</u> socially competent with their fathers (measured by warmth, self-esteem, demanding behaviour, maturity, socia-bility, independent behaviour) than intact family boys; father-custody girls were <u>less</u> socially competent than intact family girls; mother-custody boys showed higher self-esteem than in-tact family boys, but were "not fairing poorly" (contrast Hetherington et al, 1982); mother-custody girls showed lower self-esteem; mother-custody children generally were more deman-ding of their mothers than in intact families. Boys in father-custody homes were therefore more competent than boys in intact homes; father-custody girls were less competent.

Comparing father-custody with mother-custody, the findings were that father-custody boys were more socially competent than father-custody girls, but mother-custody girls were more compe-tent than mother-custody boys. Particularly significant diffe-rences in measures of social competence were found for demand-ing behaviour, maturity, sociability and independence. Mother-custody boys were also more demanding and less mature with their mothers than father-custody boys were with their fathers. Hetherington et al (1982) made a similar finding. Santrock et al (1982) conclude that "competent social behaviour is more characteristic of children whose custodial parent is the same sex as they are ... on the whole children living with the same-sex parent seem to cope better with divorce".

The findings of Hetherington et al (1982) concerning mother-custody boys, and of Santrock et al (1982) favouring a "same-sex child-custodial-parent family structure" could have important implications for same-sex custody dispositions. But Santrock et al are concerned to point out that the effects of father- or mother-custody are mediated by factors other than the child's sex. In particular they claim that quality of parenting and child-rearing practices are linked to social competence in children; authoritative parenting (Baumrind, 1971) (warmth, clear setting of rules and regulations, extensive verbal give-and-take) is significantly correlated to higher levels of competence, regardless of custodial arrangement. Mother-custody boys may not display disruption in sex-typing (Hetherington et al, 1982) when mothers "encourage masculine and exploratory behaviour and do not have a negative attitude toward the absent father" (Santrock et al, 1982:301).

Availability of support systems and additional caretakers were also positively related to the child's social competence, regardless of custodial arrangement. Fathers however made more use of these than mothers, and of particular significance, fathers enlisted the aid of non-custodial parent. Father-custody children therefore had more frequent contact with the non-custodial parent than mother-custody children; and fathers with custody reported an improvement after the divorce in the mother-child relationship, whereas mothers reported a deterioration in the father-child relationship (Santrock et al, 1982: 294-5).

The third major finding from the father-custody studies considers the custody arrangement from the parents' point of view. Fathers have reported problems of too little free social time if continuing employment with homemaking and parenting; financial problems, often due to decreased family income, or difficulties in managing a household budget; and emotional difficulties related to the expression of community attitudes, feelings of isolation or loneliness, feelings connected with sexual identity, parental competence and household tasks. Many of these concerns reported by fathers are also reported by mothers in one-parent families (Hetherington, 1981:50; Gersick, 1979). Some men report few problems running their households or in raising children (Gasser and Taylor, 1976; O'Brien, 1980). Luepnitz (1982) found that the major problem for fathers with custody was loneliness; for mothers with custody it was low income, overwork, exhaustion, anxiety, limit-testing in children. The advantages of fathers with custody were less discrimination in housing and credit; the advantages for mothers with custody were fewer custody fights than with father- or joint-custody; both father- and mother-sole custodians had the advantage of being free to take the children and leave town. The disadvantages for fathers with custody were the need for more substitute care (than joint custody parents); for mothers the disadvantages were being overwhelmed by total responsibility for the children, no break from parenting, being less likely to receive maintenance from her ex-husband (than joint custody mothers), needing more substitute care (than joint custody parents) but barely affording it. Both sole mothers and fathers missed the perspective of a second adult in disciplining.

199

Conclusion. The father-custody studies all share a measure of agreement that "there is nothing inherently pathological in the motherless family unit" (Orthner and Lewis, 1979); "on all measures of children's psychological adjustment, there were no differences by custody type. The emotional climate was as positive in families headed by a father as in those headed by a mother" (Luepnitz, 1982:149); "regardless of the custodial arrangement, we believe the quality of the ongoing relation-ship with the custodial parent is a critical factor in both the boy's and girl's social development" (Santrock and Warshak, 1979:115); "type of custody was not linked in any way with any of the children's acute reactions to the divorce" (Santrock et al, 1982:295).

Not only are the differential effects on children of the custodial arrangements apparently marginal, but both parents also may display some deterioration in parenting (Wallerstein and Kelly, 1980:36-41):

> Parents in the first year following divorce often are pre-occupied with their own depression, anger, or emotional neediness and are unable to respond sensitively to the wants of the child. The parenting practices of both mothers and fathers tend to deteriorate in the first year following divorce and recover markedly in the second year after divorce. In the immediate aftermath of divorce both parents tend to be inconsistent, less affectionate, and lacking in control over their children (Hetherington, 1981:49).

There is also unanimous agreement that while certain unsatisfactory outcomes of mother-custody and of father-custody have been noted, these effects are not necessary, and, like all consequences of divorce for children, are moderated or mediated by other factors. The particular factors considered significant are the quality of the child's relationships with both parents, custodial and non-custodial (Wallerstein and Kelly, 1980), the child-rearing practices of the custodian parent (Santrock et al, 1982), and the availability of support systems to the custodial parent (Hetherington et al, 1982; Santrock et al, 1982).

The quality of pre- and post-divorce parent-child relationships

Custody dispositions involve both material and practical con-siderations as well as the emotional interests of the child. Typically practical considerations predominate in court reports (McDermott et al, 1978) and in judgments. This may be because of practical difficulties in making assessments of parent-child relationships: obtaining adequate evidence, and assessing the data available are both time-consuming and demanding of complex judgments, obstacles not always recognised by court reports or judges.

It has been proposed however that courts ought to address the child's emotional needs in alternative custody arrangements, by evaluating the child's "longitudinal development" through "interactional analysis of the alternative family subsystems" measured by a "Parent-child interaction test" (McDermott et al, 1978). This test would measure the child's attachment behaviour towards each parent, and each parent's attachment behaviour towards the child. It has been claimed that such testing has effectively produced clearer criteria for decision-making based on the emotional interests of the child.

Clearly psychologists are able to measure attachment behaviour (Stevens and Matthews, 1978), and developmental psychology has illuminated the social and personality development and growth of children, and the impact of the parent-child relationship on behaviour such as aggression, impulsiveness, sex-typing, self-concepts and moral development (Maccoby, 1980). These understandings constitute an essential and invaluable context for family law decision-makers.

Nevertheless, apart from practical difficulties, there are theoretical problems in the proposal that a retrospective assessment of parent-child relationships should determine the custody outcome. Firstly, the more common divorce becomes, the less likely it is that custody choices will involve pathological considerations. In most pre-divorce families children will have been attached in varying degrees to both parents, so that measures such as a "parent-child interaction test" may produce no definitive answer. If tests attempt to measure parent-child interaction at the time of the divorce, how are allowances to be made for the short-term and temporary disruptions in both the parents' and the child's functioning (Hetherington, 1981). Secondly, there is the problem of predicting future outcomes for the child from past relationships. The custody decision is made at a time of crisis in the family: yet by about two years after the divorce "most children /and parents/ can cope and adapt" (Hetherington, 1981:36) to the divorce, and "the eventual outcome depends in large measure, not only on what has been lost, but on what has been created to take the place of the failed marriage" (Wallerstein and Kelly, 1980:305). The difficulty is that the custody decision takes place at a fixed point in time (ignoring variations of custody since they are rare in practice), whereas divorce is "a sequence of events involving a transition in the lives of children", a "process" of "reorganisation to an eventual attainment of a new equilibrium" (Hetherington, 1981:34-5). Furthermore, the evidence is that relationships change and that pre-divorce relationships are unreliable predictors of post-divorce relationships (see chapter 6). The appropriateness of taking a particular point in time for choosing a custodian even on psychologically suitable criteria is therefore questionable.

Chapter 8

CUSTODY CONSIDERATIONS: THE STATUS QUO

THE LAW

Judicial statements concerning the importance of the status
quo are not as frequent nor as firm as those concerning a maternal preference. But in practice the status quo has an overwhelming significance in determining the outcome of custody
dispositions (chapter 3). The most likely outcome of a custody contest is that the child will remain with the parent who
prior to the legal proceedings was caring for him. This is
true also in uncontested cases, where the private ordering of
the parents most often results in the child remaining with its
mother.
     The importance of continuity of care and the dangers of a
change of parentage were judicially recognised at the end of
the nineteenth century (Re McGrath (1893): "the duty of the
court is to leave the child alone ... nor can the ties of
affection be disregarded"; Re Gyngall (1893): to return the
child to her mother would be "a very serious dislocation of an
existing tie"; Re O'Hara (1900): "If a boy has been brought up
from infancy by a person who has won his love and confidence ...
and separation from whom would break up all the association
of his life, no court ought to sanction in his case a change
of custody"). But these opinions were always voiced in connection with children who had been fostered for a period of time,
and whose parents, even though blameless, were now claiming
them.
     The traditional judicial preference for parental rights
however has always been the underpinning for an alternative
view which emphasised the child's "transient" unhappiness at
the change of custody. In Re O'Hara (1900) a girl of 11 was
returned to her mother after two years with foster-parents:
"It is one of the advantages of youth that it can adapt itself
to altered circumstances with a facility which disappears with
advancing years. A young boy sent to boarding school often
goes with reluctance, and finds for the first few days his new
experiences unpleasant; but he soon grows accustomed to the

change and the parent continues to feel the sorrow of separation long after it is forgotten by the son". The strongest statement of the transient effects of separation appears in Re Thain (1926): "It was said that the little girl would be greatly distressed at parting from /her aunt and uncle/. I can quite understand it may be so, but, at her age, one knows from experience how mercifully transient are the effects of partings and other sorrows, and how soon the novelty of fresh surroundings and new associations effaces the recollections of former days and kind friends, and I cannot attach too much weight to this aspect of the case" (Eve J).

The introduction of psychological evidence into fostering cases in the 1960s began a movement which treated Eve J's views "much as Thomas Huxley would have regarded the suggestion that the world came into being in the manner set out in the first chapter of Genesis" (Re W (1965)). In Re C (MA) (1966) Dr Soddy, a child psychiatrist, gave a written statement that

> As a general proposition a change of mother after the age of six months is attended by a risk of lasting adverse effects, even if the substituted or second mother's care is adequate; this risk progressively increases when the change happens after six months, with a high level between 12 and 30 months, when the risk level begins to decline. ... Change between nine and 18 months is attended with a particularly serious risk of long or even permanent impairment of the child's capacity to form relationships ... A change would be to take an unjustifiable risk with the child's future.

The highpoint of the 'status quo approach' was reached, and remains until today, in J v C (1970). At first instance Ungoed-Thomas J refused to return a boy of 11 to his Spanish parents from English foster-parents with whom he had lived for 8½ years of his life: "the parents would be quite unable to cope with the problems of adjustment or with consequential maladjustment and suffering ... His return to Spain would ... be disastrous for him ... The prospect is altogether too dangerous ... It is the prospect of ruining the infant's life". The House of Lords upheld the decision:

> Some of the authorities convey the impression that the upset caused to a child by a change of custody is transient and a matter of small importance ... But I think a growing experience has shown that it is not always so and that serious harm even to young children may, on occasion, be caused by such a change. I do not suggest that the difficulties of this subject can be resolved by purely theoretical considerations, or that they need to be left entirely to expert opinion. But a child's future happiness and sense of security are always important

factors, and the effects of a change of custody will often be worthy of close and anxious attention (Lord McDermott).

The recognition of "psychological" parenthood (Goldstein et al, 1973) implicit in these cases now permeates all legal decisions between parents and third parties. The development of the 1970s was to translate the idea of the status quo into the context of parental conflict.

The current judicial attitude is exemplified by Ormrod L J in D v M (1983):

> it is generally accepted by those who are professionally concerned with children that, particularly in the early years, continuity of care is a most important part of a child's sense of security and that disruption of established bonds is to be avoided whenever it is possible to do so. Where, as in this case, a child of two years of age has been brought up without interruption by the mother (or a mother substitute) it should not be removed from her care unless there are strong countervailing reasons for doing so. This is not only the professional view, it is commonly accepted in all walks of life, and was the recommendation of the experienced welfare officer.

In this case the status quo reasoning had merit, since the child, whose parents were unmarried and had never cohabited, had lived from birth with her mother. The same reasoning is however applied to children who subsequent to the marriage breakdown have lived with one parent. Thus mothers most often get custody, because most commonly they have the care of the children on the breakup of the marriage. It also explains why statistically (see chapter 3) a father's chance of getting custody depends on his having kept the children with him after the breakup. In H v H and C (1969) custody of a boy of 3¾ was awarded to his father: the boy had lived happily with his father for 20 months, and "it would be very upsetting to remove him suddenly from the home he was used to". In S v S (1971)(a) a father was awarded custody of four children aged between 6 and 12: "During the three and a half years that they had been living with their father they had had a stable home ... Other things being equal, a whole-time mother was preferable to a part-time father ... /but/ to disturb the existing arrangements might involve more danger to them".

There are however difficulties in applying the status quo principle in divorce cases. This is partly because of its ambiguity. In some cases the issue is the continuity of the residential status quo, of not disturbing the child's home, neighbourhood and social environment. In this sense the status quo principle underlies not only custody decisions, but also the judicial preference in the financial arrangements after divorce for preserving the matrimonial home until the children

have "grown up", and for resolving any custody issue before a
decision on the disposition of the matrimonial home can pre-
empt the decision on the custodian.

In other cases the concern is for "psychological parenthood", of assessing the quality of the "ties of affection"
which the child has with alternative caretakers; the issue is
continuity of caretaker, of leaving the child alone unless
there is some good reason for disturbing him. In these cases
the application of the status quo principle to divorce is
clearly more problematic than to fostering cases. In the intact family a child will normally have lived with and developed attachment bonds with both parents. The period of separation from one parent following the breakdown of the marriage
will vary, as will the significance and degree of the separation. The choice of a "psychological parent" in respect of a
child who had and still has attachment bonds with both parents,
despite perhaps a total physical separation from one or even a
partial separation interspersed with visits, does not provide
a meaningful decision. Furthermore the issue of continuity of
caretaker introduces arbitrariness and chance, in the way that
circumstances surrounding the marriage breakdown and separation
result in immediate decisions about child-care, and the vaga-
ries of the legal process in determining the amount of time
the child will have lived with one parent pending the custody
decision. At present the status quo principle tends to uphold
current arrangements; advice to parents suggests that the
early decisions on care of the children are crucial since they
are usually confirmed subsequently in court orders. This is
why fathers who are actually caring for children will usually
get custody of them. The status quo principle therefore operates both arbitrarily but also in effect as a rubber-stamp to
the private arrangements made by parents, possibly as short-
term decisions in emotionally difficult circumstances. It may
also encourage "kidnapping", or tactics to delay a case coming
to hearing, in an attempt to consolidate the status quo.

Despite general judicial support for the status quo principle, there are nevertheless some circumstances in which
judges may be reluctant to give effect "to the old fallacy
that possession was nine points of the law" (Stamp L J in
G v G (1976)); for example where a parent has unilaterally and
suddenly removed the child from the other parent, even though
strictly this is not unlawful. In these "kidnapping" cases
judges do not feel bound by the status quo, but tend to follow
their instincts in deciding what is in the child's welfare.
The child's own wishes and views may also be important: in
cases where despite a custody order in favour of one parent a
child has chosen to live with the other parent, judges will
not lightly interfere with the child's clearly expressed
preference.

The status quo principle as developed in fostering cases
does not transfer easily to the divorce context. Continuity

and stability in the child's life, environment and care may be
protected by continuing the current caretaking arrangements,
but the child's psychological relationships cannot thereby be
protected in divorce as they can be in fostering cases where
the child has lost contact with his natural parent(s). The
difficulties of the status quo principle in divorce therefore
relate to how physical and legal caretaking arrangements can
protect the child's attachment with both parents. The issues
of the nature of custody orders, access and joint custody to
which this discussion gives rise will be addressed subsequently.

THE SOCIAL CONTEXT

The status quo principle seeks to maintain continuity and stability in the child's upbringing. This section will address
the evidence for the legal policies upholding the status quo
in its two dimensions: the psychological and the physical.

Continuity of relationships

The development of attachment bonds between a child and its
caretaker has already been discussed (chapter 7). It has been
seen that this development is determined by the quality rather
than the quantity of care, and that (apart perhaps from a very
short period) there is no evidence that bonds with the mother
are necessarily stronger or of a different quality from bonds
with the father, although the nature of the parent-child interactions differ as between father and mother (Rutter, 1981).
The formation of attachments within the first years of life
(the first three years is often noted) is thought to be essential for healthy development (Rutter, 1981; Wolff, 1981;
Kellmer-Pringle, 1976); but this must be distinguished from the
disruption of already existing bonds or discontinuity in attachments consequent upon family breakdown.
    The legal status quo principle is predicated on the view
that discontinuity will be damaging to the child. The most
famous statement of this is John Bowlby's claim that it was
essential for mental health that the child should experience a
warm, intimate and continuous relationship with his mother.
In particular early disruption and separation were claimed to
affect the child's emotional security so as to leave a permanent scar (Bowlby, 1951). Continuity of an attachment relationship thus came to be considered the most important consideration in decision-making about children (Maccoby, 1980). Goldstein, Freud and Solnit, following Bowlby, thus recommended
that the variation of custody orders, joint or split custody,
and access orders were all undesirable because of "the need of
every child for unbroken continuity of affectionate and stimulating relationships with an adult (1973:6) ... Continuity of
relationships, surroundings, and environmental influence are

essential for a child's normal development" (1973:31).
While there is no disagreement that separation from an
attachment figure causes acute short-term distress to a child
(Rutter, 1981:32), more recent research has shown the complicated mechanisms involved in the longer-term deleterious
effects of separation. Firstly, Rutter rejects the view that
separation as such causes damage:

> Antisocial disorders were linked with broken homes not
> because of the separation involved but rather because of
> the discord and disharmony which led to the break.
> Affectionless psychopathy was due not to the breaking of
> relationships but rather to the initial failure to form
> bonds. Intellectual retardation was due to a lack of
> appropriate experiences and not to separations (Rutter,
> 1981:131).

Rutter claims therefore that the conduct disorders and anti-
social behaviour previously associated with divorce are all
associated not with separation but with disturbed interpersonal
relationships caused by family discord and disharmony (Rutter,
1981:135).
The second aspect concerns the long-term effects of early
life experiences, and separation in particular. Freudian and
psychoanalytic approaches are based on a view that each stage
of childhood can set a unique and permanent stamp on future
personality (for example, Erikson, 1950; Wolff, 1981) and it
is widely believed that early experience (in the first year of
life) is causally related to later disturbances in social development. But these beliefs cannot be substantiated by sound
empirical research (Shaffer and Dunn, 1979; Lamb, 1978), and
research on long-term effects of child-rearing practices is
lacking (Richards, 1981). Rutter, however, while concluding
that there is simply a lack of conclusive evidence, is now
attracted to ideas of human resilience, and is sceptical of
earlier beliefs in critical or sensitive periods in early years
for bonding:

> Continuities between infancy and maturity undoubtedly
> exist, but the residual effects of early experiences on
> adult behaviour tend to be quite slight because of both
> the maturational changes that take place during middle
> and later childhood and also the effects of beneficial
> and adverse experiences during all the years after infancy.
> While it is clear that the long-term effects of early de-
> privation depend heavily on whether or not the deprivation
> continues, it would be premature to conclude that infant-
> ile experiences are of no importance in their own right
> (Rutter, 1981:197).

A review of literature on the effects of early experience

208

concluded with a plea "for a greater recognition of the possibility of personal change following misfortune ... Perhaps the single most important finding is that for an unknown number of children the options for personal change following environmental change are open during the whole of development, even up to young adulthood (Clarke and Clarke, 1976:271). Thus transient disturbances may result in recovery, enduring influences may result in enduring effects.

Thirdly is the recent emphasis on individual differences in children's responses to deprivation or separation, so that some children come through the most stressful experiences relatively unscathed and with a stable healthy personality development. Rutter (1981) identifies six factors which influence the child's response: a multiplicity of stresses, and persistence of family discord are both disadvantageous; the child's sex, temperament and genetic background influence its response; factors in the family, such as a good relationship with one parent and readily available sources of emotional support, and authoritative parenting (i.e. well-understood rules and effective supervision) (Herbert and Wilson, 1978) can protect children against "serious maladaptive and disruptive influences" (Rutter, 1981:214); coping skills can be learned which foster resilience in the face of stress; and there are protective factors outside the home, such as school and neighbourhood environment (Rutter, 1981:208-216).

The fourth aspect is the most interesting in the context of divorce, for it mirrors the findings already discussed that the damaging effects of divorce can be mediated or mitigated by satisfactory post-divorce arrangements. Research on separation has shown that "children can recover from separation quite fully if their new circumstances are adequate" (Maccoby, 1980:98). Adoption studies in particular have shown that "the child's later adjustment will be primarily determined by the quality of the relationship with the new caretakers, not by the experience of (or the degree of disturbance at) separation" (Maccoby, 1980:99); "It appears that there is virtually no psychosocial adversity to which some children have not been subjected, yet later recovered, granted a radical change of circumstances" (Clarke and Clarke, 1976:268).

This has important implications for child custody. The dangers of a change of custody have probably been overstated. Judicial acceptance of medical evidence that removal from a mother or a change of custody entails "a particularly serious risk of long or even permanent impairment of the child's capacity to form permanent relationships" (Re C (MA) (1966) is probably not justified. Indeed Eve J's view in Re Thain (1926) of the "mercifully transient" effects of partings may no longer appear as outrageous as it once did.

Nevertheless it is important to keep in mind the issue in custody decision-making. In a claim by natural parents for the return of their child who has been fostered, the social science

evidence may support a judicial preference for leaving the
child in the care of adults who are his "psychological parents"
through "day-to-day interaction, companionship, and shared experiences" (Goldstein et al, 1973:19). Any separation of a
child from persons to whom he is attached will cause some degree of stress, so any decision to separate a child must be
based on a calculation that the stress of separation will be
outweighed by its advantages, and vice versa. The advantages
and disadvantages in fostering cases may be reasonably clear,
taking into account considerations such as the reasons why the
child was initially fostered, the strength of the alternative
attachment bonds and the quality of alternative care-taking
facilities. The evidence that the effects of separation are
mediated by other factors, are reversible, and may not have
long-lasting effects is therefore not in itself justification
for returning the child to its parents; disrupting the status
quo must be based on the greater good which is predicted to
derive from the change.

The application of these arguments to divorce is more
difficult. Other than in the case of a very young infant who
has not yet developed an attachment to both parents, the marriage breakdown will inevitably result in some acute separation
distress. The effect of separation in <u>disrupting</u> attachment
bonds is however controversial. Goldstein et al (1973) representing a psychoanalytic view of child development and based
on Bowlby's theories (1951), in particular emphasising critical periods and need for absolute continuity of relationships:
("where there are changes of parent figure or other hurtful
interruptions, the child's vulnerability and the fragility of
the relationship becomes evident. The child regresses along
the whole line of his affections, skills, achievements and
social adaptation"(1973:18)) believe that an absent parent can
never be a "psychological" parent to a child: "An absent biological parent will remain, or tend to become a stranger"
(1973:17).

Another distinctive feature of attachment bonds is that
they "<u>persist</u> over time during a period of <u>no contact</u> with the
person with whom bonds exist ... it is certainly unjustified
to assume that separation is synonymous with bond disruption.
In some circumstances children can maintain bonds through
quite prolonged separations" (original emphasis) (Rutter, 1981:
142, 112). Rutter claims, therefore, that separation does not
necessarily involve disruption of bonds: "it seems probable
that environmental conditions as well as age influence a
child's ability to maintain a bond during a person's absence"
(1981:25).

The application of the status quo principle to considerations of continuity in attachments or psychological parenthood
on divorce is therefore weak. The existence and intensity of
attachment bonds between child and each parent will vary according to individual families, but there is no empirical

evidence that the physical separation caused by divorce dis-
rupts these bonds. There would therefore seem to be little
social science justification for legal policies which as a
general principle identify the present caretaker as the child's
only "psychological parent" or which insist on the absolute
continuity of that caretaker's care. The child may have strong
attachment bonds to his absent parent, despite his absence, and
the effect of removal to that other parent (as a result of a
custody order or variation of custody) may cause little more
than short-term distress, assuming that the separation is not
surrounded by other disadvantageous circumstances, in particular family conflict. Separation per se does not disrupt bonds,
nor any consequent longer-term psychological disorders.

Continuity of environment

It has been seen how the status quo principle imports the
notion of continuity of physical care in the sense of maintaining stability in the child's home and environment, and how this
judicial policy underlies both custody decisions and the disposition of the matrimonial home.
    One of the most important findings of the recent American
custody studies concerns the importance of post-divorce relationships and circumstances in the successful adjustment of
children to divorce. One of the most important of these post-
divorce circumstances concerns the "continuity of support systems and environment" in mediating the psychological distress
of divorce. The danger of discontinuity has been noted particularly in connection with the downward economic mobility of
divorced-mother-headed families, although in theory the problem is non-gender specific. Both mothers and fathers with custody may have to move for financial reasons (Luepnitz, 1982:
63; Hipgrave, 1982:177):

    Following divorce, families are likely to shift to more
    modest housing in poorer neighbourhoods or to relocate
    into a combined household, usually with the mother' fam-
    ily of origin. The greater social isolation of families
    following divorce may be exacerbated by moving. For the
    child such moves not only involve losses of friends,
    neighbours, and a familiar educational system but also
    may be associated with living in an area with high delin-
    quency rates, risks to personal safety, few recreational
    facilities, and inadequate schools. Most people experi-
    ence relocation as a stress. For children involved in
    family dissolution such moves represent further unraveling
    of the skein of their lives at a time when continuity of
    support systems and the environment can play an ameliora-
    tive role (Hetherington, 1981:46).

    There is a lack of empirical evidence on the disposition

211

of the matrimonial home after divorce, and a lack of attention to this particular post-divorce arrangement in divorce and custody literature. It has however been suggested that English judicial practice results overwhelmingly in the wife custodian and children remaining in the family home after divorce, whereas in California, for example, which is a community of property jurisdiction (i.e. spouses share family property) most family homes will be sold at divorce (Weitzman, 1983). Nevertheless Murch (1980) has shown that children of 40% of petitioners had had a change in living arrangements though staying in the care of the same parent between separation and divorce. Wallerstein and Kelly noted that 20% of the children in their study moved "within the first six months following separation, and ... considerable talk of moving was in the air for many other children, and such anticipated moves tended to produce as much anxiety and sense of uncertainty as the actual event" (1980:25-26). By five years after divorce, "almost two-thirds of children had moved their place of residence, and a substantial number of these had moved three or more times"(1980:183). Moves were dictated by the sale of the home in the financial settlement of divorce, or for economic reasons, such as cheaper housing, better jobs, or child-care arrangements. Despite the considerable mobility of both parents, however, this was "confined to a small geographical area, enabling parents and children to remain in contact with each other if they so chose" (1980:183).

Both the disposition of the family home, and the effects of relocation following divorce have been little investigated, and conclusions are therefore premature. The availability of support systems i.e. the non-custodial parent, relatives, friends, school, care-taking facilities, however is generally considered to be an important mediator for children of divorce (Hetherington et al, 1981:280; Santrock et al, 1982:294). The effect of relocation on the availability of support systems is therefore significant: for example, it may increase social isolation, or it may increase the availability of support systems, in particular in the extended family. This is in addition to the effects of relocation resulting in loss to the child of a familiar environment, peer group and school.

CONCLUSIONS

The discussion suggests that judicial espousal of the status quo principle is based on inconclusive social science evidence. The protection of continuity of caretaker from a psychological point of view in divorce cases, though not in fostering cases, is too simplistic. Apart from circumstances where one parent has "disappeared" from a child's life for some length of time, a child who has lived with both parents in an intact family will have attachment bonds with both parents, regardless of who his physical caretaker is for the time being. The case for continuity of environment appears to be stronger, although the evidence is still inadequate. But continuity of environment is not directly related to who is the caretaker. Both parents may choose to remain in the pre-divorce neighbourhood so that the child's environment is minimally disturbed. Wallerstein and Kelly (1980) found that divorced parents predominantly remained within a small geographical area. Another possibility is that whoever gets custody should remain in the matrimonial home. Indeed until Richards v Richards (1983) reversed this well-established trend this represented judicial policy in respect of domestic violence injunctions excluding one parent from the matrimonial home: "It was unfortunate that the matter of custody had not come earlier before the courts because the order of events ... must really be that the order for custody had to be made before it could be decided what should happen with regard to the matrimonial home" (Wood v Wood (1979)). It is also the practice of the courts when dealing with the matrimonial home in the financial provision on divorce. Where custody to the mother is not in issue "the availability of the house as a home for the wife and children should ordinarily be ensured while children were being educated" (Smith v Smith (1975)); where a father had custody, he was allowed to remain in the matrimonial home with the children (Eshak v Nowojeski (1980)).

The association between custody and the matrimonial home, which appears to be supported by the social science evidence, does however have difficult and unfortunate implications for the legal process. It widens the economic bargaining context of custody, for the custody decision will not only determine with whom the children live, but also who remains in and who moves out of the matrimonial home (Richards, 1982).

Indeed the status quo principle in general has an impact on bargaining and private ordering. The predominance of the status quo arises from the private parental arrangements made for child-care after divorce, and which the courts are usually asked to confirm in an order. Judicial acceptance of the status quo in practice has also however become the norm, so that judges expect to continue the status quo, and even in contested cases. The knowledge that the judge will expect to see the status quo continued, then, as mediated by lawyers, influences the private ordering of parents who believe that the status quo must be maintained in order to receive the court's approval. The problem with this process is however that the making of formal arrangements may occur some time after the parents have separated, and the child-care arrangements made at the point of separation may be quite "arbitrary":

> Frequently the spouses are very upset at this time and perhaps least able to make long-term decisions about their children. Usually, they will not know anything of the status quo principle and will make their first decisions

without the benefit of legal advice. Often people have a rather unreal belief that the courts or their solicitors will "sort everything out" and do not realise that their short-term arrangements may have a great bearing on what will eventually become the long-term pattern (Richards, 1982:135).

The status quo principle may also be used "to influence the outcome of a custody hearing":

> For instance, the party who has actual custody of a child may try to delay a hearing so that the period of this custody is as long as possible. The extent of this problem is unknown but despite the very strong arguments for the rapid resolution of custody disputes delays are often significant. Another difficulty is that a parent may try to obtain the actual custody of a child by undesirable means before a case comes to court in order to establish the status quo they desire (Richards, 1982:135).

So the impact of initial child-care arrangements originating at an early stage of the divorce process, if arranged without legal advice, will increase the "arbitrary quality" of the eventual custody decision, and indeed may even make it extremely unjust. If the initial arrangements are arranged with legal advice, the parents may become polarised and harden their bargaining positions. Arrangements which make "good legal" but "bad psychiatric sense" may predominate over "bad legal" but "good psychiatric" ones (Andry, 1968:580). A major conclusion from the review of the social science literature does suggest that ideally continuity and stability in a child's relationships and environment should be protected. The status quo principle as presently understood by the legal process interprets that finding to require continuity of the pre-trial and trial-date arrangements in the divorce court orders. The artificiality of the pre-trial and trial-date arrangements is however ignored. Whereas in the context of maintenance the principle that the court should "so far as it is practicable" attempt to place the parties in the position "in which they would have been if the marriage had not broken down" (Matrimonial Causes Act 1973, s 25) is no longer supportable (Law Commission, 1981), the principle does have attractions in the context of custody. It affirms the comment by Latey J that "a marriage could be dissolved, but not parenthood" (L v F (1978)). The principle of continuity therefore lends itself to a much wider interpretation than that presently given.

Instead of continuity of an arbitrary caretaking status quo, the evidence suggests that the law should be concerned with the child's successful adjustment to divorce by protecting continuity in the child's relationships. Empirical studies are

214

unanimous that one of the most important indicators of success
is the quality of post-divorce relationships with both parents.
Disruption of bonds with the absent parent as a result of divorce needs to be minimised. The principle of continuity is
therefore less relevant to the question of which parent gets
custody, where the child commonly has an attachment to both
parents, but is of far greater relevance to issues of how to
minimise the effects of divorce by maintaining so far as is
practicable his relationships with both his parents. In other
words the principle of continuity, rather than suggesting a
custodian, indicates that the courts' concern ought to be to
ensure that the best possible custody and access arrangements
are made so as to protect the child's relationship with both
parents. The principle of continuity is therefore the central
concern in discussions of joint custody and of access.

The status quo or continuity principle nevertheless does
have an application to the custody issue, but not in terms of
which parent should be custodian. It indicates that, whoever
is custodian, continuity in the child's environment, including
the matrimonial home, should be protected. To the judges'
credit, this represents current practice on divorce, although
the House of Lords in Richards v Richards (1983) has reversed
previous policy that protection of the home for the children
is the "first and paramount consideration" in granting injunctions excluding a spouse from the matrimonial home pending
divorce.

Chapter 9

CUSTODY CONSIDERATIONS: THE WIDER FAMILY

The legal system takes a very limited view of the child's kinship network. The law of divorce is almost exclusively interested in the parent-child relationship, and only marginally in
the child's relationship with other kin, in particular his
siblings and grandparents. Social science research on these
wider family relationships is sparse, and understandings of
their implications for divorce are almost negligible. This
chapter is therefore merely an attempt to explore some issues
which have suggested themselves from the literature.
    Step-parents raise different considerations. Whereas di-
vorce may threaten pre-existing relationships with the wider
family, recently arrived step-parents and step-siblings create
a demand for new attachments to be formed. The parental requirement that the child accept new members of his family may
exacerbate, or re-open, the problems the child faces in adjusting to the divorce. But the presence of a step-parent also
threatens the child's relationship with and loyalty to his
absent parent: the designation of the step-parent as part of
the wider family rather than as a parent-substitute may be a
crucial factor in the success of the step-family for the child.

SIBLINGS

The current judicial attitude is that "it is desirable that all
children should be with one parent but this can not always be
achieved" (Sir Seymour Karminski, Bowden v Bowden (1974)).
This comment encapsulates the practice, since the undesirability of splitting siblings is usually only expressed when the
court is in fact about to split them.
    There are no statistics available indicating how often
the courts allow the splitting of siblings between parents in
contested or uncontested cases. There are cases however where
the custody of siblings is granted to one parent against the
other's opposition (Bowden v Bowden (1974); Ward v Laverty
(1925)). The general impression however (Eekelaar et al, 1977;
Maidment, 1981) is that more often regret is voiced followed

217

by a splitting of the siblings between parents (Re P (1967);
Re O (1962)).

The desirability of keeping siblings together is said to
be that "a separation of the children is inevitably such as
must cause to them unhappiness" (Lord Evershed M R, Re O
(1962)). The judges thus recognise the existence of attachment bonds between siblings, and that separation causes short-
term distress. Indeed in Re O the court ruled that the long-
term prospects for the boy would be better in Sudan with his
Sudanese father, while his sister remained with her English
mother, and echoing Re Thain (1926), despite the "immediate
unhappiness of the inevitable parting".

The psychological evidence for attachment between siblings
derives from the same understandings about bonds between children and their parents or other adult caretakers. Rutter notes
that "bonds form with people who have no caretaking role towards the child and the presence of a peer or sib reduces
stress in similar fashion to the presence of a parent-surro-
gate" (1981:40). The evidence of effects of separation from
mother ignores that "in fact they consist of separation from
mother and father and sibs and the home environment" (1981:50).
Further, there is no evidence that a "first or main attachment
differs in kind from all other subsidiary ones" including
attachment to sibs (1981:141).

Recent research on sibling relationships has begun to
focus on siblings as "agents of socialisation" creating within
the family's social system "a network of relationships within
which each individual has the potential to influence every
other member both directly and indirectly" (Lamb, 1982):

> Among home-reared children, siblings are the most regular -
> often the only regular - playmates available to both older
> and younger siblings, and for the younger members of sib-
> ling pairs, older brothers and sisters are the primary
> models of interesting childlike activities ... Siblings
> commonly become primary confidants and sources of emotion-
> al support in pre-adolescence, and these mutually import-
> ant relationships usually persist well into adolescence
> and young adulthood ... During adolescence ... siblings
> provide the most reliable and consistently supportive re-
> lationships (Lamb, 1982:5-6).

The realisation that "siblings exercise a much greater influence over life decisions than we allow" (Sutton-Smith, 1982:
384) has hardly begun to be examined in the context of divorce.
But it is a fair assumption that the complex network of relationships within a family of parents and several children is an
important mediator in reducing the effects of divorce (Andry,
1968:567-8). For example, sibling composition may influence
the impact of father absence on the child's cognitive abilities
(Sutton-Smith et al, 1968). Wallerstein and Kelly found that

older siblings may take on an active role in the household, helping the custodian mother with her responsibilities: younger children sometimes appreciated this, though others felt cheated of their mother's care (1980:115). The presence of siblings is always mentioned as one of the ingredients of a support system which can minimise the effects of divorce (Wallerstein and Kelly, 1980:138; Hetherington, 1981:54).

The presence of siblings may not however always be beneficial. It is well documented that children from large families are disadvantaged physically, socially and educationally, regardless of social class (Pilling and Kellmer-Pringle, 1978: 13). Wallerstein and Kelly noted that the sharing of visits by siblings to the non-custodial father was a source of frustration, particularly where ages and interests diverged (1980: 139). "Some parental patterns or sibling patterns bind the siblings together and others force them into competitive relationships" (Sutton-Smith, 1982:383), so that keeping siblings together may not always be desirable and "brothers are less close to each other in subsequent years than sisters".

The finding of Santrock et al (1982) that same-sex custody seems to be more successful could have important implications for the splitting of siblings between divorced parents; they themselves however are unwilling to reach this conclusion in the absence of further exploration of sibling relationships on divorce (1982:303).

Indeed the lack of research in this area makes it impossible to reach any conclusions. It would seem that the effects of divorce on sibling attachments and the significance of siblings as a support in mediating the effects of divorce remain important areas for investigation.

GRANDPARENTS

Grandparents in particular grandmothers have always played a role in child-caring, especially of orphans (Anderson, 1971), although that role as the role of the extended family generally may have decreased in this century (Young and Willmott, 1973). The law however denies any special recognition to grandparents vis-a-vis their grandchildren. Grandparents who cared for grandchildren would be treated on the same basis as strangers, so benefiting from the status quo principle when it became ascendant. In W v W (1926) a wife's application for custody of a boy of five was refused on the grounds that the child had lived with its grandparents since birth, and in Re Collins (1950) a contest between two sets of grandparents over an orphaned grandson of 6½ was resolved, despite religious differences, by leaving the child with the maternal grandparents who had been caring for the child for two and a half years. Grandparents may not intervene in custody suits between parents as of right, unlike step-parents who since 1977 may intervene without leave (Matrimonial Causes Rules 1977, rule 92(3)), but

are commonly given leave to intervene, in one example in respect of the custody of their deceased daughter's child (Pryor
v Pryor (1947). The divorce court may grand custody to grandparents (or anyone else) under its general power to make "such
order as it thinks fit" for custody (Matrimonial Causes Act
1973, s 42(1); Re R (1974)), although when the custodianship
provisions of the Children Act 1975 come into force non-parental custody will only be available by a custodianship order.
The divorce court could equally make an order for access to
grandparents under the same statutory provision. The magistrates' courts were not able to make custody or access orders
in favour of anyone who was not a party to the proceedings, nor
could such a person initiate any such application. As a result
of a private Member of Parliament initiative, a new provision
was introduced in 1978 to allow grandparents to apply for
access whenever there is a custody application or order in the
magistrates' court (Domestic Proceedings and Magistrates'
Courts Act 1978, s 14; Guardianship of Minors Act 1971, s 14A
(1)) or where one of the parents is deceased (Guardianship of
Minors Act 1971, s 14A(2)).

Grandparents have also been allowed to prevent a step-
parent adoption taking place in respect of their deceased son's
son, on the grounds that the child should continue the family
name and business, and that it was not for his welfare to be
severed from his wider family (Re L A (1978)).

The attitude of the law may be summed up as: sympathetic
reception but no special status. Apart from the access provision, grandparents are given no special recognition in legal
provisions in respect of their grandchildren. When grandparents do appeal to court for protection of an existing tie with
a grandchild however, it is clear that the courts enthusiastically seek to recognise the claims of the child's wider family.

Nevertheless it is still the case that the law does not
actively support the continuance of the child's relationship
with his wider family. Indeed it has been said that the present system of divorce actually "sanctions the dropping of
links between grandchildren and grandparents" (Mead, 1970:110).
The problem is most acute for the family of the non-custodian
or deceased parent, in whose interests the new access rules
were introduced.

From the child's point of view, divorce "may shatter the
marriage household, but not the kinship network that children
create by their existence" (Bohannan, 1970:249). The significance of the wider family on divorce for the child is therefore
twofold: firstly, attachments may be disrupted, and secondly
valuable supports for post-divorce adjustment may be lost or
unexploited. Both these issues have been discussed in respect
of siblings, and the same considerations apply.

There is a considerable lack of evidence on the role of
the extended family. On the one hand it is claimed that in the
last half century "in most, though not all, parts of the UK,

the extended family has virtually disappeared. In many areas
it is rare for relations to be near at hand to give the kind
of assistance with children and in emergencies that has always
been the norm in small, static communities" (Seear, 1982:389).
Others claim that in compensation for the breakdown of the
"two-parent ideal ... the vertical ties between ascendants and
descendants (grandparents, parents and children), which seemed
to be weaker in recent years, may now be strengthening again"
(Willmott and Willmott, 1982:354). Research is beginning to
show "the continuing strength of extended family networks and
their value for material help, the transmission of values and
attitudes, and generally for social relationships within the
family" and how in the USA these can continue to function in
spite of geographical separation, through cheap telephones and
transport (Fogarty and Rodgers, 1982:12-13). Psychologists
too are beginning to show interest in the influence of grandparents and parents' siblings on a child's development
(Sutton-Smith, 1982:384).

Divorce studies have tangentially considered the influence
of the wider family. Luepnitz (1982:63) noted that some custodian mothers are forced for economic reasons to return to their
parents' home; but Wallerstein and Kelly (1980:43) in California found that during the family crisis about "three-quarters
of the children were not helped by grandparents, uncles or
aunts, many of whom lived in different parts of the country".
Subsequent to the divorce however "half the maternal grandparents, and fewer paternal grandparents maintained considerable interest in and regular contact with other grandchildren,
although many lived at some distance" (1980:150).

Nevertheless the extended family may be an important influence in the divorce process, both negatively and positively.
The approval or disapproval which parents themselves receive
from their own parents in respect of their parenting, may be
allowed to affect the child's emotional relations with both
sets of grandparents, as well as the child's access to the
grandparents, and the availability of child-care and substitute parenting by the grandparents (Beal, 1979:152). The most
significant influence however is as part of the support system
to parents which can mediate for the child the effects of divorce. Wallerstein and Kelly noted that grandparents who did
"live close by /during the family crisis/ were very helpful
and provided special treats and took children into their homes
occasionally. These children appeared to benefit considerably
from this special concern and care" (1980:43):

> Those children who had extended families, especially
> grandparents who were close by or who kept up a continu-
> ing interest from a distance were very much helped by this
> support system. Several children, when asked about what
> had helped them the most, told us about loving, devoted
> grandparents who kept them in mind and provided summer

vacations for them, telephone calls at frequent intervals, and an ongoing relationship attentive to the needs of the children (1980:222).

"The increased contact with the mother's own kin, particularly the children's grandparents, has been shown to have positive effects on lone mothers and their children" (Hetherington, 1981:53). Parents too tend to find support after divorce in the family: contact increases with parents and siblings, financial help may be given, as well as material services such as baby-sitting or car repairs, and confidence and caring (Luepnitz, 1982:127; Hetherington, 1982:53). There are also negative aspects however; mothers often resent having to return home to their own parents (Luepnitz, 1982): their independence is threatened and conflicts about child-rearing may arise (Hetherington, 1981:53). Custodian mothers may increase contact with their own kin (and it has been noted generally that wives keep more contact with their own families than do husbands (Rapoport et al, 1977:338)), but will usually decrease contact with their husband's kin (Marsden, 1969): "For children this often means the loss of contact with the parents of the non-custodial parent. Depending on the closeness of the child's relationship with the grandparent, this loss can exacerbate the child's anxiety about the dissolution of his or her intimate affectional network" (Hetherington, 1981:53). The recent legal provision for grandparents' applications for access is a recognition of this problem, from both the grandparents' point of view and from the point of view of the child's interests.

STEP-PARENTS

The recent growth of the divorce rate has resulted in consequential rates of remarriage and step-parenting. Leete (1979: 6) estimated that one-third of people now divorcing will remarry, particularly younger divorced women; and in 1976 it was calculated that about seven per cent of all children under seventeen have step-parents (Burgoyne and Clark, 1982:290). There has been a parallel upsurge in research into step-families, but this has mainly concentrated on the process of family reconstruction from the step-parent's perspective and on the difficulties of the step-parent role (Green, 1976; Rapoport et al, 1977; Maddox, 1975), rather than on the effects on or reactions of the child. Burgoyne and Clark in particular (1981, 1982) have shown that the attempt of step-families to reconstitute 'normal' family life is hindered by the social and legal "legacy of divorce"; and Maddox (1975) has urged that the successful step-family must openly come to terms with its origins.

The purpose here is not to describe the valuable information and understanding now becoming available on the process of reconstituting families after divorce and remarriage. Discussion is limited to the relevance of the step-family in the legal context of divorce and custody decision-making.

Step-parents and custody

At the time of the initial custody decision the custodian may already be cohabiting even though not legally divorced (Burgoyne and Clark, 1981:136; Wallerstein and Kelly, 1980:288), or may have remarried if the custody decision is delayed for a welfare report or for a contested hearing. A step-parent may also have emerged by the time of a variation of custody order. In principle the presence of a third party in the child's home must be relevant to a consideration of the child's welfare. In practice where custody is uncontested or uninvestigated as in the majority of cases, the step-parent's presence will either not be known or will be ignored (Andry, 1968:582). It is really only in contested cases that a step-parent's presence, if there is one, is considered. The courts will take account of both the ability and character of a step-parent. In Re F (1969) where both father and mother were cohabiting with new partners following their divorce, one of the determining factors in awarding custody to the mother was the role of the step-parents:

> I must consider Mr D and Miss G. I do not think it necessary to discuss their characters, although I must consider briefly what sort of a father-substitute and mother-substitute they would respectively be ... Miss G has the difficulty that, lying ahead, there is her confinement and the birth of her first child. With that in mind, as well as my assessment of the characters of these two, I can only say that on the whole I think Miss G is not likely to prove quite so adequate a mother-substitute for the ward as Mr D is likely to prove a father-substitute for her. In saying this, I give full weight to the consideration that the demands of a younger girl on her mother-substitute are likely to be heavier than her demands on her father-substitute (Megarry J).

In S v S (1973) it was said that it was preferable for the judge to actually see any substitute parents, e.g. newly-acquired spouses. In Allen v Allen (1974) one of the factors in giving custody of two teenage boys to their mother was that the younger boy, aged 12, did not like the lady friend of his father: "It is not suggested that there is any improper relationship between the husband and Miss Bush, but she is a friend of his, and she comes in practically every evening to keep him company and I daresay, to help him to some extent in the running of his house". If a child's dislike of a friend can contribute to losing a parent custody, how much more so a

cohabitee or new spouse, as in <u>Hutchinson v Hutchinson</u> (1978).
The mother left home when the baby was eight months old; at
the time of the case the child had been living for three months
with the maternal grandmother; the mother was now cohabiting
with another man, a Mr Harvey. According to the judge:

> Normally, the interest of the child dictates that the
> child should stay with the mother. The question is does
> the character antecedent impression of the mother's co-
> habitee out-balance the desirability of the mother having
> the care of the child? ... Mr Harvey is not a satisfac-
> tory person to bring this child up at all. The evidence
> indicates the relationship is unstable, there are long
> odds on a rapid breakup of relationship between Mr Harvey
> and the child's mother ... He has been described as evil,
> bad, without principles and he uses women. There is no
> doubt that he is a mountebank and a philanderer ...

The mother thus lost custody both because of the character of
her cohabitee and because of the instability of their relationship. The judge felt that she had a clear choice, but "time
and time again, consciously, she had made a choice which has
been Mr Harvey and not her child".

Step-parents and access

Unlike the custody decision, access for the child to his absent
parent requires delicate ongoing arrangements for both custodial and non-custodial families. The presence or later introduction of a step-parent can present one of the most difficult
aspects of access, and will be considered in chapter 10.

Step-parents and the child's adjustment to divorce

If the legal procedures for divorce are concerned with creating
a scenario in which the child's adjustment to divorce can be
maximised, then understandings about the role of the step-parent in this process are important. The step-parent represents
another variable in the ability of the child to cope, and understandings of the step-parent role may assist in predicting the
success or failure of the child's post-divorce adjustment.
Research suggests a number of ways in which the step-parent
role may be considered.

<u>The step-father as compensation for the absent father</u>. One of
the noted consequences of father-absence may be adverse effects
on the child's intellectual and cognitive abilities (although
the explanation is not the absence itself but the circumstances
in which the absence occurs). The presence of a step-father
has been found to mitigate these effects, but other research
suggests that these adverse effects may be increased (Pilling

224

and Kellmer-Pringle, 1978:205). The presence of a step-father is however related to greater masculinity and sex-role development in younger father-absent boys (Pilling and Kellmer-Pringle, 1978:209); and in terms of the emotional and social adjustment of father-absent children, evidence also conflicts on whether the presence of a step-father has any effect (Pilling and Kellmer-Pringle, 1978:214). In general then the research is inconclusive; Pilling concludes that "the child's age at his mother's remarriage, the quality of the mother-child relationship, and her attitude to the step-father are all likely to affect the relationship established with the step-father and its influence on the child" (Pilling and Kellmer-Pringle, 1978:214).

Step-fathers v step-mothers. Re F (1969) expressed a view that a step-father finds it easier to take on his role than does the step-mother, especially where she herself has children of the remarriage. Burgoyne and Clark (1981) show that step-parents tend to mirror societal expectations of 'normal' parenting in intact families. Fathering is less clearly defined, and traditionally assumes an indirect role of providing material and emotional support to the mother; mothering is more closely and clearly defined, and assumes the everyday care but also responsibility for child-rearing. It is therefore "a much bigger step /towards family reconstitution/ when a step-mother joins a motherless family than when a step-father joins a fatherless family" (Burgoyne and Clark, 1981:138); the step-mother is expected to , and herself expects to, become an "instant" mother and to "recreate a satisfying domestic life for their new family". Burgoyne and Clark note however that step-mothers (and step-fathers too) find the parental role easier to achieve the younger the child is (this was also noted by Wallerstein and Kelly, 1980:289); they also found that all ex-.cept one step-mother in their study of 40 step-families had had children of their own, and that this was particularly important for previously childless step-mothers in order to "confirm their authenticity as mothers and to make sense of any difficulties they had with their step-children" (Burgoyne and Clark, 1981:139).

Megarry J in Re F (1969) therefore appreciated that a step-father's social role is easier to assume than a step-mother role, but may have been incorrect in seeing a step-mother's own child as a disadvantage.

Step-parents and successful family reconstitution. On a family interaction view, the child's successful adjustment to divorce and remarriage will depend on the success of the step-parent's adjustment to his or her new role, and the success of the re-constituted family in general. Maddox claims that the key to the successful step-family is "facing up to remarriage", "more honesty and less pretending"; "if step-terms were used more

openly, the step-relationship would come out from under cover
... there are informal ways that the status might be recognised and a social role defined" (Maddox, 1975:165).

Burgoyne and Clark touch on this problem in their conclusion that although step-families are a distinct family form,
step-families are as varied as intact families (1981:145).
Moreover, what distinguishes the step-family from the intact
family is the evident "lack of planning", the "discrepancy and
asymmetry" for example in the ages and names of the children
(1982:293), which Maddox (1975) argues should be overt, with
no attempt at hiding. The attempts which step-families do
make (Burgoyne and Clark, 1981) to reconstitute and "pass" as
"normal" families are inevitably hampered by the personal and
structural constraints of the legacy of divorce; reconstitution can only take place in the light of an existing heritage
of legal decisions which continues to affect decisions and
family organisation (Burgoyne and Clark, 1982). Children also
share in attempts at normality: one response to the arrival of
a step-father is to feel "relieved to be a two-parent family"
(Wallerstein and Kelly, 1980:290), and most children want
their custodial parent to remarry (Santrock et al, 1982:295).

The problem for the step-family is that society has not
yet "faced up to remarriage" (Maddox, 1975:160). Mead's in-
sight that all societies have an ability to allow a contrast
between life as people believe it to be ("ideals") and life as
it is actually lived ("practices") has resulted in the context
of divorce in the failure to provide any terminology for "step"
relationships and the wider family created by them (Mead, 1970).
Children have problems in knowing what to call a step-parent
(Green, 1976:137). This may be surprising in view of the fact
that historically step-families have always been common, though
the cause of remarriage was death rather than divorce (Laslett,
1977). Bohannan (1970) suggests that it is this lack of a
social structure for divorce which necessitates appeals to
court for legal decisions over questions such as access or
names.

Children of divorce studies. Much of the published literature
concerns the difficulties of the step-relationship, in particular the role of the step-father (Green, 1976) as reported by
step-parents or by children. The recent research interest in
children of divorce is only beginning to consider the effects
on children of step-families, but as yet very few direct observations have been made (Santrock et al, 1982).

The divorce studies to date have nevertheless produced
some findings which indicate factors with important effects on
the child's successful adjustment within a step-family. Step-
mothers married to non-custodial fathers seem to have little
direct influence on the child; but they can be an important
influence on the father's attitude towards his children, and if
supportive the father's contact with his children can increase

226

to the benefit of the child (Wallerstein and Kelly, 1980:299). Equally step-mothers can adopt damaging strategies, such as encouraging the father to seek custody, or to lessen his contact (Hetherington et al, 1982:282). Step-mothers in father-custody families have problems of fulfilling a domestic and mothering role, as already described. In addition, the sex differences noted in respect of custody placements (that same-sex custody placements appear to be more successful) are replicated in step-families: girls who were doing less well in father-custody families appear to adjust better to the father's remarriage than boys who were doing well but now find the arrival of a step-mother produces conflict and the need to share the father (Santrock et al, 1982:311).

The transition from single-parent to step-family is difficult for children whatever the sex of the step-parent. While the security of a two-parent family is welcome, it also threatens the closeness of the child with the custodial parent (Wallerstein and Kelly, 1980:291; Santrock et al, 1982:311). The presence of step-siblings is also potentially disadvantageous: unusually large households create heavy domestic demands, particularly for the wife; some children reported valuing new friendships, but others found the tensions of living with a larger group of other children difficult (Wallerstein and Kelly, 1980:297). Hetherington et al also noted that where the step-father had children, particularly in the new household, "both parents were more likely to report high rates of marital conflict, disagreement about child rearing, dissatisfaction with the spouse's parental role, differential treatment of natural children and step-children" (1980:283).

Sex differences appear to be important in respect of step-fathers, as well as step-mothers. Step-fathers report that taking on the role of father to his wife's children is more difficult in respect of boys (continuing the difficulties of boys in mother-custody families), but an authoritative step-father whose involvement was welcomed by the mother could produce positive advantages. Age differences may be a crucial variable: boys of nine or ten or under "often formed intense attachments and warm companionate relationships with their step-fathers", but boys aged nine to fifteen "were less likely to accept even a good step-parent" (Hetherington et al, 1982: 283-4).

The age of both boys and girls has been noted as one of the critical variables. This is true not only for older boys' non-acceptance of their step-father; older girls also find the arrival of a step-mother difficult, while step-fathers' relationships with children of both sexes under eight years "took root fairly quickly and were happy and gratifying to both child and adult" (Wallerstein and Kelly, 1980:299, 289).

The problem of visiting parent versus step-parent most clearly arises in the context of access and will be addressed in chapter 10. It is necessary here however to consider what is widely believed to be a crucial factor in the child's successful development, i.e. the child's need for a positive relationship with both his parent and step-parent: "For sons a continued positive relationship with the natural father played an important role in the development of social and cognitive competence even if a supportive step-father was available" (Hetherington et al, 1982:284).

> Many children were able to maintain and enjoy both relationships. The father and step-father did not occupy the same slot in the child's feelings and the child did not confuse the relationship with the two men ... Children with good step-fathers ... did not turn away from fathers, whom they continued to visit ... Neither divorce nor remarriage appeared to change substantially the importance or the emotional centrality of both biological parents for the growing child (Wallerstein and Kelly, 1980:292-3).

Both parents and step-parents can therefore be influential in different ways; the step-father need not replace the father, and indeed any attempt to do so, creating conflict or rivalry between the two men, will disturb the child, causing the child to experience "painful psychological conflict which he is unable to resolve" (Wallerstein and Kelly, 1980:294). Maddox calls for the recognition of the difference between step-parents and real parents, and of the positive dimensions of step-families for the child (Maddox, 1975:167). The practice of the judges therefore in referring to step-parents as "parent-substitutes" (as in Re F (1969)) may, in cases where contact with the natural parent is maintained, be both inaccurate and positively detrimental to the child's welfare.

Names. The law's ambiguity concerning change of a child's surname following his custodian mother's remarriage has already been noted (chapter 2): formal changes are not allowed except with the father's or the court's consent, but there is some reluctance to outlaw informal changes.

There is some evidence that changing names is commonly desired. In a step-parent adoption study 11.5% of parents had already changed the child's surname by the time of the adoption application, and a further 88% wished to do so after adoption (Masson and Burgoyne, 1979). Burgoyne's study of step-families also shows the importance of names: often the children themselves asked for the change because of difficulties and potential embarrassment of everyday relationships at school etc, and in many cases an informal change of name had been made (Masson and Burgoyne, 1979).

There are two purposes of changing the child's name. The first is to hide the fact of remarriage, by removing overt discrepancies which show up the step-family as not 'normal': differences in surname "single the family out for unwelcome scrutiny" in public, for example, schools, doctors etc (Burgoyne and Clark, 1982:286). This is commonly linked with arguments about administrative convenience, though the two points are quite distinct and different. This secretive attempt to hide the past may be analogous to the way in which illegitimate children are "shut away psychologically" by mothers hiding the origins of their birth, and which is considered to be damaging to the child's sense of identity (Wolff, 1981), or by the secrecy surrounding the origins of the adopted child which is considered equally unsatisfactory (Houghton Committee, 1972; Children Act 1975, s 26). The child's need of identity is similarly threatened by divorce (Bohannan, 1970).

Secondly, the change of a child's name, in passing the step-family off as 'normal', is an attempt to create a "sense of unity", in the same way that a child born of the remarriage is deemed by parents to create a "bond" or "seal", "bringing everyone together" in one unit (Burgoyne and Clark, 1981:142).

Maddox, in her claim for honesty and openness in step-families, argues forcibly against name-changes:

> There should be a general acceptance of two last names within a family. A society that wants ... divorce ... cannot afford to be embarrassed when the children in a household don't have the same surname as their father and mother. Like millions of other children, they have their father's name and their mother has remarried. What is difficult about that? (Maddox, 1975:166).

CONCLUSIONS

The significance of this chapter has been to consider the impact of divorce on the child's wider family. Though the law has traditionally taken a narrow view of family relationships beyond the nuclear family, and for the most part creates no legal relationship or rights and duties between other than parent and child, it is clear from psychological and sociological interest in the wider family that divorce not only breaks a marriage but threatens other relationships ("kinship network") created by marriage. Divorce is not just an event which affects parent-child relationships. The child's attachments with members of the wider family, notably siblings and grandparents, parents' siblings and their families, are at risk. The converse is that these attachments need to be protected by the legal system, not only to save the child unnecessary distress, but also because the wider family can play an important part in the post-divorce support systems which can mitigate or compensate for the inevitable disruption of divorce. It is this positive approach to the wider family which the law at present fails to recognise, and fails to exploit to the benefit of the child.

Step-parents do not give rise to the same problems of

protecting the child's existing attachments, but they do become part of the child's post-divorce environment, and can hinder or help the child's adjustment to divorce for many years after the legal termination of the marriage. Along with parental contact, absence of parental conflict, and adequate support systems, positive acceptance of a step-parent as another attachment object who is not attempting to replace the absent parent, is yet another indicator of a child's ability to successfully cope with divorce.

If the law of divorce wishes to protect the welfare of the children of divorce, then divorce and custody decision-making must be alive to the impact of the wider family on the divorce process.

Chapter 10

ACCESS

Access or visitation arrangements whereby the child and non-
custodian parent maintain a relationship with each other, encapsulate and epitomise the "fundamental dilemma" (Murch, 1980:
93) of post-divorce adjustment for both children and parents
in a way that the custody decision does not. Access requires
on-going arrangements which must accommodate different needs,
interests and resources, both material and emotional, of all
the participants, and which may change over time. The inability of the legal system to deal adequately with access, at the
time of separation, divorce and post-divorce has already been
seen: actual access arrangements may bear little relation to
the legal orders which are made (Hall, 1968; and see chapter
3); and the legal system is ineffective in resolving access
disputes, and is infrequently resorted to. Courts cannot
solve the human problems of adjustment to divorce; only parents
can make custody and access arrangements work if they want them
to (Despert, 1953).

THE LAW

Access questions are in law governed by the same welfare of
the child principle as governs custody decisions. Historically
therefore the same interpretations of the welfare of the child
were imported into access questions, and were tied up with
whether an adulterous mother was unfit to have access. The
Custody of Infants Act 1839, the first statutory inroad into
the father's sole right at common law to custody, made express
provision for access by the mother except where she was adulterous. But the principle of not awarding access to an adulterous wife had already been imported by the judges into the statutory power of the Divorce Court to make custody orders after
the decree, even though no specific mention was made of access
or of depriving an adulterous wife of it (Clout v Clout and
Hollebone (1861); Manders v Manders (1890)). This principle
was perpetuated in the Divorce Courts even after the exception
in the 1839 Act was repealed by the Custody of Infants Act 1873.

Thus in <u>Handley v Handley</u> (1891) it was said that though the court could make an order in favour of a guilty wife, as a general rule it would not unless there were exceptional circumstances. Such a principle was of course never operated against a guilty husband (<u>Hyde v Hyde</u> (1859)). But alongside the <u>Handley v Handley</u> approach there were also decisions like <u>Symington v Symington</u> (1875) in which the House of Lords seems to have turned attention away from the conduct of the mother to the interests of the children. Access might therefore be refused in the interests of the child's health (<u>Philip v Philip</u> (1872)). This view was reinforced in <u>Stark v Stark and Hitchins</u> (1910):

> The matrimonial offence which justified the divorce ought not to be regarded for all time and under all circumstances as sufficient to disentitle the mother to access to her daughter, or even to the custody of her daughter ... The court ought not to lay down a hard and fast rule on this subject ... And it is always to be borne in mind that the benefit and interest of the infant is the paramount consideration, and not the punishment of the guilty spouse;

and upheld in <u>B v B</u> (1924).

The same view had been expressed of the Guardianship of Infants Act 1886, s 5, which allowed the mother to apply for custody or access to her child. The court was directed to have regard for the welfare of the infant, and the conduct and the wishes of the parents. It was said in <u>Re A and B</u> (1897) that s 5 gave the court the widest discretion, which, though it had to be exercised judicially, meant that a mother could be given custody (and thus also access) notwithstanding that she had been guilty of matrimonial misconduct.

Around the turn of the century, therefore, access was no longer refused automatically because the mother was guilty of adultery, although stringent conditions might still be imposed (<u>Re L</u> (1962)). The judges certainly from 1875 and statute from 1886 were also concerned about the welfare of the child, and in 1925 the welfare of the child principle was by statute applied to all custody and access issues (Guardianship of Minors Act 1971, s 1; Matrimonial Causes Act 1973, s 52).

In the 1960s however the courts developed a line of cases which viewed access as a "basic right of any parent", only to be refused where the parent was not a fit and proper person to be brought into contact with his children; a wife's desertion or adultery was insufficient to lose access:

> Here the wife is asking for no more than periodic access to her own children. In the ordinary way that would be no more than the basic right of any parent. I agree ... that to deprive a mother altogether of access to her own

children, particularly to two small daughters, is a "very strong thing to do". I should be disposed to go so far as to say that the court should not take that step unless satisfied that she is not a fit and proper person to be brought into contact with the children at all. Such a situation might arise, for instance, if she were a person with a criminal record, or one disposed to act with cruelty against children, or something of that sort. To say of a woman that she is a bad wife or mother may be an excellent reason for not giving her care and control, but, in my view, is not sufficient ground for depriving her of any kind of access (S v S and P (1962)).

In C v C (1971) a mother was refused access to her five children on the grounds that she was mentally unstable (though another psychiatrist thought she was well enough mentally to have access), evidenced in particular by a wild outburst by the mother in court, and by her life style (her husband had found photos of her posing in the nude). Davies L J concluded that "(t)he children were living in a happy secure and serene household. If that state of things was to be interrupted by short visits by the mother there were almost bound to be disagreements and scenes which might seriously affect the children. Visits by the mother could do no possible good to the children". On the other hand in Re R (1963) an epileptic father was held to be a perfectly fit and proper person to have access.

Other cases did not dwell on the 'fit and proper' issue, but simply refused access because it was not in the child's interests. In B v B (1971) a boy of sixteen was quite adamant that he did not want to see his father. The court reluctantly refused the father access: "(N)ormally it is the basic right of every parent to have access to the child ... But there are exceptions to every rule ... There is now no suggestion in the present case ... that the father is in any way an unfit person to have access to this boy". But "(i)t would do no good at all for this boy to be forced against his will to go and see his father; on the contrary, it might well do him harm". The principle that access was not in the child's interests if there was a possibility of harm to the child, was followed in M(P) v M(C) (1971) where a father was refused access on the basis of a welfare officer's report. The court said that the children were living in a perfectly stable environment, and the event in their lives which caused upset was the access. This had only emerged after the original access order, but the consequence was that it was not in the best interests of the children to allow access at the present time. Access was also refused to a father who was in prison; it was thought better that access be resumed when the father came out of prison in two years' time (Anon (1963)). And in G v G (1963) it was held that access to a mentally ill father would be harmful to the children, and therefore since the paramount consideration was the welfare of the children, the decision to refuse access to the father was right.

Until 1973 therefore while access was a basic right of any parent, there were two exceptional circumstances where the court was prepared to deprive a parent of his right: where the parent was not a fit and proper person to have access, or where for some other reason access was not in the interests of the child's welfare. Nevertheless, the courts were very reluctant to deny access: "For a court to deprive a good parent completely of access to his child is to make a dreadful order. That is what has been done here, and the impact on both parent and child must have lifelong consequences. Very seldom can the court bring itself to make so Draconian an order, and rarely is it necessary" (B v B (1971)).

The modern definitive interpretation of the welfare principle appears in M v M (1973): first, the overriding consideration is the child's interests: any right of a parent to access would always take second place to the child's interests: "Where one finds ... a reference to the basic right of a parent to access to the child, I do not accept that the meaning conveyed is that a parent should have access to the child although such access is contrary to the child's interests" (Latey J). Thus, to say that the parent wanting access was not a fit and proper person to have contact with the child would be one consideration in deciding whether the order would be in the child's interests. On the other hand, that parent might be perfectly fit and proper, but still access might not be in the child's interests. On the particular facts of the case, access was refused to the mother, although she was a fit and proper person, because there was evidence that access was unsettling and disturbing the boy and affecting his general development. Secondly, access was not to be regarded as a "basic right in the child":

> (T)he companionship of a parent is in any ordinary circumstances of such immense value to the child that there is a basic right in him to such companionship. I for my part would prefer to call it a basic right in the child rather than a basic right in the parent. That only means this, that no court should deprive a child of access to either parent unless it is wholly satisfied that it is in the interests of that child that access should cease, and that is a conclusion at which a court should be extremely slow to arrive (Wrangham J).

Wrangham J's "basic right of a child to access" was attempting a subtle change of emphasis. But while it is true that the right of a parent can no longer be seen as a proprietorial right to access, the logic underlying the argument is that because it is a right of the child not to be deprived "of an

234

important contribution to his emotional and material growing up in the long term", therefore it becomes the corresponding right-duty of the parent to make that contribution. In other words, save in exceptional circumstances, a child, and thus a parent, will not be deprived of access. Indeed judicial practice concerning parental applications for access has hardly changed since 1973.

Judicial interpretation of the child's welfare as the first and paramount consideration in access cases therefore holds that, whether access is called a right of the child or a right of the parent, the welfare of the child imports a prima facie presumption that access is in the child's interests. Thus access will always be awarded to the non-custodian unless it is shown that there are exceptional reasons justifying its refusal. Access to the child is the norm; refusal will not be lightly undertaken. (Indeed courts may be too keen to grant access, for example, to violent fathers where children may be physically at risk (Pizzey, 1974)). A major purpose of this chapter is therefore to test whether this prima facie presumption in favour of access can be justified in the light of understandings and information available from other disciplines concerned with child welfare.

THE SOCIAL CONTEXT

The most striking aspect of the legal regulation of access is the significant lack of interest in the problem. One of the most important statutory provisions regarding the welfare of the children of divorce does not even specifically mention access, except as an interpretational afterthought (Matrimonial Causes Act 1973, s 52). Among the legal profession generally access is not considered a serious problem; indeed few cases come to the higher courts for rulings on whether access is in the interests of the child's welfare. This lack of interest is matched by much academic legal writing in which thought and effort is given to custody issues, but access is often ignored or merely mentioned in passing. It is true that the initial custody decision is the major issue, since it is custody which will determine more than anything the main influence in the child's life (and is unlikely to be varied except in extreme cases). On the other hand, access, though of lesser importance at the time of divorce or separation, subsequently becomes a much larger problem because it involves continuing human relationships, between parent and child and between the separated parents. Custody tends to be, and is intended to be, a once-and-for-all decision, either because the parties agree (however reluctantly) or because variation of a custody order becomes more difficult the longer the status quo exists. On the other hand, until the access order runs out because of the child's age, access can constitute a continuing source of controversy, rather like maintenance.

The problem of access

Most noticeable in the writings of sociologists and psychiatrists on the subject of marriage breakdown has been access as a potential source of difficulty both for the parents and the child. It might be that their accounts are unrepresentative, that they focus on the abnormal, rather than the normal situation which, because it works, does not get mentioned. Yet it appears that access is a greater problem than lawyers realise. The stresses of access to the child are widely documented: in Re J (1973) the child "showed a number of signs of stress immediately following each period of access followed by more or less lasting symptoms of insecurity and tension"; and Hunt has described the difficulties for the child in the following way: "The children are exposed, year after year, to two different styles of life and sets of values - each of which belongs to a parent ... For years he may oscillate wildly in his feelings and actions, sometimes abjuring one way of life or the other; if he is unlucky, he may never solve the problem as long as he lives" (1968:239). By contrast however Murch reported that few parents attributed disturbances specifically to access arrangements rather than to the separation or marital tensions generally (1980:84); and in Goode's study only 25% of the mothers thought the child was harder to handle after the father's visits (1956:323).

Even where relations between the parents are good: "(a)ccess, even at best, is unsettling. A child may appear to be coping with the emotional strain, but there are still the practical problems of too little time and of opportunities having to be missed. This is one of the hard facts about divorce. Parents can help by accepting it and showing restraint in the demands they make" (Sanctuary and Whitehead, 1970:133). However access also provides the perfect opportunity for continuing the battle and bitterness between the couple (Despert, 1953; Watson, 1969; Hunt, 1968). Thus children may actually be used by the parents for their own ends:

> Whatever the custodial arrangements, these marriages usually continued after the divorce, through the lives of the children ... This relationship is often the only channel through which the other spouse can make legitimate demands upon the other: (a) the wife by support demands; (b) the husband by visitation demands. It may also offer the most convenient means for learning about the activities of the other spouse. Further, this relationship contains the most important weapons in the conflict of wills between ex-spouses, both during the divorce conflict and afterwards. This exploitation of the parent-child relationship may, of course, be unconscious, since few parents can admit that they use their children as punitive instruments (Goode, 1956:313-4).

236

The two main techniques for using the children are: (a) threatening to withhold visits, or making them difficult; and (b) persuading the children to dislike or be suspicious of the other parent. But even where the parents are not consciously or unconsciously using the children in this way, there is also the problem that the visits themselves will cause stress.

> Tensions were most pronounced in the minority of families where the father had continued to visit frequently after separation or divorce. If the mother still had a lingering affection for him she fostered the children's loyalties and memories and supported his visits. But where, as usually happened, resentment built up between the parents, all too easily the father's visits or contacts with the children became a battle for their affections. Young children soon forgot even violence and neglect and were puzzled and distressed that the father could not stay. Happy visits when he was able to indulge their wants contrasted with the pinching and scraping and bad temper which were too often the result of the mother's financial position (Marsden, 1973:145-6).

> The relationship between the usually absent parent and the child at such visits is nagged by the fact that the parent and child will separate once again; that the advice and corrections of the absent parent will be overruled; while the assurances of love must carry their own proof during his absence. Since it is a rare young child who sees any reason for his parents to divorce, the haunting suspicion of abandonment gnaws at the enjoyment of the visits (Goode, 1956:322).

The result of these problems associated with access seems to be that visits become less frequent and regular.

> In the light of these difficulties it was easy to understand why only one of the fathers who now visited had been coming for as long as five years. The usual story appeared to be that visits which began well tailed off ... Repeated contacts with the father only served to dramatise and exacerbate the conflict of affection, and by active discouragement - or by an equally eloquent display of "neutrality" when the child appealed to her for a decision about writing to or seeing the father - the mother worked to bring the relationship to an end (Marsden, 1973:146).

A study of motherless families reported similar findings: "Our impression from the fathers' answers is that there is a tendency for visits to diminish in frequency and regularity with passage of time ... (M)others, fathers, and children find that visits make demands on them all which generate stresses and conflicts that eventually tend to reduce the frequency of visits" (George and Wilding, 1972).

Recent empirical data supports the view that for many non-custodial parents, divorce not only ends their marriage but also their participation as parents. In the Keele and Oxford studies (Maidment, 1976; Eekelaar et al, 1977) access appeared not to be taking place at all at the time of the divorce petition in about one-third of cases, and in the Keele study regular access took place in less than another third. In an American study (Fulton, 1979) 20% of custodial parents reported a steady pattern of visitation, 44% a tapering off in visitation, 6% only one or two visits a year and 28% reported no visits at all. In a Gingerbread study in London (Willmott and Willmott, 1982) about half of the children had no contact at all with the non-custodial parent or saw him or her only seldom; about a quarter saw him or her occasionally or irregularly; and a quarter had regular contact, usually weekly. In another Gingerbread study of access (Gingerbread/Families Need Fathers, 1982) less than half (43%) the respondents (both custodial and non-custodial parents) reported regular access; 39% reported rare visits; 18% reported no access, of which 69% were by choice of the non-custodial parent; some custodial parents were happy about the lack of access; others were not. These were all cases where access had been ordered; indeed only 3 out of 219 parents were actually refused access by the court. Murch (1980) found that no access was taking place in nearly a third of undefended divorces, but in only 5% of cases referred for a divorce court welfare report; access once a fortnight or more occurred in 41% of the undefended divorces, and in 62% of the welfare report cases; infrequent access (i.e. between once a month and every six months or only on holiday) in 28% and 31% of cases respectively. Murch also found that most of the non-access cases concerned children who were very young when the parents separated; and that staying overnight access was in only 26% of the undefended divorce cases, but 48% of the welfare report cases. In this study access arrangements were made by agreement in two-thirds of cases.

Luepnitz (1982) also found that less than half of the children in her study had frequent or continuous access. But she found very different patterns according to which parent had custody; non-custodial fathers visited either frequently or rarely if at all; non-custodial mothers however visited frequently or occasionally, but rarely failed to visit at all. This supports Santrock et al's finding that father-custody children have more contact with their non-custodian parent than mother-custody children (1982:294), but whether this is because of the mother's greater desire for involvement as Luepnitz suggests (1982:34) or because the father is more in need of child care support as Santrock et al suggest (1982:294) is unclear.

Hetherington et al (1982:251-2) also noted that "divorced

fathers became increasingly less available to their children and ex-spouse over the course of the 2-year period", although at two months after divorce some fathers had actually maximised their visitation rights and had more contact with their children than before the divorce. They also observed (as did Hess and Camara (1979)) that "the frequency and duration of paternal visits was greater with sons than with daughters".

Wallerstein and Kelly's study (1980) contrasts with the general pattern, but no indication is given or can be inferred as to the explanation for this, except that it may have been significant that most parents remained geographically close after the divorce. After separation 40% of children saw their fathers at least once a week, over 25% saw him two to three times a month, 25% saw him infrequently or erratically, and only 5% did not see him at all. At five years after separation while the nature of the father-child relationship was different from in an intact family, and had changed in duration according to the child's age, the authors were surprised that 25% of children still saw their fathers at least once a week, 20% two or three times a month, 17% infrequently or erratically and only 9% not at all.

The reasons for the often reported tailing off or the absence of visits is not well-understood. Suggestions appear in the literature:

> The husband is likely to have exaggerated notions about how much visiting he can do, and the wife may have equally unreal notions about how much visiting he will do. Most of her complaints were against the man as husband, not as parent, and she has little grounds for refusing liberal visiting privileges. His insistence on these rights, becomes, in turn, an assertion that as parent he wants to do his duty. Even when it was his decision that broke the marriage, he is likely to feel that he has been made an outsider when he recognises that the children and wife will be together. Consequently, he may make promises, to himself and possibly to the children, to visit as often as permitted ... Nevertheless, in general, these promises are not oriented to the realities of time, energy, and money, and the visits will probably become less frequent with time (Goode, 1956:314-5).

The factors which contribute to this result are:

i   the expense of entertaining the children
ii the time spent in travelling, and the consequent loss of his own social activities
iii the tension between the ex-spouses at every visit
iv the non-paternal goals of such visits diminish as both create new lives
v   the children lose interest in the visits because of

the tension, and the desire to carry on a normal
life, for example, playing with friends
vi   if the father misses a visit the child covers its
disappointment by withdrawing emotionally
vii   the daily activities of the child become less familiar to the visiting parent (Goode, 1956:315).

Goode does not claim that visits will always diminish, but he
does suggest that there is "a general set of structural ele-
ments in the post divorce situation ... and the visits will
decline in frequency unless there are unusual counter-factors
at work" (1956:316).

The fact of numerically declining visits is sometimes
matched by the custodial parent's desire for less visits, or
no visits (Goode, 1956:324). Three types of attitude may be
shown by the custodian: (i) the custodial parent may object
strongly to the visits, irrespective of the court decision
(this suggests that the law's view of access as a right of the
non-custodial parent even against the wishes of the custodial
parent is pervasive); (ii) if the custodial parent approves of
the visits it is only for the sake of the children, and he admits that he himself does not like them; (iii) the custodial
parent usually had no feelings either way, i.e. he neither
encouraged nor discouraged the visits. But if trouble arose
he was "more likely to influence the child against rather than
in favour of further contacts ... Because of the nature of
the situation (he is) not so neutral as it appears at first"
(George and Wilding, 1972:61). Goode suggests some of the
reasons why the custodial parent may not like visits: (i) the
mother sees her relationship with the child as more important
than the father's; (ii) the mother feels that the father may
have forfeited some of his parental rights by his marital behaviour; (iii) ex-spouses gradually come to have less friendly
or positive attitudes towards each other as time goes by, and
are therefore less willing to make concessions to each other;
(iv) his visits cannot ordinarily be fitted into her life or
the children's without much time and energy, and they are anyway not pleasurable for her (Goode, 1956:323).

In a study of children-of-divorce cases referred to welfare officers for reports, thus by definition perceived by the
courts to be 'difficult' cases and containing a large percentage of contested cases, welfare officers reported that access
was taking place frequently in 45.9% of cases, infrequently in
23% and not at all in 28.7%. The reasons ascribed by the
officers for non- or infrequent exercise of access were 35%
practical difficulties, 22% lack of interest by absent parent,
10% consideration for the children, 8% opposition by children,
8% hostile attitude of other parent, 8% injunction against
absent parent, 3% consideration for other parent; no significant variations were found related to age or sex of the child,
except that children under three were visited less frequently

240

(Eekelaar, 1982). This study did not attempt to explain these reasons, but Wallerstein and Kelly (1980) have suggested some of the mechanisms including the practical and emotional difficulties of role adjustment for the absent father. They note that "the relationship between the visiting parent and the visited child has no counterpart, and therefore no model, within the intact family" (1980:121), and this partly explains the problem of access (see also Burgoyne and Clark, 1982:299). The relationship between parent and child becomes "structured by the constraints and pattern of the visits". The visits themselves give rise to practical problems, of spending time with children of different ages and interests, of finding parameters for the new role of part-time parent, of constraints of time and space; fathers also have emotional difficulties, of dependence on children for their own self-esteem, of fears of rejection; both parents find the visit "an event continually available for the replay of anger, jealousy, love, mutual rejection, and longing between divorcing adults"; some parents actively compete for the affection and loyalty of their children. Wallerstein and Kelly found that in the first year after separation, two-thirds of the mothers and 80% of the fathers were stressed by the visits. The father's exercise of access was however not related to the child, but to his own psychological dilemmas: fathers depressed after divorce found it painful to visit their children, often visiting irregularly or not at all; fathers who felt guilty either allowed visits to decline or initiated a "guilt-ridden flurry of visiting which was rarely sustained"; fathers who sought to harass the mother through access tended to decrease visits and often ended them abruptly. The father's social role is also ill-defined both within marriage and after divorce; access may demand greater participation and responsibility for child-care than the father is used to. Society may also contribute to access difficulties by viewing contact or co-operation between ex-spouses as "incestuous" (Mead, 1970:121); thus even good intentions concerning access may be in this way undermined (Burgoyne and Clark, 1982:300).

The evidence suggests then that the access situation is by its very nature fraught with potential difficulties. It may further be surmised that access disputes which reach the courts are no more than the tip of an iceberg (Southwell, 1982). The feeling must be fairly common that however unhappy the custodial parent is about visits, he nevertheless is under a duty to allow them (George and Wilding, 1972:62, as evidenced in comments such as "If I could change legal access I would" or "I don't like it for myself but they have a right to see her"). The question is therefore in what sense can access be in the child's interests. In contrast to the practice there is a very widely held view that access is a "good thing". Certainly the judges have consistently held that "(i)t is important for children that they ... should know both their parents" (from

Taylor v Taylor (1870) to D v B (1977)). This has so often
been stressed by the courts that they have further held that
"generally speaking, it is the duty of parents, whatever their
personal differences may be, to seek to inculcate in the child
a proper attitude of respect for the other parent" (B v B
(1971)).

Such intuitive statements on the part of judges have
largely been supported by psychiatrists and others advising on
divorce: "The loss of easy access to both parents is one of
the principal tragedies of the disrupted marriage so far as
children are concerned ... Every effort should be made to ensure that ... access continues" (Watson, 1969). The main burden of divorce manuals, when considering the effect on the
children, is to point out that because access can so easily
become a source of argument and bitterness therefore parents
should try to make access work. To this end practical advice
is often given to help parents behave reasonably towards the
visits: "When both mother and father realise the child's needs
for a stable, continuing relationship with his father, they
are less impelled to use calendar and clock as weapons against
each other. The father's time with the child becomes no longer
a visitation, either of angel or scourge, but simply a visit"
(Despert, 1956).

Effects of separation from parent

Psychological evidence which could support such popularly held
views about the value of contact between the child and the
absent parent concerns the effects on a child of separation
from its parent. From the child's point of view a broken marriage, with custody awarded to one parent and access to the
other, means that the child is separated physically from one
parent. The effect of separation will depend on what relationship the child had with that parent. It is clear from
psychological research (Rutter, 1981) that attachment bonds
can and often do develop from a very early age between the
child and both parents and that such attachment is created by
psychological interaction even for short periods rather than
by satisfying the child's physical needs (Schaffer, 1971).
Separation from either parent with whom an attachment bond has
developed will have different effects depending on the age or
developmental stage of the child, the quality of the pre-separation parent-child relationship, and also temperamental or
sex differences in response to stress (Rutter, 1981).

Nevertheless, although separation from the object of
attachment behaviour can cause distress (according to Rutter,
only a short-term effect) which may lead to depression, or
anti-social or delinquent behaviour (according to Rutter, long-
term effects), the latter are more associated with the broken
home and family discord that accompanies separation rather than
the separation itself. Many factors also modify the effects of

separation, for example, the maintenance of bonds with the absent parent or siblings, the age of the child, good alternative "maternal" care, a good relationship with the custodian parent, or the "subsequent childhood environment after parental loss" or "the psychological reconstruction phase following the divorce" (Dominian, 1968:124).

Rutter's main thesis however is that separation need not necessarily involve disruption of bonds: "but that raises another issue: if bonds can be maintained during a separation then obviously bonds cannot be equated with attachment behaviour. But in that case how should one measure the strength of a bond (or even its presence) when the person with whom bonds have developed is absent? Further elucidation of the bonding process requires resolution of that difficulty" (Rutter, 1981: 126). Maintenance of bonds depends on the ability of the child to maintain a mental image of the parent during his absence. This is easier the older the child is. If maintenance of bonds is the significant factor, and can occur despite physical absence, then the non-custodial parent's absence will not necessarily disrupt the child's bonds with that parent. On the other hand, it is obvious that contact, i.e. access, will be more effective in preventing disruption of bonds and its consequent damage to the child, such as lack of trust or self-esteem, and feelings of abandonment (Benians, 1982). Little evidence exists on the effect of periodic but regular separation as occurs in a successful access arrangement, as opposed to transient or permanent separation, but the significance of the maintenance of bonds through contact is suggested by a study of delinquent boys where the highest number were those who never saw their father after the divorce (Dominian, 1968: 124-6). This suggests that contact with the father, even if only sporadic, is important for the child not to feel rejected and thus fall into delinquent behaviour. In the access situation it is open to the custodial parent to help the child maintain the bonds with the absent parent. It is also possible, by the custodial parent's behaviour and attitude, for the bonds to be disrupted.

It may be concluded, inferentially, that access is desirable in order to assist in the maintenance of bonds where they exist with the non-custodial parent, and so prevent disruption of bonds and its consequent damaging effects. The other way of considering this problem is to assess the effect of parental absence. The effects of father-absence on cognitive abilities, sex-role development, and emotional and social adjustment have already been discussed (chapter 7). The conclusion was that research apparently showing adverse effects of father-absence is in fact inconclusive when the material deprivations of and reasons for father-absence are taken into account. In addition there may be differential effects according to the stage of development, age or sex of the child. Little also is understood of modifying factors (Pilling and Kellmer-Pringle, 1978).

Most importantly however, research on father-absence has tended to focus on prolonged absence; "the effect of the degree and quality of the contact with the father himself, where this is possible, has been ignored in most studies" (Pilling and Kellmer-Pringle, 1976:200). In other words, research on access arrangements themselves is lacking.

Psychoanalytic literature, based on untested understandings of the Freudian theory of children's emotional development, tends to accept most psychological research on the effects of separation. It does however emphasise the particularly harmful effects of stress and separation in the sensitive stages of children's development. Thus Wolff, a psychiatrist in the psychoanalytic school, says:

> A major contribution of the psychoanalysts has been to show that at each stage of social and emotional development the child is concerned with particular aspects of his relationship with the people in his environment: that each stage presents its own problems to be solved; that different sources of anxiety exist at different stages; and that with increasing maturity the child's responses to excessive stress undergo progressive changes (Wolff, 1981:12).

Thus psychoanalysts claim that behaviour disorders occur most often during pre-school years (i.e. the genital stage of emotional development) and again at puberty, and that until a child is seven or eight and becomes a rational human being, stressful experiences can affect a child in such a way that disorders may persist into adult life.

Psychoanalysts also emphasise the child's sex. This follows from a belief that "during the genital stage of development children model themselves on the parent of the same sex ... When a parent is absent during these critical years, personality development is impaired and the task of identity formation at adolescence is likely to be difficult" (Wolff, 1981: 96). Thus some studies have supported "the idea that an important cause of delinquency is loss of the parent of the same sex, and the consequent lack of an identification model" (Wolff, 1981:107). Nevertheless other studies have not found the same link: "Both parents influence their children's development and which parent is more important varies with the child's age, sex, temperament and environmental circumstances ... It may well be that youngsters who have developed bonds with adults of only one sex are at a disadvantage later with respect to heterosexual relationships and to the development of sex-appropriate attitudes and behaviour. It is probable that for optimal development bonds need to be formed with people of both sexes" (Rutter, 1981: 115, 108). The psychoanalytic view on the loss of a parent has been summed up:

Even when social stimulation is adequate and the child's intellectual development and his capacity to form emotional relationships with others are unimpaired, the absence of a parent can have profound psychological effects. These are greatest when the loss occurs in the child's third or fourth year of life and when the absent parent is of the same sex as the child (Wolff, 1981:108).

The psychoanalytic view of child development leads in two directions. Depending on the child's age and sex, custody to one parent may be indicated; but failing that contact with the non-custodial parent of the same sex is presumably desirable. It is not clear whether a non-parent, for example, a step-parent can equally provide a sexual identification model for the child.

The other path of psychoanalytic theory leads to a view of access or contact with a non-custodial parent as threatening to the child's continuity of relationship with the custodial parent. This view, propounded by Goldstein et al (1973) has been influential (Wolff, 1981) though in practice rejected for the most part (Katkin et al, 1974; Benedek and Benedek, 1977).

Goldstein, Freud and Solnit's "Least Detrimental Alternative". Goldstein et al's proposals for the law of child placement (1973) are premissed on their view that the law is incapable of protecting a child's "best interests"; it can only attempt to secure the "least detrimental alternative" by protecting the child's relationship with his psychological parent(s). Their argument is based on:

the need of every child for unbroken continuity of affectionate and stimulating relationship with an adult ... (This) calls into question those custody decisions which split a child's placement between two parents or which provide the non-custodial parent with the right to visit or to force the child to visit. Such official invitations to erratic changes and discontinuity in the life of a child are but illustrative of many determinations in law which run contrary to the often professed purpose of the decisions themselves - to serve the best interests of the child (1973:6-7).

Therefore the only relationship which matters to a child is that with a psychological parent:

(F)or the child, the physical realities of his conception and birth are not the direct cause of his emotional attachment. This attachment results from day-to-day attention to his needs for physical care, nourishment, comfort, affection and stimulation. Only a parent who provides for

these needs will build a psychological relationship to
the child on the basis of the biological one and will
become his "psychological parent" in whose care the child
can feel valued and "wanted". An absent biological parent
will remain, or tend to become, a stranger (1973:17).

Thus an absent parent cannot be a psychological parent.
"Whether any adult becomes a psychological parent of a child
is based thus on day-to-day interaction, companionship, and
shared experiences ... A "visiting" or "visited" parent has
little chance to serve as a true object for love, trust, and
identification, since this role is based on his being available on an uninterrupted day-to-day basis" (1973:19, 38).
Finally, visits by an absent parent are harmful to the child:
"Where there are changes of parent figure or other hurtful
interruptions, the child's vulnerability and the fragility of
the relationship becomes evident. The child regresses along
the whole line of his affections, skills, achievements and
social adaptation". Further, "children have difficulty in relating positively to,profiting from, and maintaining the contact with two psychological parents who are not in a positive
contact with each other. Loyalty conflicts are common and normal under such conditions and may have devastating consequences
by destroying the child's positive relationships to both parents" (1973:18, 38). The upshot of this argument is that
courts would no longer make access orders:

> Once it is determined who will be the custodial parent,
> it is that parent, not the court, who must decide under
> what conditions he or she wishes to raise the child.
> Thus, the non-custodial parent should have no legally
> enforceable right to visit the child, and the custodial
> parent should have the right to decide whether it is de-
> sirable for the child to have such visits. What we have
> said is designed to protect the security of an ongoing
> relationship - that between the child and the custodial
> parent. At the same time the state neither makes nor
> breaks the psychological relationship between the child
> and the non-custodial parent, which the adults involved
> may have jeopardised. It leaves to them what only they
> can ultimately resolve (1973:38).

Under this scheme access could only operate as a voluntary
arrangement. Once custody has been decided it would be unconditional and final. The court would have no part in establish-
ing or enforcing visitation rights (1973:101).
    Goldstein et al's psychoanalytic approach is in direct
contrast to modern psychological thinking which rejects separation per se from an attachment figure as harmful and which
recognises the importance of the maintenance of bonds despite
absence or through periodic contact for the child's successful

246

development. In their emphasis on the exclusivity of custody, which will usually mean that the mother's relationship with the child is protected while the father disappears from the child's life, they also ignore the modern trend towards greater father-participation within marriage and after divorce, and ignore evidence now emerging from the children-of-divorce studies which emphasise the importance of the child's continuing relationships with both parents.

The significance of access

The psychological literature suggests that although bonds may be maintained despite absence, even where it is prolonged, access or contact may help to prevent bond disruption and its consequent harm to the child. Access also helps to overcome the child's shattered identity resulting from divorce (Mead, 1970). Benians (1982), a child psychiatrist, has identified five ways in which access, by allowing continuity of relationships with both parents, contributes to the "psychological well-being of the child": it prevents disruption of attachment; provides for a reciprocal and continuous relationship encouraging trust and confidence in relationships with others; provides the child with an example of parents who "care for themselves and their children"; provides models with whom the child can identify; and provides the child with knowledge of his origins, a sense of continuity with his "genetic inheritance".

These values of access to the child in the longer-term have therefore been considered to outweigh the well-documented short-term distress caused by access arrangements: "Where the parents have separated and one has the care of the child, access by the other often results in some upsets in the child. These upsets are usually minor and superficial. They are heavily outweighed by the long term advantages to the child" (Latey J in M v M (1973)); "The fact that a change of custody or liberty of access may unsettle the mind of the infant is only a circumstance to be considered, and ought not to be regarded as a complete bar to any change or new order for access" (Stark v Stark and Hitchins (1910)). Watson, a child psychiatrist, agrees: "While there will be some distress caused by movement back and forth between the parents, in the end such movement is necessary to growth. Every effort should be made to facilitate visitation" (1969:85).

It is in particular the child's desire and need in later life to know his origins, by analogy with current thinking in adoption practice to allow adopted children to search out their original birth certificates (Children Act 1975, s 26), which has been emphasised by judges as a reason for access:

> the long term advantages to the child of keeping in touch
> with the parent concerned so that they do not become
> strangers, so that the child later in life does not resent

247

the deprivation and turn against the parent who the child thinks, rightly or wrongly, has deprived him, and so that the deprived parent loses interest in the child and therefore does not make the material and emotional contribution to the child's development which that parent by its companionship and otherwise would make (M v M (1973)).

The unique role of parents is their "intimate knowledge of their child over the years (which) plays a part in the shaping of his self-image" (Newson and Newson, 1978:44). A clinical study by Tessman (1977) found that older children and young adults are often involved in an "unwilling quest" for the absent parent:

> Input derived from continued contacts about what the parent was really like could help transform the magical images of childhood to both less fearsome and less magnetic proportions. This process was not available to some, either because of the withdrawal of the absent parent or the hostility of the remaining one. It seemed particularly difficult in some of the cases in which divorce coincided not only with the pubescence of the child, but also with the devaluation of the parent in the human support network surrounding the child.

The weight of current opinion then is that continuity of relationships with both parents after divorce conduces to the child's continuing sense of stability and security. The contribution of the recent children-of-divorce studies has been to investigate the benefits to children of continuing contact, and children's own feelings about contact with their non-custodian parent.

Children-of-divorce studies

Empirical research directly comparing different access arrangements and their effects on children is scarce. Research on the children of divorce generally, however, includes parent-child relationships after divorce, and all reach the same conclusion: that children usually cope better with divorce if contact with both parents is maintained. Access protects the child "against the pain of loss and the psychological impact of that loss" (Wallerstein and Kelly, 1980:239).

Hess and Camara (1979) found that "parental harmony is less important for most child outcomes variables /i.e. social relations with peers, aggression, work style at school, but not indicators of stress/ than are the affective relationships that are maintained after divorce between the child and his or her parents ... It is the quality of relationship between the child and parents that is most crucial in divorced families (and) the most powerful influence on the child's social and school adjustment after the divorce" (1979:91-2). The quality of the relationship with the non-custodial father does not depend however on the extent of contact: "The child's confidence, or lack of it, in the tie with the father apparently depended less on frequency of scheduling than it did on the quality of the interaction that took place when they did meet". Hess and Camara conclude that it is the post-divorce family relationships and processes which are significant for the child's adjustment and "the child's relationship with the father without custody is of equal importance to his or her well-being and separate from the relationship with the custodial mother" (1979:94).

Wallerstein and Kelly agree that parental friction does not necessarily result in fewer visits, indeed it may increase them; and the significance of the mother's negative attitude towards visiting faded over time. Nevertheless parental harmony and the mother's interest in maintaining the father's visits did encourage visiting, and continued and frequent visiting (1980:126). Hetherington et al prefer to emphasise the importance of a good relationship between parents for the success of access:

> When divorced parents agreed about child-rearing, had positive attitudes towards each other, and were low in conflict, and when the divorced father was emotionally mature - frequent contact between father and child was associated with positive mother-child interactions and positive adjustment of the child. Where there were disagreements and inconsistencies in attitudes towards the child and conflict between the divorced parents, or when the father was poorly adjusted, frequent visitation by the father was associated with poor mother-child functioning and disruptions of the child's behaviour (Hetherington et al, 1978:173).

The Gingerbread/Families Need Fathers study of access also found a positive correlation between bitter divorces and negative attitudes by custodians towards access (1982:35).

Wallerstein and Kelly's major contribution to this discussion however lies in their finding that:

> The relationship that evolved within the constraints of visiting was diminished in its power and influence as compared with that in the intact family, but its importance to the child remained over the years. Whether the father maintained his presence by regular visiting or attenuated his contact to the vanishing point, he continued to influence the thoughts and feelings of his children, and, most particularly their self-concept and self-esteem (1980:235) ... We observe the sadness, disappointment, and anger of the infrequently visited youngsters, and

contrast their pain with the enhanced self-esteem and
pleasure of the children and adolescents whose fathers
gave continual evidence of their interest and love in the
post-divorce family (1980:238) ... Successful outcome at
all ages, which we have equated with good ego functioning,
adequate or high self-esteem and no depression, reflected
a stable, close relationship with the custodial parent
and the non-custodial parent. In such cases the friction
between parents had largely dissipated. The visiting
pattern was likely to be regular and dependable, and encouraged by the custodial parent and related to the
child's age and interests. In these arrangements the
child or adolescent essentially enjoyed the supports of
the intact family (1980:215) ... The role of the father
was two-fold in its potential effect on the child's psychological and social development. The negative effect of
irregular, erratic visiting was clear. The father's
abandonment, relative absence, infrequent or irregular
appearance, or general unreliability, which disappointed
the child repeatedly, usually led the child to feel rejected or rebuffed and lowered the child's self-esteem. We
soon learned that the unvisited or poorly visited child
was likely to feel unloved and unlovable, nor did anger
at the rejecting father always undo the child's unhappy
conclusion about his or her unlovability. The father's
direct contribution to the child's psychological health
and competent coping was not so clearly discernible either
at the time of counselling or at the eighteen-month follow-
up. At five years, however, this positive contribution
of the father's role emerged with clarity. Specifically,
good father-child relationships appeared linked to high
self-esteem and the absence of depression in children in
both sexes up to and including those in the thirteen-to-
twenty-four age group (1980:218-9).

Their key to "the continuing psychological importance of two
parents" lies in their observations concerning the child's
widespread and intense "yearning" for the absent father: "The
intensive longing for greater contact persisted undiminished
over many years, long after the divorce was accepted as an
unalterable fact of life" (1980:134). This desire for increased contact existed regardless of whether actual visits were
frequent or non-existent, and despite the difficulties which
burdened the actual visits. In the year after divorce only
20% of the children were reasonably content with the visits;
satisfaction depended less on amount of contact, than on ease
of access to the absent parent. One-third of children were
disappointed at their father's apparent lack of interest; one
fifth, mainly older children, suffered internal conflict between desire and anger; some aligned with their mother and
shared her hostility; 11% were genuinely reluctant to see him.

250

At five years "for all the children and adolescents a good re-lationship with the custodial parent was the key to good func-tioning in the post-divorce family" (1980:217); "divorce appeared not to diminish the importance of the psychological link between father and child" (1980:219). For all age groups, good father-child relationship, high self-esteem and absence of depression were related. "Those children who had been for-tunate enough to enjoy a good father-child relationship on a continuing stable basis over the years were more likely to be in good psychological health" (1980:219).

Wallerstein and Kelly conclude that "regardless of the legal allocation of responsibility and custody, the emotional significance of the relationship with each of two parents did not diminish during the five-year period" (1980:308). Good parenting by the custodian as well as the quality of the rela-tionship with the absent father are necessary to successful adjustment. Wallerstein and Kelly's finding of a striking discontinuity between the pre-divorce and post-divorce father-child relationship also makes the significance of post-divorce visiting therefore quite independent of prior relationships within the intact family. Moreover unless the relationship is actually psychologically or physically harmful to the child, "the maintenance of some continuity of the father-child relat-ionship appeared preferable to complete loss of contact, even though the relationship may have been impoverished from its conception or gradually deteriorated during the years (1980: 239).

Others too have noted the child's desire for contact with the absent parent (Murch, 1980:91). In Luepnitz's study about half the children wanted more visits; even 40% of those child-ren who already had frequent or continuous visitation desired more. Those who wanted less access were disturbed by being a pawn in parental conflicts (1982:35). Santrock et al reported that children enjoyed visiting the non-custodial parent, and the majority would have liked more visits (1982:295). Hether-ington likens the pre-school child's wish to maintain contact with its father to "mourning" (1981:50).

Access and child maintenance

There is a widely held belief that access and financial support by the non-custodial father are linked. Some fathers are said to believe that if they did not exercise access, they are not required to pay maintenance; others believe that the paying of maintenance entitles them to access (Burgoyne and Clark, 1981: 137; Richards, 1982:147). Wallerstein and Kelly report some post-divorce litigation seeking to link child support with visitation rights (1980:186). Burgoyne and Clark however found many mothers prepared to forego maintenance if it meant they were no longer inconvenienced by visits from their ex-partner (1981:137). Another study however found that overwhelmingly

251

divorced parents did not consider access as a reward for paying maintenance (Gingerbread/Families Need Fathers, 1982:27).

Access and the step-family

In practice re-marriage and the creation of step-families have important consequences for access arrangements (Burgoyne and Clark, 1981, 1982; Murch, 1980). Pre-eminently access interferes with the ability of reconstituted families to pass as "normal". Access, more than any other legal legacy of the first marriage, impedes the "normalisation" attempts of the step-family, and increases its fragility. Conversely, remarriage, both his own and the custodial parent's, creates conflict for the non-custodial parent regarding continuing commitment to his children. Mothers who are in any case prepared to trade off maintenance for no access, may be fortified by remarriage and the new source of financial security provided by the step-father: "contact with the non-custodial father no longer merits the social costs involved" (Burgoyne and Clark, 1981:137). Step-parent adoption thus provides a legal opportunity to terminate access in exchange for terminating financial support which is no longer needed.

The step-parent's own eagerness to succeed in a parental role to his step-children may be "shattered" by the child's rejection of his authority, and the child's continued disturbance at the absence of the natural parent. The step-parent must always live in the shadow of the natural parent's influence, the more so when that parent remains a physical visitor (Maddox, 1975). Access only increases the fears and fantasies, jealousies and hostility between natural parent and step-parent (Rapoport et al, 1977:113; Murch, 1980:87).

The presence of a step-father has also been found to exacerbate the uncertainty and ambiguity of fathers as to their parenting role, which is highlighted after divorce in their difficulties of role adjustment and over how to continue parenting in the artificial access situation. In Burgoyne and Clark's study (1981, 1982) these difficulties were found to lead to failure of fathers to maintain contact with their children, although ironically these absent fathers often became step-fathers to children of their second partner. But Wallerstein and Kelly found to the contrary that fathers continued to visit despite the mother's remarriage, although less so where the father himself had remarried. Nor was the step-father's enormous influence undone by the father's continued visits. "Many children were able to maintain and enjoy both relationships. The father and step-father did not occupy the same slot in the child's feelings and the child did not confuse the relationship with the two men" (1980:292). The step-father only "replaced" the father where the father had abandoned the child, or where the child voluntarily rejected the father. Children's ability to "enlarge their view of the family and make room" for both

father and step-father was not however always matched by the
adults, many of whom formed rivalries which were often bitter
and long lasting. Indeed this adult rivalry caused the child
to suffer painful conflict of love and loyalty between father
and step-father, and psychological damage to the child was
caused by the adult conflict and unresolved anger of the divorce, and the jealousies of remarriage between father, mother
and step-father. According to Wallerstein and Kelly, the child
has no difficulty in coping with a visiting parent and resident
step-parent as long as the adults have been able to resolve
their own conflicts. Murch notes too the need for reasonable
and trusted communication between former partners (1980:85).

Access following remarriage is then a problem, not for
the child, but for the adults. Access to the natural parent
may even be of greater significance for older children who do
not easily accept step-fathers and resent their presence in
the family (Wallerstein and Kelly, 1980:220). Antagonism between the adolescent boy and his step-father has been found to
be a factor in delinquency; so also in lack of contact with
the natural father (Dominian, 1968:124-6). The main thrust
then of Wallerstein and Kelly's findings is that:

> Within the post-divorce family, the relationship between
> the child and both original parents did not diminish in
> emotional importance to the child over the five years.
> Although the mother's caretaking and psychological role
> became increasingly central in these families, the
> father's psychological significance did not correspond-
> ingly decline. Even with remarriages, at least during
> the earlier years of these remarriages, though the step-
> father often became very quickly a prominent figure to
> the children, the biological father's emotional signifi-
> cance did not greatly diminish, although his influence
> on the daily life of the child lessened ... Their self-
> images were firmly tied to their relationship with both
> parents and they thought of themselves as children with
> two parents who had elected to go their separate ways
> (1980:307).

Conclusion

Apart from Goldstein et al's particular and idiosyncratic rejection of access as a threat to the security of the child's
relationship with his custodial parent, there is currently
widespread professional agreement that it is in the child's
interests to maintain a continuing relationship with both natural parents, and the closer and more normal that relationship
can be, for example through staying access, the better it is
for the child. That is not to deny the extreme difficulties
which access may create, both material and emotional. But it
is clear that these difficulties are more the parents', than

the child's, unless the child becomes the victim of the parents' problems.

Where the custodian is not remarried or cohabiting, contact with the non-custodian parent provides the child with positive emotional, material and social advantages of having two parents, which are the opposite of the disadvantages for children of one-parent family upbringing. These have already been discussed in some detail (chapter 7). Two parental relationships must be better than one (Weinraub, 1978). Indeed the terminology "one-parent family" in this context is a misnomer if it suggests that the child necessarily has only one parent after separation or divorce.

Where the custodian has remarried, the child's need for his natural parent seems to be undiminished even in the presence of a successful relationship with a step-parent; and all the more so where this relationship is stressful.

The two main mechanisms in the child's need for continuing contact relate to the issue of separation and loss, and of identity. The loss of an attachment object, while not resulting in enduring psychological disturbance, explains much of the child's distress after divorce and the child's "yearning" for his absent parent. But the degree of distress will depend on the existence or strength of bonds with the absent parent or the ability to maintain bonds despite absence; thus the younger child may suffer less from the loss, while the older child will suffer more. Age may be of less significance to the other mechanism, the sense of individual identity which is created by the biological family: "understanding one's origins and having a sense of place within a family's history" (Group for the Advancement of Psychiatry, 1981:88).

The law's current insistence that access, continuing contact with the non-custodial parent, is the right of the child to "know" both his parents despite their divorce, thus accords with the policy implications of the social science evidence. Yet the legal regulation of access is not unproblematic. The legal system is clearly incapable of and lacks the resources to enforce and supervise access orders once made, except in rare cases where supervision orders are made. There is some dispute as to whether this is even necessary. Murch found that the majority of access arrangements, where they do take place, are satisfactory to the participants (1980:71). The Gingerbread study (1982:22) however reported that 61% of custodial parents were satisfied but only 35% of non-custodian parents. It may be that the difficulties of access have generally been exaggerated through clinical impressions.

In practice since most orders are for "reasonable" access, the parents are left to make their own arrangements. On one view this imposes an enormous responsibility upon them, since the importance to their child of access may not be fully apparent to them, nor may they be capable of adopting successful and reasonable arrangements without professional assistance

254

(Maidment, 1975). On another view, "reasonable access" is preferable to formally defined or rigid access orders, since it allows for "a more open and flexible arrangement (which) requires a degree of communication, understanding and goodwill between parents. Any means of encouraging and fostering the necessary goodwill and communication is bound to be in the better interests of children" (Gingerbread/Families Need Fathers, 1982:21).

There is widespread agreement currently that whether the law adopts a more interventionist role in access arrangements or not, for many divorced families successful access will require the professional help of divorce conciliation or counselling services (Murch, 1980; Wallerstein and Kelly, 1980; Parkinson, 1982). This is a recognition of access, not "in terms of enforcing rights, or of making families abide rigidly by a particular code of practice", but as a process of "reorganisation" of the "family's social structure" of "how parental responsibilities are defined and new boundaries drawn around family relationships. These adjustments take time. They often proceed by painful trial and error before the family as a whole and its individual members can discover an acceptable equilibrium" (Murch, 1980:93).

At present the embryonic welfare services provided by divorce courts make some attempt to offer help with access difficulties. Welfare reports are often ordered where there is an access dispute (Maidment, 1976); welfare officers may informally offer conciliation or counselling although this is not their statutory function (Murch, 1980); and supervision may be ordered (Griew and Bissett-Johnson, 1975; Southwell, 1982). But the success of intervention will depend on the extent to which the particular welfare or supervising officers are convinced of the need for and benefits of access (Southwell, 1982). In practice professional social work opinion is divided on this (Murch, 1980:67); it may be that social workers and probation officers, the only agencies with professional responsibility for dealing with access, allow the practical problems of access to devalue its importance to the child.

Hall (1968) noted that at present "there is no machinery to safeguard the child against subsequent disadvantageous changes in the arrangements" apart from the supervision order. In general these orders are rare, but Hall suggested that greater use be made of them, and that the "exceptional" conditions be removed. A further suggestion mooted was that a lesser order should be possible, for example requiring a wel-officer to visit annually or twice yearly with a duty to report if a change in the arrangements appeared desirable. The idea that the parties themselves should be bound to report to the court a material change in the arrangements was rejected as impractical since the court was powerless to enforce such a rule. The somewhat optimistic conclusion was: "If there is reason for anxiety a supervision order can be made. Otherwise the parent will simply have to be trusted; and fortunately it is the case, no doubt, that the great majority of parents can be relied on to do their best for their children anyway" (Hall, 1968:41).

The law's ineffectiveness and lack of resources to provide a framework for the process of family reorganisation encapsulated in the access order, other than in cases of dispute, does not altogether invalidate the intervention of the law in these matters however. An awareness of parental responsibility is an important factor in the parent's emotional relationship with the child (Newson and Newson, 1978:439). The law performs an important function in embodying the right of the child to maintain contact with his non-custodial parent through the moral authority of an access order. Wallerstein and Kelly have argued that "there is some evidence that legal account-ability may influence and shore up psychological and financial responsibility. Furthermore there is evidence in our findings, that lacking legal rights to share in decisions about major aspects of their children's lives, that many non-custodial parents withdrew from their children in grief and frustration" (1980:310).

Social science evidence thus currently supports the law's view of access as the right or need of the child of divorce. While the legal system is in a weak position to actually ensure that this right is enjoyed (as opposed to ancillary conciliat-ion or counselling services), nor has "capacity to predict future events and needs, which would justify or make workable over the long run any specific conditions it might impose con-cerning for example ... visitation" (Goldstein et al, 1973:50), the law nevertheless embodies a moral authority to encourage parental responsibility towards children despite marriage breakdown. In this sense access as a parental duty and respon-sibility could be made more prominent in divorce procedures. Thus for example <u>both</u> parents should be required to attend the Children's Appointment, and the importance of access to their children should be explained to them (see for example the Code of Practice for access recommended by Justice (1975)). Hall's comment in 1968 has lost none of its pertinence: "The gravity of the consequences for the child of the disruption of the marriage must be made quite clear to the parents, and they must be left in no doubt that in consequence they now bear a special responsibility to the child ... Perhaps the greatest weakness of the present procedure is that (the method used to obtain the required assurance) sometimes gives the impression of super-ficiality" (Hall, 1968:37-8).

Chapter 11

JOINT CUSTODY

DEFINITION AND PURPOSE

The term joint custody is often used loosely to describe various different custody arrangements in which both parents participate. It is also often referred to by alternative labels,
such as shared parenting or co-parenting, or as divided or
split custody. Confusion however arises from a failure to distinguish between the concepts of legal and actual custody, i.e.
between parental rights and responsibilities for children, and
their physical care and control (see chapter 2). Legal and
actual custody may be jointly held by both parents, but need
not be. Most commonly joint custody is defined by lawyers to
mean joint <u>legal</u> custody; in this case the actual custody may
or may not be joint, and the court may or may not specify the
terms of the child's actual custody. Joint legal custody thus
means that both parents jointly share the rights and responsibilities for major decisions concerning the child's welfare,
such as education, health, and religion. 'Divided' or 'split'
custody will be reserved for cases where children of the family are split between parents, each of whom have sole custody
of the children allocated to them.

    The confusion over the meaning of joint custody is not
purely one of terminology. Feminist opposition to joint custody might well turn on objections to a father acquiring joint
legal rights of decision-making while leaving the burden of
physical child-care solely with the mother. Examples of fathers
seeking joint custody for this purpose, for example, to retain
decision-making power over the child's education, are not unknown (<u>Dipper v Dipper</u> (1980)). But current enthusiasm for
joint custody (Family Advocate, 1982) derives from the greater
participation of fathers in child-care and from the desire of
mothers to share the responsibilities and burdens of bringing
up children. Joint custody therefore seeks to allow fathers
to increase and mothers to decrease their participation in
physical child-care and its responsibilities. Joint actual
custody is thus nowadays an important purpose of joint custody

arrangements, although its terms may not necessarily be specified in the court order. In this chapter then joint custody
will be used to mean joint legal custody together with some
degree of joint physical care of the child, although the degree
of physical care may vary from very little to a great amount.

The distinction between joint custody and the equal parental rights which exist during a subsisting marriage is not
easy. Equal parental rights are "exercisable by either without the other" (Guardianship Act 1973, s 1); joint custody requires that no disapproval of its exercise has been signified
by the other joint custodian (Children Act 1975, s 85(3)). In
practice both types of parental rights may be indistinguish-
able; certainly some judicial opinion is of this view (Dipper
v Dipper (1980). Joint custody orders may even be technically
superfluous if the aim is to preserve the equal parental rights
of the subsisting marriage for the post-divorce parent-child
relationships. Indeed equal rights may be preferable to parents if the technical distinction with joint custody is valid;
Families Need Fathers for example describes itself as "A Society for Equal Parental Rights".

THE LAW AND ITS PRACTICE

In England and Wales divorce courts may make "such (custody)
order as the court thinks fit" (Matrimonial Causes Act 1973,
s 42). The divorce courts are thus free to make joint custody
orders of all kinds in their discretion. The magistrates cannot technically make joint orders, but in practice by granting
legal custody (which by definition includes actual custody) to
one parent, and by granting such "parental rights and duties
comprised in legal custody" as are specified (but not actual
custody) (Domestic Proceedings and Magistrates' Courts Act
1978, s 8(4)) to the other parent, they can in fact achieve an
order tantamount to joint legal custody; but they cannot order
joint actual custody. In this respect the magistrates cannot
achieve a full joint custody order.

Judicial interpretation has established that joint custody
may be granted where this is for the welfare of the child. In
Jussa v Jussa (1972) (a case arising under the Guardianship of
Minors Act 1971, but equally applicable to divorce) it was held
that joint legal custody with care and control (actual custody)
to one parent was appropriate "where there was a reasonable
prospect that the parents would co-operate for the well-being
of the children for whom both had affection." Joint custody
was not to depend on exceptional circumstances, but whether it
was in the child's interests. In this case the purpose of
joint custody was to give the 'innocent' father "a voice in
his children's future". This principle has been subsequently
deemed to apply to all forms of joint custody, both legal and
actual: it is that the order must be for the welfare of the
child, and this will depend on the parents' co-operation.

258

In practice few joint custody orders are made, although they are said to be increasing. According to the Lord Chancellor (Hailsham, 1981) some 2 to 2.5% of orders were for joint custody; in the Oxford study it was 3.4% (Eekelaar et al, 1977). The Lord Chancellor, echoing the judiciary and legal profession generally, explained this low percentage as resulting from fear of damage to children from hostility between parents who under joint custody would need to agree on decisions concerning the child. Others explain it as resulting from failure of the legal profession to explain to clients the possibility and advantages of joint custody (Richards, 1982; Parkinson, 1981; Murch, 1980; Luepnitz, 1982).

There is also some evidence of the reluctance of the judiciary to approve joint custody even where this is agreed between parties. A recent Practice Direction (1980) has ruled that the judge should not dismiss an agreed joint custody application at the Children's Appointment, but should adjourn the matter for hearing. Similarly, where one party applies for joint custody, and one applies for sole custody.

In practice too there is some evidence that joint custody, far from being ordered to co-operating parents for positive purposes, may be used as a compromise between warring parties. The Oxford study noted "a greater readiness to make joint custody orders in contested than in uncontested cases which suggests that they may be used more as a compromise solution to a difficult problem than as a creative attempt to involve the absent parent in the child's future" (Eekelaar et al, 1977: para 13.16). It has also been reported in the United States that parents with "chronic, severe marital conflict often decided on joint custody largely because of their inability to decide where the children should live. These decisions reflected less of what was best for the children and more of the parents' own indecision and conflict" (Beal, 1979:151; also New York Times, 1980).

The appropriateness of joint custody where parents are in conflict over their children is controversial. Despite Jussa v Jussa (1972) emphasising the need for parental co-operation, other judicial opinion asserts the value of joint custody to the parent, usually the father, denied day-to-day care:

> There are cases in which the party who has not got the day-to-day control of the children is anxious to preserve as much of his or her contact with them as is possible in the new circumstances ... and there is a good deal to be said for recognising the responsibility and the concern of the father in this case by making an order which shows that the court recognises that he is anxious to take an active part in their upbringing. Therefore, a joint custody order meets his problems as far as it can be met in the physical circumstances and should at least help him to get over the bitterness he is bound to feel (C v C (1980); H v H (1981)).

259

Professional child care opinion on this is also divided, and will be explored subsequently.

Legal encouragement of joint custody is most evident in the United States, where it is said to be growing in popularity (Wallerstein and Kelly, 1980:121). Almost every state has in the past few years enacted joint custody laws (Family Advocate, 1982); California was the first to write into law that agreed joint custody is presumed to be in the child's best interests, and that consideration of joint custody is mandatory in all cases (Goldzband, 1982). Joint custody in this modern American usage usually envisages joint physical custody; the purpose of the new laws has been to ensure that the child maintains frequent contact with both parents. Many examples of American divorced parents sharing physical custody of their children have been reported (New York Times, 1980), ranging from arrangements for overnight stays which in practice differ little from access, to children spending alternate years with each parent. English law by contrast has, as far as reported cases are concerned, largely been concerned with joint legal custody orders, which ostensibly conducing to the child's welfare, address the needs of fathers who wish to continue participating in their children's lives without taking on the responsibilities of sole custody and/or care and control. In these cases joint custody owes more to a reaction against the presumption of sole custody to mothers (the maternal preference).

THE CASE AGAINST JOINT CUSTODY

The main case against joint custody has been made by Goldstein et al (1973, 1979). Their insistence on the child's need for one psychological parent who provides the child with the security and stability of one home and one decision-maker has led logically to policy conclusions which not only encompass unconditional and final custody orders, and no court-sanctioned access, but also no joint custody. According to Goldstein et al therefore joint custody by definition can never be in the child's best interests; a child needs one "anchor", he finds "shuttling between homes" bewildering. Others also of a psychoanalytic persuasion echo this view: "What is especially hard for young children is to have to break and remake their ties with parents repeatedly ... Whenever he moved from one parent to the other, he had to reconstruct his world" (Wolff, 1981: 122-3).

A related objection to joint custody is that it makes of the child a "yo-yo", "whose loyalties are divided and whose stability is undermined by shifting living arrangements" (Roman and Haddad, 1978:118). Without doubt joint custody can result in such problems for children, but it is clear that this is not necessarily so. Many reports of joint custody attest to children coping well with two homes, even where parents' life-styles and values differ (Abarbanel, 1977; New York Times, 1980). Professional opinion agrees that where joint custody does not work, it can be disastrous for the child. The child may become the cause of the continuing conflict between the parents; in the same way as children may feel responsible for their parents' divorce, the child may feel responsible for the continuing conflict over joint custody decision-making and practical arrangements.

There is also the argument that joint custody "won't work", or "it will cause more fighting" (Wallerstein and Kelly, 1980: 134). "However good their initial intentions, parents may find themselves in disagreement about their children's future; circumstances can change radically, and attitudes with them ... neither parent can make a decision that prevails" (Wilkinson, 1981:35). On this view parents can consult over their children when they choose to do so regardless of a court order, so that "when the order works it is unnecessary and when it is necessary it is unworkable." (Wilkinson, 1981:35). Similarly, "parents who could not reconcile conflicts while living together are even less likely to be accommodating to one another while living apart" (Roman and Haddad, 1977:115). But the evidence emerging on the practice of joint custody indicates that this is not so. Even where custody has been contested, it appears that some parents are able to successfully separate their marital conflicts from their parental roles (Parkinson, 1981; Beal, 1979; Roman and Haddad, 1977: Steinman, 1981). This issue will be explored further subsequently.

Another objection to joint custody may be labelled: "It just isn't done" (Wallerstein and Kelly, 1980:134). On this view, fathers who want to participate more, and mothers who wish to share child-care with the father are made to feel guilty, that their desires are socially unacceptable. Ex-partners are not expected to get on well together, and contact between them is disapproved, almost as if it was "incestuous" (Mead, 1970). Parents who desire joint custody are deemed to be "unable to separate in a healthy way, and use the arrangement and by implication their children, to stay together in some fashion" (Roman and Haddad, 1977:116). "Therefore, even if divorced parents consciously desire to continue to exercise a shared responsibility for the care of their children there are important informal pressures tending to undermine this intention especially where one or both of them has remarried" (Burgoyne and Clark, 1982:300).

Perhaps the strongest argument against joint physical custody is the logistical one: the practical problems created by housing, mobility and remarriage. Unless parents are able to remain living within close physical proximity of each other, so that children's school, neighbourhood and peers are unaffected by the joint custody arrangement, then there must be doubts about whether joint custody is in the child's best interests. As chapter 6 has indicated, stability in the child's post-divorce environment appears to be a crucial factor in the successful adjustment to his parents' divorce. While this does not indicate which parent should have custody, it does indicate that a child's ability to cope with his parents' divorce is enhanced if the social support systems outside of the nuclear family are maintained. Joint custody arrangements therefore which alternate homes are acceptable so long as they do not also entail concomitant changes outside of the homes.

THE CASE FOR JOINT CUSTODY

The case for joint custody lies essentially in the arguments against sole custody, and is the logical extension of the arguments in favour of access. These have been fully rehearsed in chapter 10 and need not be repeated here. The arguments for joint custody however must be viewed from two perspectives: that of the child, and that of the absent parent under a sole custody order (Parkinson, 1982).

From the child's point of view, recent custody studies have unanimously supported Wallerstein and Kelly's finding that "the central hazard which divorce poses to the psychological health and development of children ... is in the diminished or disrupted parenting which so often follows in the wake of the rupture and which can become consolidated within the post-divorce family" (1980:316). Wallerstein and Kelly also made the critical finding concerning children's "intense longing for greater contact (which) persisted undiminished over many years, long after the divorce was accepted as an unalterable fact of life" (1980:134). These findings "point to the desirability of the child's continuing relationship with both parents during the post-divorce years in an arrangement which enables each parent to be responsible for and genuinely concerned with the well-being of the children" (1980:310). The crucial importance of access to the child and parent has already been illustrated (in chapter 10), but the logical extension of these arguments must lie in creating the maximum contact between child and parent in the physical circumstances dictated by divorce.

The case for joint custody then is that "it approximates most closely the traditional marital situation in that it gives the child the greatest exposure to both mother and father. It is also a more flexible and natural arrangement. Having to make an appointment to see your father can be hard on kids" (Gardner, 1980). Joint custody is the nearest possible arrangement to living with two parents. The child does not feel deserted or abandoned by an absent parent, he does not "lose" his father, or suffer the pain of visits, or the inconvenience of visiting schedules. The child continues contact with both parents; the child is able to continue to enjoy "the permanent loving relationship", to be "dependent on his parents' role as a memory bank to which he can continually refer for evidence of himself as an individual with a history", to maintain both parents' "uniquely caring" and "partial" force in his development (Newson and Newson, 1976:437-444). The virtues of joint custody, if it can be achieved in practice, are almost universally accepted (Parkinson, 1982). Only Goldstein et al (1973, 1979) and their school of thought differ. Much scepticism is voiced however over whether the practical difficulties of organising joint custody can be overcome to the child's benefit. Little empirical research on joint custody families exists as yet. Steinman (1981) has reported however on 24 joint custody families with 32 children in California. In all cases joint custody was agreed without outside advice or encouragement. Physical custody was shared either by splitting the week (50%) or alternating weeks (25%), or alternating homes every day, every two weeks, every three months, or alternate years. The particular arrangements were related to the geographical proximity of the parents' homes. Steinman reported that all the children had two psychological parents and were attached and had strong loyalty to both. They were aware of the differences between the two homes, and their parents and their values; but they did not feel confused by these differences, except where the parents were in conflict over child-rearing values. The children did not suffer the crippling loyalty conflicts which exist where parents fight over the children; the children were free of such conflicts because each parent supported a positive relationship with the other. The children were nevertheless highly concerned with issues of loyalty and felt responsibility for being fair to both parents. Most children were not confused by living in two homes and were able to maintain complex schedules, but 25% did experience confusion and anxiety about schedules and switching houses, mainly four and five year old girls and seven to nine year old boys. The geographical distance between homes did not worry many of the children or they were able to master their stress, but some found travelling a frightening experience. Continuity of friendships and school was very important for all the children. Many of the children had fantasies of reconciliation between their parents, but did not suffer feelings of rejection or abandonment by either parent. Paradoxically while joint custody seems to enhance children's sense of self-esteem and sense of continuing importance to their parents, at the same time parental co-operation seems also to "keep alive the wish for a reunited family" (Steinman, 1981:413).

Nevertheless Steinman concludes that joint custody was more successful for the parents than for the children; this provides a further example of the conflict of interests created by parents' wish to divorce, where children repeatedly report a desire for a parental reconciliation (Steinman, 1981: 413; Wallerstein and Kelly, 1980). In Steinman's study one third of the children "felt overburdened by the demands and

263

and requirements of maintaining a strong presence in two homes"; the considerable demands on the child of joint custody "need to be evaluated with regard to the capacities and emotional concerns of the individual child" (1981:414). For those children who could cope, the "co-operative and respectful relationship ... attitudes, values and behaviour of their parents" was the more significant feature of joint custody in helping the children adjust to divorce, than the exact amount of time the child spent with each parent.

Many claims for joint custody however concentrate on the benefits to the otherwise absent parent, which by allowing him to share in the rights and responsibilities for his children after the divorce ensure his continued participation in the children's lives. Wallerstein and Kelly having noted the practical and emotional problems for fathers and children created by access arrangements, concluded that "a rethinking of visiting issues must include the concept that both parents remain centrally responsible for and involved in the care and psychological development of their children" (1980:134). The positive benefit of a joint custody order is that the "legal accountability may influence and shore up psychological and financial responsibility" (1980:310). The negative effect of a sole custody order is that the law is seen to be designating one psychological parent for the child, an interpretation which can be devastating to both child and parent (1980:311). "The non-custodial parent's lack of legal responsibility may have a negative impact: many non-custodial parents withdrew from their children in grief and frustration. Their withdrawal was experienced by the children as rejection and was detrimental in its impact" (1980:310).

Others too have objected to the "winner takes all" effect of a sole custody order; to the creation of the "weekend parent" or "visitor"; the "either/or" world of child custody (Roman and Haddad, 1977); and the psychological effect this has on non-custodial parent and child.

It is claimed that only equal legal rights and responsibilities for children of divorce can create a situation in which parents are able to continue their role to the benefit of the child. Greif studied 40 American divorced and separated fathers; she reports: "the more opportunity fathers have to act as fathers, the more they see themselves as fathers and seek to continue that involvement" (1979:313) and vice versa. "A clear danger of child absence is perceived role loss, leading to further withdrawal from the child" (1979:314). Those fathers who had joint custody reported higher satisfaction with their post-divorce relationship with their children than non-custodial fathers. The positive benefit of joint custody was "the daily intimate contact that living together, rather than visiting together, provides" (1979:315). Green speaks of fathers learning to "enjoy" their children (1976:132). The father with joint custody will also not be excluded socially from his

child. A repeated complaint of non-custodial parents relates
to their inaccessibility to aspects of their child's life,
such as school meetings and reports, and medical decisions
(Goldzband, 1982:35).

Luepnitz's study of 16 custodial mothers, 16 custodial
fathers and 18 joint custody parents sought to compare and
contrast the different forms of custody. She concludes "that
joint custody at its best is superior to single-parent custody
at its best".

1. Contrary to the warnings of many judges, there was no
   evidence that the joint custody families in this
   study sustained more post-divorce conflict than
   single-parent custody.
2. Contrary to the warnings of Goldstein, Freud and
   Solnit (1973), there was no evidence that children
   experienced a great disruption from living in two
   houses. In fact, most children felt their new life-
   style held certain advantages over the nuclear-family
   household.
3. Whereas many single parents had "split the scene",
   forfeiting all contact with the children, no joint
   parent had done so.
4. Approximately half the children in single custody
   desired more contact with their noncustodial parent.
5. No joint father had ceased to support the children
   financially, as many noncustodial fathers had.
6. There was some evidence in the sample that joint children had maintained meaningful relationships with both
   parents, in contrast with the single-custody children
   for whom the "visit" was a vacation.
7. Single-custody parents reported feeling "burned out"
   and "overwhelmed" in a way that joint parents did
   not (1982:53).

The main claim for joint custody then is that it maximises
the parent-child contact which is considered to be critical to
the child's ability to adjust to his parents' divorce. Joint
custody does this on two levels: the practical level of daily
living, and the emotional or psychological impact on the parents who both retain legal and practical responsibility for
the child's upbringing. Nevertheless as Steinman (1981) has
shown, joint custody may be easier for parents to operate than
for children. In particular the positive experience which
joint custody can provide will depend on the child's emotional
and practical abilities, but also on the degree of parental co-
operation or conflict.

PARENTAL CONFLICT

There is widespread acceptance that successful joint custody
depends on the ability of the parents to isolate their marital
difficulties from their parental role (Steinman, 1981; Greif,
1979), and to communicate with each other about their children
(Goldzband, 1982:35). Joint custody which becomes the opportunity for continued conflict over the child, where the child
becomes the spy or the weapon, or the cause of continuing conflict, is detrimental to the child. Where joint custody represents a parental value, that they "view themselves as equally
significant to the children and jointly responsible for their
physical, emotional, intellectual and moral development"
(Steinman, 1981:404), then it most closely approximates to
parent-child relationships within marriage. The child retains
two parents in a more flexible and natural arrangement; there
is no winner or loser in the parents' custody battle.
   Attempts are being made therefore to identify families
where joint custody can be successful. Steinman emphasises co-
operation and respect between parents over child-rearing, and
support of each other's relationship with the child (1981:414).
Beal suggests that families with a "severe degree of child
focus", and chronic severe marital conflict may choose joint
custody because of their own indecision and conflict, and thus
intensify loyalty conflicts for the children (1979:151). In
families with a mild degree of child focus by contrast,
spouses may "assume the overly responsive/adaptive role towards
one another", may make no decisions except with total agreement, may be equally involved in child-rearing, and thus agree
to joint custody (1979:147).
   What remains controversial is whether joint custody can be
a solution to parents who are in legal conflict over custody.
It has already been seen that English courts sometimes use
joint custody as a compromise in these cases. Some professional opinion rejects such compromises (Goldzband, 1982:35); Beal
argues that joint custody here reflects indecision (1979:151).
Others suggest that legal conflict is not necessarily a predictor of failure. Parkinson reports on the experiences of the
Bristol Courts Family Conciliation Service that "hostility and
conflict at the time of separation do not rule out joint custody. Lasting agreements are reached in many fiercely disputed
cases in which both parents had expected to either 'win' or
'lose' custody. If there is a fight over custody, everyone
loses" (1981:12). Greif points out that legal conflict over
custody may be dissipated if parents are able or helped to
separate the marital from the parental issues, to recognise
their mutual love for the child, and trust the other parent's
competence (1979, 1980). Burgoyne and Clark suggest that parents who recognise the legal and structural factors which prevent step-families passing as "ordinary" unbroken families will
find joint custody (or access) arrangements workable (1982:301).

CONCLUSION

This discussion has illustrated some of the confusion and controversies associated with joint custody. The English judges'
presentation of joint custody as a mechanism for maintaining
a father's "say" in his child's life (Hailsham, 1981) is inconsistent with the now more common orientation of many of its
proponents. To these, joint custody "does not mean a precise
apportioning of the child's life, but a concept of two committed parents, in two separate homes, caring for their youngster
in a post-divorce atmosphere of civilised, respectful exchange"
(Brown et al, 1976:32). Joint custody thus means parents sharing authority and responsibility for their children, because
this is in the best interests of the children of divorce, to
maintain the fullest possible contact with both parents.

As this chapter and the chapter on access suggests, the
critical question for the child's emotional health is the "co-
parental relationship" between the parents (Ahrons, 1981), i.e.
"the relationship between both parents that permits them to
continue their child-rearing obligations and responsibilities
after divorce" (Bohannan, 1971). Ahrons (1981) claims that a
"mutually supportive and co-operative coparenting relationship"
is the key to successful joint custody. It results in "a bi-
nuclear family system", i.e. one family system of two inter-
related households, maternal and paternal, with "kin or quasi-
kin" qualities. But Ahrons also notes that a court order for
joint custody does not necessarily create such a system; legal
structures do not necessarily influence the fabric of family
life (Wallerstein and Kelly, 1980:310). Thus sole custody
with access may produce similar relationships and patterns in
practice to joint custody if the coparenting relationship is
comparable (Ahrons, 1981:425). In practice certain forms of
joint custody may differ little from sole custody with liberal
or staying access. It is this concern for the underlying
parental relationship rather than the formal court order which
leads experts such as Wilkinson to comment that where there is
conflict joint custody is unworkable, and where there is co-
operation, joint custody is unnecessary (1981:35).

The view taken here however is that joint custody differs
from liberal access not just as a matter of degree, but as a
matter of substance. "Responsibility" is the prime function
of the parental role (Newson and Newson, 1976:437); the practice of divorce is that sole custody orders are made in over
90% of cases which legally remove that responsibility from one
parent for no reason other than that his marriage is dissolved.
Some fathers may not want that responsibility; but there is
ample evidence that many do, as is apparent from the existence
of pressure groups such as Families Need Fathers. The psychological impact of the loss of legal rights for non-custodial
parents, usually fathers, and for children, has been documented. The judges bemoan the fact that divorce in practice ends

not only the marriage but also parenthood; the confusion in the definition of "custody" in Dipper v Dipper (1980) displays a reluctance by the judges to allow a custody order to exclude the non-custodial father from participating in his child's life; judges insist on access as the right of the child to the companionship of his parent. The logical conclusion of all these movements is to joint custody. The legal system in making sole custody orders is failing to encourage that sense of responsibility for children which is said to be the role of parenthood.

Yet there are difficulties with joint custody. There are some parents and some children who do not want or cannot accept the concept of two committed and co-operating parents who are no longer married to each other. There are also economic and logistical problems of providing two homes within geographical proximity, which militate against joint physical custody. Joint custody arrangements must also be flexible to change over time to suit changing conditions (Luepnitz, 1982:152). The case for mandatory consideration of joint custody in all cases in the interests of the child's welfare would appear however from the evidence presented here to be unanswerable.

Chapter 12

CHILDREN OF DIVORCE: SOME CONCLUSIONS

PARENTS V CHILDREN: THE CUSTODY DILEMMA

This book has attempted to explore the current dilemmas of
child custody law and practice. While divorce is now more
widespread than ever, and consequently more children of divorce are living apart from one of their parents, at the same
time the previous certainty and prevailing understandings of
the proper legal and social arrangements for the care of these
children have receded. No longer are a father's legal rights
over his children sacred, a mother's matrimonial offence no
longer disqualifies her from legal control of her children,
nor is maternal care considered critical to a child's satisfactory physical and emotional development. It is the erosion
of these earlier legal and social rules for child responsibility and care that has opened up the law of child custody to
challenge. This challenge has come mainly from the social
changes in parenting and life-styles of recent years: in particular the new interest of fathers in their children's upbringing and the greater equality of women in the workplace and at
home. But older attitudes die hard too. Child custody law
and practice is still imbued with such ideas as that children
are inevitably damaged by divorce, that younger children need
their mothers, or that boys need their fathers (Ellsworth and
Levy, 1969). These "myths" are perpetuated not only be an inherently conservative legal system and its practitioners.
Parents too by their private ordering of the consequences of
divorce in the vast majority of cases are also responsible,
though parental behaviour is influenced by the supposed requirements of the legal system. Thus fathers may not seek
custody because of the expectation that their claims will fail.
      The purpose of this book has therefore been to explore the
dilemmas, the challenges and the "myths". It has done this by
investigating social science knowledge of marriage, divorce,
the family and parent-child relationships. In the past decade
the amount of research concentrating specifically on divorce,
and its effects on children, has grown rapidly, and provides

new and important understandings of the problems of child custody. It is further asserted that such knowledge cannot be ignored by the legal system if it is to retain its credibility in child custody decision-making. Earlier religious, moral and social values which created legal rules for the determination of custody cases have already been eroded; in the spirit of the second half of the twentieth century the legal system will be at fault if it fails to use the increasing understandings of the social sciences to improve the quality of custody decisions. It is not only a question of the credibility of the legal system, though that is an important matter; it is also in the spirit of the law since the late nineteenth century that the child's welfare is "the first and paramount consideration". It is hoped then that this account of child custody law in its social context will have not only described current understandings of the issues that arise in custody cases, but also conduce to the welfare of the child in the form of "better" decisions.

The nature of social science knowledge is problematic. Indeed it has been often said, particularly by lawyers searching for new certainties in child law, that the present state of knowledge makes its positive application in the determination of legal issues inappropriate (for example, Ellsworth and Levy, 1969; Mnookin, 1975; King, 1980). It seems to this writer that the search for absolute solutions is misplaced. Social science knowledge will increase, fluctuate and change in the same way as do philosophical, ethical or social values. This is because they are all created and influenced by the same prevailing social and political interests. There is therefore no reason not to use such social science knowledge and understandings as currently exist, even if these are shown subsequently to need revision. Nor is it a slight on the judiciary if decisions based on the current social sciences are subsequently seen to be inappropriate. It is argued here that the default of the judiciary is greater if it fails to recognise the existence and relevance of such knowledge.

There are nevertheless concrete problems in applying the body of social science knowledge in legal decision-making. In particular there is the difficulty of applying general understandings to particular cases. For example, access may be of critical importance to the healthy adjustment to divorce of children generally, but in the particular case the child may be damaged by it. For each generalisation presented in this book, there may be particular cases to which it should not apply. Researchers are aware of this danger (for example, Santrock et al, 1982:303), and the suggestion is in no way being made here to limit judicial discretion to deal with each case on its own particular facts and merits. The most that is being claimed is that the judiciary be aware of the general findings, of the probablities, as well as the limitations of current knowledge; that particular problems can be identified as such from a basis of knowledge of the general pattern; and that a priori assertions give way to informed and reasoned choices.

There remains the problem of judical discretion versus the application of rules. Previous certainty has already been eroded; the current width of judicial discretion is deplored by lawyers and clients of the legal system alike; thus the hope that the social sciences can fill the void with clear, certain, absolute answers. Ellsworth and Levy (1969) recommend for example assessment procedures to match parenting skills, custodial arrangements, and children. An example of this is McDermott et al's parent-child interaction test, an assessment procedure which focusses "on the emotional and psychological aspects of custody alternatives". McDermott et al argue that the custody decision-making process must include "a comprehensive framework of custody criteria which includes emotional and psychological criteria and allows for the changing developmental needs of children ... An ordering of criteria priorities is required" (McDermott et al, 1978:116). McDermott et al claim the value of psychiatry in creating clear legal criteria. The Group for the Advancement of Psychiatry (1980) advocate criteria on the basis of a family systems approach. Others recommend criteria on the basis of particular professional experience or expertise, or particular research findings.

The proponents of clear criteria for determining child custody all share a concern for the child's welfare, though solutions may differ. In contested cases where the exercise of the judicial function is unavoidable, rules or criteria are seen to be preferable to unlimited judicial discretion. In uncontested cases the role of these criteria is in a supervisory capacity; in theory at least parental autonomy to decide on the post-divorce arrangements for the children is assumed to be limited by criteria for state intervention in the best interest of the child; though in practice parental private ordering goes largely unchecked. The justification for state intervention on behalf of the children of divorce has been explored in chapter 6; it lies essentially in the potentiality of damage to these children, and in the new understandings of how such damage can be minimised. But the very notion of the welfare or best interests of the child is itself controversial, so that formulations of child custody criteria not only vary through different professional or research perspectives, but also through different understandings of the ultimate aim of the law which makes the welfare of the child "the first and paramount consideration" in custody cases.

It has already been seen that the welfare principle is essentially indeterminable. The substance of what conduces to the welfare of the child has changed and will change, but the very concept itself is open to differing interpretations. The most fundamental difference is between interpretations that seek to protect the child's welfare, and those that seek to attribute to children 'rights' to determine their own choices, between the right to protection and the right to self-determination. The use of the term 'right' in both these cases is confusing; in a legal context the former makes the child the object of legal intervention in the interests of his welfare: the latter at most makes the child the subject of legal rights which he may take steps to enforce, or at the least the subject of claims to a legal right for which he may seek recognition as an enforceable legal right. The former is the more common use of the term "children's rights" and permeates the child-saving or child protection philosophies; Freeman (1983a) describes it as the "rights as welfare tradition". The latter represents a more radical approach of "child liberation" (Freeman, 1983a). This seeks to give children legally enforceable rights of decision-making. Thus the right of children to choose their own post-divorce arrangements has been advocated (Bersoff, 1976). English law in fact recognises no cases where the child is the subject of legal rights which he may enforce. There are no available procedures whereby children can enforce their own rights, whether these are to protection, maintenance etc. (with the exception of the wardship procedure, which it has been argued could be initiated by children themselves (Lowe and White, 1979), but this is never done). In practice all children's rights are enforced on their behalf by adults, such as their parents or the state.

Freeman (1983a) observes that "in many cases where the case for children's rights is put, there is no conflict between children and their parents". It is where children's rights are claimed against their parents, that the "gravest of problems" arise (Freeman, 1983a). In divorce, it is now becoming apparent, the main interests of children and parents are usually in direct conflict. Children are repeatedly reported as expressing a wish that their parents were still married or would reconcile (Wallerstein and Kelly, 1980:306; Santrock et al, 1982:295; Steinman, 1982; Mitchell, 1983). A marriage which is unhappy for the parents may nevertheless be "comfortable" and "gratifying" for the children; there is no evidence that divorce is more beneficial or less stressful for children than an unhappy marriage (Wallerstein and Kelly, 1980:305-7). In divorce therefore the right of parents under the law to break up the marital home and family life is dramatically opposed to the wishes of the child. Only very few would deny the right of parents to divorce in the interests of their children's welfare. Wolff, for example, argues that divorce should be delayed until children are older (1981:123). More commonly the right to divorce may be surrounded by more complicated procedures and formalities where there are dependent children (as for example in Sweden). The parental right is thus given precedence; and children of divorce are not deemed to require legal intervention for the protection of their "rights as welfare", in the way that children who are abused or neglected by their parents are. Similarly access, sole custody or joint custody orders are made to parents, more in recognition of parental legal rights than in recognition of children's "rights as welfare".

The concept of children's rights to self-determination is therefore inappropriate from the very nature of the divorce context. It is also inappropriate, it is argued, as a matter of social fact. Divorce is not, legally or socially, treated as a circumstance in which the child's right to protection warrants state legal intervention to restrict parental autonomy. The fact of marriage breakdown with otherwise good parenting is not deemed to warrant upholding a child's right to protection. On divorce therefore parents and children are still considered to be part of a social unit, the family, in which interests and rights are not opposed to a degree requiring legal intervention, but in which interests and rights must be accommodated. How such interests and rights are accommodated depends, within a system of family autonomy, on the family decision-making process. It is common within this process for parents to impose decisions upon their children; indeed the decision to divorce is the major example of this, and one which society sanctions through its non-intervention. Similarly decisions giving sole custody to the mother.

The special psychological relationship of parent and child (usually created by a biological tie although not necessarily, i.e. the relationship may exist without a biological link as in adoption, or it may not exist despite the biological link: in other words the special relationship is in fact a social function) forms the context in which parental power of decision-making over children is sanctioned. Despite this position of power, there have been complaints that the needs of parents have been repressed by the twentieth century "ethos of child-focus" (Rapoport et al, 1977:3), that the process of reaction against the patriarchal family by "a child-focused, mother-oriented, expert-guided society" has produced its own crisis for parenthood: "Children first, last and always is no longer a tenable maxim for family life, on anyone's account" (Rapoport et al, 1977:14). Rapoport et al suggest therefore "an approach that clarifies the nature of the fit between parents' and children's lives ... a new conception based on an appreciation of how parents' preoccupations, needs and requirements can be reconciled with those of children" (1977:14).

This emphasis on parent-child or family interaction is particularly pertinent to the divorce process. The "fit" or accommodation of each parent's interests to or with the interests of their children must be worked out in a way that is acceptable, to the individuals concerned and to society. "Family systems" theory and family therapy thus seek to understand the origins of family problems and to resolve them in terms of interactions between the individuals, adults and children, who make up the family. There is nevertheless an ethos of child protection which must also be accommodated into the process. It is also a legal requirement of divorce through the welfare principle. This requires that "child-appropriate" decisions are made by parents. On divorce this means that parents' rights of self-determination must be exercised in such a way so as to minimise the damaging effects of those decisions on their children. It also suggests child-centred parental behaviour, i.e. "the parents' recognition of the child's status as an individual with rights and feelings that are worthy of respect. Although clashes of interests will inevitably arise between children and adults, child-centred parents voluntarily relinquish the authoritarian stance, and instead deliberately concede to the child the right to exercise choice and autonomy, to participate in decision-making, and generally to be taken seriously as a member of the family community" (Newson and Newson, 1976:312).

The view taken here then is that children's "rights as welfare" on divorce should require as a matter of law that parental decision-making within a system of family autonomy accommodates the interests of children in two ways: (i) by taking steps to minimise the known damaging effects for children of divorce, and (ii) by respecting the wishes and feelings of the children, even though these cannot be overriding. The parental duty to accommodate the interests of their children represents the right of parents to divorce but only if it is exercised responsibly. This concept of parental responsibility will be returned to subsequently.

THE WISHES OF THE CHILD

English statute law does not require that the wishes or views of a child, of any age, should be taken into consideration in custody cases. Other legal systems have made such provision for older children: in Australia for example the court may not make an order contrary to the wishes of a child over 14 years unless there are special circumstances (Family Law Act (Australia) 1975, s 64). English law has also provided that in reaching decisions relating to children in care, local authorities "shall so far as practicable ascertain the wishes and feelings of the child regarding the decision and give due consideration to them, having regard to his age and understanding" (Child Care Act 1980, s 18).

Judicial interpretation of the welfare principle has not produced any explicit policy concerning the wishes of the child, except that these may be taken into account in the judge's discretion. It has been seen that there are procedures available whereby the child's wishes may be made known to the court: welfare reports, judicial interviews, expert witnesses and separate legal representation (chapter 3). The main purpose of these procedures is not however to present the child's wishes, although in practice welfare officers do consider this to be an important function, and will usually consult children over the age of seven (Eekelaar, 1982:84). But in most cases, even contested ones, none of these procedures will be utilised. In most cases therefore the child's wishes may not in fact be known to the court at all, and certainly in uncontested cases parental private ordering will predominate.

Where the issue of the child's wishes has arisen, the courts have taken a pragmatic view. In B v B (1971) a boy of 16 wanted "to have nothing to do with his father". The court suspected that the boy's attitude was a result of his mother's and maternal grandfather's indoctrination and pressure. Although sympathising with the unimpeachable father, the court ordered that all access should cease, since to force the boy against his will to see his father "would do no good at all, on the contrary, it might well do him harm". In Re S (1967) a boy of 13½ wished to continue his education in England rather than go to California with his mother who had remarried. The court allowed the child's wishes to predominate; there was no suggestion of paternal pressure. But courts are also sceptical of deciding in accordance with the child's wishes. In Re S (1967) the court added:

> There are occasions when the wishes expressed by a boy of thirteen and a half may count for very little. In many cases it is unfortunately plain that they are reflections of the wishes of one of the parents which have been assiduously instilled into the ward and are not anything which could be called an independent exercise of his own will. Sometimes again the child's wishes, although genuinely his own, are so plainly contrary to his long term interest that the court may feel justified in disregarding them.

The suspicion of parental pressure or influence then is often raised, and used as a reason for dismissing consideration of the child's wishes. So also is concern for the long-term interests of the child.

Wallerstein and Kelly's observations lead them to similar conclusions. Noting particularly that 9 to 12 year olds displayed anger, hostility, willingness to be co-opted, take sides and label parents as "good" or "bad", they "doubt their capacity to make plans which would be in their best interests":

> Although the wishes of children always merit careful consideration, our work suggests that children below adolescence are not reliable judges of their own best interests and that their attitudes at the time of the divorce crisis may be very much at odds with their usual feelings and inclinations ... These observations and the fact that several of the youngsters with the most passionate

275

convictions at the time of the breakup later came shame-
facedly to regret their vehement statements at that time,
have increased our misgivings about relying on the expressed opinions and preferences of youngsters below adolescence in deciding the issues which arise in divorce-rela-
ted litigation (1980:314-5).

There is however another dimension to this issue: the burden which the very act of expressing a wish can place on some
children (and of which parents may be unaware) (Luepnitz, 1982:
52). Judges have recognised this problem. In Doncheff v Doncheff (1978) scepticism was voiced of the undoubted expression
of wishes by two girls of 15 and 13 and a boy of 9 to return
to live with their father:

> These children were on the horns of a dilemma. No doubt,
> if they were asked whether they would prefer to live with
> mother or father or both, they answer would be "with both".
> They had no such choice available to them and, in the
> difficult position in which they are placed, (influenced
> ... no doubt by the father) they had said: "with the
> father".

This view of the child's only real wish that his parents
had not created a situation in which the child was forced with
making a choice is one which is fully supported by the empirical evidence, as already described. It also leads to a further
reason for reducing the significance of the child's wishes.
This is that a requirement, either legal or informal, that the
child expresses a wish or makes a choice is actually invidious.
Indeed there are "explicit taboos" against children expressing
preferences between their parents (Newson and Newson, 1976:
293). If it is in the child's best interests to maintain a
continuing relationship with both parents after divorce then
the less opportunity there is for the child to feel guilt or
show conflicting loyalties between his parents the better.
Indeed post-divorce arrangements for children could seek to
minimise such 'either/or' choices completely, both for the
child and as already discussed for the parents. Certainly it
would not be in the child's interests to allow the custody
decision to be determined by the child's choice.
    Yet there is a certain distaste for suggesting that child-
ren's wishes should be ignored or overridden by parental autho-
ritarianism, even if out of concern to relieve the child of the
burden of the decision. A child-centred decision-making process must allow the child to be heard, especially in circumstances where family behaviour results in choices having to be
made. The weight of expert opinion would endorse such a view.
The Group for the Advancement of Psychiatry (1980) for example
recommends that "a child's opinion in custody disputes has
relevance but it is only one part of the evaluation".

The reality of parental private ordering of divorce and custody however is more often that the child is excluded not only from the decision-making process, but also from knowledge of its existence. Wallerstein and Kelly note that one-third of the children had "only a brief awareness of their parents' unhappiness prior to the divorce decision ... four-fifths of the youngest children were not provided with either an adequate explanation or assurance of continued contact" (1980:38-39). A British study confirms this pattern (Mitchell, 1983): two-thirds of parents avoided giving children an explanation of their break-up; half the children thought their family life had been happy; one-third of the children had never discussed with anyone their feelings about their parents' separation. Mitchell concludes that there is considerable misunderstanding by parents of their children's perceptions and needs.

Wallerstein and Kelly are concerned at the failure of parents to tell their children about the divorce:

> No single family in our study was able to provide the children with an adequate opportunity to express their concerns, to recognise with them that the divorce was indeed a family crisis ... No parent recognised that "telling" was not a pronouncement but should properly initiate a gradual process which would help the child both understand and integrate the important changes in his life. The parents' ability to be helpful to their children at this time undoubtedly contributed to the intensity of the children's response and, most particularly, to their fearfulness (1980:40).

"Telling the child" is thus not only "a signal opportunity (for the parents) to help the child cope with the crisis ... and a central component in the supportive role of the parent" (Wallerstein and Kelly, 1980:40); it may also be the preliminary to eliciting the child's opinion.

The dilemma is then how to accommodate the child's opinion to conflicting parental wishes. The reality of family life is that in many cases parental wishes will predominate over the decision to divorce itself, less so over consequent arrangements for child-care. The most that a requirement to consider the wishes of the child can achieve is to ensure that parental decisions are taken in the knowledge of the child's opinion. In this sense the decision-making process will respect the child as an individual, and may produce more child-appropriate or child-centred decisions. The fear that the burden on the child of expressing an opinion will be too great is nevertheless an important issue. There would be however a contradiction in parents recognising the need of the child to be told, and then excluding the child completely from the decision-making process. This is clearly a matter that requires sensitive handling by parents.

The age, or stage of emotional development, of the child has already been noted as a factor in determining the degree to which a child's opinion or wishes should be elicited or allowed to influence the decision, particularly in relation to pre-adolescent children (Wallerstein and Kelly, 1980:314-5). The age of the child may also be a factor in the timing of the parents' decision to divorce. One of the major contributions of Wallerstein and Kelly's study (1980) has been to explore the different responses of children to divorce according to their stage of development: pre-school and kindergarten (three to five year olds), young school-age (six to eight), older school-age (nine to twelve) and adolescent (thirteen to eighteen). The association between the timing of divorce and different kinds of vulnerabilities according to age and sex of the child has been confirmed (Hetherington et al, 1982; Kalter and Rembar, 1981). But the age and sex of the child were not thought by Wallerstein and Kelly (1980), nor by Kalter and Rembar (1981), to determine the later outcome of the divorce for the child. According to Wallerstein and Kelly, at five years after divorce, age or sex of the child were not relevant: "the factors which contributed to good outcome and to poor outcome were related to the quality of the relationship with both parents, the quality of life within the divorced family, and the extent to which the divorce itself provided the remedy which the adults sought" (1980:313).

TOWARDS A CONCEPT OF RESPONSIBLE DIVORCE

This review of current social science understandings of the consequences of divorce for children has led to two main conclusions, both of which turn on the concept of responsibility, that of parents and that of the legal system.

The main focus of this discussion is 'ordinary' divorces, presumably the vast majority where apart from the marriage breakdown there are otherwise two good parents. It has been seen that in these cases the formulation of the custody issue as one of "which parent?" is misguided both in its intention and effect. There is nothing inherent in either the psychological or social roles of mothers or fathers generally which indicates which is the 'better' parent. It is also argued that in 'ordinary' divorces there is usually nothing in the relationship of particular parent and child which suggests that one parent is 'better' than the other. Attempts at psychological assessment of the child's relationship with each parent are thus not only unproductive, but also ignore the social context which in practice most often dictates the custody decision. Mothers get custody thus, not because they are better parents but because both they and their husbands and the legal system normally expect that mothers will perform child-care functions.

The conclusion to be drawn from the evidence presented here is therefore that the question "which parent?" not only poses an unrealistic choice, but also an improper one. The phrasing of the question suggests that parental rights over the child are in issue, and that on divorce only one parent can have such rights. The evidence however is that neither implication is appropriate. The weight of expert opinion now is that the most critical factor in the child's successful adjustment to divorce is his continued contact with both parents. The child's right to be protected against the damage caused by losing one parent should thus be seen as creating a correlative duty or responsibility on each parent to continue his role as parent to his child. In the process the parent will benefit too: divorced parents grieve for an "absent child" as well as children grieve for an "absent parent" (Greif, 1979). This concept of parental responsibility means that parents should not be allowed to abandon the parenting role merely because the marriage which produced the children in question has ended. The parent's duty is to protect his child against the known damaging consequences of divorce by continuing the parent-child relationship to the maximum possible extent in the physical limitations imposed by the absence of one family home.

This concept of parental responsibility must in turn be promoted by the legal system. A law which in practice allows sole custody rights to one parent in the majority of cases, and which allows access decisions and practice to go largely unchecked is by implication encouraging parental irresponsibility on divorce:

> We believe that a societal attitude, and a consequent judicial attitude, that focused less on parental rights to custody and visitation and more on parental responsibilities and on the rights of children to have access to both parents would promote more constructive custody decisions (Group for the Advancement of Psychiatry, 1981:87).

More specifically it is proposed here that access or parental contact arrangements be a mandatory consideration and a presumption in all children of divorce cases, whether contested or not, and whether the parent applies for an access order or not.

The case for joint custody is a logical extension of these arguments, and is forcefully argued by many in the same spirit. The view taken here is slightly different. English law already provides for equal parental rights within marriage, and a joint custody order in practice adds little to the existing legal framework. Rather than make any order for custody whatsoever therefore, preservation of equal parental rights in the post-divorce situation is a more appropriate symbol of the continuing parent-child relationships, and their immunity to the breaking of the marital role. Preservation of the pre-divorce parent-child relationships will not only encourage a sense of continuing parental responsibility for children, but will also

279

by eliminating sole custody orders prevent the legal system either allowing or forcing parents to abdicate such responsibility. It will at the same time remove the opportunity for hostility and rejection which the 'either/or' world of present custody law encourages and allows.

These proposals have been made in the spirit of encouraging continuing parental responsibilities; they have also been made in the spirit of 'lowering the stakes' of custody cases. The fact that custody orders grant sole rights to one party and remove them from the other makes the stakes of the judicial decision, even if initiated by private ordering, too high. As Parkinson says, in contested cases, parties may believe they can 'win' or 'lose', but in fact everyone loses (1981:13). But this may also be true in uncontested cases, although the parents may not realise this at the time of the court order. The non-custodial parent may lose his child; the custodial parent may lose the opportunity to share the chores of childcare, and to enjoy well-adjusted children whose close relationship with their other parent is critical to their welfare.

Sole custody orders therefore have damaging consequences for a number of reasons: they impose a winner/loser choice, they encourage legal irresponsibility, and there is too much at stake in the decision. The judges themselves have recognised the validity of the last point. It has been seen that 'custody' did not always refer to full parental rights over children but was more akin to 'care'; Dipper v Dipper (1980) was an unsatisfactory attempt to revert to that earlier meaning of 'custody' in the interests of continuing a divorced and absent father's participation in his children's lives.

The solution proposed here in the interests of 'lowering the stakes' of custody decisions is a presumption that the equal parental rights of a subsisting marriage should continue after divorce, and that the only order a court makes should relate to the physical care of the child. In the interests of reducing confusion in terminology, this order might be called a "children's residence order". Such an order would specify where and with which parent the child will live; it could thus be for a joint, shared or sole residence in the same way that custody orders are. The purpose of the order from the point of view of the legal system will be less one of enforcing or supervising any particular arrangements but of requiring parents to take responsibility at the time of divorce for making arrangements for the physical care of their children and for both parents' participation in this. Residence orders, and also access or parental contact arrangements, will thus be made in the knowledge that both parents will continue to exercise legal responsibility, and rights, over major issues in the children's upbringing.

The objections against such a presumption are obvious; it is clear that there are some parents who, having to share legal rights over their children, will cause more damage to their children by their inability to co-operate, than in a 'winner-takes-all' scenario. The option must always be open to remove parental rights in the interests of the child, but only where serious attempts have been made to create a spousal relationship where equal parental rights can operate. But more importantly the presumption of equal parental rights gives rise to the same practical difficulties that have been noted in respect of joint custody. It may be that those issues over which consultation ought to take place should be specified in the law, or that greater use will be made of the power to apply to court for resolution of differences as provided for in the Guardianship Act 1973, s 1(3), and as recommended in Dipper v Dipper (1980).

The claim here is that with adequate counselling and conciliation support services the ideal of equal parental rights could work out far more often in practice. Moreover the benefits of a legal system which is seen to be taking positive steps to encourage continuing parental responsibility and participation after divorce will outweigh the practical disadvantages. The symbolic value of this new approach will doubtless also increase the number of cases where co-operation is feasible; the symbolic and educative function of the law should therefore have a powerful influence over parental behaviour in relation to their children after divorce. The responsibility of the legal system is thus to encourage parental responsibility; particularly through the types of orders which are available on divorce and the presumptions of equal parental rights, parental contact orders and residence orders.

The responsibility of the legal system however goes further. Current social science understandings of the effects of divorce for children now provide sufficient indicators or criteria of successful outcome for children for new legal procedures and principles to be devised. The criteria on which such procedures and principles should be based, and which are drawn from the body of evidence presented in this book are:

1. that society cannot afford to treat the children of divorce as pathological, to dwell on the damage of divorce, or attribute typical problems of childhood and adolescence to divorce;
2. that children can be damaged by divorce, especially where there are multiple stresses (in particular economic ones):
3. that the interests of parents and children on divorce are not coterminous, but at the same time are in 'ordinary' divorces interdependent, so that solutions must take account of the two-way process of parent-child interaction and reach a family resolution;
4. that the most important factor in the child's adjustment to divorce is the quality of the post-divorce arrangements for all members of the family: and these

can be quite independent of pre-divorce relationships;
5. that the seemingly most important element in the
   child's adjustment to divorce is a continuing relationship with both parents; the two other important
   factors are the quality of parenting given by the parent in charge of the child, and the existence of
   satisfactory support services which in the absence of
   extended families can mitigate the problems of isolation nowadays experienced by the nuclear family, particularly middle-class families.

The role of the legal system is to embody and pursue these
current interpretations of the welfare of the child. As a
matter of principle, in addition to the children's orders and
presumptions already discussed, these criteria could be written
into legislation (as some American states have listed factors
which are presumed to be in the best interests of the child
(Michigan Child Custody Act 1970, 722.23)), according to which
the welfare of the child must be measured. Procedures must
also be devised by which the legal system can seek to minimise
the known damage of divorce and to maximise the known factors
which result in successful coping. The Children's Appointment
is an obvious stage in the present procedure (although many
would say too late in the divorcing process) at which the welfare criteria could be operated, but at present it only pays
lip-service to the welfare of the child; partly because of the
cursory operation of the procedure, but partly also because
the legal system does not provide support services for counselling and conciliation by which a meaningful concern for the
child's welfare can be effected. The case for such support
services seems to be incontrovertible (Fine: 1974; Parkinson,
1982; Wallerstein and Kelly, 1980); it merely requires the
political will to provide them.
There remains the question of the role of the legal system
in respect of private ordering of divorce. In contested cases,
judicial decision-making is necessary, but support services
which offered counselling and conciliation might produce resolutions which allowed the presumptions of equal parental
rights, children's residence orders and parental contact
orders to stand. There should certainly be mandatory consideration of these presumptions in all cases. In uncontested cases,
the court's function must be to supervise parental agreements
on the basis of the welfare of the child criteria, in order to
identify cases where parental interests are in conflict with
children's interests, or where parents are failing to create
post-divorce arrangements which maximise the child's ability
to cope successfully with divorce. In many cases the role of
the court or its support services in uncontested cases may be
one of giving information or advice to parents on how they
might achieve more satisfactory post-divorce arrangements.
In cases of clear conflict or obvious damage to the child,

uncontested cases may be picked out for further investigation and support (as they already are by referral for a welfare report).

Children of divorce can be protected against damage to their psychological or emotional health and development. A society which desires and allows divorce on the scales now experienced is irresponsible if it fails to provide a legal system which encourages and helps parents to fulfil their responsibilities to protect their children. This is what "the welfare of the child is the first and paramount consideration" currently requires.

Buckley v Buckley (1973) Times 13 March   178
Buckley v Rice-Thomas (1554) 1 Pl Com 118   xii

Re C [1964] 3 All ER 483   80, 81
Re C 1973 (1979) 9 Family Law 50   75
Re C [1978] 2 All ER 230   36, 49
Re C(A) [1970] 1 All ER 309   156, 159, 177
Re C(MA) [1966] 1 WLR 646   81, 161, 204, 209
C v C (1971) Times 28 May   41, 233
C v C (1980) Court of Appeal, April 17. In M P M Richards
   (1982): Post-Divorce Arrangements for Children: A Psycho-
   logical Perspective. Journal of Social Welfare Law: 133-151
   259
C v C (1981) Times 2 December   86
Cadman v Cadman (1982) 12 Family Law 82   79, 80, 84
Re Carroll [1931] 1 KB 317   126
Cartlidge v Cartlidge (1862) 2 Sw & Tr 567   120
Charlton v Lings (1868) LR 4 CP 374   119
Clarke-Hunt v Newcombe (1983) 13 Family Law 20   54, 58
Clissold v Clissold (1964) 108 Sol Jo 220   24, 29
Clode v Clode (1982) 3 Family Law Reports 360   55
Clout v Clout and Hollebone (1861) 2 Sw & Tr 391   95, 120, 231
Codrington v Codrington (1864) 3 Sw & Tr 496   95, 120
Re Collins [1950] 1 All ER 1057   219
Condom v Vallum (1887) 57 L T 154   24, 125
Cook v Cook [1978] 3 All ER 1009   19
Crick v Crick (1977) 7 Family Law 239   51
Re Curtis (1859) 28 LJ Ch 458   97

Re D [1973] 3 All ER 1001   44
Re D [1977] 1 All ER 145   47, 178, 181
Re D (1980) Adoption and Fostering, Part 4 p 58   47
D v B [1977] 3 All ER 751   41, 242
D v B [1979] 1 All ER 92   51
D v D (1980) 10 Family Law 53   78
D v M [1982] 3 WLR 891   55, 57, 179, 205
D'Alton v D'Alton (1878) 4 P D 87   100, 103
De Manneville v De Manneville (1804) 10 Ves 52   95, 112, 114
Dipper v Dipper [1980] 2 All ER 722   27, 28, 257, 258, 268,
   280, 281
Dodd v Dodd (1906) Times 28 April   132, 140
Doncheff v Doncheff (1978) 8 Family Law 205   276

Re E [1964] 1 WLR 51   80
Re E [1967] 2 All ER 811   159
Re EO (1973) Times 15 February   81
Re Elderton [1883] 25 Ch D 220   98
England v England (1980) 10 Family Law 86   19
Eshak v Nowojeski (1980) Times 19 November   213
Eyre v Shaftesbury (1722) 2 P Wms 112   112

Re F [1969] 2 All ER 766   16, 17 223, 225, 228
Re F [1976] 1 All ER 417   55
F v S [1973] Fam 203   32
Faulkner v Faulkner (1981) 2 Family Law Reports 115   55, 57
Re Fynn (1848) 2 De G and Sm 457   96, 97, 123, 155

Re G [1899] 1 Ch 719   155
G v G (1963) Times 3 May   233
G v G (1976) 6 Family Law 43   206
G v G (1981) 11 Family Law 149   178
Re Goldsworthy [1876] 2 QB 75   98, 124, 155
Goodfellow v Goodfellow (1968) 112 Sol Jo 322   156
Greenhill v Greenhill (1836) 1 Curt 462   113
Re Gyngall [1893] 2 QB 232   31, 78, 100, 153, 157, 203

Re H (1974) Times 26 November   44
Re H (1980) Times 19 July   178
H v H [1974] 1 All ER 1145   79
H v H (1981) Court of Appeal, June 11. In M P M Richards
   (1982): Post-Divorce Arrangements for Children: A Psycho-
   logical Perspective. Journal of Social Welfare Law: 133-151
   259
H v H and C [1969] 1 All ER 262   160, 205
Re Halliday's Estate ex p Woodward (1852) 21 LTOS 17   98, 124
Hamilton v Hector (1872) LR 13 Eq 511   98, 121
Handley v Handley [1891] P 124   131, 155, 232
Hart v Hart (1881) 18 Ch D 670   122
Heathcoat v Heathcoat (1864) 10 L T 389n   96
Hewer v Bryant [1970] 1 QB 357   24, 25, 27
Ex p Hopkins (1732) 2 P Wms 152   78, 94
Hunt v Hunt (1884) 28 Ch D 606   122
Hutchinson v Hutchinson (1978) 8 Family Law 140   224
Hyde v Hyde (1859) 29 LJ PM & A 150   121, 232

Re J [1973] Fam 106   236
J v C [1970] A C 668   3, 15, 16, 80, 81, 105, 159, 160, 204
Jump v Jump (1883) 8 P D 159   98, 122
Jussa v Jussa [1972] 1 W L R 881   29, 33, 258, 259

Re K [1977] 1 All ER 647   16, 156
Re K [1977](a) 2 All ER 737   42, 178
Re K (1978) Law Society Gazette 12 July   48

Re L [1962] 3 All ER 1   15, 156, 232
Re LA (1978) Times 27 April   47, 220
L v F (1978) Times 1 August   53, 214
Laxton v Laxton [1966] 2 All ER 977   157
Ex p Lytton (1781) cited in 5 East 222   94, 111

Re M [1967] 3 All ER 1071   28, 157
M v M [1973] 2 All ER 81   22, 34, 40, 41, 234, 247, 248

M v M (1980) 1 Family Law Reports 77   56-58, 156, 177, 179
M(P) v M(C) (1971) 115 Sol Jo 444   233
Manders v Manders (1890) 63 Law Times 627   231
Re Mathieson (1918) 87 LJ Ch 445   101
McDermott v McDermott (1980) 10 Family Law 145   19
Re McGrath [1893] 1 Ch 143   5, 99, 103, 131, 157, 160, 203
Monk v Monk (1979) Law Society Gazette 31 January   33

Re N [1974] Fam 40   22, 37-39, 42, 43
Re Newton [1896] 1 Ch 740   100
Noble v Thompson (1979) New Law Journal 11 October   81

Re O [1962] 2 All ER 10   218
Re O [1964] 1 All ER 789   160
Re O'Hara [1900] 2 IR 232   78, 158, 203
Official Solicitor v K [1965] AC 201   75, 78, 160

Re P [1967] 1 WLR 818   218
P v McK (1973) Times 28 June   75
Philip v Philip (1872) 41 LJ P & M 89   96, 121, 232
Re Plomley (1888) 4 TLR 256   99
Practice Direction [1980] 1 All ER 813   72, 259
Practice Direction (Joint Custody) [1980] 1 All ER 784   29
Practice Direction [1980](a) 1 All ER 1040   40, 86
Practice Direction [1981] 1 WLR 1162   74, 75
Practice Direction [1982] 3 All ER 988   70
Practice Direction [1982](a) 1 WLR 118   84
Practice Direction [1983] 1 WLR 416   85
Pryor v Pryor [1947] P 64   220
Ex p Pulbrook (1847) 11 JP Jo 102   124

Re R (1963) Times 8 October   233
Re R [1974] 1 All ER 1033   13, 220
Re R(M) [1966] 3 All ER 58   159
R v R (1980) 10 Family Law 56   42
R(BM) v R(DN) [1978] 2 All ER 33   50, 51
R v Austin [1981] 1 All ER 374   22
R v Clarke (1857) 7 El & Bl 194   126
R v De Manneville (1804) 5 East 221   94, 112
R v Dobbyn (1818) 4 Ad & El 644n   94
R v Greenhill (1836) 4 A & E 624   94, 113
R v Gyngall [1893] 2 QB 232   31, 78, 100, 153, 157, 203
R v Isley (1836) 5 Ad & El 441   94
R v Smith in Re Boreham (1853) 22 LJQB 116   122
Rashid v Rashid (1979) 9 Family Law 118   41
Richards v Richards [1983] 3 WLR 173   213, 215
Roach v Garvan (1748) 1 Ves Sen 157   112

Re S [1958] 1 All ER 783   156, 159
Re S [1967] 1 All ER 202   32, 79, 80, 275
Re S (1975) 5 Family Law 88   47

Re S [1977] 3 All ER 671   46, 47
S v O (1978) 8 Family Law 11   41
S v S (1968) 112 Sol Jo 294   24, 25
S v S (1971) Times 15 July   79, 178
S v S (1971)(a) Times 24 March   205
S v S (1973) 177 Sol Jo 34   223
S v S (1980) 1 Family Law Reports 143   178, 181
S v S and P [1962] 2 All ER 1   233
S(BD) v S(DJ) [1977] 1 All ER 656   16
Re Scanlon (1888) 40 Ch D 200   99
Shears v Shears (1973) 3 Family Law 45   42
Shelley v Westbrooke (1817) Jac 266   112
Shillito v Collett (1860) 24 J P 660   123
Re Smart [1892] AC 425   130, 151
Smith v Smith (1745) 3 Atk 304   94
Smith v Smith [1975] 2 All ER 19   178, 213
Smith v Smith (1980) 10 Family Law 50   179
Re Spence (1847) 2 Ph 247   154
Spratt v Spratt (1858) 1 Sw & Tr 215   120
Stark v Stark and Hitchins [1910] P 190   131, 152, 155, 232,
   247
Swift v Swift (1865) 4 De GJ & Sm 710   121
Symington v Symington (1875) LR 2 Sc and Div 415   95, 121, 232

Re T [1963] Ch 238   34, 50
Re T (1974) Times 16 January   78
Re T (1980) 1 Family Law Reports 59   75
Re Taylor [1976] 4 Ch D 157   98
Taylor v Taylor (1870) 39 LJ (P and M) 23   242
Re Thain [1926] Ch 676   5, 158, 159, 204, 209, 218
Thomas v Roberts (1850) 3 De G & SM 758   124
Thompson v Thompson (1975) Times 12 March   75
Re Turner (1872) 41 LJQB 142   126

Ullman v Ullman (1912) 151 AD 419, 135 NYS 1080   155

Vansittart v Vansittart (1858) 4 K & J 62   121
Villareal v Mellish (1737) 2 Swans 533   112

Re W (1963) cited in Re C [1964] 3 All ER 483   81
Re W [1965] 3 All ER 231   159, 160/161, 204
Re WG (1976) 6 Family Law 210   53, 54
Re W(JC) [1963] 2 All ER 706   24, 155
W v A [1981] 1 All ER 100   53
W v W [1926] P 111   159, 219
W v W (1971) Times 1 April   74
Wakeham v Wakeham [1954] 1 All ER 434   24, 155
Ward v Laverty [1925] AC 101   217
Warde v Warde (1849) 2 Ph 786   97, 121, 124
Wellesley v Duke of Beaufort (1827) 2 Russ 22   95
Westneath v Westneath (1821) Jac 264   111

BIBLIOGRAPHY

Abarbanel, A (1977), 'Shared Parenting after Separation and
  Divorce: A Study of Joint Custody', American Journal of
  Orthopsychiatry 49: 320-329
Ahrons, C (1981), 'The Continuing Co-parental Relationship
  between Divorced Spouses', American Journal of Orthopsychia-
  try 51: 415-428
Ainsworth, M D S, Bell, S M and Stanton, D J (1976),
  'Infant-Mother Attachment and Social Development' in
  M P M Richards (ed) The Integration of a Child into a Social
  World, Cambridge: Cambridge University Press
Alexander, S (1976), 'Women's Work in Nineteenth Century
  London, A Study of the Years 1820-50' in J Mitchell and
  A Oakley (eds) The Rights and Wrongs of Women, Harmondsworth:
  Penguin
Anderson, M (1980), Approaches to the History of the Western
  Family, 1500-1914, London: Macmillan
Anderson, M (1971), Family Structure in Nineteenth Century
  Lancashire, Cambridge: Cambridge University Press
Andry, R G (1968), 'Family Relationships, Fathers and the Law'
  in E Miller (ed) Foundations of Child Psychiatry, Oxford:
  Pergamon
Aries, P (1962), Centuries of Childhood, Harmondsworth:
  Penguin, 1973

Backett, K C (1982), Mothers and Fathers, New York: St Martin's
  Press
Bates, F (1976), 'Expert Evidence in Cases involving Children'
  in F Bates (ed) The Child and the Law, New York: Oceana
Bauer C and Ritt L (1979), Free and Enobled, London: Pergamon
Baumrind, D (1971), 'Current Patterns of Parental Authority',
  Developmental Psychology Monographs 4 (2)
Beal, E (1979), 'Children of Divorce: A Family Systems Per-
  spective', Journal of Social Issues 35: 140-154
Beales, H L (1966), 'The Victorian Family' in Ideas and Beliefs
  of the Victorians, New York: Dutton
Bell, R and Harper, L (1977), Child Effects on Adults,
  New Jersey: Lawrence Erlbaum
293

Benedek, R S and Benedek, E P (1977), 'Postdivorce Visitation: A Child's Right', Journal of American Academy of Child Psychiatry 16:256-271

Benedek R S and Benedek E P (1979), 'Children of Divorce: Can We Meet Their Needs', Journal of Social Issues 35: 155-169

Benians, R (1982), 'Preserving Parental Contact' in Family Rights Group, Fostering Parental Contact, London: FRG

Bernal, J H (1976), 'Attachment: Some Problems and Possibilities' in M P M Richards (ed) The Integration of a Child into a Social World, Cambridge: Cambridge University Press

Bersoff, D (1976), 'Representation for Children in Custody Decisions', Journal of Family Law 15: 27-49

Besant, A (1893), Autobiography, London: Unwin

Bevan, H (1973), The Law Relating to Children, London: Butterworths

Bevan, H and Parry, M (1978), Children Act 1975, London: Butterworths

Black, E C (ed) (1973), Victorian Culture and Society, London: Macmillan

Bohannan, P (ed) (1970), Divorce and After, New York: Doubleday

Bowlby, J (1951), Maternal Care and Mental Health, Geneva: WHO

Bowlby, J (1969), Attachment, Harmondsworth: Penguin

Bowlby, J (1972), Child Care and the Growth of Love, Harmondsworth: Penguin

Bradley, D (1976), 'Realism in Divorce Law', New Law Journal December 6: 1204

Bromley, P (1976), Family Law, 5th edition, London:Butterworths

Bromley, P (1981), Family Law, 6th edition, London:Butterworths

Brophy, J (1982), 'Parental Rights and Children's Welfare: some problems of feminists' strategy in the 1920s', International Journal of the Sociology of Law 10:149-168

Brown, C A, Reldberg, R, Fox, E M and Kohen, J (1976), 'Divorce: Chance of a New Lifetime', Journal of Social Issues 32

Brown, J A C (1961), Freud and the Post-Freudians, Harmondsworth: Penguin

Burgoyne, J and Clark, D (1982a), 'Reconstituted Families' in R N Rapoport, M P Fogarty and R Rapoport (eds), Families in Britain, London: Routledge & Kegan Paul

Burgoyne, J (1982b), 'Contemporary Expectations of Marriage and Partnership' in Change in Marriage, Rugby: National Marriage Guidance Council

Caird, M (1890), 'The Emancipation of the Family' in P Hollis, Women in Public: The Women's Movement 1850-1900, London, George Allen & Unwin

Change in Marriage (1982), Rugby: National Marriage Guidance Council

Christ, C (1977), 'Victorian Masculinity and the Angel in the House' in M Vicinus (ed) A Widening Sphere, Indiana: Indiana University Press

Clarke, A M and Clarke, A D B (1976), Early Experience: Myth
and Evidence, London: Open Books
Cooper, E (1982), 'Children and Marriage' in Change in
Marriage, Rugby: National Marriage Guidance Council
Coveney, P (1967), The Image of Childhood, Harmondsworth:
Penguin

Dally, A (1982), Inventing Motherhood, London: Burnett Books
Davidoff, L, L'Esperance, J, and Newby, H (1976), 'Landscape
with Figures: Home and Community in English Society' in
J Mitchell and A Oakley (eds) The Rights and Wrongs of
Women, Harmondsworth: Penguin
Davis, G and Bader, K (1983), 'In-Court Mediation Observed',
New Law Journal April 15 and 29: 355-357, 403-405
Davis, G, McLeod, A and Murch, M (1983), 'Undefended Divorces:
should s 41 of the Matrimonial Causes Act 1973 be repealed?'
Modern Law Review 46:121-146
Davis, G and Murch, M (1977), 'Implications of the Special
Procedure in Divorce', Family Law 7: 71-78
de Mause, L (1974), The History of Childhood, New York: Psycho-
history Press
Departmental Committee on the Adoption of Children (1972)
(Houghton Committee), Cmnd. 5107, 1972. London: HMSO
Despert, J L (1953), Children of Divorce, New York: Doubleday
Dickens, B (1978), 'Representing the Child in the Courts' in
I Baxter and M Eberts (eds) The Child and the Courts, Toronto:
Carswell
Dickens, B (1981), 'The Modern Function and Limits of Parental
Rights', Law Quarterly Review 97: 462-474
Dingwall, R, Eekelaar, J and Murray, T (1983), The Protection
of Children: State Intervention and Family Life, Oxford:
Blackwell
Dodds, M (1983), 'Children and Divorce', Journal of Social
Welfare Law: 228-237

Eekelaar, J M (1973), 'What are Parental Rights', Law Quarterly
Review 89: 210-234
Eekelaar, J, Clive, E, with Clarke, K and Raikes, S (1977),
Custody After Divorce, Oxford: Centre for Socio-Legal Studies
Eekelaar, J (1982), 'Children in Divorce: Some Further Data',
Oxford Journal of Legal Studies 2: 63-85
Ellsworth, P C and Levy, R J (1969), 'Legislative reform of
child custody adjudication', Law and Society Review 4:
167-233
Elmy, E (1886), English Woman's Review: 221
Elston, E, Fuller, J, Murch, M (1975), 'Judicial Hearings of
Undefended Divorce Petitions', Modern Law Review 38: 609
Erikson, E (1950), Childhood and Society, Harmondsworth:
Penguin
Eversley, D and Bonnerjea, L (1982), 'Social Change and Indi-
cators of Diversity' in R N Rapoport, M P Fogarty and

R Rapoport (eds) Families in Britain, London: Routledge & Kegan Paul

Families Need Fathers (1974), A Society for Equal Parental Rights, London: FNF

Family Advocate (1982), 'Joint Custody: Whose Needs does it Serve?', Family Advocate 5, 2

Ferri, E (1976), Growing Up in a One Parent Family, Slough: NFER Publishing Company

Finer Report (1974), Report of the Committee on One Parent Families, Cmnd 5629, London: HMSO

Flandrin, J-L (1979), Families in Former Times, Cambridge: Cambridge University Press

Fogarty, M and Rodgers, B (1982), 'Family Policy - International Perspectives' in R N Rapoport, M P Fogarty and R Rapoport (eds) Families in Britain, London: Routledge & Kegan Paul

Foster, H and Freed, D (1972), 'Bill of Rights for Children', Family Law Quarterly 6: 343

Freeman, M D A (1977), 'First Considerations in Adoption Law', New Law Journal July 14

Freeman, M D A (1983), 'Freedom and the Welfare State: Child-Rearing, Parental Autonomy and State Intervention', Journal of Social Welfare Law 70-91

Freeman, M D A (1983a), 'The Concept of Children's Rights' in H Geach and E Szwed (eds) Providing Civil Justice for Children, London: Edward Arnold

Fuller, R and Stevenson, O (1979), The Impact of Social Policy on Transmitted Deprivation: A Literature Review, DHSS/SSRC Transmitted Deprivation Programme, University of Keele

Fulton, J (1979), 'Parental Reports of Children's Post-divorce Adjustment', Journal of Social Issues 35: 126-139

Gardner, R (1980) in New York Times Magazine, February 3: 32-46

Gasser, R D and Taylor, C M (1976), 'Role Adjustment of Single Parent Fathers with Dependent Children', The Family Co-ordinator 25: 397-401

Gavron, H (1966), The Captive Wife, Harmondsworth: Penguin

George, V and Wilding, P (1972), Motherless Families, London: Routledge & Kegan Paul

Gerard, A (1981), The Frustrations of s 41, unpublished manuscript presented to International Society of Family Law/ Society of Public Teachers of Law Family Law Group, University of Newcastle

Gersick, K (1979), 'Fathers by Choice: Divorced Men who Receive Custody of their Children' in G Levinger and O Moles (eds) Divorce and Separation, New York: Basic Books

Giller, H and Maidment, S (1983), 'Representation of Children: Does More Mean Better?' in J M Eekelaar and S N Katz (eds) The Resolution of Family Conflict, Canada: Butterworths

Giller, H and Morris, A (1982), 'Independent Social Workers and the Courts: Advise, Resist and Defend', Journal of Social Welfare Law: 29-41

Gingerbread/Families Need Fathers (1982), Divided Children: A Survey of Access to Children after Divorce, London: Gingerbread and Families Need Fathers

Goldberg, S (1977), The Inevitability of Patriarchy, London: Temple Smith

Goldstein, J, Freud, A and Solnit, A J (1973), Beyond the Best Interests of the Child, New York: Free Press

Goldstein, J, Freud, A and Solnit, A J (1980), Before the Best Interests of the Child, London: Burnett Books

Goldzband, M (1982), Consulting in Child Custody, Lexington Massachusetts: D C Heath

Goode, W J (1956), After Divorce, New York: Free Press

Gowler, D and Legge, K (1982), 'Dual-worker Families' in R N Rapoport, M P Fogarty and R Rapoport (eds) Families in Britain, London: Routledge & Kegan Paul

Graveson, R H and Crane, F R (1957), A Century of Family Law, London: Sweet and Maxwell

Graveson, R H (1948), 'The Restless Spirit of English Law' in G Keeton and G Schwarzenberger (eds) Jeremy Bentham and the Law, London: Stevens

Green, M (1976), Goodbye Father, London: Routledge & Kegan Paul

Greif, J (1979), 'Fathers, Children, and Joint Custody', American Journal of Orthopsychiatry 49: 311-319

Griew, E and Bissett-Johnson, A (1975), 'Supervision Orders in Matrimonial and Guardianship Cases', Social Work Today: 322

Group for the Advancement of Psychiatry (1980), Divorce, Child Custody, and the Family, San Francisco: Jossey-Bass

Guardian (1976) November 12

Gurin, G, Veroff, J and Feld, S (1960), Americans and their Mental Health, New York: Basic Books

Hall, F, Pawlby, S J and Wolkind, S (1979), 'Early Life Experiences and Later Mothering Behaviour: A Study of Mothers and their 20-week old Babies' in D Shaffer and J Dunn (eds) The First Years of Life:Psychological and Medical Implications of Early Experience, New York: Wiley

Hall, J C (1972), 'The Waning of Parental Rights', Cambridge Law Journal 31: 248-265

Hart, N (1976), When Marriage Ends: A Study in Status Passage, London: Tavistock

Henderson, R W (1981), Parent-Child Interaction: Theory, Research and Prospects, New York: Academic Press

Herbert, G W and Wilson, H (1978), Parents and Children in the Inner City, London: Routledge & Kegan Paul

Hess, R D and Camara, K A (1979), 'Post-divorce family relationships as mediating factors in the consequences of divorce for children', Journal of Social Issues 35: 79-96

Herzog, E and Sudia, C E (1973), 'Children in Fatherless Families' in B M Caldwell and H N Ricciuti (eds) Review of Child Development Research Volume 3, Chicago: University of Chicago Press

Hetherington, E M (1981), 'Children and Divorce' in R W Henderson (ed) Parent-Child Interaction: Theory, Research and Prospects, New York: Academic Press

Hetherington, E M, Cox, M and Cox, R (1978), 'The Aftermath of Divorce' in J H Stevens and M Mathews (eds) Mother-Child Father-Child Relationships, Washington DC: National Association for the Education of Young Children

Hetherington, E M, Cox, M and Cox, R (1979), 'Play and Social Interaction in Children following Divorce', Journal of Social Issues, 35: 26-49

Hetherington, E M, Cox, M and Cox, R (1982), 'Effects of Divorce on Parents and Children' in M E Lamb (ed) Non-Traditional Families: Parenting and Child Development, New Jersey: Lawrence Erlbaum

Hewitt, M (1958), Wives and Mothers in Victorian Industry, London: Rockcliff

Hilgendorf, L (1981), Social Workers and Solicitors in Child Care Cases, London:HMSO

Hipgrave, T (1981), 'Child-Rearing by Lone Fathers' in R Chester, P Diggory and M B Sutherland (eds) Changing Patterns of Child Bearing and Child Rearing, London: Academic Press

Hipgrave, T (1982), 'Lone Fatherhood: A Problematic Status' in L McKee and M O'Brien (eds) The Father Figure, London: Tavistock Publications

Hoeffer, B (1981), 'Children's Acquisition of Sex-Role Behaviour in Lesbian-Mother Families', American Journal of Orthopsychiatry 51: 536-544

Holcombe, L (1977), 'Victorian Wives and Property: Reform of the Married Women's Property Law 1857-1882' in M Vicinus (ed) A Widening Sphere, Indiana: Indiana University Press

Holdsworth, W (1922-1972), A History of English Law, Volume III, London: Methuen

Hollis, P (1979), Women in Public Life: The Women's Movement 1850-1900, London: Allen & Unwin

Hooper, Anne (1981), Divorce and Your Children, London: Allen & Unwin

Horwill, F (1979), The Outcome of Custody Cases in the Family Court of Australia, unpublished paper, Melbourne: Family Court of Australia Counselling Service

Houghton Committee (1972), Departmental Committee on the Adoption of Children, Cmnd 5107, 1972, London: HMSO

Humphries, S (1981), Hooligans or Rebels?, Oxford: Oxford University Press

Hunt, M M (1968), The World of the Formerly Married, London: Allen Lane

Illsley, R and Thompson, B (1961), 'Women from Broken Homes',
  Sociological Review 9: 27-54
Infant Mental Health Journal (1981), 'Fathers and Infants',
  Infant Mental Health Journal 2: 213-292

Judicial Statistics (1980), Cmnd 8436, London: HMSO
Judicial Statistics (1981), Cmnd 8770, London: HMSO
Justice (1975), Parental Rights and Duties and Custody Suits,
  London: Justice, British Section of the International
  Commission of Jurists and Stevens

Kadushin, A (1971), 'Child Welfare' in H S Maas (ed) Research
  in the Social Services: A Five Year Review, USA: National
  Association of Social Workers
Kadushin, A (1976), 'Adopting Older Children: Summary and
  Implications' in A M Clarke and A D B Clarke Family
  Experience: Myth and Evidence, London: Open Books
Kalter, N and Rembar, J (1981), 'The Significance of a Child's
  Age at the time of Parental Divorce', American Journal of
  Orthopsychiatry 51: 85-100
Katkin, D, Bullington, B and Levene, M (1974), 'Above and
  Beyond the Best Interests of the Child: An Inquiry into the
  Relationship between Social Science and Social Action',
  Law and Society Review 8: 669-687
Kellmer-Pringle, M (1974), The Needs of Children, London:
  Hutchinson
Kessen, W (1965), The Child, New York: Wiley
King, M (1975), The Times July 18
King, M (1981), 'Welfare and Justice' in M King (ed) Childhood
  Welfare and Justice, London: Batsford
Kirkpatrick, M, Smith, C and Roy, R (1981), 'Lesbian Mothers
  and their Children: A Comparative Study', American Journal
  of Orthopsychiatry 51: 545-551
Kohn, M L (1971), 'Social Class and Parent-Child Relationships'
  in M Anderson (ed) Sociology of the Family, Harmondsworth:
  Penguin
Kotelchuk, M (1972), 'The Nature of the Child's Tie to his
  Father', doctoral dissertation, Harvard University. Cited
  in M E Lamb, 'The Father's Role in the Infant's Social World'
  in J H Stevens and M Mathews (eds)(1978) Mother-Child Father-
  Child Relationships, Washington DC: National Association for
  the Education of Young Children
Kram, S W and Frank, N A (1982), The Law of Child Custody,
  Lexington, Massachusetts: D C Heath
Kulka, R A and Weingarten, H (1979), 'The Long-term Effects of
  Parental Divorce in Childhood on Adult Adjustment', Journal
  of Social Issues 35: 50-78

Lamb, M E (ed)(1976), The Role of the Father in Child
  Development, New York: Wiley
Lamb, M E (1978), 'The Father's Role in the Infant's Social

World' in J H Stevens and M Mathews (eds) <u>Mother-Child</u>
<u>Father-Child Relationships</u>, Washington DC: National Associ-
ation for the Education of Young Children

Lamb, M E (ed)(1982), <u>Non-Traditional Families: Parenting and</u>
<u>Child Development</u>, New Jersey: Lawrence Erlbaum

Lamb, M E (1982a), 'Sibling Relationships Across the Lifespan:
An Overview and Introduction' in M E Lamb and B Sutton-Smith
(eds) <u>Sibling Relationships: Their Nature and Significance</u>
<u>Across the Lifespan</u>, New Jersey: Lawrence Erlbaum

Langner, T S and Michael, S T (1963), <u>Life Stress and Mental</u>
<u>Health</u>, New York: Collier-Macmillan

Laslett, P (ed)(1972), <u>Household and Family in Past Time</u>,
Cambridge: Cambridge University Press

Laslett, P (1977), <u>Family Life and Illicit Love in Earlier</u>
<u>Generations</u>, Cambridge: Cambridge University Press

Law Commission (1968), Working Paper No 15, <u>Arrangements for</u>
<u>the Care and Upbringing of Children</u>, London: Law Commission

Law Commission (1973), Working Paper No 53, <u>Matrimonial</u>
<u>Proceedings in Magistrates' Courts</u>, London: HMSO

Law Commission (1977), <u>Report on Matrimonial Proceedings in</u>
<u>Magistrates' Courts</u>, No 77, HC 637, 1976-77, London: HMSO

Law Commission (1981), <u>Financial Consequences of Divorce</u>,
No 112, HC 68, 1981-82, London: HMSO

Leete, R (1978), 'One Parent Families. Numbers and Characteristics', <u>Population Trends</u> 13, London: HMSO

Leete, R (1979), <u>Changing Patterns of Family Formation and</u>
<u>Dissolution in England and Wales 1964-76</u>, OPCS, London: HMSO

Levin, J (1974), 'Step-parents and Guardians', <u>New Law Journal</u>
124:507

Levitin, T E (1979), 'Children of Divorce. An Introduction',
<u>Journal of Social Issues</u> 35: 1-25

Levy, R J (1982), <u>Custody Investigations in Divorce Cases</u>,
unpublished manuscript: University of Minnesota

Lewis, C (1982), 'The development of father-infant relationships', unpublished PhD thesis, Nottingham University.
Cited in N Beail and J McGuire (eds) <u>Fathers: Psychological</u>
<u>Perspectives</u>, London: Junction Books

Lewis, C, Newson, E and Newson, J (1982), 'Father Participation
through Childhood and its Relationship with Career Aspirations
and Delinquency' in N Beail and J McGuire (eds) <u>Fathers:</u>
<u>Psychological Perspectives</u>, London: Junction Books

Lomax, E (1978), <u>Science and Patterns of Child Care</u>,
San Francisco: W H Freeman & Co

Lord Chancellor (1981), <u>New Law Journal</u>, May 21

Lowe, N and White, R (1979), <u>Wards of Court</u>, London: Butterworths

Luepnitz, D (1982), <u>Child Custody: A Study of Families After</u>
<u>Divorce</u>, Lexington, Massachusetts: D C Heath

Maccoby, E E (1980), <u>Social Development: Psychological Growth</u>
<u>and the Parent-Child Relationship</u>, New York: Harcourt, Brace
Jovanovitch
300

Maddox, B (1975), The Half-Parent, New York: Signet
Maidment, S (1975), 'Access Conditions in Custody Orders',
British Journal of Law and Society 2: 182-200
Maidment, S (1976), 'A Study in Child Custody', Family Law 6:
200
Maidment, S (1976a) 'The Step-Relationship and its Legal
Status', Anglo-American Law Review 5: 259
Maidment, S (1980), 'Step-Parents and Step-Children: Legal
Relationships in Serial Unions' in J Eekelaar and S Katz
Marriage and Cohabitation in Contemporary Societies, Canada:
Butterworths
Maidment, S (1980), 'Matrimonial Statistics 1979', New Law
Journal December 11: 1168-1170
Maidment, S (1981), Child Custody: What Chance for Fathers,
London: National Council for One-Parent Families
Marsden, D (1973), Mothers Alone, Harmondsworth: Penguin
Marshall, D (1973), Industrial England 1776-1851, London:
Routledge & Kegan Paul
Masson, J and Burgoyne, J (1979), 'The English Stepfamily',
paper presented to the Third World Conference of the Inter-
national Society on Family Law, Uppsala, June
Masson, J and Norbury, D (1982), 'Step-parent Adoption',
Adoption and Fostering 6(1): 7-10
McDermott, J (1970), 'Divorce and its Psychiatric Sequelae in
Children', Archives of General Psychiatry 23: 421-428
McDermott, J F, Wen-Shing Tseng, Char, W F, Fukunaga, C S
(1978), 'Child Custody Decision Making: The Search for
Improvement', Journal of American Academy of Child Psychiatry
17: 104-116
McGlaughlin, A (1981), 'Generational Continuities in Child-
Rearing Practices' in R Chester, P Diggory and M B Sutherland
Changing Patterns of Child Bearing and Child Rearing, London:
Academic Press
McGreal, C E (1981) in H E Fitzgerald and C E McGreal (eds)
Fathers and Infants, USA: Human Sciences Press
McGregor, O (1957), Divorce in England, London: Heinemann
McKee, L (1982), 'Fathers' Participation in infant care: A
critique' in L McKee and M O'Brien (eds) The Father Figure,
London: Tavistock
McLoughlin, D (1980), Custody and Divorce, unpublished MA
thesis, University of York
McWilliams-Tullberg, R (1977),'Women and Degrees at Cambridge
University 1862-1897' in M Vicinus (ed) A Widening Sphere,
Indiana: Indiana University Press
Mead, M (1949), Male and Female, Harmondsworth: Penguin, 1962
Mead, M (1970), 'Anomalies in American Post-Divorce Relation-
ships' in P Bohannan (ed) Divorce and After, New York:
Doubleday
Mendes, H A (1976), 'Single Fatherhood', Social Work 21:308-313
Menefee, S (1981), Wives for Sale, Oxford: Blackwell

Michaels, N (1967), 'The Dangers of a Change of Parentage in Custody and Adoption Cases', Law Quarterly Review 83: 547-568

Mill, J S (1883), The Subjection of Women, 5th edition, London

Mitchell, A (1983), New Society May 12

Mnookin, R H (1975), 'Child-Custody Adjudication: Judicial Functions in the Face of Indeterminacy', Law and Contemporary Problems 39: 226-293

Mnookin, R (1979), Bargaining in the Shadow of the Law: The Case of Divorce, Centre for Socio-Legal Studies, Working Paper No 3, Oxford: SSRC, Centre for Socio-Legal Studies, Wolfson College

Mnookin, R H (1983), 'Divorce Bargaining: The Limits on Private Ordering' in J M Eekelaar and S N Katz (eds) The Resolution of Family Conflict, Canada: Butterworths

Morgan, P (1975), Child Care: Sense and Fable, London: Temple Smith

Mueller, C W and Pope, H (1977), 'Marital Instability: A Study of its Transmission between Generations', Journal of Marriage and the Family 39(1): 83-93

Murch, M (1975), 'Divorce Court Welfare Reports - Should Parents See Them', New Law Journal: 736

Murch, M (1980), Justice and Welfare in Divorce, London: Sweet and Maxwell

National Council for One-Parent Families, The Times January 17

Neff, W F (1929), Victorian Working Women, New York: Columbia University Press

New York Times (1980), 'Is Joint Custody Good for Children?', Magazine, February 3: 32-46

Newson, J and Newson, E (1963), Patterns of Infant Care in an Urban Community, Harmondsworth: Penguin, 1965

Newson, J and Newson, E (1974), 'Cultural Aspects of Child-rearing in the English-Speaking World' in M P M Richards (ed) The Integration of a Child into a Social World, Cambridge: Cambridge University Press

Newson, J and Newson, E (1978), Seven Years Old in the Home Environment, Harmondsworth: Penguin

Nissel, M (1982), 'Families and Social Change since the Second World War' in R N Rapoport, M P Fogarty and R Rapoport (eds) Families in Britain, London: Routledge & Kegan Paul

North West Regional Divorce Court Welfare Officers' Practical Guide (1976), Welfare of Children in Divorce and Domestic Dispute, North West Regional Divorce Court Welfare Officers

OPCS (1978), One-Parent Families 1971-1976, Office of Population Census and Survey Monitor Reference FM2 78/2, London: HMSO

OPCS (1983), Monitor FM2 83/1, Divorces 1981, London: HMSO

Oakley, A (1982), 'Conventional Families' in R N Rapoport, M P Fogarty and R Rapoport (eds) Families in Britain, London: Routledge & Kegan Paul

O'Brien, M (1982), 'Becoming a Lone Father: Differential
Patterns and Experiences' in L McKee and M O'Brien (eds)
The Father Figure, London: Tavistock Publications
O'Faolain, J and Martines, L (eds)(1974), Not in God's Image,
London: Fontana
Orthner, D K and Lewis, K (1979), 'Evidence of Single Father
Competence', Family Law Quarterly 13(1): 27-47

Pankhurst, E Sylvia (1931), The Suffragette Movement, London:
Longmans, Green
Pankhurst, R (1954), William Thompson 1755-1833, London: Watts
Parkinson, L (1981), 'Joint Custody', One Parent Times 7: 10-
13
Parkinson, L (1982), 'Divorce and Families' in Change in
Marriage, Rugby: National Marriage Guidance Council
Parkinson, L (1983), 'Conciliation: Pros and Cons', Family Law
13: 22
Parmiter, G M (1981), 'Bristol "In-Court" Conciliation Proced-
ure', Law Society's Gazette: February 25
Payne, J D (1982), unpublished paper cited in L Parkinson
(1982), 'Divorce and Families' in Change in Marriage, Rugby:
National Marriage Guidance Council
Perkins, J G (1909), The Life of the Honourable Mrs Norton,
New York: Henry Holt
Pilling, D and Kellmer-Pringle, M (1978), Controversial Issues
in Child Development, London: Elek
Pinchbeck, I and Hewitt, M (1973), Children in English Society
Volume II, London: Routledge & Kegan Paul
Pizzey, E (1974), Scream Quietly or the Neighbours Will Hear,
Harmondsworth: Penguin
Platt, A M (1969), The Child Savers, Chicago: University of
Chicago Press

Rapoport, R N, Fogarty, M P and Rapoport, R (eds)(1982),
Families in Britain, London: Routledge & Kegan Paul
Rapoport, R and Rapoport, R (1982), 'British Families in
Transition' in R N Rapoport, M P Fogarty and R Rapoport (eds)
Families in Britain, London: Routledge & Kegan Paul
Rapoport, R, Rapoport, R N and Strelitz, Z (1977), Fathers,
Mothers and Others, London: Routledge & Kegan Paul
Reiss, E (1934), The Rights and Duties of English Women,
Manchester: Sherratt and Hughes
Richards, M P M (1981), 'Aspects of Development in Contemporary
Society' in R Chester, P Diggory and M B Sutherland (eds)
Changing Patterns of Child Bearing and Child Rearing, London:
Academic Press
Richards, M P M (1982), 'Post-divorce Arrangements for
Children: A Psychological Perspective', Journal of Social
Welfare Law: 133-151

303

Rimmer, L (1981), Families in Focus: Marriage, Divorce and Family Patterns, London: Study Commission on the Family

Roberts, D (1978), 'The Paterfamilias of the Victorian Governing Classes' in A S Wohl (ed) The Victorian Family, London: Croom Helm

Rogers, C M and Wrightsman, L S (1978), 'Attitudes towards Children's Rights: Nurturance or Self-Determination, Journal of Social Issues 34: 59-68

Roman, M and Haddad, W (1978), The Disposable Parent: The Case for Joint Custody, New York: Holt Rhinehart and Winston

Rosen, A (1974), Rise Up Women, London: Routledge & Kegan Paul

Rowbotham, S (1977), Hidden From History, 3rd edition, London: Pluto

Rutter, M (1973), Maternal Deprivation Reassessed, Harmondsworth: Penguin

Rutter, M (1975), Helping Troubled Children, Harmondsworth: Penguin

Rutter, M (1981), Maternal Deprivation Reassessed, 2nd edition, Harmondsworth: Penguin

Rutter, M and Madge, N (1976), Cycles of Disadvantage: A Review of Research, London: Heinemann

Ryan, A (1970), The Philosophy of the Social Sciences, London: Macmillan

Sachs, A and Wilson, J H (1978), Sexism and the Law, London: Martin Robertson

Sanctuary, G and Whitehead, C (1970), Divorce - and After, Harmondsworth: Penguin

Santrock, J W and Warshak, R A (1979), 'Father custody and social development in boys and girls', Journal of Social Issues 35: 112-125

Santrock, J W, Warshak, R A and Elliott, G L (1982), 'Social Development and Parent-Child Interaction in Father-Custody and Stepmother Families' in M E Lamb (ed) Non-Traditional Families: Parenting and Child Development, New Jersey: Lawrence Erlbaum

Schaffer, H R (1971), The Growth of Sociability, Harmondsworth: Penguin

Seear, N (1982), 'Families and Employment' in R N Rapoport, M P Fogarty and R Rapoport (eds) Families in Britain, London: Routledge & Kegan Paul

Shaffer, D and Dunn, J (eds)(1979), The First Years of Life: Psychological and Medical Implications of Early Experience, New York: Wiley

Shanley, M L (1982), 'One Must Ride Behind: Married Women's Rights and the Divorce Act 1857', Victorian Studies 25: 355-376

Shipman, M (1972), Childhood: A Sociological Perspective, Slough: NFER

Shorter, E (1977), The Making of the Modern Family, London: Fontana

Skolnick, A (1975), 'The Limits of Childhood: Conceptions of
    Child Development and Social Context', Law and Contemporary
    Problems 39: 38-77
Social Services for Children in England and Wales 1979-81,
    HC 79 (1982-83), London: HMSO
Social Trends (1976), Table 39, London: HMSO, Central Statis-
    tical Office
Social Trends (1982), The Times December 8
Southwell, M (1982), Arrangements for Children on Marriage
    Breakdown with Special Reference to Access, unpublished
    PhD thesis, University of Keele
Stapleton, W and Teitelbaum, L (1972), In Defense of Youth,
    New York: Russell Sage
Steinman, S (1981), 'The Experience of Children in a Joint-
    Custody Arrangement', American Journal of Orthopsychiatry
    51: 403-414
Stevens, J H and Mathews, M (eds)(1978), Mother-Child Father-
    Child Relationships, Washington DC: National Association for
    the Education of Young Children
Stone, L (1978), 'The Rise of the Nuclear Family in Early
    Modern England, The Patriarchal Stage' in C E Rosenberg (ed)
    The Family in History, Pennsylvania: University of Pennsyl-
    vania
Stone, L (1977), The Family, Sex and Marriage in England
    1500-1800, Harmondsworth: Penguin, 1979
Stone, O M (1982), The Child's Voice in the Court of Law,
    Canada: Butterworths
Strachey, R (1928), The Cause, New York: Kennikar
Suttie, I (1935), The Origins of Love and Hate, Harmondsworth:
    Penguin, 1960
Sutton, A (1981), 'Science in Court' in M King (ed) Childhood
    Welfare and Justice, London: Batsford
Sutton-Smith, B (1982), 'Epilogue' in M E Lamb and B Sutton-
    Smith (eds) Sibling Relationships: Their Nature and Signifi-
    cance Across the Lifespan, New Jersey: Lawrence Erlbaum
Sutton-Smith, B, Rosenberg, B G and Landy, F (1968), 'The
    interaction of father absence and sibling presence on cogni-
    tive abilities', Child Development 39: 1213-1221

Thompson, D (1976), 'Women and Nineteenth Century Radical
    Politics: A Lost Dimension' in J Mitchell and A Oakley (eds)
    The Rights and Wrongs of Women, Harmondsworth: Penguin

Vicinus, M (ed)(1977), A Widening Sphere: Changing Role of
    Victorian Women, Indiana: Indiana University Press

Wallerstein, J and Kelly, J B (1980), Surviving the Break Up:
    How Children and Parents Cope with Divorce, London: Grant
    McIntyre
Walters, M (1976), 'Mary Wollstonecraft, Harriet Martineau,
    Simone de Beauvoir' in J Mitchell and A Oakley (eds)

The Rights and Wrongs of Women, Harmondsworth: Penguin
Walvin, J (1982), *A Child's World: A Social History of English Childhood 1800-1914,* Harmondsworth: Penguin
Watson, A (1969), 'Children of Armageddon: Problems of Custody without Care', *Syracuse Law Review* 21: 55
Watson, R (1980), *The Resolution of Spousal Conflict,* Address to Australasian Conference on Family Law, Queenstown, New Zealand, July 14
Weeton, E (1939), *Miss Weeton: The Journal of a Governess,* E Hall (ed), Oxford: Oxford University Press
Weinraub, M (1978), 'Fatherhood: The Myth of the Second Class Parent' in J H Stevens and M Mathews (eds) *Mother-Child Father-Child Relationships,* Washington DC: National Association for the Education of Young Children
Weiss, R S (1979), 'Growing Up a Little Faster: The Experience of Growing Up in a Single Parent Household', *Journal of Social Issues* 35: 97-111
Weitzman, L (1983), 'Equity and Equality in Divorce Settlements: A Comprehensive Analysis of Property and Maintenance Awards in the United States and England' in J M Eekelaar and S N Katz (eds) *The Resolution of Family Conflict,* Canada: Butterworths
Weitzman, L and Dixon, R (1979), 'Child Custody Awards: Legal Standards and Empirical Patterns for Child Custody, Support and Visitation after Divorce', *University of California Davis Law Review* 12: 473-521
Wilkinson, M (1981), *Children and Divorce,* Oxford: Blackwell
Willer, D and Willer, J (1973), *Systematic Empiricism,* New York: Prentice-Hall
Willmott, P and Willmott, P (1982), 'Children and Family Diversity' in R N Rapoport, M P Fogarty and R Rapoport (eds) *Families in Britain,* London: Routledge & Kegan Paul
Wilson, E (1977), *Women and the Welfare State,* London: Tavistock
Wilson, H (1982), 'Families in Poverty' in R N Rapoport, M P Fogarty and R Rapoport (eds) *Families in Britain,* London: Routledge & Kegan Paul
Winnicott, D (1957), *The Child, The Family and The Outside World,* London: Tavistock
Wohl, A S (ed)(1978), *The Victorian Family,* London: Croom Helm
Wolff, S (1981), *Children Under Stress,* 2nd edition, Harmondsworth: Penguin
Wynn, M (1964), *Fatherless Children,* London: Michael Joseph

Young, M and Willmott, P (1973), *The Symmetrical Family,* London: Routledge & Kegan Paul

323